Praise for *Tin Can Titans*

"The strength of *Tin Can Titans* is that Wukovits has ferreted out deeply personal stories of the officers and enlisted men who experienced hell aboard these destroyers—the horrors of pitching decks, exploding shrapnel, and gut-wrenching fear."

—Walter Borneman, *Wall Street Journal*

"An inspiring story of courage, duty, sacrifice, and devotion to country in the most trying and dangerous of circumstances. It's an epic story. These are ships and Americans that should not be forgotten."

—*The American Spectator*

"[Wukovits] draws overdue attention to the heroism, dedication, and courage of the young destroyer sailors . . . . [He] does a masterful job capturing the day-to-day boredom, excitement, and fear ordinary tin can sailors experienced on routine patrols at the height of the Pacific war."

—*America in WWII*

"A story of valor, sacrifice, and endurance and one that is well told."

—*WWII History*

"Wukovits certainly joins [Samuel Eliot] Morrison and James D. Hornfischer as one of the preeminent writers on the history of US Navy operations in the Pacific theater."

—New York Journal of Books

"A well-researched, well-written, and well-edited book, sure to stir the imaginations of many veterans, and well worth the time of adventure-loving civilians."

—*Roanoke Times*

"A lively and briskly written account of destroyer squadron operations . . . Anyone interested in destroyer operations . . . will find this title worth consideration."

—*Warship International*

TIN CAN TITANS

TIN CAN TITANS

The Heroic Men and Ships of World War II's Most Decorated Navy Destroyer Squadron

---

JOHN F. WUKOVITS

DA CAPO PRESS

Da Capo Press
Hachette Book Group
1290 Avenue of the Americas, New York, NY 10104
dacapopress.com
@DaCapoPress, @DaCapoPR

Printed in the United States of America

Originally published in hardcover and ebook by Da Capo Press in March 2017

First Trade Paperback Edition: November 2018

Published by Da Capo Press, an imprint of Perseus Books, LLC, a subsidiary of Hachette Book Group, Inc. The Da Capo Press name and logo are trademarks of the Hachette Book Group.

The Hachette Speakers Bureau provides a wide range of authors for speaking events. To find out more, go to www.hachettespeakersbureau.com or call (866) 376-6591.

The publisher is not responsible for websites (or their content) that are not owned by the publisher.

Print book interior design by Trish Wilkinson. Set in 11-point Adobe Garamond Pro

Library of Congress Cataloging-in-Publication Data
Wukovits, John F., 1944– author.
Tin can titans : the heroic men and ships of World War II's most decorated Navy destroyer squadron / John F. Wukovits.
Other titles: Heroic men and ships of World War II's most decorated Navy destroyer squadron
Description: Boston : Da Capo Press, [2017] | Includes bibliographical references.
Identifiers: LCCN 2016042188 | ISBN 9780306824302 (hardcover) | ISBN 9780306824319 (ebook)
Subjects: LCSH: United States. Navy. Destroyer Squadron 21—History. | Fletcher Class (Destroyers)—History—20th century. | World War, 1939–1945—Naval operations, American. | World War, 1939–1945—Pacific Area.
Classification: LCC D769.52.D38 W85 2016 | DDC 940.54/5973—dc23 LC record available at https://lccn.loc.gov/2016042188

ISBNs: 978-0-306-82430-2 (hardcover); 978-0-306-82431-9 (ebook); 978-0-306-92190-2 (paperback)

LSC-C

10 9 8 7 6 5 4 3 2

To my granddaughter, Katie Lastra,
whose quick wit and bright smiles never fail to amaze me

CONTENTS

Map 1: Desron 21 in the Solomons *ix*
Map 2: Desron 21 in the Pacific *x*
Preface *xi*

PART I: ORIGINS OF A SQUADRON

Prologue 3
CHAPTER 1 The Destroyers Go to War 7
CHAPTER 2 Initiation at Guadalcanal 25
CHAPTER 3 Naval Slugfest off Guadalcanal 48

PART II: DESRON 21 HOLDS THE LINE IN THE SOUTH PACIFIC

CHAPTER 4 Blunting the Tokyo Express 73
CHAPTER 5 Birth of a Squadron 92
CHAPTER 6 Struggle for the Slot 116
CHAPTER 7 Kula Gulf Confrontations 136

PART III: DESRON 21 SWEEPS TO VICTORY

CHAPTER 8 Climbing the New Guinea Ladder 165
CHAPTER 9 The Philippine Whirlwind 184
CHAPTER 10 Kamikaze Carnage 206

CHAPTER 11 Eyewitness to Victory 223

Epilogue 235

Chronology *243*

Appendix I: Battle Stars Awarded *245*

Appendix II: Location of Ships at War's End *251*

Notes *253*

Bibliography *275*

Index *303*

Photos follow page 146

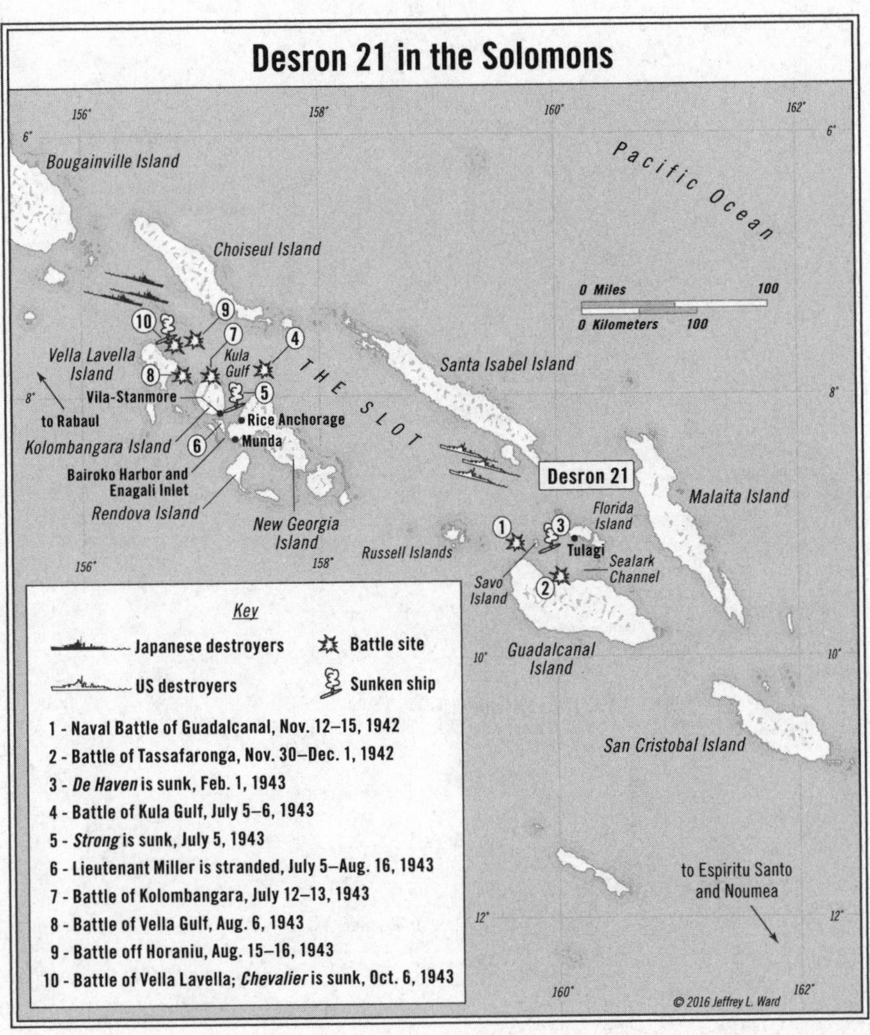
Desron 21 in the Solomons
156°
158°
160°
162°
6°
8°
10°
12°
Pacific Ocean
Bougainville Island
Choiseul Island
0 Miles 100
0 Kilometers 100
Santa Isabel Island
Vella Lavella Island
Kula Gulf
THE SLOT
Vila-Stanmore
to Rabaul
Rice Anchorage
Munda
Kolombangara Island
Bairoko Harbor and Enagali Inlet
Rendova Island
New Georgia Island
Desron 21
Malaita Island
Florida Island
Tulagi
Russell Islands
Sealark Channel
Savo Island
Guadalcanal Island
San Cristobal Island
to Espiritu Santo and Noumea
© 2016 Jeffrey L. Ward
Key
Japanese destroyers
Battle site
US destroyers
Sunken ship
1 - Naval Battle of Guadalcanal, Nov. 12–15, 1942
2 - Battle of Tassafaronga, Nov. 30–Dec. 1, 1942
3 - De Haven is sunk, Feb. 1, 1943
4 - Battle of Kula Gulf, July 5–6, 1943
5 - Strong is sunk, July 5, 1943
6 - Lieutenant Miller is stranded, July 5–Aug. 16, 1943
7 - Battle of Kolombangara, July 12–13, 1943
8 - Battle of Vella Gulf, Aug. 6, 1943
9 - Battle off Horaniu, Aug. 15–16, 1943
10 - Battle of Vella Lavella; Chevalier is sunk, Oct. 6, 1943

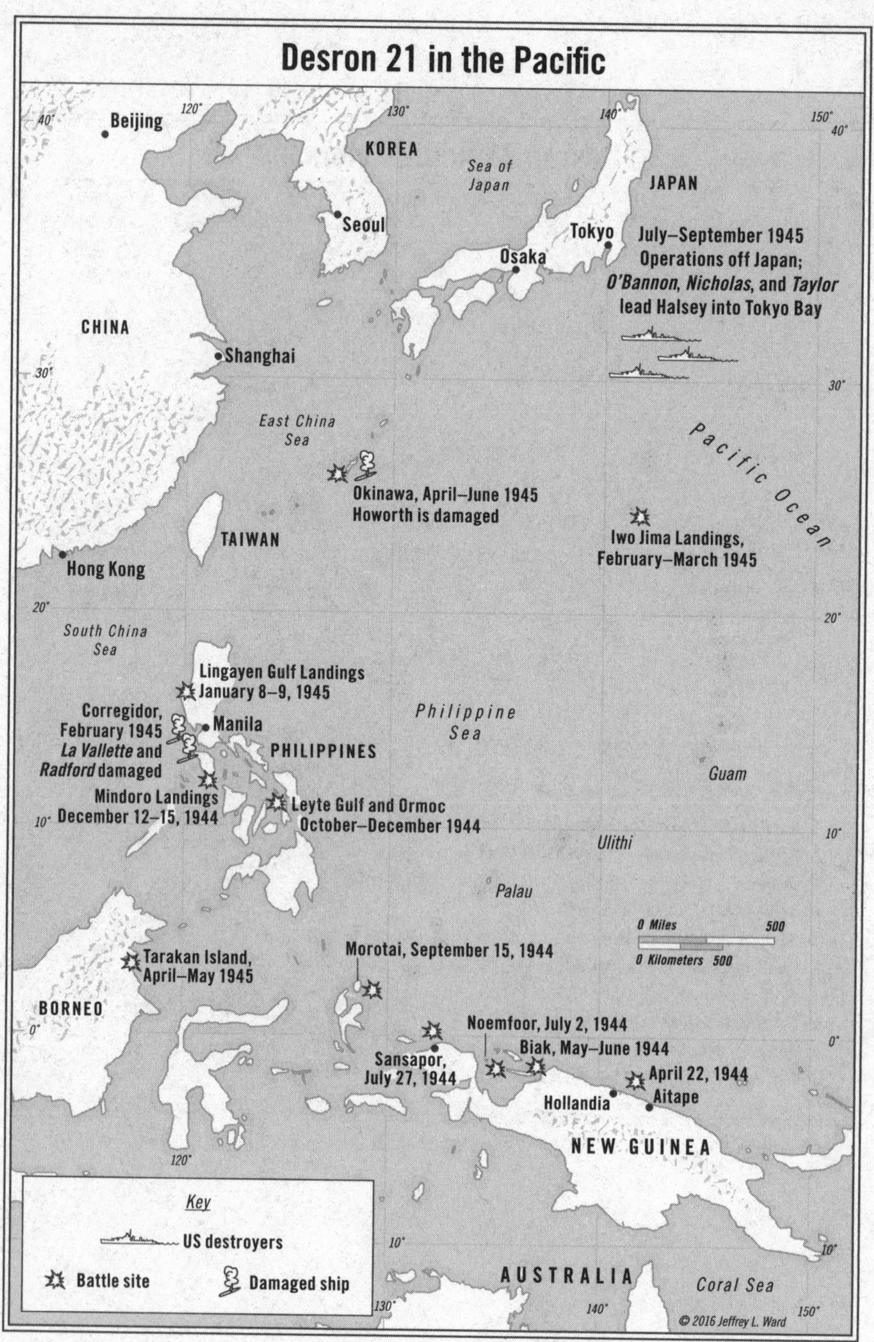
Desron 21 in the Pacific
Beijing
KOREA
Sea of Japan
JAPAN
Seoul
Tokyo
Osaka
July–September 1945
Operations off Japan;
O'Bannon, Nicholas, and Taylor
lead Halsey into Tokyo Bay
CHINA
Shanghai
East China Sea
Pacific Ocean
Okinawa, April–June 1945
Howorth is damaged
Iwo Jima Landings,
February–March 1945
TAIWAN
Hong Kong
South China Sea
Lingayen Gulf Landings
January 8–9, 1945
Corregidor,
February 1945
La Vallette and
Radford damaged
Manila
Philippine Sea
PHILIPPINES
Guam
Mindoro Landings
December 12–15, 1944
Leyte Gulf and Ormoc
October–December 1944
Ulithi
Palau
0 Miles 500
0 Kilometers 500
Tarakan Island,
April–May 1945
Morotai, September 15, 1944
BORNEO
Noemfoor, July 2, 1944
Biak, May–June 1944
Sansapor,
July 27, 1944
April 22, 1944
Hollandia
Aitape
NEW GUINEA
Key
US destroyers
Battle site
Damaged ship
AUSTRALIA
Coral Sea
© 2016 Jeffrey L. Ward

PREFACE

The idea for this book occurred when I was researching material for my previous book, *Hell from the Heavens*, the story of the destroyer USS *Laffey* (DD-724). That ship, which battled twenty-two kamikazes off Okinawa in April 1945, often operated in conjunction with other destroyers, and I wondered if there might be a squadron whose exploits offered an equally compelling tale. When my agent, Jim Hornfischer, mentioned the *O'Bannon*, I examined the squadron of which she was a part and found that Destroyer Squadron 21 more than fit the bill. Not only was the unit the most decorated destroyer squadron of the war, but the ships' feats from 1942 to war's end, where they were involved in the Solomon Islands, the Gilberts and Marshalls, New Guinea, the Philippines, Iwo Jima, Borneo, Okinawa, and the Japanese Home Islands, presented a panorama of naval conflict in the Pacific. As I dug deeper into the unit's accomplishments, I discovered dramatic surface engagements, encounters with aircraft and submarines, shore bombardments, convoy escorting, and antisubmarine patrols.

Mostly I unearthed examples of individuals reacting under the crucible of war, for the book is the story of people rather than of a unit. Inspiring leaders guided crews and ships through treacherous combat, daring sea rescues, and antiaircraft duels with kamikazes. Young sailors shook off the civilian world and blended into top-notch crews, seamen and machinist's mates ignored their anxieties to perform under fire, and a gridiron hero offered a modern version of Robinson Crusoe in battling the Japanese while stranded on an island. Men managed fears and missed loved ones. They performed their duties during moments of mind-numbing boredom and of intense action, during those dangerous nights rushing up the Slot to meet the Tokyo Express and while operating off Okinawa and its kamikaze-filled skies. They exhibited every emotion, from joy and laughter to terror and fear. And the squadron officers and crews repeatedly demonstrated heroism under fire, whether the opposition came from a Japanese warship, artillery battery, aircraft, or submarine. In telling the story of Destroyer Squadron 21, I am presenting the naval side of the Pacific war.

I have many people to thank. I received superb help from Destroyer Squadron 21 survivors—Russell Bramble, Warren Gabelman, Donald Holmes, John O'Neill, Willy Rhyne, James Setter, Douglas Starr, and Robert Whisler—who during interviews and other correspondence helped me to better understand what war on the waters was like. Dow Ransom Jr. graciously allowed me to digitize the fascinating diary kept by his father, a ship's physician aboard one of the destroyers. Thomas Chesnutt opened up the diary he kept aboard another destroyer and was most willing to answer the many queries I sent his way. Martin Johnson's interviews, combined with the compelling wartime letters he made available, proved invaluable. Fortunately, I was able to explore the vast amount of material gathered by the late Dave McComb of the Destroyer History Foundation and presented on his website, which his widow, Meredith, gave me permission to use.

With his editorial comments, Bob Pigeon at Da Capo Press expertly shepherded the manuscript into final form, and he and his team, including publicist Lissa Warren and others, developed the book's jacket and touted the book's attractions. Jeffrey Ward's skilled maps complemented the text. My writing mentor, naval biographer Thomas Buell, and my history adviser at the University of Notre Dame, Dr. Bernard Norling, profoundly influenced me with their advice. Although neither is now with us, their kind words and wise counsel remain with me each day. The support and advice of my extraordinary agent, Jim Hornfischer, helped me attain a dream that otherwise might not have been realized.

I have been blessed with the support of a nurturing family. My older brother, Tom, who served so nobly as a naval aviator during the Vietnam conflict, offers encouragement and exhibits pride in what I do. The memories of my parents, Tom and Grace, and of my younger brother, Fred, prod me to give my utmost. My daughters, Amy, Julie, and Karen, put a smile on my face with their unquestioned love and support for what I do, and make me proud of the people they have become. My four grandchildren, Matthew, Megan, Emma, and Kaitlyn, keep me young at heart with their vibrant personalities and amazing stream of achievements, and help me to remember that my main duty as an author is to make certain that the deeds of a past generation are not forgotten by those that follow. My invaluable companion of more than two decades, Terri Faitel, a marvelous mathematics teacher, scrutinized my manuscript to dig out errors and to make certain the text made sense. I rely on her more than she may realize.

John F. Wukovits
Trenton, Michigan
June 30, 2016

PART I

ORIGINS OF A SQUADRON

PROLOGUE

Admiral William F. Halsey had not been this satisfied since before the war. As he looked across the waters of Tokyo Bay on August 29, 1945, from the bridge of his flagship, USS *Missouri*—the battleship nicknamed the "Mighty Mo"—a conglomeration of battleships and cruisers steamed behind in a long line stretching to the horizon. Those ships, and others like them, had outslugged the Japanese in surface actions and pounded their installations in landings from the Solomon Islands to Okinawa. Farther out at sea, the formidable fast carrier task forces and their swarms of aircraft that dominated the naval war in the western Pacific in 1944–1945 guarded against surprise kamikaze attacks. The United States had won a long, grueling war, largely due to those ships and other weapons sent to the front lines through an uninterrupted pipeline connecting the American military to home-front factories and shipyards.

As one of the two top naval commanders in the Pacific, Halsey played a prominent part in the victory, gaining accolades and winning battles from the first day of war to the last. He became the nation's darling for his audacious actions, and for four years he looked forward to the moment he would enter the bay, promising along the way to ride Emperor Hirohito's famous white horse through the streets of Tokyo. Halsey described the entry into Tokyo Bay as "the supreme moment of my career," and said, "Every man jack among us was looking toward one moment, the moment we would anchor in Tokyo Bay."[1]

Halsey might justifiably have placed his *Missouri* in the first spot, giving the battleship the honor of taking the victorious United States Fleet into Tokyo Bay as conquering heroes come to lay claim on a defeated foe. He instead handed that recognition to a trio of destroyers, *O'Bannon* (DD-450),

Nicholas (DD-449), and *Taylor* (DD-468), smaller vessels dwarfed in size by "Mighty Mo," which followed them in line. Halsey's love of destroyers, the dashing ships whose speed and offensive punch matched his aggressive personality, had started early in his career. He considered himself a destroyerman even when he rose to higher command, for those ships that sliced low through the water, with the wind slapping his face and the sea salt coating his lips, were in his DNA. The crews of 330 officers and enlisted forged a tight unit, something that the *Missouri* and her crew of 2,700 could not hope to achieve. They were men who leaned on one another when the guns boomed and drank together when the fighting ended. They were his type of men.

Halsey did not choose the three destroyers based upon sentiment, however. He selected them because of the record they had amassed over the previous three years, and because in the bleak months of late 1942, when he most needed a weapon with which to stymie the Japanese in the Solomons, he turned to his destroyers.

O'Bannon, *Nicholas*, and *Taylor* were part of Destroyer Squadron 21 (Desron 21), the most acclaimed destroyer squadron of the war. Similar to an Army or Marine company, the squadron operated as a unit, in some ways a seagoing band of brothers. At times all of the squadron's destroyers barreled into action together, while on other occasions individual ships received separate missions, much as an infantry company dispatches smaller platoons on different assignments.

Desron 21 destroyers could be found with American forces as they steadily advanced up the Solomon Island chain, during the assaults against the Gilbert and Marshall Islands, along New Guinea's coast, into the Philippines, and north to Iwo Jima and Okinawa before participating in air and naval bombardments of the Japanese Home Islands. The squadron fought in major surface clashes and minor actions, conducted hundreds of patrols, escorted giant battleships and diminutive landing craft, scoured the ocean depths for enemy submarines, and scrutinized the skies for kamikazes. Foes charged the ships on, above, and below the surface. By appearing in almost every major assault of the Pacific war from 1942 to 1945, the squadron's exploits reflected the history of the Pacific clash itself.

Admiral Halsey wished to recognize those accomplishments by asking the three remaining operational ships of Desron 21 to lead the armada into Tokyo Bay. They had served under his command at Guadalcanal, and to the man the press called the "Bull" it seemed only fitting that they would accompany him at war's end.

"At daylight, there was my old ship, the *Nicholas*, getting under way," recalled Ensign Jack Fitch, subsequently on the Desron 21 staff, "honored to lead the entire armada, which stretched single file over the horizon into Tokyo Bay. It was and is the most spectacular sight I ever saw."[2]

In its three years of existence, Desron 21 earned three Presidential Unit Citations, one Navy Unit Commendation, and 118 battle stars—forty-eight by the trio that now steamed at Halsey's van, in front of the *Missouri*. The squadron had sunk or helped sink ten submarines and numerous surface vessels, shot down dozens of aircraft, and rescued more than eighteen hundred sailors and downed airmen, but it came with a high cost, as attested to in that only three of the twelve destroyers (counting replacements) remained to operate with Halsey and the three hundred Allied warships at war's end. Desron 21 ships were torpedoed three times, mined four times, and hit four times by shore batteries, suffering a total of 372 crewmembers killed and many more wounded.

While Desron 21's achievements were impressive, it was not a squadron of ships that registered an inspiring resume, but the people serving aboard those destroyers. Just as soldiers in an Army battalion seize a hill and Marines in a platoon storm a beach, the officers and sailors of Desron 21 issued the orders and manned the guns. They dropped depth charges and delivered shells to five-inch guns, downed enemy aircraft and rescued military brethren. They put their lives on the line not once or twice but day after day, and emerged victorious despite the worst that the Japanese could hurl at them. The united effort of career Navy officers and civilian enlisted, ship's doctors and gridiron heroes, swept the once victorious Japanese from their island bastions and rolled them back toward Tokyo. People, not metallic superstructures and hulls, won the battles.

Halsey selected the final three destroyers of Desron 21 because he knew that their endeavors epitomized all that was noble in the conflict. "The history of the Pacific war can never be written without telling the story of the U.S.S. *O'Bannon* [a key member of Desron 21]," wrote Admiral Halsey in the foreword to a book about the ship and unit. "Time after time the *O'Bannon* and her gallant little sisters were called upon to turn back the enemy. They never disappointed me. Out-numbered, out-gunned, during the dark days of '42 and '43 they stood toe-to-toe with the best the Japanese Fleet could offer—and never failed to send them scurrying home with their tails between their legs.

"No odds were ever too great for them to face," added Halsey. He said that their actions "derailed the Tokio Express so often that the Japanese admirals ran out of excuses. No medals, however high, can reward the gallant men of the tin-can fleet for their brave deeds. In her [the nation's] darkest hour their country called. They answered with flaming guns and high courage."[3]

So, too, did Donald MacDonald answer his nation's call.

CHAPTER 1

THE DESTROYERS GO TO WAR

Like most young boys, Donald John MacDonald gave little thought to the military when he was growing up in DuBois, Pennsylvania. Born on July 25, 1908, MacDonald reaped the benefits of a well-to-do family. His father was a business executive who owned a lucrative list of properties, including coal mines and a hotel. His grandfather on the paternal side came to the United States from Inverness, Scotland, and his Scots-Irish maternal grandparents arrived in the heated years leading to the American Revolution. As a representative from New Hampshire, his great-great-uncle Josiah Bartlett signed his name to the Declaration of Independence, three names to the right of John Hancock and three names above John Adams.

At DuBois High School, MacDonald proved his prowess both on the athletic field and in the classroom, where he earned valedictorian honors as well as the distinction of being named class president. Since females found the combination of good looks, brains, and athletic acumen irresistible, the outgoing MacDonald never lacked for girlfriends.

In MacDonald's senior year, his father contacted a congressman and obtained an appointment for his son to the United States Naval Academy. Being more interested in sports and girls, and never having given the military serious thought, MacDonald took the exams without studying and failed the English portion. When the congressman promised to hold an appointment for him a year from then, MacDonald cracked the books.

He attended the Werntz Naval Academy Preparatory School in Annapolis, a highly regarded preparatory school for the Naval Academy operated by Bobby Werntz, a stern taskmaster. The discipline produced quick results, with MacDonald passing the next year's exams. He earned the congressman's appointment and, in 1927, entered the Naval Academy as a plebe.

Once accepted at Annapolis, the athletic MacDonald focused more on extracurricular activities than on classroom work. "I guess I never spent enough time reading books and so forth," he said. "I was always sort of out playing golf, tennis, and anything else."[1] He lettered in soccer, but had enough natural intelligence to graduate eighty-fifth out of 441 graduates of the Class of 1931. Commissioned an ensign, MacDonald was assigned to destroyers, but he planned to remain in the Navy only until the economy, ravaged by the onset of the Great Depression, improved and allowed him to depart for a promising business opportunity.

After one month's leave, MacDonald joined his first ship, the USS *Hulbert* (DD-342), in San Diego. In no time the flustered young officer found himself in authority when the skipper, Lieutenant Commander Frederick D. "Pinky" Powers, handed MacDonald the first watch. "You know," barked Powers, "I don't want anyone on this ship who doesn't carry his own weight, so you're going to start standing watches right away."

Although MacDonald at times felt overwhelmed, he claimed that he benefited from Powers, whom he called "a pretty tough hombre." Powers put him in charge at a time when many of MacDonald's classmates wallowed at the bottom of the command chain. Instead, he began learning how to supervise men from his first hour aboard the destroyer. "This did really help me and gave me a great boost in connection with confidence."[2]

Two years later MacDonald reported to the battleship USS *California* (BB-44), where he gained additional experience by administering the junior officers' mess, commanding the Number Four gun turret, and serving as the catapult officer. This lasted until the fall of 1937, when he was assigned to the USS *Salinas* (AO-19), a Navy oil tanker whose job was to keep the shore-based oil farm tanks full for the Navy's ships and aircraft. The vessel operated along the East Coast, transporting oil from Houston refineries to a fuel farm.

Being a young, single naval officer had its benefits, and the handsome MacDonald took full advantage of the many opportunities for fun that a life of travel and glamour offered. He was comfortable in the presence of women, popular at parties, and conversant with dignitaries. "Life was very pleasant then for a naval officer. You were accepted wherever you went, not exactly always respected, but at least accepted. Naval officers were almost looked upon as catches for the daughters, because we had a little bit of stability and also independence."

The ship's base, Charleston, South Carolina, especially came alive during Christmas season. "I seemed to be very popular," he said. "I had a very hectic social schedule." He had just been advanced to lieutenant, junior grade, "and we were very much in demand by the parents of daughters they would like to see marry into the Navy at the time."[3] Debutante balls and parties followed one after the other, with the fun-loving MacDonald on each list.

So far, MacDonald had been exposed to relatively routine matters, but that changed in April 1938 when he received orders to leave *Salinas* and report to Washington, D.C., to work in the Navy Department's coding room. For the first time in his young career, as an assistant communications officer for coding arrangements, MacDonald worked closely with the Office of Naval Intelligence and with top naval officials, including the Chief of Naval Operations Admiral Harold R. Stark and his assistant, Rear Admiral Robert L. Ghormley.

It was heady company for an officer only a few years out of Annapolis, but his simultaneous duties as an aide to President Franklin D. Roosevelt at the White House were even more impressive. Roosevelt used MacDonald as a source of information for what came into the decoding room. If MacDonald read anything he judged important, especially pertaining to Great Britain's struggle with Germany after war in Europe flared in September 1939, he was to send it directly to Roosevelt.

MacDonald deciphered most of the messages darting back and forth from Winston Churchill to Roosevelt, many which related to the president's desire to help the British at a time when a majority of the people in the United States opposed intervention in what they considered a foreign war. MacDonald was authorized to phone the president directly, so that Roosevelt would have the information as soon as possible. Wherever MacDonald went in Washington, he had to leave his phone number in case an important message needed deciphering. Eleanor Roosevelt sometimes invited him and other aides to dine at the White House, where they engaged in friendly banter while enjoying a top-notch dinner. He once attended a banquet given on behalf of the king and queen of England, and at the request of the president or his wife often appeared at balls and dances hosted for Roosevelt nieces.

"It was a wonderful life. We were there so frequently that they almost got to know us like their own children. We were invited to lots of parties," he recalled. Long at ease in the presence of beautiful women, MacDonald, splendidly attired in his uniform, moved gracefully from guest to guest; "my social life was very busy in the evenings."[4] He especially looked forward to the times when Colonel George S. Patton, the commanding officer at nearby Fort Myer, hosted an affair, more for the presence of Patton's daughters than the officer.

In late summer of 1940 MacDonald jumped from the social pleasures of peacetime Washington, D.C., to the perils of wartime London when he crossed the Atlantic to be the assistant naval attaché and special naval observer under Ghormley, the naval attaché. He went from deciphering messages sent by a troubled Winston Churchill to the scene of the fighting those messages described, at a time when Churchill could not be certain his nation would withstand Hitler's assault. A German invasion seemed all too possible, and the German air arm blistered London and other British cities during the Blitz.

"Well, when we arrived there, England was in desperate straits, there's no doubt about it, and this was when Churchill came on the air with his 'blood, sweat, and tears' speech," said MacDonald. "We'd only been there about a week when he came on the air with that one. They were desperate. They had no way of defending themselves, really, because the military equipment, as far as the Army was concerned, was virtually all left on the beaches of Normandy in the Dunkirk arrangement. It was all left over there, so the only thing they had were the volunteers who were called up to bring their shotguns and a few things like that to stand by. England had a terrible time." He added, "The atmosphere at the time was that maybe England wouldn't be able to hold out, so we might not be over there too long."[5]

The group stayed at the Dorchester Hotel in a suite of rooms with two bedrooms on the top floor. When German aircraft lumbered toward the big city, rather than hasten to the basement shelters as guests were required to do, MacDonald and the other American military personnel scampered to the roof, where they observed German bombs set fire to warehouses and ships.

After one of the largest German raids, MacDonald visited the official in charge of the fire equipment in London. The man told MacDonald that his department faced nearly 2,500 fires burning at the same time all over London, and that it was impossible to extinguish them all. When MacDonald asked how he handled the situation, the official explained they had no choice but to let some burn themselves out so they could focus on the most threatening conflagrations. Under desperate circumstances the official and his crews assessed what they were able to do and then executed the tasks. MacDonald was impressed with this lesson in crisis management.

On another occasion Churchill invited Ghormley, MacDonald, and others to join him for an inspection trip to Dover. When they reached the port city, Churchill grabbed high-powered binoculars to gain a view of the

German military installations on the other side of the Channel and noticed that the enemy was constructing additional gun emplacements. In a testy mood, Churchill asked the British commander at his side to fire a few rounds across the water, but the officer advised against it. He explained that they had done that before, but the Germans responded with ten times as many shells.

Having deciphered so many of Churchill's messages to Roosevelt, MacDonald was hardly stunned when the British leader nevertheless ordered a shot fired, nor was he surprised when the Germans indeed sent back ten times as many. MacDonald saw why so many Britons rallied to Churchill's side: their leader never shrank from the aggressive course. No matter how desperate the situation—and things certainly favored the Germans at this stage of the conflict—Churchill acted with composure and optimism. MacDonald admired that quality and made a mental note of it for the day when he commanded men in battle.

Even more, he admired the resolve displayed by London's citizenry. Each day men and women left their homes, many residences showing signs of recent bombings, and traipsed to work. Fathers and mothers shook off the numbness that came from bomb-interrupted sleep or from hours spent in bomb shelters, and commenced daily schedules that had long structured their lives. Despite the dangers that had become an all too familiar part of their routines, children attended school and played with neighborhood friends. Almost daily, MacDonald observed examples, not from statesmen or admirals but from men and women, boys and girls, of how to endure under stress.

"The people over here are standing up remarkably well," he wrote his parents in February 1941. "The morale is still very high. They are quite confident that they will win."[6] Their example profoundly influenced him when he later faced trying situations against Japanese firepower.

MacDonald would have to put those lessons to the test sooner than he assumed. During a visit to friends in the English countryside on December 7, 1941, MacDonald listened to a radio broadcast announcing the Japanese attack on Pearl Harbor. He immediately departed for London, where he found Ghormley in his office trying to obtain additional information.

When a telegram shortly after the Japanese attack informed him that his father was seriously ill, in February 1942 MacDonald boarded an aircraft and arrived home in time to visit his father before he succumbed. After the funeral, the young officer contacted people in the Navy to seek a seagoing command. With the mad naval expansion then in place, both in ships and in men, it was not long before he was named the executive officer, the second-in-command, of the destroyer USS *O'Bannon*, the second of the *Fletcher*-class destroyers then being constructed at Bath, Maine.

Lieutenant Commander Donald MacDonald was off to war.

"The Deadliest Killer in the Fleet for Her Size"

Navy men have long been charmed by destroyers. Admiral Halsey claimed he owed much of his success to his destroyer commands between the wars, mainly because, like the man, the ships carried a reputation for aggressiveness and action. Although he eventually directed massive task forces consisting of aircraft carriers, battleships, and cruisers, Halsey never lost his fondness for the smaller destroyers.

The craft were originally created in the late nineteenth century to combat torpedo boats, which then wreaked havoc with ships. They slowly transformed into the offensive tool the hard-hitting admiral so loved, first by adding self-propelled torpedoes, which could be launched against surface ships, and then by carrying depth charges, to dispatch submarines during World War I. When aerial threats became more prevalent as the world wound its way toward war in 1939, destroyers enhanced their arsenal with antiaircraft batteries. Originally assigned one task, by World War II destroyers had morphed into multipurpose warships that could attack or defend.

MacDonald was fortunate to join one of the sleek, new *Fletcher*-class destroyers just then bursting out of American shipyards. *Fletcher*-class destroyers played a crucial role early in the Pacific war because when Pearl Harbor was attacked, the famed naval architectural firm Gibbs and Cox had already crafted their designs; faced with the instant need for more ships, the Navy turned to those destroyers. Ten were commissioned within nine months, with nineteen more ordered, and a total of 175 left shipyards during the conflict, more than any other class of destroyers. The ships formed the foundation for what would later become Destroyer Squadron 21.

At 376 feet long—the length of almost one and a third football fields—and forty feet across at the widest, the ships were known for speed and offensive wallop. Two turbine engines propelled the ship at top speeds approaching thirty-seven knots (42.6 miles per hour). While the thin-skinned vessels could be vulnerable to bombs and shells, the real value of the *Fletcher*-class destroyers rested in the array of gunfire and torpedoes they could bring on an enemy, which made them effective in both offensive and defensive modes.

The five 5-inch single-barrel gun mounts led the way. The guns, which could be fired automatically or manually, propelled fifty-four-pound shells at surface targets eighteen thousand yards distant or at incoming aircraft from six miles away.

Five twin 40mm antiaircraft gun mounts, positioned along the ship's length, supplemented the five-inch batteries. Situated in open gun tubs, the 40mm guns could fire 160 rounds per minute at aircraft to a range of 2,800 yards, or lower their trajectory to pour streams of shells toward close-in surface targets.

Seven single-barrel 20mm antiaircraft guns, capable of firing 480 rounds per minute, stood from bow to stern. They were generally used against aircraft that had closed to within a thousand yards, but in tight situations they could be turned against enemy crew manning the decks of ships that had drawn uncomfortably close. Crew referred to these guns as "revenge guns," because if the opponent had already pulled within their range, he had most likely already inflicted serious harm to the destroyer.

Two torpedo mounts, with five torpedoes each, carried the destroyer's main offensive weapon. Boasting five hundred pounds of explosives in their twenty-one-inch diameters, torpedoes could put out of action or even sink a cruiser if placed in a vulnerable location. Multiple torpedo hits could do the same to enemy battleships.

In addition to that firepower, two racks of eight six-hundred-pound depth charges, tasked with demolishing enemy submarines, straddled the fantail to port (left) and starboard (right), and three K-guns, situated forward of the depth charge racks, tossed additional three-hundred-pound depth charges to either side. Smoke screen generators, which emitted thick clouds of smoke to mask the destroyer or the ships she might be escorting, also stood on the fantail near the depth charge racks.

According to Captain Frederick J. Bell, skipper in the Pacific of the destroyer USS *Grayson* (DD-435), the modern destroyer was "the deadliest killer in the fleet, for her size—because of the tin fish that she carries in tubes on deck." He added, "She was made for speed; she was designed to carry the maximum fighting power in her slender hull, and there was no wasted space."[7]

Noted naval expert Bernard Brodie praised the advantages of the *Fletcher*-class ships and other destroyers. "Destroyers are multiple-duty vessels," he wrote. "They screen the battle fleet against torpedo attack and shroud it with smoke to protect it against enemy guns. With their torpedoes they attack the mightiest battleships of the enemy fleet. They protect convoys against the U-boat menace, and by that fact become the mainstay of a nation which must carry on a vast shipping in order to survive."[8]

MacDonald was impressed with *O'Bannon*, which he said "was longer, she was bigger, she was in all respects finer than anything that the U.S. Navy had seen in destroyers prior to this time."[9] He thought the destroyer compared favorably to the small cruisers of twenty years earlier, and he concluded that the vessel's lighter yet stronger metal could make her more maneuverable and harder to sink than World War I–vintage destroyers. MacDonald never expected, though, that his smaller ship might have to engage enemy battleships and cruisers in a surface duel, where fourteen-inch guns would possess a huge advantage.

"How You Going to Win a War with a Mob Like That?"

The experiences of the first three ships before leaving the United States were shared by every destroyer crew that steamed to war. After shipyard workers constructed their destroyers, a commissioning ceremony preceded the shakedown cruise in the Caribbean, where sea trials tested ship and crew. When complete, they received their assignment to either Pacific or European waters.

After a course at the antisubmarine warfare school in Key West, Florida, where American naval officers studied the Royal Navy's tactics against German U-boats, in March 1942 MacDonald traveled to Bath to help Commander Edwin R. Wilkinson prepare the *O'Bannon* for service. Named after Lieutenant Presley O'Bannon, the ship and crew faced a stern challenge in living up to the heritage established by the Marine officer. In 1805 O'Bannon commanded a Marine detachment that charged through heavy enemy musket fire to engage Barbary pirates in bitter hand-to-hand combat at Tripoli. After the victory O'Bannon's contingent raised the Stars and Stripes over foreign soil for the first time. Their exploits were later commemorated by the verse "to the shores of Tripoli" in the Marine Corps Hymn.

Bath, Maine, had once been a thriving fishing center and the home for whaling captains, but in early March, before warming temperatures had a chance to melt a hard winter's snowy residue, it left much to be desired. The town resounded to the noise of welders and other shipyard workers, who in their off-hours crowded Bath's two main streets to do their shopping or seek out food or beverages.

Wilkinson and MacDonald, as did the officers of *Fletcher* and *Nicholas*, recognized the challenges they faced. In these lean years the skipper of every destroyer earmarked for the combat zones had to rely on a small core of experienced officers, chiefs, and petty officers to work their magic in molding into a workable crew the youth who came out of Navy training camps. Only four of Wilkinson's officers had served aboard destroyers before coming to *O'Bannon*; only four were regular Navy.

At least the nucleus crew, the group of experienced officers and enlisted who arrived in Bath to prepare the ship for service, would help. Most had compiled years of service in the Navy and had come to *O'Bannon* from ships that had been damaged or sunk, mainly at Pearl Harbor. Men such as Chief Quartermaster John T. Sexton and Chief Boatswain Robert J. McGrath provided what MacDonald called the backbone of the ship's organization during training and in the battles that were to come. MacDonald wondered, though, if service aboard a ship at Pearl Harbor compared with the ordeals he observed in London. "Some of them had been at Pearl Harbor, this had made an impression but, on the other hand, so many of them did not seem to have any idea of what a real war might mean."[10]

The officers and nucleus crew spent hours at Bath, familiarizing themselves with the ship and training the few enlisted who were present. They interspersed baseball games, dances, and parties whenever they could.

MacDonald spent his few leisure hours at the Bath home he rented with three other naval officers—Wilkinson and two others from their sister ship, USS *Nicholas*. The living arrangements came naturally, as for the next year both *O'Bannon* and *Nicholas* were built side by side, making them two of the first three *Fletcher*-class destroyers launched and commissioned. The men played poker and relaxed from the rigors of training, unaware that the two ships and their crews would be inextricably linked throughout the entire Pacific war.

On June 26 *O'Bannon*'s engines turned over for the first time, and the nucleus crew took her to sea under her own power. Wilkinson set a course south for the Boston Navy Yard, where the rest of the crew would board, the ship would officially join the Navy in an impressive commissioning ceremony, and *O'Bannon* would depart for her shakedown cruise.

The commissioning ceremony varied little from ship to ship. On the *Nicholas*, after the invited guests had filed aboard, the Navy accepted delivery of the destroyer from the shipyard, and the captain, Lieutenant Commander

W. D. Brown, took command. All eyes focused on the skipper as he issued his first order to his executive officer to set the watch. "Now we had manned a living man-o'-war, United States Ship *Nicholas* (DD 449), the first of the new fleet destroyers that was an equal match of the enemy," wrote Watertender 1/c Virgil N. Wing.[11]

After the ceremony, the *Nicholas* sailors shuffled below to change into dungarees and begin their first work as a crew. The men added two coats of war paint to the brass fixtures to eliminate the gleam, and scraped paint from bulkheads until they reached metal to reduce the chances in combat of enemy shells igniting the flammable covering.

Aboard *O'Bannon*, an initial glimpse of the Boston contingent made MacDonald long for grizzled veterans. As occurred aboard the other destroyers, most recruits looked no older than nineteen, and he guessed that few had received more than a handful of hurried weeks of basic training. "An awful lot of them were very inexperienced in everything," said MacDonald, who believed that "some of them were mere children who had fibbed to the recruiting officer." However, in those early months of the war, "the services were hard-pressed for men, and a ship had to take what it could get."[12]

At least three-quarters had never been to sea. They knew only the rudiments of seamanship, many lacked a high school education, and some had no idea where Japan was. As MacDonald stared at the youths who uneasily stepped aboard, "duffle bags over their shoulders, uncertain which way to turn," a veteran petty officer with a dozen years at sea muttered, "Look at 'em. How you going to win a war with a mob like that? They don't know a gun mount from a horse. It's a sorry-looking crew."

The astute officer arrived at a different conclusion, though. Although he agreed with his petty officer that these boys required training, "what I saw coming aboard was a cross-section of my country, as it was then—raw and untrained youth that had taken freedom for granted." He described them as "timid and awkward," an assortment of "clerks, mechanics and schoolboys, of Catholics, Protestants and Jews, of Irish, Italians, Scandinavians and colored boys," but remarked that they were "all lovers of their country, would make a great crew." He believed that at the commissioning, "we were not great fighters then, not by a long shot," but he was certain that thorough training and sound direction from officers, chiefs, and petty officers would weld them into "great fighters."[13] His crew was green, but MacDonald had also witnessed London's civilians respond with courage and dignity to the bombings. He was confident this young crew would respond, too.

Fletcher's executive officer, Lieutenant Commander Joseph C. Wylie, was not concerned about the crew. His military family had showed him that an effective officer could work wonders with novitiates. His South Carolina–bred grandfather had fought nobly for the South during the Civil War, and his two sisters had married military officers, one currently in the Army and the other serving in a submarine. *Fletcher*'s first executive officer also counted on the talents of the destroyer's skipper, Lieutenant Commander William M. Cole, like Wylie a Naval Academy graduate. Together they would whip those recruits into shape.

Even though the young crew had been rushed through training camps to man ships, Wylie noticed that most were literate and patriotically motivated. Joining the military neither for career enhancement nor adventure, they had one goal in sight—to smash the enemies who threatened their nation. "Superb," Wylie said of the crew, "they were highly motivated. They just came to fight."[14] He and Cole could work with that.

"We Have to Cross the Ocean in That Small Thing?"

The transformation from recruit to seaman began almost as soon as the band at the commissioning ceremony sounded its final note. "From this day on," said MacDonald, "it was nothing but hard work for all hands in getting the ship ready to sail, getting her supplied, and in training." MacDonald added, "It never stopped, really, the training part."[15]

During the first three weeks of July *O'Bannon* operated out of Boston and New York. Old hands grew frustrated with the young sailors, who were slow in moving to battle stations and ragged in executing drills. Even though they operated within sight of New England's coastline, the veterans demanded perfection, for they understood more than did these fresh-faced youngsters that once they reached the combat zone, tardiness and errors resulted in men dying.

Seaman 2/c James F. Setter of the *Fletcher* had left his home in Richmond, Kansas, to volunteer for the Navy two months before Pearl Harbor, thus making him a wizened veteran compared to the stream of untested youngsters the Navy rushed out of training camps to the fleet. Setter had not seen his new ship before the commissioning, and while it lacked the majesty of those mammoth battleships, he liked that he was serving in one of the first of a new class of destroyers. Whether the vessel steered toward Hitler in Europe or the Japanese in the Pacific, he figured he would go to war in style. Setter suppressed a chuckle when he heard the young sailor near him mutter, "You mean we have to cross the ocean in that small thing!"[16] He'll learn, thought Setter.

For the next month *Fletcher*, often accompanied by her sister ship, *O'Bannon*, operated off Cuba, conducting antisubmarine drills, air raid alarms, and other exercises that would become an all too familiar part of their everyday lives in the South Pacific. The shakedown "took us into southern waters at a time when the submarine menace was at its peak," wrote MacDonald. Reports of U-boat attacks frequently interrupted their training regimen, and several times they were ordered to protect "poor defenseless merchant ships against this menace."

The first time *O'Bannon* arrived at the scene of an attack, only floating debris remained of what had a few hours before been a ship. Though an escort had already retrieved the survivors, the images of flotsam from the sunken ship made a lasting impression on sailors who had heretofore witnessed nothing more serious than bloody noses and scraped arms. "This was the first realization of war that nearly all my men had ever been confronted with," said MacDonald. "A ship virtually blown to bits in the middle of the night leaving behind all forms of wreckage floating around in the thick oil."[17]

On August 14 *O'Bannon* and *Fletcher* plucked out of the water eighty-nine survivors from two British freighters that had been part of a large convoy the pair had been escorting in the Caribbean. The sight of injured sailors and the knowledge that people had died at the hands of the enemy more deeply affected the crew than did debris bobbing in the waves.

A few of the *O'Bannon* sailors, convinced that their ship would be torpedoed, refused to go below at night, lingering instead on deck in their life jackets. Some came to MacDonald in tears and begged for a transfer ashore. MacDonald talked to each man, trying to help him understand that while no one aboard ship wanted to be there, everyone had a duty to defend their nation. Most listened to his words and worked through their misgivings, but Wilkinson had to transfer one sailor who shot himself in the foot to avoid battle.

Nicholas was the first to embark for the Pacific. After the ship had arrived back in the Boston area after completing the shakedown, crew scuttlebutt focused on the ship's ultimate destination. Some guessed European waters, where an assault against Hitler was bound to begin sooner than later, while others put their money on the South Pacific, then crying for destroyers and any other vessel the Navy could send. They had their answer on August 17 when *Nicholas* weighed anchor and the destroyer inched south from the New England coastline toward the Panama Canal instead of east toward Europe.

Their shakedown complete, in mid-August *O'Bannon* was under way for Boston and final preparations for heading to the Pacific. MacDonald spent as much time as he could with his fiancée, Cecilia, whom he met at one of the numerous social occasions he attended while in Washington, D.C., before his London assignment. Before he left she handed him a medal of St. Christopher, the patron saint of travelers, to keep him safe from what appeared to be a long and bloody war. MacDonald slipped the medal into his left breast pocket, and from then on made certain the keepsake was with him in every action.

In early September *O'Bannon*, accompanied by the seaplane tender USS *Albemarle* (AV-5) and her old companion *Fletcher*, left the Navy Yard at Portsmouth, Virginia, and set course for the Panama Canal. On September 9 the trio passed through the canal and exited into the Pacific. While thousands of miles separated them from the enemy, they now steamed the same waters as the Japanese, and would soon join *Nicholas* in the South Pacific to meet the urgent situation brewing off Guadalcanal.

The initial three ships paved the way for the other destroyers of Desron 21, which were either just beginning shakedown cruises or were gathering for the North African landings. The trio hurried to the Pacific before the rest for one reason—the Navy and Marines at Guadalcanal needed them as soon as possible.

One day after *O'Bannon* passed through the Panama Canal, the official record of Admiral Chester W. Nimitz, Commander in Chief, Pacific Fleet, stated that Japanese forces "for the counter attack on Guadalcanal are now approaching the area. If our information is correct, they can be expected to arrive there in great strength."[18] He needed everything he could lay his hands on now, not later.

At the same time, Admiral Ernest J. King, Commander in Chief, United States Fleet, and Chief of Naval Operations, wanted destroyers for a scheduled North African landing. Holding the reins of power, King allowed *O'Bannon*, *Fletcher*, and *Nicholas* to join Admiral Ghormley, then in command of the

South Pacific, but retained the other new destroyers emerging from the nation's shipyards, including those that would ultimately constitute Destroyer Squadron 21, for use off North Africa. Ghormley would have to wait for more significant reinforcements until after the North African landings.

The first three of the sparkling *Fletcher*-class destroyers, MacDonald's *O'Bannon*, Cole and Wylie's *Fletcher*, and Wing's *Nicholas*, hastened westward toward unknown perils, the vanguard of what would eventually be the most honored destroyer squadron of the war. For the last three months of 1942 this trio operated in the South Pacific maelstrom, where American and Japanese forces fought a no-holds-barred battle to gain supremacy in that part of the world. The three would implant a standard of excellence and would establish the criteria with which other squadron ships measured themselves for the duration of the war.

With their early arrivals in the South Pacific, the officers and crew of *O'Bannon*, *Fletcher*, and *Nicholas* would gain valuable experience that they could share with the ships that followed. There was one problem, though: once in a war zone dominated by the Japanese, would they still be afloat to welcome those destroyers?

They would find out near an island little known before the war—Guadalcanal.

As soon as *O'Bannon* and *Fletcher* left the Canal Zone on September 11, bound for Bora Bora, 4,600 miles away in the Society Islands of French Polynesia, drills intensified. Aboard the *Fletcher*, the crew griped about the incessant calls to battle stations for antiaircraft tests, abandon-ship exercises, and every imaginable drill possible, but knew that Cole and Wylie had their best interests at heart. "We had the best skipper and exec in the Navy," remembers Ensign Fred Gressard. "Capt. Cole was a wonderful person, beloved by the entire crew, who had a marvelous relationship with our XO [executive officer] Wylie. They were two of the best officers I ever met and they really had our crew trained well in such a short period of time."[19]

O'Bannon matched suit. With the destroyers steaming at 13.5 knots, Wilkinson's piercing black eyes scrutinized every exercise as he looked for imperfections that might, against the enemy, cause death or injury. Taking lessons from his coaches, the former football player believed that endless repetition created a successful rhythm that was crucial for victory. He sounded the klaxon at any hour of the day or night, sending his crew to battle stations five or more times each day.

The ships arrived at Bora Bora on September 25, completing a tricky passage between coral reefs that challenged the navigating skills of MacDonald and Wylie. They remained in the beautiful lagoon for three days, refueling and replenishing supplies, before embarking on the weeklong voyage to Noumea, New Caledonia, 950 miles east of Australia. Upon arrival, crews lined up to port and starboard as the destroyers entered the blue-green waters of the massive lagoon, but were disappointed when, instead of a tropical island replete with palm trees and jungles, they viewed what Wyle called "sort of a drab colony."[20]

Large enough to hold a major portion of the Pacific Fleet, the lagoon would become a vital naval base for operations in the coming months, but at this stage of the war, ship navigators had few charts to guide them in. MacDonald had already maneuvered through the coral reefs at Bora Bora, and he was now "leery about how to get into this place."[21]

Fortunately, Ensign Perry Hall, the junior officer-of-the-deck aboard USS *Sterett* (DD-407), noticed *O'Bannon* and *Fletcher* headed directly toward a minefield protecting the harbor. Hall informed another officer, who shouted to *O'Bannon* over the "talk between ships" radio (TBS), "Reverse your engines—you are standing into danger!"[22] Wilkinson ordered an immediate reversal, and both destroyers backed away from the minefield until *Sterett* could guide them into the harbor. Hall's quick action prevented the possible loss of both *O'Bannon* and *Fletcher*, two new destroyers whose absence over the next few months could have adversely affected the naval balance off Guadalcanal.

After the narrow escape, Wilkinson and MacDonald made the usual call on the Commander South Pacific, MacDonald's comrade from London, Vice Admiral Ghormley. Ghormley shared the most recent reports coming from the fighting off Guadalcanal, and told MacDonald that he was "trying to hold our foothold in the Solomon chain with a shoestring against very strong Japanese forces." Ghormley added that he expected help would arrive, "but none seemed very close."[23]

MacDonald was surprised both by his friend's pessimism and when Ghormley said, "You know, Donald, I don't have any fighting admirals out here."[24] Maybe *O'Bannon* and *Fletcher* could help alter that condition.

Traveling ahead of *O'Bannon* and *Fletcher*, Watertender Wing had experienced a similar Pacific crossing aboard *Nicholas*, with drills filling the hours. "Held drills and battle problems all day," he added to his diary for September

11. "I held plant drills during the battle problems. What-would-you-do-if? Some practices in thwarting disaster, because in emergencies your thoughts are scrambled and unreliable."[25]

When later that month the ship pulled into Tongatabu, part of the Tonga Islands, 550 miles southwest of Samoa, Wing chatted with the crew of other ships then in port and learned that four heavy cruisers had been lost in the August 9 Battle of Savo Island.

The sour tidings continued at their next stop, Noumea. One afternoon Wing crossed the moored ships to the USS *Manley* (DD-74), where he found an old Navy friend, Clyde Hynes, stretched out on a canvas cot. Wing sensed a different demeanor in the man, who had been known for his "energetic and tough" deportment during service on cruisers in the 1930s. "He was shook up and said so," wrote Wing. "He had been in the initial assault landing at Guadalcanal and Tulagi." Over the last month Hynes and *Manley* had ferried troops and supplies each night to the Marines on Guadalcanal, taking shelter by day underneath jungle overhang in island coves to evade enemy aircraft. Wing thought that a visit to *Nicholas*, with her guns and "our first-class equipment," would bolster his friend, "but he didn't have any of the spirit I knew in him before—his comments were feeble" after examining *Nicholas*. "He had changed. It was like hearing a whimper from Jack Dempsey."[26]

Wing could fairly easily dismiss ship scuttlebutt, but he could not ignore this evidence of war's toll. If an experienced sailor such as Hynes, a man Wing knew and trusted, could be so affected by the hazards off Guadalcanal, how might the inexperienced hands of *Nicholas* and the trailing tandem react?

"The Site of a Life-and-Death Struggle"

Wing's concerns were justified, as the operation that had begun off Guadalcanal in early August had within one month dissolved into disappointing land battles and disastrous naval encounters. September and October 1942 off Guadalcanal, a part of the Solomon Islands chain, 1,100 miles northwest of Australia, rivaled that of the December 7 catastrophe.

"We have been unable to prevent the Japs from bombarding our positions and from landing troops on either flank of the Marine Guadalcanal position," assessed Admiral Chester Nimitz's Command Summary on October 1. The summary concluded that the Japanese had been building their forces for almost two months in preparation for a major assault, with Guadalcanal as the likely target. "The enemy's most probable next moves are the recapture of the Southern Solomons, and the extension of control in New Guinea." The summary stated that the Japanese moves would be done by "a gradual infiltration followed by a major assault."[27]

Pessimism in the United States mirrored the military's uncertainty in the South Pacific. Newspaper columnists and military analysts, including the *New York Times*'s esteemed Hanson Baldwin, cautioned as far back as January that the nation was ill-prepared for the losses that lay ahead and warned that the United States could lose this war. "Is Guadalcanal to be the story of a desperate adventure? . . ." asked Charles Hurd in an October article appearing in the *New York Times*. "Brief Navy communiqués now indicate that the island is the site of a life-and-death struggle." Hurd was certain that "the tropical island is the focal point of an intent and apprehensive American interest in the war." He explained that if the Japanese triumphed and held Guadalcanal, "it would be the southern anchor of a battle line extending all the way from the Asiatic coast and a point of departure for a dangerous drive on our supply lines." However, "in Allied hands it would be a base from which to begin the task of rolling back the Japanese."[28]

While *O'Bannon* and *Fletcher* hunted German U-boats in the Atlantic during their shakedown, over in the Pacific, Operation Watchtower, as the military designated the August 1942 Guadalcanal landings, suffered a series of setbacks. Meant to halt the Japanese thrust toward Australia and New Zealand and to establish a base from which the United States could eventually launch its own offensive, US naval and Marine forces instead scraped for their lives.

In the Battle of Savo Island, in early August, the United States Navy suffered the worst defeat in its history when it lost four cruisers and more than 1,000 dead to a surprise Japanese night surface engagement, leaving Vice Admiral Ghormley only one capital ship and one carrier, *Hornet*, remaining in the South Pacific. Major General Alexander A. Vandegrift's Marines maintained a slim hold on Guadalcanal, centered on the vital fighter strip at Henderson Field, but the battle's outcome would depend upon which side could rush in enough reinforcements and supplies to withstand the other.

Some Marines on Guadalcanal compared the situation to that of their Marine compatriots who had had to surrender at Wake Island and Guam. Hanson Baldwin wrote, "We are, indeed, fighting a major war on a shoestring," and he noted that the fighting to date indicated "that the Japanese will never quit until they are killed or utterly crushed." He concluded that action off Guadalcanal "has developed into a battle for the Southern Pacific.

The battle is a sprawling, intermittent sea, air and land action in which the stakes are high—perhaps eventual victory itself."[29]

Optimism infested the other side. By early May leading Japanese militarists concluded that the United States, badly reeling from its losses at Pearl Harbor and in the Philippines, could not mount a major counteroffensive until at least the second half of 1943. The Japanese thrust southward toward the Solomons seemed to be progressing as they had hoped, and it appeared that before long, the Japanese would solidify their position in the region and threaten US supply lines to Australia.

A headline in Japan's *Asahi Shimbun* in August 1942 proclaimed, "Japan Leads the World," and an official boasted, "Soon we will be calling the sea between New Guinea and Japan the Sea of Great East Asia—the Mediterranean of the Far East."[30] Captain Hideo Hiraide, the Japanese navy's spokesman and also a popular radio personality, went so far as to announce in one broadcast that Japan was planning a naval review off New York Harbor.

Rear Admiral Matome Ugaki of the Navy's general staff tempered his enthusiasm after the blows inflicted by US surface and air forces at the May Battle of the Coral Sea and the June calamity at Midway, where US aircraft sent four Japanese carriers to the ocean's bottom. "Unless we destroy them promptly," he wrote on August 7, the day American Marines landed at Guadalcanal, "they will attempt to recapture Rabaul, not to speak of frustrating our Moresby operation. Our operations in that area will become extremely unfavorable. We should, therefore, make every effort to drive the enemy down first, even by putting off the Indian Ocean operation."[31]

The focused attention to Guadalcanal handed the advantage to the Japanese and created a desperate situation for the crews of *O'Bannon*, *Fletcher*, and *Nicholas*. "Danger lurked at every turn," MacDonald said of their arrival in the South Pacific.[32]

CHAPTER 2

INITIATION AT GUADALCANAL

The officers and crews knew enough about the Pacific war to realize the Navy rushed them to waters dominated by their foe. The Japanese had already sunk three aircraft carriers, four cruisers, and an alarming number of destroyers. Risks had to be taken if they were to reverse the situation and prevent the Japanese from dominating in the South Pacific, and risks meant death and injury.

O'Bannon, *Fletcher*, and *Nicholas* were tossed into the action as soon as they arrived in the South Pacific. For much of October the new arrivals escorted transports and other vessels along the main supply route, six hundred miles from Espiritu Santo to Guadalcanal and the nearby island of Tulagi. The task, which called for shepherding supply ships across waters heavily infested with Japanese submarines, was so dangerous that American sailors christened the area "Torpedo Junction."

"Dawn quarters is a lot more serious in this area—no laggards at all," Watertender Wing, aboard *Nicholas*, entered in his diary for October 1, about escorting the transport *Formalhaut* across prime hunting grounds for enemy submarines that lay in wait for the shipping they knew would be ferrying men and supplies to the United States Marines on Guadalcanal.[1] The next day, three days before *O'Bannon* and *Fletcher* entered Noumea, New Caledonia, one thousand miles to the south, Lieutenant Commander William D. Brown, skipper of *Nicholas*, guided his destroyer and *Formalhaut* into Lengo Channel, the southern entrance to Savo Sound, which separated Guadalcanal from Tulagi. While the crew had safely traversed Torpedo Junction, they now operated off Guadalcanal, within range of Japanese aircraft and surface ships.

In those early weeks on Guadalcanal, both sides engaged in a frantic race to build up their forces. A pattern became maddeningly familiar to every destroyer crew operating in those dangerous waters. The skippers maintained Condition Two, with half the guns manned and half the crew at battle stations, while escorting transports to the Solomons, and upped the vigilance to Condition One, with all stations and guns manned, when nearing Guadalcanal and while guarding the transports as they unloaded their cargoes. If enemy aircraft appeared, the destroyers moved the transports to sea while US fighters from Henderson Field engaged the Japanese, and returned to Guadalcanal to resume unloading when the aerial battles terminated.

Three times in the next two days *Nicholas* and *Formalhaut* had to retreat from the area due to enemy air attacks, but *Formalhaut* delivered her entire complement. Once finished, the two ships turned south, where they again entered the dangerous waters of Torpedo Junction for the jaunt to Noumea, New Caledonia. Both ships safely arrived at their destination, but instead of relaxing, of necessity Brown and his crew shifted their attention to the next of many transports waiting to be escorted to Guadalcanal.

The unrelenting state of readiness taxed officers and crew. Day and night, cooks made available coffee, sandwiches, and soup, and even delivered the items to crew manning their posts. The crews often felt as if they worked on gigantic yo-yos as their destroyers ricocheted from harbor to harbor to keep supplies and reinforcements flowing to the island. The destroyers zigzagged north to Guadalcanal, south to Espiritu Santo, east to Samoa, southwest to Noumea, back to the Solomons, again to Noumea, and so on. Destroyermen prefer offensive action, but their ability to shepherd convoys across Torpedo Junction, to sweep the harbor entrances at Espiritu Santo and Noumea, and to search for enemy submarines took precedence over what MacDonald and most officers considered the primary role of a destroyer—launching torpedoes against enemy ships in a surface action. Their desire to operate in an all-destroyer group and so engage the Japanese had to wait.

Complicating matters was that at the same time, the Japanese engaged in their own rush of men and matériel to Guadalcanal. The aptly labeled Tokyo Express operated most nights in late summer and fall. Normally consisting of one or two cruisers escorted by a handful of destroyers, the convoys departed the Japanese stronghold at Rabaul, seven hundred miles to the northwest, in the afternoon and entered Savo Sound, to Guadalcanal's northwest, two nights later, where they bombarded Henderson Field and Marine lines before dropping off supplies for their own forces ashore. After completing their delivery, the ships scurried northwest before daylight to be out of range of US aircraft operating during the day.

With the Japanese gone, the United States Navy took over by day. Wilkinson and Cole timed their arrivals to enter Lengo Channel east of the Marine perimeter around 5:00 a.m. to reach Lunga Point by daylight. While the destroyers searched the waters for enemy submarines and the skies for Japanese aircraft, the transports unloaded ammunition, rations, construction materials, and other items to Vandegrift's forces ashore. At dusk they retired south near San Cristobal Island, not far from Guadalcanal, and waited until the early morning, at which time they returned to Guadalcanal for another day of unloading.

Most crews hated pulling away from the island at night, which exposed the Marines on Guadalcanal to terrifying bombardments, but the Navy had to protect its sparse resources. Vandegrift complained about the torturous nighttime bombings, but Ghormley did not yet feel strong enough to challenge the enemy at night.

"I'll never forget the humiliation of slinking down Lengo Channel each evening in October and letting the Japs come in at night and bombard the shit out of the Marines," said Lieutenant John Everett of the *Nicholas*. "Americans are not accustomed to having the shit kicked out of them; it was very hard to take."[2]

It was difficult to swallow back home, too. In the *New York Times*, Charles Hurd described the actions off Guadalcanal as "the game of hide-and-seek being played by the opposing air and naval forces around Guadalcanal." Hanson Baldwin cautioned his readers only three days after *O'Bannon* and *Fletcher* had escorted *Copahee* to Guadalcanal that "the news from the Solomons of the last few days again showed that this campaign is likely to be bitter, unrelenting and protracted and will probably continue to involve a considerable portion of the naval strength of both sides."[3]

"I Daily Hoped for Relief"

Confident of victory, the Japanese poured in fresh commanders, troops, and supplies for a mid-October push. On October 9, Lieutenant General Harukichi Hyakutake, a brilliant tactician with experience in the jungles of New Guinea, arrived to direct the offensive. Within a week four thousand Japanese reinforcements joined the forces already on Guadalcanal. The Japanese expected to attack on October 22, by which time almost seventy ships from the Combined Fleet, including four aircraft carriers, would have arrived to keep Nimitz's fleet at a distance. Lieutenant General Masao Maruyama, commander of the crack Sendai Division, admonished his troops that they were to either defeat the Americans or die.

The Marine commander, General Vandegrift, pleaded for additional men and supplies to alleviate the dire conditions. While he possessed a significant force of Marines, he explained that because of the ceaseless combat and inadequate rations, more than half were physically unable to mount protracted operations against such a skilled enemy. On frequent visits to the front lines, Vandegrift saw repeated examples of his men's ability, but also detected signs that they teetered on the brink of collapse. Malaria-infected men remained at their posts in the unfamiliar jungle terrain, where they fought in temperatures reaching 103 degrees. They suffered from a lack of food and sleep and watched in mounting frustration as enemy ships steamed at leisure in the strait off Guadalcanal, untouched by an absent United States Navy. "I daily hoped for relief by the Army," wrote Vandegrift of the difficult September and October weeks.[4]

While Japanese submarines intensified their efforts in Torpedo Junction, on October 13 Japanese battleships lambasted Henderson Field with their mammoth twelve-inch and fourteen-inch guns, which hurled toward the Marines on Guadalcanal shells that Vandegrift later described as "monsters." The Navy's inability to prevent the bombardment infuriated the Marine commander, whose men suffered nightly while the enemy boldly steamed offshore, free to wreak havoc on Guadalcanal. "I could do nothing to disrupt the raid," Vandegrift wrote. "We owned no night fighters; our artillery could not reach the ships. Like everyone else in the perimeter I sat out the bombardment, hoping against a direct hit on my dugout."[5]

Vandegrift sent a priority dispatch to Nimitz and Ghormley. He argued that the situation called for "two urgent and immediate steps: take and maintain control of the sea areas adjacent to Cactus [code name for Guadalcanal] to prevent further enemy landings and enemy bombardments such as this force has taken for the last three nights; reinforcement of ground forces by at least one division in order that extensive operations may be initiated to destroy hostile forces now on Cactus."[6]

Two days later, again in full view of incensed Marines, the Japanese unloaded more troops and supplies off Tassafaronga. Admiral Ugaki confided to his diary on October 13, "I think a chance of turning the tables has been grasped at last. It has been a long struggle and effort, indeed."[7]

The apparent Japanese advantage rested upon a cracked foundation, however. Admiral Isoroku Yamamoto, Commander in Chief, Combined Fleet, who had visited the United States earlier in his career and witnessed that country's astounding productivity, doubted that the Americans would relinquish their slim hold on the island. They had already sacrificed the lives of many Marines and sailors, and they would continue to fight until a massive infusion of men, ships, and matériel from the United States reached Guadalcanal. He feared that optimism among the Japanese high command overlooked American determination and industrial capabilities. Yamamoto argued that the Japanese army had foolishly sent small numbers of reinforcements to Guadalcanal—fifteen hundred in August and another three thousand in September—and contended that such a piecemeal approach would allow the United States to close the military gap in the South Pacific.

Yamamoto's qualms mirrored the anxiety felt in Washington, D.C. On October 16 reporters asked Secretary of the Navy Frank Knox if Vandegrift could hold the island. The secretary declined to offer a prediction but replied, in words that were less than reassuring, that he hoped Vandegrift could resist until additional help arrived.

Both sides prepared for the decisive phase around Guadalcanal. By night the Japanese continued to rush men and supplies to the island while bombarding Vandegrift's forces, while during the day the American ships shuttled in reinforcements to those Marines and Army infantry who would have to battle Hyakutake's units.

"We have been racking our brains these days to think of some plan to destroy the enemy fleet," Ugaki wrote in his diary on October 18. Both Knox and Ugaki understood that the stakes were high, and that whichever side grabbed the upper hand at Guadalcanal would take a huge step toward controlling the South Pacific. As a captured Japanese document stated, "It must be said that the success or failure in recapturing Guadalcanal Island, and the vital naval battle related to it, is the fork in the road which leads to victory for them or for us."[8]

Fortunately, a dramatic turn of events ushered in a new commander for the South Pacific, an aggressive leader who, with sheer audacity and by the nature of his powerful personality, uplifted the Marines on Guadalcanal and invigorated the crews of his ships. A destroyerman by background, he would again turn to those vessels, including *O'Bannon*, *Fletcher*, and *Nicholas*, to help turn the tide.

"The Fightingest Admiral in the Navy"

Military visitors to Admiral Ghormley's headquarters in Noumea sensed it within minutes. Instead of originality and optimism, crucial to bolstering the Marines fighting on land and the sailors at sea, desperation prevailed in the South Pacific's central command post. The admiral and his staff rarely left the sweltering confines of their offices aboard the tender *Argonne*, a depressingly small ship that Ghormley's staff had nicknamed the "Agony Maru." Mounds of paperwork shoved sleep to the side. Frantic calls for planes, ships, and men replaced measured communiqués. Ghormley, the man who should have been a source of reassurance, was far from assured himself.

Reporters saw it, too. At Pearl Harbor Admiral Nimitz asked Hanson Baldwin, fresh from a trip to the Solomons, how he assessed the South Pacific commander. "He was really completely defeatist," the correspondent recalled of Ghormley. "He was almost despairing." Baldwin added that Ghormley was overworked, and that the admiral wondered how he could mount a successful operation when he lacked the required resources. "We're just hanging on by our teeth," Ghormley had remarked to Baldwin.

Baldwin left the *Argonne* convinced that Nimitz needed to find a replacement for a man he saw as a timid commander. Instead of hesitation, the crisis called for aggression, "because here was a time when you needed tough, hard, almost ruthless men. He was a miscast, in my opinion. He should never have been in that job."[9]

MacDonald noticed it when he first visited his London comrade upon arriving in the South Pacific and Ghormley complained that he lacked aggressive commanders. MacDonald was too polite to point out the obvious—that if an officer failed, it fell to Ghormley, the commander in the South Pacific, to replace him with someone who could succeed.

Nimitz flew to Noumea on September 28, where his concerns deepened when neither Ghormley nor his staff could adequately answer Nimitz's queries about the lack of progress at Guadalcanal. As Nimitz talked, Ghormley's chief of staff at the time, Rear Admiral Daniel J. Callaghan, walked in with a dispatch. Rather than delivering a measured reply, Ghormley exclaimed, "My God, what are we going to do about this?"[10]

During a trip to Guadalcanal the next day, Nimitz found a refreshing contrast in Vandegrift's optimism. The Marine general said he could defeat the Japanese units converging on Henderson Field, especially if he received additional men and supplies and if the Navy became more aggressive around

Guadalcanal. Vandegrift needed fighting sea commanders not only to help stall the Japanese momentum but also, and more important, to provide evidence for his Marines on the island that the Navy was willing to risk everything on their behalf.

Nimitz had no alternative but to replace Ghormley. He did not have to search for the right man, for he was then in the Pacific, a commander whose actions had already made him one of the nation's first naval heroes. The men aboard *O'Bannon*, *Fletcher*, and *Nicholas* were about to be tossed into action by a man the press loved to call the "Bull."

Vice Admiral William F. Halsey was two days into a tour of the South Pacific when Nimitz ordered him to cancel plans and report to South Pacific headquarters at Noumea. When his aircraft set down in the harbor's waters at Noumea, a member of Admiral Ghormley's staff handed him a missive. Halsey ripped open the envelope, marked "Secret," and read its contents, which named him Ghormley's replacement as commander of the South Pacific. "Jesus Christ and General Jackson!" he bellowed to his staff intelligence officer, Marine Colonel Julian P. Brown. "This is the hottest potato they ever handed me!"[11]

The combative Halsey was accustomed to handling hot potatoes, though, as his long tenure in the Navy had proven. He had spent the early portion of his career perfecting destroyer tactics that he, along with a handful of similarly minded officers, boasted were the best in the Navy. Halsey employed a dynamic approach in which his destroyers barreled at flank speed through tricky maneuvers, ignoring heavy seas and biting winds alike. If ever a ship reflected her skipper's attributes, for Halsey it was a destroyer, a vessel that darted and raced about in search of an opponent to fight.

He added to his daring reputation from the war's opening moment. On a day that saw American battleships settling to Pearl Harbor's mud and aircraft smoldering on pockmarked runways, Halsey was aboard the aircraft carrier *Enterprise* scouring the seas around Hawaii in search of the enemy. Although he failed to locate the Japanese carriers, before day's end he had muttered, to everyone's delight, that before the war ended, "the Japanese language will be spoken only in hell." Even though Halsey now commanded from aircraft carriers, according to a reporter familiar with the man, "he never lost the sense of speed and dash that the 'tin cans' develop in an officer."[12]

For his deeds at Pearl Harbor, as well as for raids against Japanese-held islands in early 1942, Halsey quickly became the darling of the home front.

Newspaper headlines shouted his triumphs and called his actions salve for an ailing nation. He had restored an optimism badly shattered on the Pacific war's first day, and then shown to the military and the public alike that the Navy, though hit hard at Pearl Harbor, retained plenty of sting.

Sailors aboard ships about Guadalcanal and Marines on land welcomed Halsey's appointment, for they knew that a fighter now stood at the helm. Marines slapped each other on the back, and some claimed that having Halsey in charge was like adding three aircraft carriers to the fleet. Military correspondents, accustomed to filing disheartening reports of the fighting, shared in the jubilation. "The effect on the men of the fleet and those ashore at Guadalcanal was electric," wrote Gilbert Cant. "Halsey had the reputation of being the fightingest admiral in the Navy."[13]

Contemporary newspapers and magazines conveyed the impact on the home front of Halsey's appointment. "New South Pacific Chief Aggressive Commander," proclaimed a *Los Angeles Times* headline. The *New York Times* joined in with "Shift to Offensive Is Seen in Washington Selection of 'Fighting' Admiral Halsey as Commander in the South Pacific."[14]

Time magazine placed Halsey on its November 2 cover. A lengthy article examined the importance of the South Pacific, where *O'Bannon*, *Fletcher*, and *Nicholas* had only recently arrived. "It has become the vortex of a naval whirlpool which may easily engulf either adversary," the magazine concluded of Guadalcanal. The profile added, "If the U.S. loses Guadalcanal, the Japanese can press on with relative ease, take the whole chain of islands down through the New Hebrides to New Caledonia, and then have only the narrow moat of the Coral Sea between them and Australia. But if the U.S. holds Guadalcanal, and can force its way up the chain as far as Rabaul, then the Allies will have a series of bases from which to build a major offensive against the Japs." The article explained that the results Halsey achieved with his bag of tricks, which prominently featured those destroyers he loved, "can mean the difference between vigorous offense and weary defense in the Pacific, perhaps between beating the Japs in two years and in ten."[15]

Halsey, a man accustomed to quick action, faced three crucial tasks—to reinforce the Marines on Guadalcanal, to prevent the enemy from reinforcing their own troops on the island, and to destroy a Japanese navy that dominated the waters around Guadalcanal. Unfortunately, he had few resources with which to execute his missions. A handful of surface ships, including *O'Bannon*, *Fletcher*, and *Nicholas*, either plied the waters or would soon be there, but he needed more of everything if he was to reverse the situation at Guadalcanal. Unfortunately for him, the United States' first land assault against Hitler, the November invasion of North Africa, took priority, and Halsey would have to make do with what he had to contain the Japanese until additional help arrived.

Five days after being named commander, Halsey met with Vandegrift in Noumea. The Marine officer described the deplorable conditions under which his Marines fought, and emphasized that while he was confident his units could hold, he needed more air and ground reinforcements than he had been receiving. Halsey promised to immediately send whatever resources he had.

True to his word, Halsey located and tossed men into action and diverted ships to the Solomons. "You can't make an omelet without breaking eggs," he said. "You can't fight a war safely or without losing ships." When one Army division arrived in the South Pacific, its commanding officer told Halsey that he needed three weeks to combat-load his transports and prepare his men. Halsey laughed and remarked, "Your division is leaving for Guadalcanal tomorrow."[16]

Halsey may have been short of crucial items, but until he possessed the tools, he would substitute attitude and grit to invigorate his forces. Halsey's Third Fleet War Diary bemoaned the paucity of South Pacific resources "in men, material, ships, planes," but boasted that the sailors under his command lacked "everything but guts."[17] This sense of urgency spread throughout the forces operating in the South Pacific in the coming months, dictating much of what MacDonald, Wylie, and the other officers and enlisted aboard the trio of destroyers would do to strike back at the Japanese and begin the long road to victory.

"Even more than the hit-&-run disaster at Pearl Harbor," intoned *Time* magazine three weeks after Halsey assumed command, "even more than the defeat in the Philippines, the prolonged Battle of the Solomons had brought the U.S. people face to face with a great and bitter truth of war. To most nations in all wars have come days filled with a succession of campaigns that were costly and not going well. Now, more than at any time since 1863, America knew such days." The magazine concluded, "In their concern, the people hoped for the best, prepared for the worst, gloomed at the sinkings and took courage from their heroes."[18]

Among those heroes were the first three crews of what would eventually become Desron 21.

"I Was Just a Country Boy"

MacDonald sensed a change right away. Destroyers, historically built to launch torpedo attacks, engaged in everything but that. Lacking items in every crucial area, including warships, in the early weeks and months Halsey utilized his destroyers as his jack-of-all-trades.

Halsey sent *O'Bannon*, *Fletcher*, and *Nicholas* straight to the Solomons, where the officers and enlisted enjoyed no breather in escorting ships north from Espiritu Santo to Guadalcanal, back to Espiritu Santo, down to Noumea, and northward again to Espiritu Santo and Guadalcanal. "The Guadalcanal Shuttle was in full operation," wrote one destroyer officer of those desperate weeks in the Solomons. "Every trip to the objective area brought about a quick turnaround. It was never-ending, escorting cargo ships one time and assault transports with reinforcements the next."[19]

Crews had to remain at their stations for long stretches because of the constant threat from enemy submarines and aircraft. "We had to be on alert pretty much all the time," said Seaman 1/c Robert Whisler of *O'Bannon*, "because the air cover was not complete until Guadalcanal was secure."[20]

At the same time, the Japanese upped the pressure. In late October, Emperor Hirohito issued a rescript to his military stating, "We believe the war situation is critical. Officers and men, exert yourselves to even greater efforts." Hirohito then said to an adviser, "Guadalcanal is the focal point of the war and an important base for the navy. So don't rest on small achievements. Move quickly and recapture it."[21] The outcome in the South Pacific, and with it possibly the future of the war itself, boiled down to what unfolded off Guadalcanal.

Every voyage across Torpedo Junction, the stretch of the Coral Sea connecting Guadalcanal to Espiritu Santo and Noumea, was rife with peril. Radarmen scrutinized the water's surface and the skies for enemy ships and aircraft, while their compatriots in sonar kept watch on the ocean's depths for Japanese submarines that silently prowled below.

No one could relax. Aboard *O'Bannon*, when he was not at his battle station as a trainer on one of the ship's five-inch guns, Seaman Whisler scrubbed decks or tended to his other duties. Whisler had only recently joined the ship in Espiritu Santo from the USS *McCalla* (DD-488) and now operated in a hotly contested battle zone, all while being, at age seventeen, the youngest member of the crew.

"I was just a country boy," said Whisler years later. He was born October 1, 1924, in Hobbs, Indiana, and his family moved to Michigan five years later. "I quit my senior year in high school to join the Navy in March 1942," he recalled. His grandmother gave him a silver dollar as a parting gift, saying it was for good luck. He placed the coin in his pocket, mostly as a way of maintaining an attachment to someone with whom he was close, but he figured it could not hurt in the luck department. He needed good fortune as the *O'Bannon* threaded her way across Torpedo Junction in late October and early November. "They kept us busy all the time with missions, training, drills, and regular watches," explained Whisler.[22]

The Tokyo Express mirrored their movements by rushing in from the north their own reinforcements and supplies. Nearly every night a cluster of Japanese destroyers escorted transports to Guadalcanal, "almost in accordance with a time table," according to MacDonald. "These nights were very hectic as we were constantly on the alert and we were maneuvering in waters which were then somewhat unfamiliar."[23]

Officers and enlisted learned that around Guadalcanal and in Torpedo Junction, each day brought its challenges. Late October for *Nicholas* was typical of what the three destroyers faced. Early in the morning of October 22 the ship anchored off Guadalcanal, where Brown called general quarters to provide protection while the transport, *Kopara*, unloaded its cargo. In midmorning three Marine officers boarded to direct fire for a bombardment of enemy positions near Marine lines on the island. From a range of 11,500 yards, Brown navigated *Nicholas* on four alternating east-west runs off Guadalcanal, each time moving the destroyer closer to shore until the gap had been cut in half. The five-inch gun crews fired more than a thousand rounds during the two-hour bombardment, creating a thrilling spectacle with the fiery explosions ashore.

Shortly after, three enemy bombers attacked. Brown's five-inch guns fired for six minutes to repel the bombers, but two minutes later three more planes charged *Nicholas*. While Brown maneuvered the destroyer to avoid the bombs, the 40mm and 20mm crews joined in, pumping almost a thousand shells skyward. Over the next twenty minutes streams of gunfire coughed from *Nicholas*'s guns to divert the enemy pilots. The Japanese fled after dropping two bombs that splashed harmlessly fifty yards to port.

When the all clear sounded at 1:45 p.m., sailors were surprised at their fatigue. The air attack had lasted only half an hour, yet they felt as if they had been fighting all day. As calm settled in, the men understood how excruciating even a brief attack could be. Given that, what must a major surface engagement be like?

Thirty-five minutes after the air attack, a Japanese shore battery opened fire at *Kopara*. The five-inch crews again jumped into action, tossing almost two hundred shells against the position; the American barrage silenced the offending guns.

As dusk set in, Brown escorted *Kopara* out to sea for the night, as he did on the following two evenings. "At sea, steaming as before in company with *Kopara* on course 176° True, speed 11.5 knots," Virgil Wing wrote in his diary on October 24. "0450 Dawn alert, but I was already on watch." With a final destination of Noumea, Brown had his men tidy up the ship. "We don't get any cleaning done in the disputed area due to full time on watches of one kind or another," added Wing.[24]

The next afternoon Brown received orders to leave *Kopara*, which would continue to Noumea, and join Task Force 64 to meet a reported Japanese surface force west of Savo Island. The battleship *Washington* led an imposing array of three cruisers—*Atlanta*, *Helena*, and *San Francisco*—and nine destroyers, including *Fletcher*. With *Nicholas* joining as a tenth, the unit formed a powerful countermeasure to the reported enemy force.

Tension mounted with each mile. When in late afternoon the task force neared the western side of Savo Island, where the Japanese were reported to be, Brown called the crew to stations. The ships formed into a long column, with six destroyers leading the unit, followed by the three cruisers, the flagship, and four more destroyers in the rear. Brown mentally questioned the formation, which split the destroyers into two groups. He, like most destroyer skippers, would have preferred collecting the ten into a unit so they could launch a massed torpedo attack. Information suggested that the enemy was expected to arrive around midnight, but when nothing was found anywhere near Savo Island, the ships retired north and west of Guadalcanal.

The previous four days had taken a toll. As Virgil Wing walked aft, a machinist's mate stopped him. During fitting out in Bath, the man had boasted about his eagerness to fight, but he was now a changed sailor. After the tension of the previous days, the machinist's mate stared at Wing and mumbled, "How much more do they think we can take?"

"This night seemed to have the elements that separated fortitude from bluster," wrote Wing on October 25. "The sailors gathered in small groups or alone." One man withdrew and refused to speak; "he looked at the eastern horizon and his face seemed to thin and sag as I watched." Nearby a sailor conveyed his intent to leave with the words "I'll get off this ship, just watch me!"[25] The man received his wish when, after refusing to eat for more than a week, the ship's doctor transferred both him and the reclusive sailor off the ship.

Fletcher and *O'Bannon* experienced the same, but a new wrinkle appeared on November 8. While *Nicholas* escorted a transport to New Zealand, *O'Bannon* and *Fletcher* departed Noumea for Guadalcanal as part of Task Force 67, consisting of four transports, the cruisers *Juneau* and *Portland*, and three destroyers. Instead of guarding transports and keeping a close eye on the waters, however, the two crews were soon to be tossed into one of the largest surface naval engagements of the war.

The Japanese were on their way.

"You Are the Son of Samurai"

Admiral Ugaki knew that the emperor was already calling Guadalcanal "the place of bitter struggles" and that some action to regain the initiative was imperative. His cohort Admiral Yamamoto believed that if the Japanese did not follow up their Pearl Harbor triumph with another convincing victory over the United States, they would face an uphill battle for the remainder of the war. Ugaki wrote a friend in early October, "Things here are proving hard going. I felt from the start that America was not likely to relinquish lightly positions established at the cost of such sacrifices, and I pressed the view that a high degree of preparation and willingness to make sacrifices would be necessary on our side, but everybody here always persists in facile optimism until the very worst actually happens."[26]

Yamamoto would not allow his nation's 1942 Pacific conquests, speedy military operations that had impressed military observers around the globe, to be wasted by defeat in the Solomons. He planned an intricate November operation to hit Halsey before the American had a chance to expand his forces. While the Japanese army rushed another sixty thousand troops to Guadalcanal and the Imperial Navy continued to bombard Henderson Field, Yamamoto's senior naval commanders would lure the United States Fleet into a night battle, where Japanese wartime experience and their superb torpedoes could crush the inexperienced Americans. Two light carriers, four battleships, eleven cruisers, and almost forty destroyers gathered at Truk for the operation, while in the Solomons, beginning on November 2 and for the following eight days the Tokyo Express maintained a constant flow of reinforcements and supplies from Rabaul to Guadalcanal.

Halsey figured that November would likely bring a surface engagement with the Japanese and countered with his own measures. A cruiser-destroyer force rushed in artillery ammunition to the Marines on October 30, and he began gathering a force that included *O'Bannon* and *Fletcher* with which to meet the enemy.

"I hope they will become prey to our attack tomorrow," wrote Ugaki on November 10. When scout aircraft located Task Force 67 under Admiral Richmond K. Turner, which included MacDonald and the *O'Bannon*, two hundred miles from Guadalcanal, Ugaki asked himself, "How shall we destroy this enemy?"[27]

Tameichi Hara, then in the South Pacific, where he began compiling a record for the Imperial Japanese Navy that was the envy of his contemporaries, wondered the same. Born October 16, 1900, in a suburb of Takamatsu City, on the northern coast of Shikoku Island facing the Inland Sea, Hara seemed predestined to a life at sea. The Japanese navy traced its origins to the city, the first major naval battle in Japanese history was fought off Takamatsu in 1185, and the Inland Sea teemed with aquatic life that formed a mainstay of the Japanese economy.

The future destroyer captain was mostly influenced by his grandfather Moichiro Hara, who had been a revered samurai in his youth. Although changes in the Japanese societal structure enacted in 1871 eliminated the influence of the samurai class, his grandfather never tired of regaling Hara with tales of the feats of famous samurai warriors. Moichiro longed to return to those years and earmarked his grandson as the person to restore military glory to the family.

When Moichiro lay dying, he called his six-year-old grandson to his bedside, handed him his treasured samurai sword, and whispered that the weapon was now his. He reminded Hara of the many samurai tales he had shared of men "who suffered great hardships to achieve their missions. Try to do likewise. Always be on guard, and redouble your efforts to better yourself." Then, near death, Moichiro said, "Tameichi Hara! You are the son of samurai and you will remember that," and repeated to his grandson the ancient adage "A samurai lives in such a way that he is always prepared to die."[28]

Tameichi followed his grandfather's words. In 1918 he entered the Japanese naval academy at Eta Jima. After graduating four years later, Hara served aboard two destroyers and forged a friendship with his squadron commander, Captain Chuichi Nagumo. The brilliant destroyer expert urged Hara to study both his tactics as well as the United States, considered by many in naval circles as Japan's next enemy, and shared books he had obtained during a visit to the United States.

The intelligent officer excelled at the mechanics and tactics of the destroyer's main offensive weapon, the torpedo attack. The navy published a new torpedo manual based on Hara's studies, which transformed the torpedo assault into a formidable weapon that wreaked havoc in the Solomons for MacDonald and other American skippers.

A second development complemented Hara's work: in 1933, the Japanese navy introduced torpedoes propelled by oxygen rather than the compressed air that had long fueled torpedoes, including those used by the United States. The dramatic change, which was introduced two years after MacDonald graduated from the Naval Academy, eliminated the long white track created at the water's surface by the compressed air, and replaced it with a nearly imperceptible track. In combination with the longer ranges and faster speeds Japanese torpedoes already possessed, the new fuel source gave Hara and other Japanese destroyer captains operating in the Solomons the best torpedo yet devised.

As his friend Nagumo guided his carriers and escorts to Pearl Harbor for the December 7, 1941, attack, Hara, then the captain of the new 2,500-ton destroyer *Amatsukaze*, took his ship southward as part of the invasion force against the Philippines. In January 1942 he participated in the invasion of the Netherlands East Indies, and fought in the February Battle of the Java Sea, June's momentous Battle of Midway, and August's Battle of the Eastern Solomons. He emerged from the operations convinced that the Japanese navy was more than a match for the United States, but believed that his nation had to defeat their foe before the American factories and shipyards began operating at peak efficiency. *O'Bannon*, *Fletcher*, and *Nicholas* had already reached the region, and more warships were certain to follow.

Hara hoped that the November surface engagement would help settle matters.

"It's a Showdown in the Solomons"

At Pearl Harbor, Nimitz received signs of imminent action in the Guadalcanal area. "There are some indications that the enemy will attempt to resume his all-out attack on Guadalcanal in the near future," concluded his daily summary for November 3. "We believe that he has superior sea power in the area, but may not know it." The Japanese continued to push in reinforcements and supplies over the next three days, and Nimitz added on November 8, "There is strong indication of a grand scale offensive aimed at Guadalcanal to be undertaken by the enemy in the very near future."[29]

On November 9 Nimitz alerted Halsey that all signs pointed to a major enemy offensive "assisted by carrier striking forces slated to support movement of Army transports to Guadalcanal." He added that "this is expected to be a major effort to recapture Guadalcanal," and that the attack was expected to occur on November 13. "While this looks like a big punch I am confident that you with your forces will take their measure."[30]

Their suspicions were confirmed on November 10 when a coastwatcher on Bougainville reported sixty-one enemy vessels in the region and Halsey's reconnaissance aircraft spotted increased enemy activity near Truk and Rabaul. Halsey canceled the orders sending exhausted crews and damaged ships to Pearl Harbor for rest and repair and ordered every ship to Guadalcanal, as he faced a moment when "even half-ships counted."[31]

"This was the tightest spot that I was ever in during the entire war," Halsey wrote after the conflict. He worried that even if he turned back the Japanese warships, his naval forces might be so weakened that they would be unable to prevent future Japanese attempts to reinforce the island. If he failed to engage the enemy at sea and allowed them to bombard Vandegrift's exhausted units ashore, the morale of those Marines would be adversely affected. He had promised Vandegrift action, and he refused to renege on his pledge the first time the enemy gathered in strength. "If I have any principle of warfare that is burned within my brain," he wrote, "it is that the best defense is a strong offense. Lord Nelson expressed this very well, 'No captain can go wrong who places his ship alongside the enemy's.'"[32]

Halsey expected the crews of every ship, including *O'Bannon* and *Fletcher*, to display the same aggressiveness. Fortunately the crews, especially those of the newer destroyers, were young and lacked the experience to be frightened. "We knew it was desperate," said Seaman Whisler, the youngest member aboard *O'Bannon*, "but we were pretty confident back then. There wasn't much fear of the Japanese. Being young, though, helped."[33]

Halsey organized four naval groups under Rear Admiral Richmond Kelly Turner. Two groups, one commanded by Turner and the other by Rear Admiral Norman Scott, would escort transports containing six thousand troops and supplies to Guadalcanal. Rear Admiral Daniel J. Callaghan, an old friend of MacDonald's, would screen and be ready to engage any Japanese surface force that appeared. A fourth group, built around the damaged carrier *Enterprise*, was still at Noumea awaiting departure as soon as the carrier was repaired. Not counting the *Enterprise* group, Turner commanded two battleships, four heavy cruisers, four light cruisers, and twenty-two destroyers, including *O'Bannon* and *Fletcher*, both serving under Callaghan.

Late in the afternoon of November 12, Callaghan and Scott escorted troop transports to Guadalcanal, where they deposited their reinforcements. While the men and matériel moved shoreward, search aircraft spotted the enemy force 335 miles north. Callaghan waited until dusk before shutting down the transports and pulling away. When he had taken the transports a safe distance from the island, Callaghan detached his flagship, *San Francisco*, a second heavy cruiser, *Portland*, and three light cruisers, including *Helena*, *Juneau*, and Scott in *Atlanta*. Escorted by eight destroyers, the ships steered north to intercept the Japanese approaching Guadalcanal.

The crews of *O'Bannon* and *Fletcher* were about to face a Japanese surface force for the first time, but despite their inexperience, they approached battle with more confidence than could be justified. "We didn't worry about going head-to-head with the Japanese," said Machinist's Mate 1/c Donald Holmes of the *Fletcher*. The crew trusted Cole, whom Holmes called "the best skipper we ever had," and "Wylie was very good, too. The Japs were ready for war and we weren't, but it didn't bother us."[34]

Those officers Holmes trusted, as well as Wilkinson and MacDonald on *O'Bannon*, had doubts about Callaghan's decision to form the ships into one long column. Instead of collecting the eight destroyers as one unit, Callaghan placed four destroyers, including *O'Bannon*, at the column's van and the other four, with *Fletcher*, bringing up the rear. Nestled in the middle steamed the five cruisers. The quartet of destroyer officers believed that by separating the ships, Callaghan had reduced their effectiveness, and that he employed tactics that seemed straight from the days of sail.

They were especially concerned with the stations of the two newest destroyers. Like most warships, both destroyers possessed search radar, model C (SC radar), which detected targets attacking from above, but they also carried search radar, model G (SG radar), installed on only the newest ships, such as *O'Bannon* and *Fletcher*. The SG radar swept twenty-five to thirty miles out and spotted surface targets on a complete 360-degree circle about the ship, differentiated ships from landmasses, and made it easier for gunnery officers to hit their targets. Rather than placing *Fletcher* and *O'Bannon* in the lead, where Callaghan could benefit from that enhanced radar, he assigned three destroyers lacking that device ahead of *O'Bannon* and placed *Fletcher* in the final slot of the column.

As far as Wylie was concerned, Callaghan's move was akin to placing a blind man in the lead while a person with perfect vision had to follow behind. "I can't figure out any rhyme or reason why we were so formed or allocated," he said after the war. "We had no idea what we were going to do if we met some Nips. No battle plans, no coherence to the formation. It was just one bloody long column. That dates back, last time anybody tried that was before Trafalgar. Well," Wylie added exasperatedly, "even Nelson did not do that."[35] In the coming fight, Callaghan would have to turn to what was certain to be a heavily used TBS to call on *O'Bannon* for the enemy's ranges, course, and bearing, each call delaying decisions at a time when every second could mean the difference between being the first to launch an attack and being the first to be hit.

"Again it's a showdown in the Solomons," wrote the perceptive correspondent Hanson Baldwin. He claimed that the Japanese had assembled what was probably the largest fleet they had yet gathered to make a "major effort to expel us from the Solomons." With the United States committing vast resources to the recent landings in North Africa, thereby shrinking the number of ships it could dispatch to the Solomons, the Japanese "no longer fear surprise" from Halsey. "The issue in the Solomons is again in doubt," concluded Baldwin.[36]

"They Didn't Know Hell"

As transports poured supplies shoreward on November 12, radar operators aboard *O'Bannon* and *Fletcher* scoured the surface and the skies above Ironbottom Sound, the appellation Americans gave the waters between Guadalcanal and Florida Island because of the alarming number of vessels sunk in those waters. At the same time, sonarmen swept the depths for submarines, ready to take action against any contact.

Three waves of Japanese torpedo planes, each approaching from different sectors, interrupted the unloading in the early afternoon. "At last we were in action!" MacDonald later said. "This was our first actual contact with the enemy."[37] Since he and the crew had arrived in the Pacific a month earlier, *O'Bannon* had escorted transports and hunted enemy submarines, but they had not been in what MacDonald considered a combat encounter with the Japanese. Young sailors such as Bob Whisler, who didn't know what to expect, and veterans such as Wilkinson and Cole, who wondered how the young crews would fare against the Japanese navy, would soon have their answers.

Crews on all ships buttoned their shirts to the neck and rolled down their sleeves to prevent flash burns should a shell strike. At his post deep in the ship's bowels, engineering officer Lieutenant Carl F. Pfeifer glanced at the young men in the engine room who were about to risk their lives in battle for the first time. He had been at Pearl Harbor on December 7, but few among the crew could claim battle experience. Those boys standing at their stations far below the main deck, cut off from their shipmates above and blind to what was about to occur, "were representative of the entire ship's company. The ship was green, they were green and so were most of the officers." Pfeifer liked that their executive officer, MacDonald, was "a seasoned veteran of London air raids," and he knew the crew had performed well in shakedown and gunnery practice. "But now we were playing for keeps and I wondered how we would take it."

Pfeifer observed no outward manifestations of fear. If they were anything like him, Pfeifer concluded that their insides must be churning at top speed, because every sailor in the Black Gang, the crews that worked below in the engine and firerooms, knew what to expect "if an enemy torpedo strikes—an explosion, flame, live steam and sudden death."[38] Happily, concluded Pfeifer, his crew seemed to be handling matters well.

The sound of muffled thunderclaps above snapped Pfeifer out of his musings. The big guns had jumped into action. For Pfeifer and his boys, the time for thinking was over.

As the torpedo planes raced in, *O'Bannon*, *Fletcher*, and the other escorts formed a tight circle about the transports. Wilkinson zigzagged his ship to present a more elusive target, and while a handful of enemy aircraft evaded the fire and launched their torpedoes, most burst into flames and spiraled seaward, where they momentarily skidded along the surface before exploding. "The air seemed to be filled with crashing and burning planes and bullets," said MacDonald, who had made certain that the St. Christopher medal Cecilia had given him rested in his left breast pocket. "This was our first opportunity to see at close hand what an enemy plane looked like."[39]

At Lieutenant Pfeifer's side in the engine room far below the action, Fireman 2/c Charles H. Hagy Jr., connected to the bridge as Pfeifer's telephone talker, listened to what occurred and relayed it to the group. "We just shot down a Jap plane! We just got another!" Hagy shouted. The men in the room grinned—even the tiny bits of information Hagy conveyed were treasured, for they made the engine room crew feel a part of the fighting above. "The engine room gang never sees a gun fired, but these boys wear the results," said Pfeifer. "Now their faces glistened and their dungarees were dark and wet from profuse sweating under the 120-degree heat. They were black and grimy from cork dust and burned powder being sucked in from the decks above."[40]

O'Bannon gunners, busy loading clips of ammunition or aiming guns, directed more than eight hundred rounds at the attacking aircraft in the forty-three-minute action. Wilkinson reported afterward that their stout defense had shot down two aircraft for certain, with two probables.

Fletcher gunners claimed an even more impressive tally, splashing five of the ten torpedo planes that attacked. On his forward 20mm gun Seaman 1/c D. H. Dahlke directed such accurate fire that, according to Wylie, he "literally cut pieces out of the nose and cockpit of one plane," while on another 20mm gun close by, Seaman 1/c E. G. Walker "opened up on the nose of a dive bomber and continued to hit until after the plane crashed in the water."[41]

One bomber passed along *Fletcher*'s starboard, a second astern, and a third to port in the eleven-minute duel, including one that starboard side gunners shredded from nose to tail, but none succeeded in breaking through the thick antiaircraft blanket to harm the *Fletcher*. "Enemy's aircraft was a complete failure," concluded *O'Bannon*'s war diary for that day. "No casualties in this vessel."[42] The Japanese damaged only one ship, the cruiser *San Francisco*.

Both Wilkinson and Cole were pleased with how their men responded to their initial battle test. In the ship's recesses, Pfeifer gave high marks not only to the young men sweating and laboring in the engine room but also to the crew as a whole. "We knew now that she [*O'Bannon*] could take it and dish it out, and so could her crew. This crowd of boots and feather merchants [reserves] had performed like veterans in the first battle."[43]

As daylight blended into dusk, the screen escorted the transports eastward. Wilkinson would have liked to give his men time to relax, but mid-November off Guadalcanal was not the time for a break. If this torpedo attack was the harbinger of a stronger surface assault, his men needed to be ready.

MacDonald had hoped to return to Espiritu Santo for at least a day's respite, but instead Wilkinson, as part of Callaghan's task force, received orders to return to the Guadalcanal area to intercept an enemy surface force steaming southward from Rabaul to bombard Henderson Field and land infantry reinforcements. "We were very happy when that day was over," recalled MacDonald, "thinking we were going back to port to sort of relax a little bit, and then we were turned around and ordered back." He knew the sailors were already exhausted from the earlier air attack and from guarding the transports; "hadn't they just had a battle?"[44]

At headquarters, Admiral Halsey regretted the need to send smaller destroyers such as *O'Bannon* into action against Japanese battleships and cruisers, but he had no alternative. Should the Japanese succeed in destroying the airstrip on Guadalcanal and landing those reinforcements, his ability to hold the line in the South Pacific would be tenuous at best. Should his ships triumph, Halsey would gain both a reprieve while the Japanese pulled back to regroup and additional time to rush more men, ships, and equipment to Guadalcanal. Halsey was playing a high-risk game, but the old destroyerman wagered that the destroyer crews would come through for him.

O'Bannon and *Fletcher* steamed westward, two destroyers in a long column that comprised five cruisers and eight destroyers. Wilkinson placed *O'Bannon* in her assigned fourth slot, behind the destroyers *Cushing*, *Laffey*, and *Sterett*, while astern followed the cruisers *Atlanta*, *San Francisco*, *Helena*, *Portland*, and *Juneau*. Four destroyers formed the rear section, with *Aaron Ward*, *Barton*, *Monssen*, and *Fletcher* steaming in that order. MacDonald, Cole, and Wylie hoped that Callaghan's decision to form a single column, which the admiral believed would enable the ships to better navigate the tricky waters off Guadalcanal, would not boomerang and cost the lives of their officers and sailors.

A gentle breeze in the moonless sky wafted off the riggings as the unit sliced through calm seas. The pitch-black night challenged the eyesight of on-deck observers, who after a few moments gazing into the void felt as if they were staring through dark velvet. As Callaghan's force steamed through the narrow waters off Guadalcanal, sonar and radar crews aboard *O'Bannon* and *Fletcher* kept a close watch for submerged outcroppings and reefs as well as for enemy ships.

At midnight on November 13 the ships entered the eastern end of Lengo Channel and moved westward along Guadalcanal's northern coastline. An hour later *O'Bannon* lookouts spotted a bright light coming from Guadalcanal on the port bow. At the same time an announcement over the loudspeaker alerted the crew to a possible air raid against Henderson Field. Tension mounted when half an hour later reports came that a torpedo had passed ahead of the ship from starboard to port.

"At this time the sky was quite dark," Wilkinson later recorded in his action report, the "moon had become hidden behind dark clouds, a limited number of stars were visible, and there was a slight breeze from north northeast. The sea was smooth."[45]

Radar pips at 1:30 a.m. indicated enemy units ahead and on *O'Bannon*'s starboard bow. At the same time *Fletcher*'s radar spotted ships southwest of Savo Island, where a few months earlier a handful of Japanese cruisers had outclassed a numerically superior American force. One group crossed ahead of the American column from port to starboard, another steamed on the column's port bow, and a third barreled in on the port beam. The sightings indicated that the Japanese were out in force.

Callaghan turned his column northward to meet the enemy's triple threat. Crews snapped into action as general quarters sounded on all ships. Seaman Whisler raced to his station on the *O'Bannon*'s fantail five-inch gun, heard the gun turret doors slam shut, and prepared for a mighty explosion as the gun's shells raced toward their targets. Aboard *Fletcher*, Machinist's Mate Holmes slid down ladders to man the steam pump in the forward engine room, while not far away, Fireman Setter stood ready at his post in the forward engine room. Both listened to chief petty officers bellow instructions to feed more oil to the engines and remind the men to keep sharp, as they were likely to soon be executing a rapid series of course and speed corrections. Damage control parties collected at their assigned spots on deck and below, ready to man hoses to battle fires or to grab pumps to contain any flooding. Antiaircraft gunners stood by their weapons, intent on adding their fire if the Japanese warships came within range of their guns. Radar and sonar crews tracked waters now dissected by a score or more of ships.

With combat imminent, Seaman Whisler touched his grandmother's lucky silver dollar. Although he knew the coin would hardly determine whether he lived or died in the next few hours, its presence comforted Whisler. He vowed that if he survived this battle, he would keep the coin in his pocket throughout the war.

Aboard the *Fletcher*, Machinist's Mate Holmes trusted that if every man aboard the ship did his job, and if luck was on their side, he would emerge in one piece. "I knew we were going into battle around 2:00 a.m.," explained Holmes. "The captain said it over the speaker. So, we were ready for them. We knew it was pretty serious out there in the Solomons. We needed to be ready for them. We trusted our officers. We had no control over anything. You don't worry about being killed or wounded because there was nothing you could do about it anyway, so why worry?"[46] The more superstitious among them tried to forget that they were steaming into battle on Friday the thirteenth, or that Callaghan's cruisers and destroyers totaled thirteen, or that the digits in *Fletcher*'s hull number, DD-445, added up to thirteen.

At the front of the column *O'Bannon*, fourth in line, was cutting through the waters in the darkness when, "all of a sudden, there were a number of ships around." From MacDonald's vantage, it seemed "they were about to meet the whole Japanese South Pacific fleet." He would now find out if the training had sufficiently transformed these young civilians into an efficient crew. "After a little less than five months aboard the *O'Bannon*, he wrote, "they knew the ship, the sea, and their guns. But they didn't know hell."[47]

CHAPTER 3

NAVAL SLUGFEST OFF GUADALCANAL

The man who would do everything in his power to bring hell to the American fleet was then on the bridge as his destroyer, *Amatsukaze*, raced south from Truk toward Guadalcanal. One week before leaving Truk, Tameichi Hara had visited his mentor, Admiral Nagumo, after the admiral had been relieved of his duties. Hara thought his friend, who had been in battle since leading the Pearl Harbor attack force almost one year earlier, appeared haggard and in need of recuperation back home, but Nagumo talked only of what lay ahead for the junior officer. He warned Hara of bitter fighting to come, and he feared that Hara and his fellow ship commanders would steam into battle with a disadvantage now that most of Japan's carriers were either sunk or being repaired and many of their most gifted aviators had been killed.

In mid-November the Japanese planned a joint operation to defeat the United States Marines on Guadalcanal and to restore naval supremacy in the Solomons. While the land forces assaulted Vandegrift's lines, the navy would send a unit of battleships, cruisers, and destroyers to bombard Henderson Field and to defeat any American warships that appeared.

The Japanese army took the first step by committing the 38th Division to Guadalcanal. In four speedy runs to Guadalcanal in the month's first ten days, destroyers landed the entire Japanese division without encountering opposition.

Hara's skilled senior commander, Rear Admiral Koki Abe, had a reputation for being overly cautious, but Hara dismissed those concerns as he steamed out of Truk with the light cruiser *Nagara* and seven other destroyers to join Abe's two battleships and three destroyers near Shortland Island on the morning of November 12. Any hope for surprise ended that same morning when, while still three hundred miles from Guadalcanal, an American bomber spotted them. The plane turned away without attacking, but Hara knew that with this sighting, the enemy would be alerted to their presence and would have time to amass a naval force to greet them.

Abe reacted by altering the formation from a single column into a double semicircular formation. Hara and four other destroyer skippers spread out in a five-mile arc ahead of *Nagara*, while the other destroyers formed a second arc about *Nagara*. Abe's flagship, *Hiei*, and its sister ship, *Kirishima*, both 27,500-ton battleships, followed in a column behind *Nagara*.

As the Japanese neared Guadalcanal, heavy rains disrupted the formation. For seven hours the force navigated blindly through rough seas, which broke Hara's arc into groups of two and three destroyers and pushed the ships farther apart. With the possibility of engaging the enemy more probable, Hara "trembled in excitement and breathed deeply of the balmy night breeze." He glanced at the crew about him; "silence prevailed in our ship as every man went to his battle station."[1]

He stood silent as well, proud that he led an able crew and sturdy ship into action. Hara remembered Nagumo's insistence that their nation required convincing victories, and, bolstered by his grandfather's deathbed admonition that a samurai must always be prepared to die for his emperor, Hara steamed by Savo Island toward Guadalcanal, directly into *O'Bannon*'s radar range and on a collision course with Callaghan's cruisers and destroyers.

Hara intended to deliver such a triumph—if need be, with his death.

Both sides in the November Naval Battle of Guadalcanal agreed that one factor dominated: confusion. Fighting in the dark of night, the ships became so tangled in the waters off Guadalcanal that Samuel Eliot Morison, in his epic account of the United States Navy in World War II, concluded that opposing vessels "mingled like minnows in a bucket." In his description of the fighting, Tameichi Hara said the battle was "one of the most fantastic sea battles of modern history in that it was fought at almost point-blank range between 14 Japanese and 13 American warships," and he added, "The battle was extremely confused."[2]

Shortly after 1:00 a.m. on November 13, the thirteen US ships entered Ironbottom Sound and steamed eastward along Guadalcanal's northern coast, passing Koli Point and Lunga Point in their search for the reported enemy force. At the same time Admiral Abe and his fourteen ships, including Hara's *Amatsukaze*, sliced through the waters separating Savo Island and Cape Esperance on Guadalcanal's northwest corner, thirty nautical miles from *O'Bannon*. Rather than advancing in an orderly single column, as Hara hoped, Abe's formation steamed southeastward in three groups. With the battleship *Kirishima*, the cruiser *Nagara*, and three destroyers, Admiral Abe in *Hiei* moved closest to the Guadalcanal coast, while a few hundred yards ahead and to Abe's left a pair of destroyers led the way. On Abe's port side the other six destroyers, including Hara and the *Amatsukaze*, constituted the left flank.

Thirty minutes later Callaghan ordered a course change from west to north. As his ships turned in unison, *O'Bannon*'s radar screen filled with contacts, and the first destroyer in the column, *Cushing*, three ships ahead of *O'Bannon*, reported over the TBS the presence of ships on his starboard bow and to his port.

Across the waters, Admiral Abe faced a predicament. He had not expected to run into a surface force until after he hit Henderson Field, and had thus ordered his battleship gun crews to be ready with incendiary shells for that bombardment. With American ships suddenly materializing, Abe now needed the armor-piercing shells resting in magazines below. He immediately ordered a switch, but feared that he would be under fire before he had a chance to rearm.

Hara concluded the same from the bridge of *Amatsukaze* and was certain the enemy would open the action. Inexplicably to Hara, however, eight minutes passed without a shell coming from the American side as the two forces closed at thirteen hundred yards per minute, a lapse Hara contended "saved us from catastrophe."[3] During those unexpected minutes, Japanese crews rushed the armor-piercing shells from their magazines to the deck gun crews. In their haste, the men stacked shells all about the deck, which could ignite a violent explosion if an American salvo landed in their midst.

The combat commenced when *Hiei* shone her searchlight in an attempt to find *Nagara*'s location, and two Japanese aircraft dropped flares that illuminated *O'Bannon* and her companion van destroyers. *Atlanta* instantly responded with her five-inch guns, and *Sterett*, immediately in front of *O'Bannon*, opened fire, signaling a naval free-for-all. Now within point-blank range at 5,500 yards, *Hiei*'s guns swung portside and powered fourteen-inch shells into *Atlanta*'s bridge, killing Rear Admiral Scott and most of the other bridge officers of that cruiser.

Events occurred rapidly as the two forces groped for each other in the darkness. Wilkinson was preparing to launch *O'Bannon*'s torpedoes when at 1:48 Callaghan, seeing that the three enemy groups were attempting to box him in to the front and on his flanks, issued an order for the odd ships in line to fire to starboard and the even ships to port. *O'Bannon*, fourth in line, had been ready to fire to starboard, but as MacDonald recalled, with the new order "the firing got all messed up and they said shift the other way. By that time the Japs were coming down that [port] side and we were running right into them. That was a real close-range battle if there ever was one."[4]

Wilkinson ordered his batteries to extinguish a Japanese searchlight on the port bow that lit up the destroyer *Cushing*, three ships ahead of *O'Bannon*. Tracers from their five-inch guns sparked a slender path toward the Japanese vessel, shattered the searchlight, and splintered against the ship's forward superstructure.

"The action now reminded me of a no-holds-barred barroom brawl, in which someone turned out the lights and everyone started swinging in every direction—only this was ten thousand times worse," wrote the assistant engineering officer aboard *Sterett*, Lieutenant C. Raymond Calhoun. "Shells continued to drop all around us, star shells and flares hung overhead, tracers whizzed past from various directions, and everywhere we looked ships burned and exploded against the backdrop of the night sky. I could not tell where our forces were. We seemed to be in the midst of about ten Japanese ships without a friend in sight."[5]

The prospect had to be unsettling to destroyer crews that largely consisted of novices who had rarely traveled outside the confines of their home counties, let alone the hemisphere. They were about to engage, in the dead of night, veteran Japanese crews who in the Solomons had inflicted an unbroken string of naval defeats on American surface units. The odds did not favor those untested Americans, but the Marines on Guadalcanal, Admiral Halsey, and the nation called on them to step into the gap and deflect a feared enemy from further withering Vandegrift's already depleted lines.

Ships on both sides turned Ironbottom Sound between Guadalcanal and Tulagi into a modern-day version of a Western shootout. Operating in the early morning darkness, destroyers fired at cruisers and cruisers targeted cruisers, while Abe's two lumbering battleships trained their batteries on any target that came into view. Large gray ships momentarily loomed out of the darkness, illuminated by flashes as shells raced from guns, giving *O'Bannon*'s gunnery officer, Lieutenant George Philip Jr., only seconds to aim his fire.

"They were like giant, ghostly light bulbs being turned off and on in the twinkling of an eye," said MacDonald of the nighttime clash.[6]

Abe erred in using *Hiei*'s searchlight, as it permitted *O'Bannon* and her three van companions to concentrate their firing on the flagship. Gunfire from *O'Bannon* and *Cushing* zoomed at and over *Hiei*, with some shells splashing near Hara's *Amatsukaze*. Hara, seeing that he was moving uncomfortably close to Florida Island and its treacherous reefs on his port side, shouted, "Gain speed! Let's get the hell out of here to starboard!"[7] He put distance between the reefs and his ship before turning back to the fray.

In the confusion of battle, the three ships in front of *O'Bannon* slowed, causing the column to bunch. Wilkinson ordered a speedy turn inside to avoid colliding with *Sterett*, while to his rear, the cruiser *Atlanta* maneuvered to avoid *O'Bannon*. Japanese shells striking *Sterett*'s stern slowed that ship and required Wilkinson to make a hard right and emergency full astern to avoid smashing into her fellow destroyer. *Sterett* "was virtually blown out of the water, and the other two ships ahead [*Cushing* and *Laffey*] were both torpedoed," wrote MacDonald.[8] Wilkinson's quick thinking and skilled navigation, combined with the efforts of the engineering officer, Lieutenant Carl F. Pfeifer, and his engine room crew, enabled *O'Bannon* to clear *Sterett*'s stern by only ten yards.

"Our Navy Was There": *O'Bannon* in Battle

The *O'Bannon* crew avoided one possible catastrophe only to face another when a shell exploded behind *Hiei* and silhouetted the battleship, which was four thousand yards away. Wilkinson, who realized that he was taking his destroyer into point-blank range of a warship ten times her size and packing more power in a single turret than all of *O'Bannon*'s deck guns, set a course to shorten the distance and launch torpedoes. With the three American destroyers ahead either damaged or sinking, *O'Bannon* now led the way. "No man can adequately describe the shock and terror and tremendousness of a great naval battle fought at close range in the dead of night," MacDonald later said. "It was the most terrible experience that I've ever endured."[9]

Lieutenant Pfeifer and his Black Gang turned dials and manned pumps to give Wilkinson added speed for the run toward *Hiei*. Gun flashes illuminated the waters around *O'Bannon* and shell bursts lit the sky as the destroyer shaved the yardage between her and Abe's giant vessel. But the *O'Bannon* was sufficiently shrouded by the darkness that by the time Abe's lookouts spotted her, the Japanese battleship could not depress her fourteen-inch guns low enough to hit the American destroyer.

O'Bannon moved in so close to *Hiei* that MacDonald swore he could hear enemy shells swish overhead and zip between the masts. *O'Bannon*'s bullets and shells growled a response, gouging chunks of metal out of *Hiei*'s superstructure, and "flashes and sparks were coming out of her pagoda tower. Enormous flames began to appear in and around the ship, her fire ceased and the ship appeared to be dead in the water."[10]

Seaman 1/c Louis F. Cianca was at his station on the flying bridge near Wilkinson when the action started. He felt exposed as "showers of shell wadding and burning cork flew about us." Sheets of flames shot up from *Hiei* hundreds of feet into the air, and when Cianca looked elsewhere, he saw other ships explode in similar fashion. "It seemed as if someone had opened the door to Hell that night. Our guns never stopped," said Cianca. He believed that in a small way *O'Bannon*'s crew was avenging what had been inflicted on the United States Navy the previous December 7: "We felt we were paying back some of our debts."[11]

Twenty-three-year-old Lieutenant Lendall Knight watched the action from the turret door of a five-inch gun. "I could see star shells, ships blowing up and it became a melee," he said. His and the other *O'Bannon* guns sprayed *Hiei*'s decks "up and down until it turned cherry red."[12]

In his gun mount, Seaman Whisler tried to breathe slower and remember his training as he aimed the gun at *Hiei*. Despite wearing headphones connecting him to the radar room, he could hear the battle raging outside his mount. Whisler wished he could observe the action unfolding around *O'Bannon*, but he had his duties to perform. "I don't think anyone knew who was who," he said of the surface ships that intermingled off Guadalcanal that night. "We were pretty busy. We were so busy that we didn't think about our not being able to see anything. You think about your task and have no time to think about anything else."[13]

Men belowdecks tried to forget that they could be trapped should a Japanese torpedo explode against *O'Bannon*'s hull or a fourteen-inch shell rip into the engine room, but the specter of a fiery or watery death was difficult to ignore. "The thunder of the terrific firing ripped through our ears, but down there we could just wonder and hope and work," said Lieutenant Pfeifer. They were outmatched as to weight and size, "and our five-inch batteries looked like seagoing pea-shooters alongside the fourteen-inch guns she [*Hiei*] mounted fore and aft." As *O'Bannon* moved within fifteen hundred yards, her shells sparked against *Hiei*'s decks and cut into Japanese sailors. Pfeifer, connected to the bridge, heard Lieutenant Philip whisper, "This is murderous. This is murderous."[14] Pfeifer wondered whether Philip was referring to carnage on the battleship or was instead talking about *O'Bannon* shipmates above.

In the forward engine room twenty-one-year-old Machinist's Mate 1/c Willy Rhyne, who had joined the Navy the day after Pearl Harbor because he "wanted to go and beat 'em up," heard the five-inch shells boom from Knight's and Whisler's guns as he manned his station. "They shook the ship enough that the steam lines shook," he said. His biggest fear was that a torpedo would smash into the ship and leave Rhyne little time to exit the engine room before the waters engulfed him. "During the fight," he said, "we tried to focus on our task, but it was always in the back of my mind that something can happen."[15]

Opponents intermingled in the narrow channel, firing madly at targets that unexpectedly appeared and just as suddenly disappeared mere hundreds of yards away. Guns so fiercely rolled thunderclaps over Guadalcanal that Marines ashore were glad they were not at sea. "The battle would have pleased Mars," Vandegrift wrote. "For nearly an hour we watched naval guns belch orange death with such rapid vehemence that the island seemed to shake beneath us." The earsplitting booms from Abe's battleships nearly drowned out the softer fire from *O'Bannon*'s and *Fletcher*'s five-inch guns, presenting, according to Vandegrift, "a fantastic spectacle which offered no clue as to victor or vanquished."[16]

New York Times correspondent Ira Wolfert, on Guadalcanal to cover Marine operations for his newspaper, watched that night with hundreds of Marines as *O'Bannon* and the other twelve ships grappled with Abe's force. The Japanese navy had been a frequent and unwelcome guest, making nightly runs to bring in reinforcements or to bombard the Americans' airfield and front-line positions, and now the Marines' naval comrades were rushing to their defense. From their foxholes and bunkers Marines strained seaward in hopes of glimpsing some hint that indicated the American ships had gained the upper hand. According to Wolfert, "The action was illuminated in brief, blinding flashes by Japanese searchlights which were shot out as soon as they were turned on, by muzzle flashes from big guns, by a fantastic stream of tracers, and by a huge range of colored explosives" as three ships in sequence exploded within minutes. "From the beach it seemed like a door opening and closing and opening and closing, over and over again," as warships exchanged gunfire. Two Japanese aircraft "were caught like sparrows in a badminton game and blown to bits."

Wolfert noticed that the ships, exchanging blows in a watery arena bound by Guadalcanal on one side and Florida Island on the other, so stirred Iron-bottom Sound that waves crashed against the rocks and swirled onto the beaches near his position. He was uncertain of the battle's outcome but admired the sailors, for "our Navy was there, incredibly, . . . like the hero of some melodrama."[17]

While her deck gun crews pounded the battleship with accurate fire, by 2:00 a.m. *O'Bannon* had drawn within twelve hundred yards of *Hiei*. Flames sprouted from several spots on the Japanese ship, and *Hiei*'s gunfire had slackened. Now in range, Wilkinson launched two torpedoes at the damaged ship and had just fired a third when a tremendous explosion rocked the battleship and spread flames from bow to stern. Men on *O'Bannon*'s exposed forward antiaircraft guns dodged burning particles and fragments of eight-inch shells from *Hiei*, and one shell struck the door to the right barrel of the forward torpedo mount, knocking it out of commission before ricocheting downward and crashing into the deck just forward of the Number Two stack.

Having launched the torpedoes, MacDonald repeated Wilkinson's order for hard right and emergency full astern to clear the damaged battleship. As the destroyer swerved away, MacDonald turned to look at the fires engulfing *Hiei*. They reminded him of the conflagrations he had witnessed in London, but with one key difference: here, in the waters off Guadalcanal, he was no longer a neutral observer of someone else's war, but an active participant in a close-range duel with an enemy who wanted to kill him.

While others credited divine intervention, MacDonald could thank his medallion and Whisler his lucky coin for their deliverance from an action that should have ended in their fiery demise. A destroyer rarely challenges a battleship without paying a stiff price, but besides a damaged torpedo mount and a brief shower of razor-sharp shrapnel, the crew of *O'Bannon* had suffered neither death nor injury in the bold charge.

Would their luck hold? Gun flashes or shell explosions lit up the darkened waters, and when MacDonald counted five burning or exploding vessels on the starboard quarter and another off the port side, he thought he might never see the next day.

The next three minutes packed enough action and scares for a lifetime. In the madness of battle, MacDonald thought that the Japanese ships were firing indiscriminately at each other. He admitted that even with radar, at this stage "you couldn't tell friend from foe. A ship in flames sometimes has no identity."[18]

At 2:01 a.m. the bow of a ship suddenly loomed ahead. The white numbers painted on her bow denoted it as American, and MacDonald, at the helm for Wilkinson, ordered a hard left rudder to avoid a collision with what turned out to be a fellow destroyer, *Laffey* (DD-459), which had been caught in a crossfire and was sinking. The helmsman, Quartermaster 3/c Richard N. Lanham, responded instantly, and narrowly averted running into *Laffey*. MacDonald concluded that at least twice, had Lanham not reacted so quickly, *O'Bannon* would have been damaged. "His work was so well done," MacDonald put in his action report, "that in my mind if he had not acted correctly and quickly we would have had two collisions, one with the *Sterett* and one with the wreck of the *Laffey*."[19]

The course change veered the destroyer directly past a group of survivors swimming on the surface and screaming for help. Low on ammunition and uncertain as to how the battle was going, Wilkinson could not stop to rescue the men, but ordered his deck crew to toss life jackets overboard.

One minute later two torpedo wakes crossed ahead of *O'Bannon*, forcing another hard left turn. A rumbling underwater explosion ensued close aboard on the port beam, either from *Laffey*'s depth charges triggering as the destroyer plunged to the bottom or from a torpedo detonating at the end of its run. The eruption so violently rocked the ship and lifted the stern out of the water that MacDonald feared *O'Bannon* was going down.

"We were shaken good," said Machinist's Mate Rhyne, then in the forward engine room. "It felt like it lifted the ship out of the water. Why it didn't break our steam lines I don't know."[20] Men in the aft engine room were flung against the bulkhead, lights went out, and alarm bells and sirens blared as the ship lurched.

Not far from Rhyne, Lieutenant Pfeifer was certain that an abandon-ship order would soon come down from the bridge, but he and his men remained at their posts and kept power coursing to the engines and throughout the ship. Pfeifer's calm lent stability to an engine room filled with young sailors in their first surface action.

In the aft engine room Lieutenant Douglas P. Bates, the assistant engineering officer, was equally pleased with the men. Some officers and chiefs had claimed that the new recruits would never rise to the skilled level of their veteran shipmates, but Bates no longer held such doubts. "From that moment on I knew we had no reason to worry about the men of the *O'Bannon*," Bates said. "From their actions at a time when they were convinced death was but minutes or seconds away, I was certain we had a four-O crew of topnotch men."[21]

While the ship had momentarily slowed and lost power, *O'Bannon* otherwise appeared to be in good shape. Their concerns dissipated when repair parties and the engine room reported no major damage.

Across the waters, the Japanese destroyer *Akatsuki* fired torpedoes at *Atlanta*, but was quickly caught in crossfire and sunk by the cruiser *San Francisco* and a US destroyer. As that occurred, the battleship *Kirishima* moved in and battered the American cruiser with her fourteen-inch batteries, badly damaging the warship and killing more than seventy men, including the cruiser's skipper, Captain Cassin Young, and Admiral Callaghan.

Admiral Abe, with his flagship's internal communications dead, now chose to withdraw, accompanied by *Kirishima*. *Hiei* might have escaped a fatal hit during the battle, but the next day American bombers sent her to the bottom off Savo Island.

As the fighting around *O'Bannon* blazed, MacDonald saw a column of Japanese destroyers race past *O'Bannon*'s starboard side. On their way toward *Fletcher* and the rearguard destroyers, the Japanese warships, according to MacDonald, "had a field day torpedoing our ships at the end of the column."[22]

"The Lord Was on Our Side": *Fletcher* in Battle

"Hey, this is just like the Fourth of July out here!"[23] Commander Cole shouted across the bridge to his executive officer, Lieutenant Commander Wylie. In an early version of what evolved into the combat information center (CIC), which the two later helped develop, instead of asking Wylie to man the aft steering position, which many skippers did with their executive officers during battle in case the bridge was hit, Cole stationed Wylie on the radar in the chart house a few feet aft of the bridge, close enough so that the two could verbally communicate with each other through a ventilation port. Cole believed this would result in a smoother flow of information to the bridge, which he believed was crucial during battle. Standing within earshot of Cole and connected with headphones to the gunnery officer and torpedo officer,

Wylie could assess the situation from the radar screen and quickly relay to Cole information about surface contacts, potential targets, and where to concentrate fire. Based on Wylie's feedback, Cole could then issue his orders. A few seconds could mean the difference between victory and defeat, and Cole thought he could find those crucial seconds by having Wylie close at hand. This battle was the first test of their system.

The clash would also test Seaman 2/c Jacob Thomas Chesnutt Jr., who had only recently joined *Fletcher*. Born in Hope Hull, Alabama, in 1921, Chesnutt enlisted after the ship had been commissioned. "I'd hardly ever been out of Alabama," he said. "I was a green hick who didn't know anything, but I was raring to go!" Chesnutt reached Pearl Harbor in late September, where "they marched us to a baseball field. They named 150 of us out of 2,800, the men whose last name began with *C*, and told us we would be joining the cruiser *Juneau*." As the ship was then already in the South Pacific, Chesnutt and his companions boarded a ship bound for Espiritu Santo, but when the *Juneau* was tardy in returning to that port from the Guadalcanal area, superiors instead placed Chesnutt aboard *Fletcher*. Before arriving in the South Pacific, Chesnutt thought Guadalcanal was another body of water like the Panama Canal, and when he stepped aboard the destroyer, Wylie asked if he wanted to work with the radar. "'What's radar?' I asked."[24]

Shortly before 2:00 a.m. Cole opened fire on a cruiser to his rear. *Fletcher* gunners poured a stream of shells portside that, along with the fire of other American ships, left the Japanese vessel in flames.

A few minutes later Cole turned his batteries on another cruiser astern of his first target but was interrupted when the American destroyer *Barton*, two ships ahead of *Fletcher*, "exploded and simply disappeared in fragments" that spiraled onto *Fletcher*'s deck. With enemy batteries zeroing in, the rear column was soon in disarray. The damaged *Aaron Ward* limped out of the line, *Monssen* sat low in the water, and *Fletcher* dodged a flurry of incoming shells. "Medium caliber shells were splashing on both sides of us," wrote Cole in his action report. Fire on both flanks was "heavy and sustained," and "the situation at this time became very confused."[25] At first Seaman Chesnutt ducked when shells splashed near the ship, but stopped when he decided that nothing on the destroyer could shield him from enemy shells if they hit the lightly armored *Fletcher*. He was admittedly nervous during his first action, but he focused on his job in the radar room. "You let everything else go, and let others do their job. You knew you could go at any time from a shell or a torpedo, but you can't do anything about it, so I didn't worry about it. You had to do your job so the other guys could do theirs."[26]

From a distance of only one hundred yards Japanese ships, including *Amatsukaze*, launched torpedoes at the rearguard destroyers. "Everything we had was shooting at them," recalled Wylie, as five-inch gun crews on *Fletcher* maintained their fire to fend off the threat.[27]

Shells cut fiery paths toward their targets and explosions dotted the night-time sky, but Machinist's Mate 1/c Donald Holmes and the other crew belowdecks never saw the pyrotechnic display. They could still hear shells impacting the water, however. "I was down in the bottom of the ship, the lowest level, right above the bilges," said Holmes of his station on the steam pump in the forward engine room keeping the feed pumps running. "The entire ship was above me, and I was scared as can be! I could hear guns firing and splashes, but I didn't know what was going on or know what was happening at all. I was by myself in the bottom of the ship. That was a hard thing."

The hard-nosed chief who had trained them, Machinist's Mate 1/c James F. Gebhardt, stood in the engine room with a forty-five-caliber sidearm holstered to his waist. During exercises he had cautioned the young sailors that when the real deal occurred, he would not hesitate to use the weapon should anyone think of abandoning his post. Holmes and his buddies had joked about the comment but wisely decided not to test their chief. "I wanted to leave but knew better. Gebhardt never had to use the pistol. We were all in it together."[28]

Illumination from *Barton*'s flames and from ships' guns revealed enemy torpedoes cutting toward *Fletcher*'s starboard side. On deck, Fire Controlman Douglas J. Huggard braced for an impact, but one torpedo passed fifty yards ahead of *Fletcher*, and three slid harmlessly underneath the ship. In the engine room, Holmes heard the torpedoes pass mere feet beneath the hull, only failing to smash into *Fletcher* because they had apparently been set at the deeper depths designated for cruisers. "Yes, the Lord was on our side that night," said Wylie.[29]

Having dodged the enemy's torpedoes, Cole implemented maneuvers to set up a torpedo attack of his own. He turned the destroyer hard right and raced through the maelstrom of ships, firing to port and starboard as he wound his way. In the chart room, Wylie counted radar pips and guessed that twenty-eight ships then stood in a three-mile-wide circle. "Hey," shouted Cole to his executive officer, "aren't you glad our wives don't know where we are right now?"[30]

Wylie agreed, and then informed Cole that radar had plotted another cruiser. When a star shell illuminated a Japanese vessel close on the starboard side, which some crew claimed was the largest enemy ship they had yet seen in the war, *Fletcher*'s fate seemed sealed. Men on deck waited for the inevitable roar from guns that could have demolished the destroyer with one salvo, but no sound rent the night. In the darkened madness of the battle, the Japanese failed to spot the *Fletcher* and steamed by without firing.

When at 2:22 a.m. the torpedo officer alerted Cole that the torpedoes were ready, Cole gave the order, and within one minute ten torpedoes, the ship's entire supply, were on their path toward their target, three and a half miles away.

Wylie momentarily moved outside to the flying bridge and pulled out a stopwatch to time the torpedoes' run. At the moment he figured the torpedoes would hit, he and men near him thought they heard booms and detected flames in the distance, but in the confusion they could not be certain their ship had inflicted the damage. "We felt at the time that we did because the running time was right and we did see flashes," said Wylie. "The other side of the coin is that this was the era when, God knows, we couldn't have more useless torpedoes. They all ran too deep and the magnetic exploders didn't work."[31]

When Cole asked Wylie for their location, he answered that as far as he could tell, they were sitting in the middle of the entire Japanese fleet. "Wylie stayed in that room on that scope, guiding us and calling out to Captain Cole," recalled Ensign Fred Gressard. "Then Cole said, 'How do we get out of here?' and Wylie gave him a course—they were always within earshot during battle; a great team."[32]

Meanwhile, Cole's counterpart aboard *Amatsukaze*, Tameichi Hara, had to make split-second decisions of his own. As he related in his book, *Japanese Destroyer Captain*, early in the battle he noticed that *Hiei*, then trading blows with *O'Bannon*, was aflame. He thought of rushing to her assistance until a cluster of US ships—*Fletcher* and the other three rear destroyers, then under attack from *Yudachi*—burst out of the darkness on a parallel course to his starboard. "Get ready, fishermen!" he shouted to his torpedo crew, and moments later eight torpedoes dunked into the turbulent waters. Two minutes later a pair of explosions dissected *Barton*, two ships ahead of *Fletcher*, and sank the destroyer. Hara's other torpedoes churned on, some being the ones Holmes heard pass beneath the *Fletcher*.

After Hara launched four more torpedoes, shells inundated the waters about Hara's ship. The cruiser *Helena* had taken advantage of Hara's focus on the American destroyers to creep in on his port side. A shell exploded so close to *Amatsukaze* that "I hunched my back and clung to the railing. The blast was so strong, it almost threw me off the bridge. The detonations were deafening. I got sluggishly to my feet, but my mind was a complete blank for several seconds." A second shell smashed into the deck immediately below the bridge and exploded in the radio room, killing everyone there. On the bridge near Hara one man, his head a bloody mess from shrapnel, slumped dead over the range-finding gear. Another sailor had been obliterated, with only part of his legs remaining. The shells had killed forty-three of his men "while I stood uninjured in their midst."

Hara ordered his gunners to open fire at *Helena*, but the American shelling had destroyed the hydraulic system and immobilized the gun turrets. With near misses rattling his ship and damaging her rudder, Hara could now neither fire his deck guns nor maneuver as normal. "If the enemy closed," he wrote, "we would be as defenseless as a bull in a slaughterhouse."[33] Expecting the worst, Hara gratefully watched *Helena* cease fire and pull away when three Japanese destroyers came to *Amatsukaze*'s rescue and forced the American ship to retreat.

Amatsukaze was in no shape to continue the battle. Hara lacked full rudder control, dead sailors littered the bridge, and holes punctured the ship's hull. The Japanese commander had no choice but to join Abe in withdrawing, and he turned north to exit Ironbottom Sound.

"The *Juneau* Had Disappeared"

Shortly after 2:00 a.m., Wilkinson and Cole came to a similar conclusion. While Cole retired eastward through Sealark Channel and down Indispensable Strait, Wilkinson turned southeast to locate and attack any Japanese transports that might have sneaked through. After Wilkinson investigated the Guadalcanal coast near Kukum without result, he turned through Lengo Channel to join *Fletcher* and the other surviving American ships.

At daylight three cruisers, *San Francisco*, *Helena*, and *Juneau*, joined with *O'Bannon*, *Fletcher*, and *Sterett* to continue their retirement. The sister ships had been fortunate, as *Fletcher* escaped without damage and *O'Bannon* had suffered only minor harm. According to MacDonald, however, *San Francisco* "was in a bad way. She had received numerous hits above decks and a large number of her personnel had been killed."[34] Wilkinson and other skippers sent their doctors and pharmacist's mates to the flagship to help treat the wounded before the group retired southeastward toward Espiritu Santo.

A heartrending episode ensued. *Helena*'s skipper, Captain Gilbert C. Hoover, now the senior surviving officer after the deaths of both Admirals Callaghan and Scott, ordered Wilkinson to take *O'Bannon* fifty miles north and radio his preliminary report of the battle to Admiral Halsey. In doing so, *O'Bannon* would be far enough from the other ships that Hoover believed Wilkinson could radio the report and risk Japanese interception without endangering Hoover's crippled cruisers and destroyers as they retired toward Espiritu Santo.

Among Hoover's ships was the cruiser *Juneau*. An hour before noon on November 13, Japanese Commander Minoru Yokota in the submarine *I-26* sighted five vessels, including *Juneau* and *Fletcher*, as he prowled the waters southeast of Guadalcanal. Yokota fired a spread of five torpedoes that raced past *San Francisco* and smacked into *Juneau* with such force that men aboard *Helena* were blown against bulkheads from the concussion.

In *Fletcher*'s chart house, Cole and Wylie were about to enjoy a few ounces of medicinal whiskey sent to the bridge by the ship's doctor when *Juneau* erupted. "There was an enormous explosion," said Wylie, "and we both rushed out and looked back. The *Juneau* had disappeared and there was a lot of smoke. We could see this debris rising high in the air." Cole called for full speed while Wylie rushed to the loudspeaker to tell the crew to take cover from the debris that was about to rain on them from the stricken cruiser, now enveloped in flames and sinking, less than one mile away. Moments later, an intact five-inch twin gun mount zoomed directly over *Helena* and splashed in *Fletcher*'s wake one hundred yards astern of the destroyer.

Even though few aboard *Fletcher* believed anyone could have lived through such a titanic explosion, Cole turned *Fletcher* to where *Juneau* had gone down, intent on rescuing any survivors. They were halfway to the site when a message from Hoover ordered Cole to turn back and resume her station with the other ships. "We were very irate," said Wylie of an order telling them to abandon fellow Americans in the water.

Fifteen minutes later Captain Hoover sent Cole a long message explaining his decision to leave *Juneau*. Hoover understood Cole and his crew were upset with his decision, but he had received information that more than one enemy submarine operated in those waters, and he had a responsibility to shepherd his remaining ships to Espiritu Santo and safety. At that time

Helena, lightly damaged in the battle, was the only cruiser in the South Pacific available for combat. *Sterett* was already burying her dead, *San Francisco* needed significant repairs, and with *O'Bannon* split from the unit, *Fletcher* was the only ship under Hoover's command that had sonar and antisubmarine search-and-attack capability. He could not allow *Fletcher* to utilize time searching a large area of water for survivors few believed existed, all the while exposing his other ships to enemy submarine attack.

"That was probably the most courageous single decision I've ever seen a man make," said Wylie, "because everybody's instinct is to go after survivors. He knew the submarines were there and he also knew he had the only cruiser left in the South Pacific that wasn't damaged, that was *Helena*."[35]

Unfortunately, more than one hundred *Juneau* survivors floated in the waters as Hoover left the scene. Rescue craft eventually picked up ten men eight days later, but almost seven hundred *Juneau* sailors perished, either in the horrible explosion or from exposure or sharks, including five Sullivan brothers from Waterloo, Iowa.

While Cole departed with Hoover's ships, to the north Wilkinson completed his mission, transmitted the report to Halsey, and reversed course to catch up with Hoover. Later that afternoon, *O'Bannon* passed the area where *Juneau* went down, but unaware of the tragedy, Wilkinson maintained course to the south. He did not learn about *Juneau*'s absence until the next morning.

In a controversial decision even he later regretted, in the heat of the moment Halsey relieved Hoover from command of *Helena* as soon as the ship returned from the action. To avoid a repetition of what happened to the Sullivan family, who lost five sons in one battle, the Navy altered its policy and banned the posting of multiple family members to the same ship. Cole, whose crew included five father-son combinations, had to arrange transfers so that only one member from each family remained aboard.

When Seaman Chesnutt learned that the cruiser had sunk, he could not help but think how close he had been to joining her at Espiritu Santo the previous month. Only an unexpected delay on *Juneau*'s part had caused him to be posted to *Fletcher* rather than *Juneau*, a delay that saved his life. "I didn't realize it at the time," he confided to his diary on November 13, "but it was the Lord protecting me—not only in battle, but not allowing me to catch up with the *Juneau* which went down."[36]

Callaghan had sacrificed much, including his life, to save Henderson Field and keep the Japanese from strengthening their position on Guadalcanal.

Against one Japanese battleship and two destroyers sunk, Callaghan lost two cruisers and four destroyers, with two other ships badly damaged. However, his unit's actions, including those of *O'Bannon* and *Fletcher*, checked the enemy's momentum in the South Pacific.

"As the day ends it seems most probable that while we have suffered severe losses in ships and personnel," concluded Nimitz's command summary of November 13, "our gallant shipmates have again thwarted the enemy. If so, this may well be *the* decisive battle of this campaign."[37]

"My Pride in You Is Beyond Expression"

The Japanese were not finished. With Callaghan's forces pulling away to Espiritu Santo, two Japanese cruisers raced toward Guadalcanal and, for thirty minutes during the night of November 13–14, bombarded Henderson Field with almost a thousand eight-inch shells. The damage they inflicted would have been much worse had Callaghan and Scott not already dented the Japanese.

A second threat ensued when eleven Japanese troop transports bearing more than ten thousand reinforcements reversed course and again headed toward the island. However, Henderson Field fighters and bombers, assisted by *Enterprise* aviators, eliminated the threat by sinking one cruiser, damaging three other ships, and destroying all eleven transports.

The Japanese used their final card in the three-day Naval Battle of Guadalcanal during the night of November 14–15 when Vice Admiral Nobutake Kondo's battleship, *Kirishima*, four cruisers, and nine destroyers moved south to blast Henderson Field. Two American battleships and their four escorting destroyers engaged in a fierce thirty-minute brawl that, despite the loss of the four American destroyers, sank two Japanese ships and sent Kondo reeling to the north.

"We've got the bastards licked!"[38] Halsey shouted to his staff in the aftermath of the momentous sea action. He had a right to be elated, as his scrappy ships, including *O'Bannon* and *Fletcher*, had gained a clear-cut victory. He had thrown everything in his meager arsenal at the Japanese, with orders to Wilkinson, Cole, and the other skippers to take the fight to the enemy.

Halsey's aggressive attitude set the tone for Callaghan's crews. Their naval roadblock halted Japanese reinforcements from reaching Guadalcanal, where they would have tested Vandegrift's weary Marines, while at the same time bringing in more forces to support those same Marines. With Henderson Field and its vital fighters preserved, aircraft based there slaughtered the eleven Japanese troop transports that otherwise would have strengthened their position on the island.

Though both sides suffered similar losses in the three-day battle—Halsey lost two cruisers, seven destroyers, and more than seventeen hundred men against Yamamoto's two battleships, one cruiser, three destroyers, eleven transports, and almost nineteen hundred men—the Japanese were unable to replace lost men, ships, and aircraft as readily as the United States. American industrial might had yet to fully flex its muscle, but already the nation's factories and shipyards were sending the first of what became a burgeoning flow of ships, guns, and planes to the war fronts.

After the war, in gathering material for his autobiography, Halsey termed the Naval Battle of Guadalcanal "a decisive American victory by any standard" and called it a turning point in the Pacific war. He contended that had he lost, the Marines on Guadalcanal might have been forced to surrender, but with the American victory, Japanese momentum in the South Pacific had been irrevocably halted. "Until then he had been advancing at his will," he wrote of the enemy. "From then on he retreated at ours."[39] Although Japanese reinforcements would trickle into Guadalcanal over the next two months, their focus now turned to rebuilding the empire's naval forces and strengthening her posts in the northern Solomons. The arena of battle was gradually shifting north of Guadalcanal, to the risky waters known as the Slot.

Halsey credited the officers and crews of the ships that had steamed into battle and slugged it out with the enemy. In a message read to the crews of both *O'Bannon* and *Fletcher*, as well as to those of the other participating ships, Halsey said, "Your names have been written in golden letters on the pages of history and you have won the everlasting gratitude of your countrymen. No honor for you could be too great. My pride in you is beyond expression. Magnificently done. To the glorious dead: Hail heroes. Rest with God. God bless you all."[40]

MacDonald was proud of how his young crew had performed in their first major action against the Japanese: "The Japs tried to knock us out and, if they had knocked us out that night, they would have had Guadalcanal." MacDonald said that in the nighttime encounter, only their collection of cruisers and destroyers had stood between the Japanese and Vandegrift's defenders. "Stood in between all right," MacDonald proudly added, "there's no doubt about that."[41]

Commander Wilkinson wrote in his action report, "The officers and men of this vessel handled the ship and themselves excellently." He said that he could not too highly praise the "manner in which they remained unflinching and steadfast at their posts with shells from all sides falling short and over." In answer to those who harbored doubts that the country could so speedily fashion a professional fighting force out of civilians, he concluded, "It is believed a tribute to the spirit and indoctrination of the Naval Service that a group of American men and boys, many of them never having seen a ship, could be welded into an organization that would stand up so calmly under fire in the short period of this vessel's official life, June 26 to November 13. The officers and men of this crew, each and every one, handled themselves like veterans and are greatly deserving of all meritorious considerations."[42]

The Navy thought highly of *O'Bannon*'s senior officers as well. For their actions in the battle, Wilkinson was awarded the Navy Cross, while MacDonald and Pfeifer received Silver Stars.

Aboard *Fletcher*, Cole was equally effusive about his men. Cole tipped his hat to Wylie for creating a more efficient system of obtaining, assessing, and relaying information under fire. "From his station at the SG Radar screen he kept the Commanding Officer continuously advised of the tactical situation (which was often visually obscured), selected targets, and directed gun and torpedo control. The effectiveness of the *Fletcher*'s engagement was due principally to his intelligent analysis and cool judgment."[43]

Obsessed as they were with the ill fortune often associated with the number thirteen, as far as the men of the *Fletcher* were concerned, luck had also played a major role. Having avoided harm, they nicknamed their destroyer "Lucky 13" and considered *Fletcher* a lucky ship for having stared down so many intimidating omens.

The battle, though, exacted a toll. Lieutenant Malcolm M. Dunham, *O'Bannon*'s doctor, was among those whom Wilkinson sent over to aid the wounded aboard *San Francisco*. He treated so many broken limbs, ghastly cuts, and burned faces, and witnessed such destruction while on the cruiser, that when he returned he was noticeably affected. He told MacDonald that being on the *San Francisco* "was like walking through a death chamber, people were wounded and dead every place you turned, the ones who were not wounded give the impression of being very severely shocked for days." As MacDonald talked with the physician, he noticed that "the realization that he might have to go through another [battle] again bothered him."[44] MacDonald made a mental note to keep tabs on how Dunham fared as the weeks passed.

On *Fletcher*, the twenty-one-year-old Chesnutt heard and saw enough to believe that his future was drastically limited. Only in the Guadalcanal area a few weeks, he told himself, "Forget it! You'll never live through this war."[45]

Action reports also included recommendations. MacDonald urged that the TBS be used only when necessary, as he found that in the heat of the fight, the channel became cluttered with too many unnecessary communications. He was pleased with the contribution made by the ship's advanced radar and advised the Navy to install the equipment on other ships as quickly as possible, but he was disappointed that the enemy had opened fire first. Had Callaghan better arranged his ships, with *O'Bannon*, *Fletcher*, and other radar-carrying vessels in the van, he might have seized the advantage. Their radar would have detected the Japanese sooner, and the destroyers could have gathered for a massed torpedo attack to be delivered before Callaghan's cruisers opened fire with their batteries. In splitting his destroyers, though, Callaghan had negated that impact.

Unfortunately, even had a coordinated torpedo charge been conducted, the results most likely would have been disappointing. At this stage of the war American destroyers and submarines were, almost criminally, sent into battle with faulty torpedoes. Unlike the Long Lance, the vaunted Japanese torpedo that packed double the explosive power and which could be fired at longer ranges than the American counterpart, *O'Bannon* and *Fletcher* carried torpedoes that either ran too deep to strike against enemy hulls or exploded before reaching their targets. Tests conducted in August, three months before the action off Guadalcanal, revealed that a ten-foot error in depth performance afflicted many of the torpedoes, but the information had yet to be disseminated throughout the Pacific.

Commanders at headquarters and in South Pacific officers' clubs heatedly discussed the dismal performances posted by the US torpedoes, and even Halsey scoffed at the weapon's value. "There was a saying in the South Pacific Forces at this and later times," he wrote of the latter months of 1942 in the South Pacific, "that every time a Japanese torpedo hit our ships stopped, and that every time one of our torpedoes hit the Japanese ship made two knots extra speed."[46]

Mixed impressions marked the Japanese reaction. On November 13 Commander Hara joined Vice Admiral Kurita's fleet 250 miles north of Guadalcanal. The admiral relayed his congratulations to Hara over the battle, but Hara "felt no triumph at all."[47]

Accompanied by Kurita and the remnants of the force from Guadalcanal, the next day he anchored *Amatsukaze* at Truk, the vast Japanese naval bastion in the Caroline Islands. When he was able to inspect his ship, Hara counted thirty-two holes in her hull larger than one yard in diameter and another forty-five smaller ones, a sign both of the ferocity of the battle as well as of his good fortune in surviving it.

Radio Tokyo boasted of a victory. Captain Shoichi Kamada, chief of the Japanese Navy press section at Shanghai, claimed that the battle was "a heavy blow dealt at the United States," and Domei, the Japanese news agency, added, "The Japanese have the Americans where they want them, and mean to keep them there until no American warship is left in active service."[48]

Those in the know, such as Hara, understood that Pacific reality clashed with propaganda announcements. Many senior officers termed the battle a defeat because the Americans had retained their hold on Henderson Field, the Guadalcanal landmark that stood like an unsinkable aircraft carrier from which hundreds of aircraft would soon bomb Japanese installations in the Central Solomons. "Up until this battle," explained Captain Toshikazu Ohmae, Chief of Staff, Southeastern Fleet at Rabaul, "we were determined to retake Guadalcanal," but the naval encounter forced them to reexamine their plans.[49] In a sign that the military was not as elated as the news accounts, the Japanese relieved Admiral Abe of his command.

The American home front resounded with praise for its navy. *Time* magazine highlighted the encounter in successive November issues, placing Halsey on the cover of the November 30 edition and stating that the Japanese naval advantage "had been whittled down" and that "the forces under Vice Admiral William F. ('Bull') Halsey met the Japs and slugged it out. Three bloody days later the Japs were retreating northward from Guadalcanal waters and the Navy had won one of the most satisfactory victories of the war."[50]

The magazine explained that a confident Japanese force had steamed south toward Guadalcanal, as "the U.S. Navy had not, in over three months of fighting, done much fighting with surface units: only once (on the night of Oct. 11–12) had the Japs met a determined effort to cut their line of reinforcements. They had a surprise in store." Instead of the "hit and run" operations that marked September and October, "this time there was a new spirit in the U.S. task forces. The Americans came in slugging again and yet again." *Time* stated that *O'Bannon*, *Fletcher*, and every other ship under Callaghan and Scott had "saved Guadalcanal" by repulsing "the strongest

Japanese attempt to take Guadalcanal," and in the process "restored the Navy's confidence in itself and public confidence in the Navy."[51]

The *New York Times* said the victory handed the Navy and the nation "badly needed proof that in slugging contests at sea our leaders, men and ships can out-think and outfight the Japanese," and that the victory was further evidence of the startling transformation of civilians such as Robert Whisler and Willy Rhyne into able sailors and soldiers.[52]

Making their triumph all the more remarkable was that as this battle raged in the Solomons, on the other side of the world another American armada had the week before launched its first major operation against Hitler's armies in North Africa. Japanese leaders noted, with fear and respect, that the United States was able to wage war on two fronts simultaneously. If the country could conduct such campaigns now, what might their military be able to do once America's factories and shipyards began turning out ships and weapons in abundance?

The eloquent Vandegrift had the final word with the message he sent to Halsey on behalf of all the Marines on the island. He wrote, "Our greatest homage goes to Scott, Callaghan and their men who with magnificent courage against seemingly hopeless odds drove back the first hostile stroke and made success possible. To them the men of Cactus lift their battered helmets in deepest admiration."[53]

In the battle's aftermath, Roosevelt nominated Halsey for promotion to full admiral. When Halsey received the four stars denoting his new rank, he removed the three-star clusters from his uniform and asked that one cluster be sent to Mrs. Callaghan and the other to Mrs. Scott. "Tell them it was their husbands' bravery that got me my new ones."[54]

Halsey's aggressive spirit had spread to *O'Bannon* and the other ships that participated in that night encounter. While the next months would concentrate largely on what Admiral Nimitz called a battle of supply, as both sides reinforced and prepared for future offensives, Halsey would continue to push his forces to keep their foot on the pedal. Except for one surface action involving *Fletcher*, the crews of *O'Bannon*, *Fletcher*, and *Nicholas* now faced an indeterminate period of exhausting patrols and escort missions.

PART II

DESRON 21 HOLDS THE LINE IN THE SOUTH PACIFIC

CHAPTER 4

BLUNTING THE TOKYO EXPRESS

Although the crew of *O'Bannon* exceeded MacDonald's expectations in the recent engagement, he worried about their reaction to the event. While they had emerged from their first major action without casualties, some of the crew doubted that their good fortune would continue. The ship was certain to be involved in many battles before Japan was defeated, with each action diminishing their odds of surviving. "The boys were interested in living," MacDonald said, "and some of them got a little worried."[1]

They might have been more concerned if they had known about Halsey's correspondence with Admiral Nimitz over the alarming shortage of destroyers. Halsey needed to strengthen his grip in the southern Solomons and establish a base from which to mount offensive strikes northward, but he could not do that without aid. *O'Bannon*, *Fletcher*, *Nicholas*, and the other units required reinforcements.

"This is a most acute shortage," he wrote Nimitz in early December.[2] Halsey explained that in order to escort transports to Guadalcanal, he had to pull his destroyers from antisubmarine screen duty around his aircraft carriers, which consequently limited the carriers' utility. Nimitz sympathized with his admiral but told him he would have to wait until US shipyard production increased or more were released from actions in the Aleutians and in the European theater.

Despite the deficiencies, Halsey exuded confidence that he would wrest control of the Solomons from the Japanese. "Everyone here is working like a beaver," he wrote to Nimitz. "We shall lick hell out of the yellow bastards every time an opportunity presents. That is a promise." He explained that a lull following the Naval Battle of Guadalcanal had handed them "the first breathing spell we have had," and that he was using it to build up the Marine defenses. He wrote that "we have been piling things into Cactus, as fast as possible," including a shipment of turkeys for Thanksgiving.[3]

The lull to which Halsey referred did not extend to the crews of those transports and their escorting destroyers that rushed supplies and reinforcements to the island. Halsey admitted that he had no choice but to keep throwing his destroyer crews into harm's way, even though "these splendid men are pretty well shot" after the November surface engagement.[4] If Vandegrift was to succeed, those transports and destroyers had to keep the aquatic pipeline going.

Nonstop escorting action became the norm for the crews of *O'Bannon*, *Fletcher*, and *Nicholas*. "We had hardly returned to base when we were ordered out again—up to Guadalcanal," MacDonald wrote of the days immediately following the Naval Battle of Guadalcanal. "*My God,* they [the crew] said, wasn't it over *yet*? No. It hadn't begun. We went up again and again."[5] Sleep was a rare commodity. Seaman 1/c Whisler learned to catch a few hours' nap in between the duties and watches that kept him active around the clock.

In a grueling pattern that lasted into the middle of 1943, the destroyers escorted transports to and from Guadalcanal, searched the seas for enemy submarines and the skies for Japanese aircraft, and bombarded enemy land positions. The weeks taxed the destroyer crews, who longed for a breather in Australia or Noumea. "At that point of time, the US did not have the equipment, ships or supplies that they needed," Seaman 2/c Chesnutt wrote in his diary a few days after the major November surface engagement. "We actually just limped along getting by with whatever was available."[6]

Not yet assigned to the permanent squadron that would soon garner praise throughout the Pacific—such organization would come only when more ships reached the Pacific—the three destroyers often worked together, but at other times left Espiritu Santo or Guadalcanal alone or with other units. Operating in waters around Guadalcanal and south to Espiritu Santo that Lieutenant Pfeifer noted "virtually belonged to Hirohito," the destroyers helped bolster Halsey's land units both at Guadalcanal and for what looked to be a long, difficult drive up the Solomons.[7]

They steamed through channels made treacherous by uncharted submerged reefs and underwater rock formations, often relying on out-of-date charts that cautioned, "Mariners are warned to navigate this area with great caution."[8] Cole and Wilkinson relied on their ship-handling skills, sharp-eyed lookouts, and luck to maneuver through the islands. Crews, faced with the dual threats posed by the Japanese and the tricky waters, could never let their guard down.

The destroyers' war diaries read like long litanies of actions. In early December, for instance, Wilkinson daily called *O'Bannon*'s crew to general quarters because of contacts picked up by his radarmen and sonarmen. The ship barely avoided a torpedo that passed ahead of the destroyer, patrolled off Guadalcanal while transports unloaded their supplies, shepherded the transports into Tulagi Harbor for the night, formed a nightly screen to protect those vessels from submarines and surface raiders, patrolled the entrance to nearby Gavutu Harbor, provided gunfire support for Marines near Togama Point, and conducted five depth charge attacks on possible enemy submarines spotted off Guadalcanal. Only then did *O'Bannon* leave the Guadalcanal area, not for a respite but to escort a transport across Torpedo Junction to Espiritu Santo.

After completing the dangerous trip to the New Hebrides, *O'Bannon* waited three days for another transport convoy to assemble. During the interim, *O'Bannon* patrolled the waters off Espiritu Santo's entrance and conducted military exercises and drills. After taking on supplies and fuel on December 11, *O'Bannon* again escorted more transports across Torpedo Junction to Guadalcanal, where she repeated the fatiguing schedule of patrolling and screening. Combat in the lower Solomons became an unrelenting series of missions that, while lacking the drama and headline-grabbing actions of major surface engagements, nonetheless carried the same deadly risks to crews and ships.

The tired men needed no excuse to vent their anger. One day Wylie and other sailors on *Fletcher* followed a dogfight between American and Japanese pilots. During the action, an American pilot parachuted out of his damaged fighter and was floating down to the water when "four Nips came by and shot him while he was in the air." Angry crew yelled obscenities at the Japanese pilot, and Wylie's "hatred for the Japanese increased."

Wylie and others wanted payback. When Cole took the ship near two enemy pilots who also had parachuted into the water, the Japanese swam away. Still upset at watching the American pilot being gunned down, Wylie ordered the deck gunners to open fire "because I didn't want them to get back to shore and fly again. They were within swimming distance of the beach." The savagery that marked the Marine combat on Guadalcanal extended to the water, and Wylie and his crew had no reservations about shooting the Japanese after their enemy had declined help from the Americans. "The bitterness was incredible," said Wylie.[9]

On the other side, the Japanese had lost so many destroyers and transports trying to push food, supplies, and reinforcements to their comrades on Guadalcanal that on November 16, two days after Wilkinson and Cole had helped repel Abe's surface units, authorities in Tokyo turned to submarines for help. Each day at Buin on Bougainville, the northernmost Solomon Island standing 470 miles north of Guadalcanal, the Japanese loaded rations and other supplies onto destroyers and submarines, which rushed them down the Slot to Makino Point at the west end of Guadalcanal.

When Hara asked Commander Yasumi Toyama, chief of staff on Rear Admiral Razio Tanaka's Destroyer Squadron 2 at Rabaul, his opinion of the squadron's work, Toyama protested, "We are more a freighter convoy than a fighting squadron these days." His squadron ships carried cargo to "that cursed island, and our orders are to flee rather than fight. What a stupid thing!" Toyama groaned that the destroyers' decks were stacked so high with supplies for Guadalcanal that they could carry only half of their usual ammunition, thereby reducing their ability to fight. Hara agreed that "we must always be ready for battle. I think it is wrong ever to consider fighting as merely secondary," and he added that "excessive caution is crippling."[10]

Hara, Toyama, and other officers stifled their complaints in light of what was at stake for their countrymen on Guadalcanal. "More than one hundred men are dying from hunger daily," explained Vice Admiral Teruhisa Komatsu, commander of the submarine force. "Many of the rest are eating grass. Very few men are fit for fighting. What are we to do, let our countrymen starve to death in the jungle? We must help them, no matter what sacrifices must be made in doing so!"[11]

Much as *O'Bannon*, *Fletcher*, and *Nicholas* escorted transports to and from the island, Japanese destroyers carried the bulk of the load on their side. In the operation nicknamed "Tokyo Express" by their American counterparts and commanded by Rear Admiral Tanaka, already noted for his surface exploits around Guadalcanal, each destroyer on the Express delivered one hundred drums of supplies per run. The destroyer skippers brought their ships within two to three hundred yards from shore, where they dropped the drums over the side to float them toward the island. The emergency delivery system proved haphazard at best, as some drums sank or drifted away before reaching the infantry, but it was the most they could do under the circumstances.

Operating in what he labeled "the savage waters of the Solomons," Hara asserted that "the destroyers of the celebrated 'Tokyo Express' were the real workhorses of the South Pacific."[12] Often heading out unaccompanied by the more powerful cruisers or battleships, as did *O'Bannon*, *Fletcher*, and *Nicholas*, Hara's *Amatsukaze* sailors and other destroyer crews grudgingly deemphasized their offensive capabilities to focus on resupplying their harried comrades on Guadalcanal.

Success in November and December around Guadalcanal rested on the overburdened American destroyer crews who repeatedly transited Torpedo Junction to bring in more men and equipment than did the Japanese. Combat in the lower Solomons pitted destroyer against destroyer, Hara versus MacDonald, in a single-minded contest to keep open those vital lifelines to Guadalcanal.

The Japanese assessment of the situation was gloomy: for every submarine or destroyer that delivered supplies to their forces on Guadalcanal, the Americans sent two. "The enemy foothold is thus being strengthened day by day," Ugaki posted in his diary on November 26. "If things go on at this rate, we'll soon be unable to do anything about the situation." Eleven days later he commented of the supply runs made by *O'Bannon* and the other US destroyers: "So frequent are they that it is rather too much trouble to make note of them." He said the Japanese struggled to ship even the most basic of supplies to Guadalcanal, even by submarine, and wrote on December 10, "The only ways left for us now are either to fire materials packed in waterproof bags from torpedo tubes while submerged or to chute them from planes." Ugaki concluded that evacuation of the island, once scoffed as incredulous, was now being considered and is "the most urgent matter."[13]

Japanese resupply efforts continued until December 11, when Tanaka sent the final naval supply run to Guadalcanal. Evacuation increasingly seemed the only option, with Japan pulling her forces off Guadalcanal, digging in on islands to the north, and renewing attacks from those locations. Even without Guadalcanal, the Japanese would still hold the rest of the Solomons. Hundreds of inlets and harbors dotted the island chain across hundreds of miles, providing bases from which Japanese ships or aircraft could emerge to strike the Americans. Should they abandon Guadalcanal, the Japanese intended to make Halsey sweep them from each location, a monumental task that would further challenge the destroyer crews who daily plied the dangerous waters.

"We Are Out to Win a War"

With major surface engagements certain to occur in forcing the Japanese out of the Solomons, however, and disappointed with the tactics utilized in the mid-November naval battle, Halsey asked Rear Admiral Thomas C. Kinkaid, a veteran of naval encounters since Pearl Harbor, to examine the previous engagements off Guadalcanal. As Wilkinson, Cole, and other destroyer officers had urged, Kinkaid's study recommended placing destroyers with the latest radar, such as *O'Bannon*, *Fletcher*, and *Nicholas*, in a van group to provide a better chance of spotting the enemy before the Japanese detected them. He also urged that destroyers act as independent units rather than being shackled to a cruiser column, and that cruisers hold their fire, which divulged a ship's position, until after the destroyers had launched their torpedoes. Kinkaid believed his suggestions increased the odds for American forces to deliver a surprise attack with both torpedo and cruiser fire before the Japanese had a chance to respond.

The plan might have worked at Tassafaronga, the next engagement, had the battle-tested Kinkaid been there to implement it, but immediately before the action he was shifted to the Aleutian campaign. His successor, Rear Admiral Carleton Wright, lacked Kinkaid's experience, but with Kinkaid's blueprint, he stood an excellent chance of winning.

On November 29 American intelligence intercepted a Japanese message indicating that another of Admiral Tanaka's Tokyo Express would arrive near Guadalcanal the next day. Admiral Wright steamed out in his flagship, *Minneapolis*, to meet the eight Japanese destroyers, but instead of positioning his ships into two groups, one comprising his six destroyers and the other containing his five cruisers, as Kinkaid suggested, Wright placed them in the familiar column formation. Leading the way were Cole and Wylie in *Fletcher*, followed by three destroyers, a quintet of cruisers, and two rear destroyers.

Cole and Wylie tried to alert Wright of their radar capabilities, but again their entreaties fell on deaf ears. When dusk settled in and Wright instructed them to hold fire until they received his permission, Wylie was furious. His ship and the other destroyers needed to strike upon first sighting, not wait for an admiral four ships back to give his approval. Wright's move struck Wylie as "the most stupid thing that I have ever heard of."[14]

In the late hours of November 30, just as Wright's force arrived southeast of Savo Island, seven of Tanaka's destroyers formed a single column in preparation for delivery of the drums, with the eighth, *Takanami*, prowling as scout 3,300 yards in the van. Since oil drums cluttered the decks of each destroyer, Tanaka lacked his usual complement of ammunition and torpedoes, but he hoped to sneak in close along Guadalcanal's coast, deliver his cargo, and beat a hasty retreat northward before the Americans could pounce on him.

With Cole again working on the bridge and Wylie feeding him information, *Fletcher*'s radar picked up Tanaka's ships at 7,000 yards. Cole relayed the enemy's course, bearing, and speed to Wright, and requested permission from Wright to mount a torpedo attack. The admiral, who did not want to release his destroyers until he knew the enemy's precise location, refused.

Not until five minutes after *Fletcher*'s radar detected Tanaka's destroyers did Wright give the command to open fire. By that time, ships on both sides had so changed their relative locations that Wright missed an opportunity to launch a torpedo attack at optimal position and handed Tanaka the time he needed to fire his deadlier, more accurate torpedoes.

Without waiting for orders, as Cole was forced to do, *Takanami* launched her eight torpedoes and opened fire at the American force. A few moments later, Cole received permission to launch his ten torpedoes, at which point, according to Seaman Chesnutt, "hell broke loose."[15] American cruiser fire sank the lead Japanese destroyer, but the other seven Japanese destroyers turned parallel to Wright's ships and launched their torpedoes, which crashed into four of the five American cruisers, leaving only *Honolulu* unscratched. Two torpedoes shattered *Minneapolis*'s bow and a third torpedo rammed into *New Orleans* and ignited two of her ammunition magazines, while a fourth struck *Pensacola* and set her fuel tanks afire. Finally, two torpedoes punctured *Northampton*'s port side, sparking a tremendous explosion that engulfed the cruiser in flames.

As soon as his torpedoes were away, Tanaka changed course to the northwest and raced away at full speed, leaving Wright behind with a shattered cruiser force. Tanaka failed to deliver the supplies earmarked for Guadalcanal, but in the fifteen-minute battle he had damaged four cruisers.

Cole rushed to the assistance of the damaged *Northampton*. Upon nearing the stricken ship, Cole reduced speed and carefully backed *Fletcher* into thick oil alongside the cruiser, now engulfed in flames. For almost three hours Cole's crew brought survivors over from the sinking ship, much like fishermen hauling in a school of fish. *Fletcher* crewmen tossed cargo nets into the water and put every available sea ladder over the side to aid in the rescue. In the whaleboat, Ensign Gressard towed rafts packed with *Northampton* survivors to *Fletcher*. Several men, including Fireman 1/c J. E. Howell, Torpedoman 2/c D. E. Krom, Seaman 1/c D. Strickland, and Seaman 1/c H. W. Thomas, jumped over the side to help exhausted *Northampton* men to the ship.

In the middle of the rescue operation, *Northampton*'s stern began settling. The final man off the cruiser, Captain Willard A. Kitts, grabbed on to a line strung from *Fletcher* to his cruiser, but as he slid across, the line became entangled around his ankle, flipping the officer upside down. Facing the prospect of being dragged downward to a watery death by his sinking cruiser, Kitts grabbed the sheath knife he carried and cut himself free before the ship sank. Captain Kitts's extraction from near death provided a powerful example for many of Cole's crew, who had resisted carrying the knives because they were an annoyance. "We never had any more trouble getting our men to carry knives," said Wylie.[16]

Fletcher sailors gently peeled the soiled clothing off the oil-covered *Northampton* survivors. After hosing them down, they handed them spare clothing from the ship's stores or shirts and trousers donated by the crew. While *Northampton* cooks joined their *Fletcher* counterparts to prepare meals for both crews, exhausted *Northampton* sailors slumped onto unoccupied spaces on deck and below and fell into deep slumbers.

Seaman Chesnutt, who had now survived two major engagements in as many weeks, wrote that *Northampton* men so filled *Fletcher*'s decks that "we could hardly walk without stepping on somebody." The rescue made the young radar operator think about his own mortality. "I always wondered how bad it must have been for them as their ship sank," he said, "and then when they were in the water. It makes you think—I could be one of those guys one day."[17]

Fletcher and a second destroyer helped rescue almost seven hundred *Northampton* officers and men. Among those plucked from the waters was Radioman 3/c Jason Robards Jr., who after the war won two Academy Awards as a noted Hollywood film actor. With the rescue operation complete and more than one thousand men cramming every deck of his destroyer, Cole steered *Fletcher* from the area and retired through Sealark Channel on a course to overtake Wright's other ships, then on their way to Espiritu Santo.

In Noumea, Halsey raged over the outcome off Tassafaronga. Despite commanding a superior force, Wright lost one cruiser, limped away with another three damaged, and suffered four hundred dead while sinking only one Japanese destroyer. Halsey wrote Nimitz that he felt Wright had mismanaged the battle and that the surprising defeat was "entirely due to the way we must throw destroyers and cruisers into action without organization."[18] Halsey stressed the need to revise tactics in line with Kinkaid's suggestions, especially with the large number of new destroyers due to arrive in 1943.

The outcome underscored that some American task group commanders relied too heavily on their cruisers while underplaying the importance of destroyers such as *Fletcher*. Halsey and Nimitz understood that evolving naval tactics demanded a closer examination of the new radar and of the massed torpedo attack, both of which would assume greater importance in the 1943 surface engagements bound to occur in Solomon waters, and turned a spotlight on previous encounters.

In light of the poor showings posted in Solomon waters, beginning with the disastrous Battle of Savo Island in August and terminating with Wright's disappointing performance at Tassafaronga, Nimitz asked Halsey to "please be utterly frank with me regarding flag officers. We are out to win a war and not to please individuals. Those not in line for the first team must be sent ashore."[19] That determination to promote aggressive-thinking commanders would elevate executive officers and other worthy men, including MacDonald of *O'Bannon*, to ship command.

The first destroyer commander casualty hit *Fletcher* shortly after the ship reached Espiritu Santo. Wright unfairly shifted blame for the battle to Commander Cole, who Wright contended had not adequately supported his cruisers. Halsey, uncertain that he had all the facts, reluctantly replaced Cole on December 11 with Lieutenant Commander Frank L. Johnson, but later promised Cole a new posting when Halsey learned how gallantly the *Fletcher* had performed in mid-November. Cole eventually became commander of destroyers in the South Pacific.

Admiral Tanaka deserves much credit for Tassafaronga's outcome. Hara called it remarkable that Tanaka inflicted so much damage on the enemy while losing only one ship, and naval historian Samuel Eliot Morison concluded that Tanaka "made no mistakes at Tassafaronga" in sinking one American cruiser and putting three others out of action for much of the next year. "It is always some consolation to reflect that the enemy who defeats you is really good, and Rear Admiral Tanaka was better than that—he was superb," he wrote.[20]

Destroyer commanders and their crews would have to be superb if they were to grab the initiative from Tanaka, Hara, and their other Japanese counterparts. Naval combat for the next year would be frequent, violent, and costly, with the victor grabbing control of the entire Solomon Islands chain, asserting dominance in the South Pacific, and taking a giant step toward victory in the Pacific war.

"I Actually Believed That I Would Get Killed"

After the draining succession of escort runs across Torpedo Junction, *O'Bannon* received a welcome break when the ship was ordered to accompany troop transports carrying the 1st Marine Division to Australia for rest and relaxation after their three-month campaign on Guadalcanal. MacDonald could not have been prouder in "bringing out our very famous First Marine Division who had done such wonderful work in holding Henderson Field," and the added bonus of a few days enjoying Australia's food, bars, and women was like an early Christmas present.

A four-day trip southward brought *O'Bannon* into Brisbane on December 19, the start of a glorious three days in the city. The chance to drop their concerns about enemy air or submarine attacks worked wonders for the crew, both mentally and physically, and MacDonald noticed that the men "certainly did make the best of that short stay."

War duties returned all too soon, and with minor damage repairs complete by December 22, *O'Bannon* reentered the active zone and steamed northeast to Espiritu Santo, where, as New Year's Eve approached, they patrolled the entrance to the harbor while preparing for another task. "The Japanese," wrote MacDonald, "had become very active again and the Tokyo Express was once again running in accordance with their daily time schedule."[21] After a series of bitter clashes on land and at sea, both combatants pulled back to regroup, replenish their forces, and prepare for the next round of fighting.

During December's final week, the crews of *O'Bannon* and her sister ships, also in Espiritu Santo, celebrated the holidays. Catholic officers and sailors attended a Christmas Eve midnight mass celebrated aboard another ship, and clusters of men sang carols, a remarkable contrast to the violence they had recently witnessed. On New Year's Eve men sat in the cooler air topside to watch *Disputed Passage*, a 1939 war film starring Dorothy Lamour and Akim Tamiroff. The movie helped divert their attention from the fighting to the north, but the rapidly increasing number of ships pulling into the harbor hinted that action was close at hand.

As the New Year approached, Tameichi Hara enjoyed time with his family to end the year, but Admiral Ugaki could not share in the happiness. "Guadalcanal is now hopeless," he concluded. After a spectacular first five months of war that had brought triumph and honors to Japan, the United States Navy halted their momentum at the Battle of the Coral Sea and at Midway, and now a combined American Marine-Navy effort had stymied them on Guadalcanal. "The invasions of Hawaii, Fiji, Samoa, and New Caledonia, liberation of India and destruction of the British Far Eastern Fleet have all scattered like dreams," Ugaki wrote in his diary on the last day of 1942.[22]

In Tokyo, Emperor Hirohito was not as pessimistic. In his annual New Year's Day Imperial Rescript, issued December 26, he expressed disappointment in the losses that had marked the latter half of the year, but promised that "dawn is about to break in the Eastern Sky. Today the finest of the Japanese Army, Navy and Air units are gathering. Sooner or later they will head toward the Solomon Islands where a decisive battle is being fought between Japan and America."[23]

Across the waters, Nimitz concluded, "Until we have the requisite numbers of fresh troops to take and keep up the offensive our situation in the Solomon Sea Area will be unsatisfactory from the viewpoint of getting along with the war. Results in 1942 are gratifying considering the fact that we have not had enough tools to work with. While we have managed to stop Jap advances toward Australia and the supply lines thereto, we have not impaired Jap capacity to defend gains of 1942." He added that nothing substantial could be accomplished until more ships, aircraft, and other matériel arrived from the United States. "All this means only one thing for 1943—more tools to work with than are now in sight. In addition, we must improve material, such as torpedoes and radios."[24]

Hanson Baldwin conveyed similar thoughts to his readers back home. He explained that in the aftermath of Tassafaronga, both sides prepared for the next phase in the Solomons fighting. "The job at the moment is supply; the inexorable laws of logistics have forced one of those temporary lulls peculiar to all great wars. But it is certain that great blows are being prepared by both sides and soon again the armies, the navies and the flying fleets will surge back and forth in intensified struggle across the global map of battle."[25]

Countless patrols and frequent escort duties, interrupted only by battles large and small, awaited *O'Bannon*, *Fletcher*, and *Nicholas* in 1943. They welcomed on December 13 the added presence of the fourth ship of what would become Desron 21, the USS *De Haven* (DD-469), under Commander Charles E. Tolman, and looked forward to the arrival of another six *Fletcher*-class destroyers in the coming weeks. But with such bounties at stake, the costs were bound to be high. Halsey's destroyers were certain to absorb a large percentage of those casualties. "I actually believed that I would get killed during some of the battles," explained Seaman Chesnutt of his thoughts for the future. "I didn't see any way in the world that I could live thru the fighting day by day and felt sure the war would last 4–5 years, especially, if we had to take Japan."[26]

The New Year brought hope that 1943 would be better than the year that had expired, but the crews of the four destroyers already in the South Pacific, as well as the six additions in place by February, instead encountered six weary months of patrols, bombardments, and escorts in the Slot, a stretch of water that would burn itself in their memories, followed by three major surface engagements. No one, whether MacDonald, Whisler, or Chesnutt, would think that 1943 was an improvement.

In the first week of the new year, Halsey used a quick trip to New Zealand to boost his forces' morale. When reporters asked the admiral what he thought Japan's next move might be, Halsey shot back, "Japan's next move will be to retreat. A start has been made to make them retreat. They will not be able to stop going back." He added, "All the Axis is hearing the tolling of the bells. And we are doing 'the rope pulling.'" His prediction was "victory for the United Nations. Complete, absolute defeat for the Axis Powers." Then, in words directed at both his forces and the home front, Halsey said that each of his men was the equal to twenty Japanese, and that "under my command the United Nations in the South Pacific have the finest fighting men our country ever produced. They are imbued with a fighter instinct and it is conceded we will not stop until there is a complete victory."[27]

Halsey understood that the situation around Guadalcanal did not support his boisterous comments, but he hoped his words would resonate not only with men and women in the United States but also with his weary forces in the Solomons. He later explained, "My forces were tired; their morale was low; they were beginning to think that they were abused and forgotten, that they had been fighting too much and too long." He said that in Pearl Harbor's aftermath, some people saw the Japanese as "supermen. I saw them as nothing of the sort, and I wanted my forces to know how I felt."[28]

After the four-day trip to New Zealand, Halsey returned to his headquarters to oversee the buildup of his forces. He arrived with the confidence of his commander in chief in his back pocket when, in a message to Congress, President Roosevelt echoed Halsey's optimism by asserting that the country's military forces in the South Pacific were switching from a defensive stance to an aggressive one.

Reporters noticed a difference as well. In an article titled "What Comes Next in the South Pacific?" John G. Norris wrote in the *Washington Post*, "Reinforcements had been landed at Henderson Field, and sizable reserves of food, fuel and ammunition installed there. Bombers, escorted by fighters, were taking off from the Guadalcanal airfield for daily air raids all over the middle and northern Solomons." He concluded, "The trend of war in the Pacific definitely is in our favor."[29]

Part of that trend would be the first offensive operation undertaken by *O'Bannon* and *Fletcher*, as well as the arrival of six more *Fletcher*-class destroyers to bolster the four that already operated in Solomon waters. Their addition was the first step toward organizing them into a fighting unit that would garner more acclaim and awards than any other Pacific squadron.

"Get a Staff Together and Get Going"

Halsey had become aware of a new enemy threat in early December when reconnaissance aircraft spotted the beginnings of a Japanese airfield at Munda on New Georgia Island, 180 miles northwest of Guadalcanal. Once the airfield was operational, it could house the fighters needed to escort Japanese bombers on their runs against Henderson Field. "The airfield that the Japs have put in Munda is a thorn in my side," Halsey wrote to Nimitz in December. He urged immediate action, and promised on his end to "give it all the Hell we can from the air."[30]

Henderson Field fighters mounted the first air strike on December 6, followed three days later by a major B-17 bomber raid. Into the New Year, American aircraft pounded Munda almost daily, but to Halsey's dismay, the Japanese quickly recovered after each raid, filling bomb craters and patching damaged installations. Halsey concluded that only a land assault against New Georgia would knock out the threat.

Halsey brought in a new admiral, Rear Admiral Walden L. "Pug" Ainsworth, to take over his sparse collection of cruisers and destroyers, but offered Ainsworth few specifics as to what his first steps should be. Improvisation was the order of the day until more of everything arrived from the United States. "I was told by Admiral Halsey to get aboard the *Louisville* and get a staff together and get going and he would tell me what to do," recalled

Ainsworth. The admiral would have to make do with a ragtag collection of cruisers and destroyers—"we seldom had full destroyer squadron strength"—that bore little resemblance to the mighty armadas that would hunt down the Japanese in 1944–1945.[31] His principal tasks were to keep the Guadalcanal area secure from enemy attacks and prevent the Tokyo Express from reinforcing Japanese land forces still on the island.

After putting his cruisers and destroyers, organized as Task Force 67, through five days of training and exercises off the Santa Cruz Islands east of Guadalcanal, on January 2 Ainsworth led two groups of ships out of Espiritu Santo for his first offensive strike against the Japanese. Once they had escorted the transports to Guadalcanal, the ships, which included Ainsworth's flagship, the cruiser *Nashville*, six additional cruisers, and their escorting destroyers, including *O'Bannon*, *Fletcher*, and *Nicholas*, would hasten northwest to bombard the Japanese airfield and other installations at Munda. Ainsworth planned to travel at high speed once darkness settled in, with the goal of arriving off Munda by midnight. There, aided by black-painted Catalina amphibious planes (nicknamed "Black Cats"), whose pilots spotted targets and observed the firing, he would conduct the bombardment early in the morning. Speed and timing were crucial, as Ainsworth needed to move into position the night before, try to remain unobserved by enemy aircraft, run the gauntlet of Japanese heavy guns and airfields that protected Munda, conduct the bombardment, and race back to American air cover near Guadalcanal before pursuing Japanese ships caught up to them.

Under overcast skies late in the evening on January 4 Ainsworth started his run into Munda with *O'Bannon* and *Fletcher* screening for *Nashville*, *Helena*, and *St. Louis*. Ainsworth was reluctant to trust the radar aboard *O'Bannon* and *Fletcher*, which had never been used to guide ships in a nighttime offensive. As backup, the submarine *Grayback* waited at her preassigned position off the entrance to the bay leading to the airfield to act as a navigational aid into the unfamiliar waters.

Shortly after midnight on January 5, radar picked up *Grayback* off Banyetta Point, at which time the column slowed to eighteen knots and turned onto the course along New Georgia's western shore. The plan called for a ten-minute bombardment of the white coral airstrip and adjoining installations by each of the three cruisers, after which *Fletcher* and *O'Bannon* would turn their batteries on the island in a joint bombardment.

The cruisers opened fire shortly after 1:00 a.m. Streams of fire rent the nighttime darkness as shells arced toward the airstrip, reminding MacDonald of "watching a hose spraying bullets over there on the target."[32] After each cruiser pounded the airstrip with a thousand shells, *O'Bannon* dropped seven hundred yards astern of *Fletcher* and the pair of destroyers opened a ten-minute bombardment from twelve thousand yards.

Fletcher's new skipper, Lieutenant Commander Johnson, stood on the bridge next to Captain R. P. Briscoe, Commander Destroyer Squadron 5. When lookouts spotted a large vessel five thousand yards to their west, Johnson brought the ship hard left, increased his speed to twenty-five knots, and ordered his torpedo battery to stand by. He asked Wylie to confirm the sighting, but the executive officer replied that the radar screen revealed no such contact.

Wylie wondered who was right. Radar had contributed to the success of the November surface engagement off Guadalcanal, but Johnson, a skipper new to South Pacific combat, insisted that the radar was malfunctioning. "The bridge insisted that a ship was there," said Wylie, "and radar, with the PPI screen, insisted that there was no such ship." Wylie "was perspiring freely" when he learned that the ship's torpedomen were preparing to launch torpedoes, and agreed with the radarman third class next to him, who shook his fist at the radar screen and growled, "Oh you bastard, if you let us down now!"[33]

On the bridge, Briscoe also had difficulty balancing Wylie's conclusions with what materialized before his eyes. He and Johnson became more perplexed when the image imitated *Fletcher*'s course change and also turned to the left. They also noticed that when *Nashville* ceased firing, the image disappeared, only to reappear moments later with more gunfire. The commanders suddenly realized that what they saw was *Fletcher*'s own shadow outlined in the haze by the cruisers' bombardments. Johnson belayed his order to the torpedo crew, forestalling what would have been an embarrassing torpedo attack against thin air. The captain wrote in his action report that the image had seemed so real that it might explain conflicting reports of enemy locations during earlier night engagements.

This first offensive naval bombardment was a success. Ainsworth punished Japanese installations at Munda without sustaining any damage, and the operation handed him and his commanders their first opportunity to conduct a radar-guided bombardment at night. According to Lieutenant Commander Dennis Crowley, one of three Navy aviators spotting for Ainsworth's ships, it was "the most accurate big gun fire we have ever seen or hope to see." Crowley added, "The ships didn't need much help. The first shell struck directly on the runway a third of the way from the west end. Following shells worked toward the western end, then switched back and in neat succession ran the length of the runway down to the east end just like a plane taking off. That done, the firing next fell in a pattern on both sides, covering a large area around the field." Crowley guessed that the enemy was taken completely by surprise and that many Japanese must have perished from the voluminous shelling. "The warships looked afire as they poured out their shells hot and heavy. It was almost as light as day in the space between the fleet and the beach."[34]

After the bombardment, *Fletcher* and *O'Bannon* guided the cruisers out of the bay toward the rendezvous point near Guadalcanal to join *Nicholas* and the support group. As they arrived, thirteen enemy dive-bombers bracketed *Honolulu* with bombs, showering her with water and bomb fragments, while another bomb struck a gun mount on the cruiser *Achilles*, killing thirteen crew. Antiaircraft gun crews aboard the cruisers laced the sky with their bullets, shooting down two aircraft, while Henderson Field fighter aircraft splashed four more.

When Ainsworth learned of two downed enemy pilots floating in the water, he ordered Wilkinson to retrieve them. Wilkinson moved *O'Bannon* alongside the pair, now clinging to debris and in obvious need of medical attention, but when a boatswain tossed life rings to them, the Japanese shoved the rings aside and began swimming away. The crew retrieved the first pilot from the water, who died from his wounds soon after, but the second continued to resist. MacDonald used a whaleboat to approach the man, but "as we got alongside to grab him, he reached down and pulled a revolver and held it at me. He actually shot, but the bullet didn't go off." With that failed attempt on their executive officer, men with machine guns standing on *O'Bannon*'s bridge "just let him have it and blew his head right off."[35]

The use of radar "under all conditions of visibility permits both exact navigation in strange waters and successful conduct of night bombardment on practically any type of area target," wrote a convinced Johnson in his action report, handing Wylie credit for promoting the device. Johnson was so impressed with radar's capabilities that he urged that "no combatant vessel should fire a planned night bombardment unless equipped with Sugar George [surface] Radar," and suggested that there was no longer any need for a submarine or other type of vessel to wait ahead of the force as a navigational aid. Wilkinson agreed with his fellow skipper, claiming that the use of SG radar for both accurate bombardments and for navigation "makes a night bombardment of this sort simple and deadly."[36] Other officers said that because of radar, bombardment vessels could open fire at longer ranges and enjoy greater accuracy, and claimed that even if all radar did was help ships navigate the tricky Solomon waters, that would justify its use.

These comments confirmed what Wylie had suspected. In his brief time with the destroyer, he had helped develop an early version of what would soon become the combat information center (CIC). Wylie's enhancements in relaying crucial information to the skipper during surface engagements soon gained notice at headquarters.

In June 1943 Wylie was detached and sent to Pearl Harbor to compile a handbook outlining the tools a CIC should possess, how the room should be arranged, and how it could be properly managed. The CIC, in effect, would analyze and deliver material to the captain, who could then make the speedy decisions that demanded his attention.

Wylie spent six weeks developing the *CIC Handbook for Destroyers Pacific Fleet*. The twenty-page handbook placed the SC radar (air-search) on one side of CIC, the SG radar (surface-search) on the other, and the air plot and surface plot forward of them. "That was the first time there had been brought together a concept and a process for the management of all information relating to the enemy."[37]

Wylie's renovation soon became an established part of each ship. Older vessels set up the CIC in the division commander's cabin, which was not often utilized anyway, while newer vessels had the CIC incorporated into the ship designs. In addition, Wylie started an informal destroyer school in Espiritu Santo, called Coconut College, for exchanging ideas and bringing newly arrived ships up to speed on current tactical developments. Wylie's contributions in formulating the CIC and disseminating information to commanders when they most needed it became one of the most important advancements in handling ships while in a combat zone.

"We Are in the Big Leagues"

Wylie's innovations arrived at the right time, as the Navy speedily expanded to meet the dual threat posed by Germany and Japan. Senior commanders, including Halsey and Nimitz, scoured the Naval Academy's rosters for viable candidates to man and skipper the new ships.

The first four vessels that would eventually coalesce into the United States Navy's most honored destroyer squadron had already arrived. *O'Bannon*, *Fletcher*, and *Nicholas* had come onto the scene in September, gaining valuable experience in escorting, patrolling, and surface combat. The recently arrived *De Haven* was the fourth destroyer, but her crew lacked the experience to know what South Pacific combat was like.

The commanders of what would by early February be a full squadron of ships were already acquainted with one another. They had graduated from the Academy in the mid-twenties, taken classes together, participated in common exercises, and held the same hopes for promotion during a naval career. Commanders of the first three destroyers had already established an efficient working relationship, systems that evolved during the shakedown cruises and then during combat with the enemy. The more recent commanders had yet to pass through those stages.

Skippers of the newest seven destroyers benefited from preliminary experience in escorting transports before they reached the Pacific. During the fall of 1942, while the first three *Fletcher*-class destroyers battled the Japanese off Guadalcanal, six arrivals were initiated in Atlantic waters. The USS *Radford* (DD-446), under Lieutenant Commander William K. Romoser, helped tow a burning transport to Halifax, while the other five destroyers participated in the November 1942 invasion of North Africa. The USS *Taylor*, with skipper Lieutenant Commander Benjamin J. Katz, Lieutenant Commander Harry H. Henderson's USS *La Vallette* (DD-448), the USS *Strong* (DD-467), commanded by Lieutenant Commander Joseph H. "Gus" Wellings, and the USS *Chevalier* (DD-451), led by Lieutenant Commander Ephraim R. McLean Jr., escorted transports across the Atlantic to North Africa. The USS *Jenkins* (DD-447), under the command of Lieutenant Commander Harry F. Miller, also screened for battleships as they bombarded German positions ashore.

One by one these ships departed the Mediterranean or Canada; they gathered in the United States, then embarked on the longer voyage through the Panama Canal to the South Pacific. Like every commander who entered Pacific waters, the captains of each of these vessels, aware that each mile they steamed west brought them a mile closer to the fighting, conducted daily drills to prepare the young crews for battle. Operations in European or Canadian waters carried the risk of being attacked by German U-boats, but Pacific combat would add perils from surface warships and from the air that were not as predominant off North Africa or North America. The crews had to be prepared for those new threats.

As the *Chevalier* left the Panama Canal to enter the Pacific Ocean, Lieutenant Commander McLean announced over the loudspeaker in the booming voice to which the crew had quickly become accustomed, "All hands not on watch lay aft to the fantail." One of his young crew, Yeoman R. H. Roupe, wondered what McLean was doing. "As the fantail slowly filled with men, the Captain appeared and climbed to the top of the after five-inch gun turret. On watch in sky-aft, we crowded the edge of the gun-shield and strained our ears to hear."

McLean's strong voice cut through the ocean breezes to announce, "We have now joined the Pacific Fleet." He added that he had been looking forward to engaging the Japanese for almost two decades, and now that they were in the same waters as the enemy, he expected the crew to keep their life jackets close by at all times. "All hands be on your toes," he said. "We are in the Big Leagues."

Chevalier and her crew would soon be battling toe to toe with the Japanese, which meant they could no longer afford to commit any amateurish blunders. "We realized that we were in the Big League, all right," said Roupe, "and probably on the first team, too."[38]

In the South Pacific, MacDonald and the crew of his *O'Bannon* wondered about the proficiency of the new arrivals. MacDonald said that he "only hoped that any new ship that joined up and hadn't been in one of these battles could control itself to the point of not shooting some of its own friends, also at some of its own friendly aircraft. This is one of the things that you gain by experience and experience only, because the great tendency is to be trigger-happy once you start opening fire."[39]

The first few months of 1943 would begin providing answers.

CHAPTER 5

BIRTH OF A SQUADRON

Foster Hailey knew a story when he saw it. The veteran *New York Times* reporter had left his New York home at 11:00 p.m. on December 7, 1941, anxious to rush to the Pacific, where, he hoped, he could make sense out of the catastrophe at Pearl Harbor and bring the drama of war to his readers. If a reporter wanted to convey the emotions and significance of an event, Hailey believed, he had to be where the action occurred and stand among the participants. His search for the next story took him to the Coral Sea for the May 1942 naval battle, to Guadalcanal to experience a thundering Japanese bombardment of Henderson Field, and to the offices of Admiral Bull Halsey to study the war as orchestrated from above.

He now sought stories from the naval spectrum's tail end, where sailors took center stage. He had already seen war from the trenches during his tenure with the Marines on Guadalcanal, and he now wished to add a different perspective by heading to the sea. He shunned the glamorous aircraft carriers and their squadrons of fighters—the reading public already knew about those vessels and their flyboys—and turned instead to some of the smallest ships then prowling the Solomons, the speedy destroyers. "That is one of the lures of the tin cans," Hailey wrote, "they travel fast. They're hard-hitting, tough-living, hell-for-leather ships, the cowboys of the fleet."[1]

Hailey wanted stories that illuminated men more representative of the American home front than the generals and admirals. He found what he sought among the officers and crews of Admiral Halsey's first destroyer squadron to populate the Solomons, a unit anchored by *O'Bannon*, *Fletcher*, and *Nicholas*.

Like Admiral Halsey, Hailey recognized that at this stage of the Pacific war, success and victory rested on the outcome of the fierce land and sea battles waged in the islands and waters of the Solomons. The combatants stood at opposite ends, with the Japanese based at Rabaul in the northwest and the US military operating from Guadalcanal to the southwest. In between lay an eight-hundred-mile arena consisting of narrow channels, sharp underwater ridges, bays and harbors, and Japanese-held islands and airfields.

The opponents would contest that stage over the next year with planes and PT boats, Army infantry and Marine battalions, cruisers and destroyers. Day after day the destroyers steamed into the Slot, the narrow body of water separating the Solomons' two island arms. Stretching from southeast to northwest, it offered a compact battle area that made daily encounters almost inevitable. Upon MacDonald and Whisler on *O'Bannon*, Chesnutt and Holmes on *Fletcher*, and every officer and enlisted aboard the destroyers that gathered off Guadalcanal in January 1943 would depend victory or defeat in the Solomons. For much of that time, Hailey mingled with those men, interacting with officers and chatting with enlisted so that he could sufficiently convey that Solomon Islands drama to home-front audiences.

"Anxious to see some action, I joined a destroyer squadron which had been operating with Admiral Ainsworth's force and was being sent to Tulagi to do any odd chores that might be found, such as sidetracking the Tokyo Express if it should attempt resumption of the old schedule down 'the slot,'" he wrote.[2] Hailey found a home with the men of *O'Bannon* and *Nicholas*, soon to be operating as a unit called the Cactus Striking Force.

"Fighting and Killing Is Now Their Job"

Upon emerging from the desperate November days, and with the arrival of new destroyers such as *De Haven*, Admiral Halsey finally saw an opportunity to mount minor strikes against the Japanese. Nimitz's headquarters had estimated that naval superiority in the Solomons would not come until the spring arrival of additional ships and aircraft, but until then, Halsey intended to keep the Japanese off guard by sending his destroyers and a handful of cruisers north for quick nighttime bombardments. Unwilling to risk his few battleships in such forays, Halsey turned to his *Fletcher*-class destroyers, such as *O'Bannon*, as being perfectly suited for the task. The missions would also sate the old warrior's passion to be freed from the defensive shackles required around Guadalcanal and allow him to seek out the enemy.

In mid-January Halsey organized a fast-moving destroyer unit to mount those raids. "As a destroyer sailor of long service," he wrote Nimitz on January 11, "it has broken my heart to see the way these ships were of necessity abused materially and in the way of personnel." He said that squadron and division organization had been wisely abandoned in the early months off Guadalcanal, but explained, "With our new organization, which I shall use my utmost endeavor to keep going, this handicap should be overcome. In other words, I believe at long last we are in sight of a position where we can use destroyers as they should be used." Excited at the prospect of allowing his destroyers to seek out the enemy rather than escorting transports, Halsey added, "It is the first offensive force that we have had in the South Pacific. I hope it grows larger and larger and that the 'Yellow Bastards' forces grow smaller and smaller."[3]

Based out of Tulagi and nearby Purvis Bay on Florida Island, thirty miles northeast of Guadalcanal across Ironbottom Sound, Captain R. P. Briscoe's Cactus Striking Force of *O'Bannon*, *Nicholas*, *Fletcher*, and *De Haven*, plus the newly arrived *Fletcher*-class destroyer *Radford*, were given three principal tasks. During daylight hours the unit was to support the infantry fighting the enemy on Guadalcanal, mainly by bombarding Japanese shore positions between Point Cruz and Cape Esperance, while at night the ships would intercept the Tokyo Express or, more important, join with cruisers to bombard enemy installations to the north. His directive offered little rest for sailors already weary from two months of naval action but promised they would at least be taking the offensive, as indicated by the inclusion of the word "striking" in their unit name.

"This was to be one of the most exciting periods of our entire stay in the South Pacific," said MacDonald later.[4] His destroyer and the four companions now had a home. While still occasionally dashing to Espiritu Santo, the force principally operated in one area, with Florida Island's dual harbors at Tulagi and Purvis Bay, shielded by hills ringing the harbors and a wall of jungle stretching to the water's edge, offering havens for the unit.

The switch handed MacDonald and other destroyer officers the opportunity for advancement. With aircraft carriers and battleships either damaged or being withheld from combat until more vessels arrived from American shipyards, destroyer commanders occupied center stage. Upon Wilkinson's departure, MacDonald received command of *O'Bannon* on January 10. Lieutenant Commander Andrew Hill became skipper of *Nicholas* when Commander Brown left to join the staff of Rear Admiral Aaron S. "Tip" Merrill.

Should they and the other skippers excel at their duties, additional promotions were certain to follow.

Their task would not be easy. "We will have to call on all our patriotism, stamina, guts, and maybe some crusading spirit or religious fervor thrown in, to beat him," said Lieutenant General George Kenney, commander of the air forces in Douglas MacArthur's Southwest Pacific Area, of the Japanese. "No amateur can take this boy out. We have got to turn professional. Another thing: there are no quiet sectors in which troops get started off gradually, as in the last war. There are no breathers in this schedule. You take on Notre Dame, every time you play!"[5]

A pattern developed in the coming weeks. With the US infantry shoving the Japanese into Guadalcanal's western corner, during daylight hours the destroyers prowled offshore to provide fire support for the Army units, directed by a liaison officer who boarded the destroyers to help pinpoint the targets. By night, *O'Bannon* and the other *Fletcher*-class destroyers steamed the waters north of Guadalcanal to tangle with the Tokyo Express. Leaving Tulagi, which destroyer crews labeled the "Sleepless Lagoon" because they enjoyed so little rest there, they swept up the Slot as far as the Russell Islands, thirty miles northwest of Guadalcanal, searching for enemy surface craft bringing supplies or reinforcements to the island, or dropping depth charges on Japanese submarines detected by their sonar.[6] Crews aboard older destroyers lacking the advanced radar wished they could join the quartet in their northward dashes to meet the enemy, while sailors aboard the five *Fletcher*-class destroyers developed a squadron esprit de corps for the first time. The Cactus Striking Force quickly crafted a reputation in the South Pacific as Halsey's first offensive response to the Japanese and became a foreshadow of what the ships, soon to be organized as Desron 21, could achieve.

Aboard the USS *Sterett*, the ship into which the *O'Bannon* had nearly collided in the November battle, Ensign C. Raymond Calhoun prayed that his older destroyer could join the five in pursuing the enemy. "The crew watched with envy as the new 'cans' (*Fletcher*-class destroyers) dashed up the slot to Munda, Rendova, and New Georgia, where the action was now furious." According to Calhoun and his *Sterett* shipmates, that quintet "was intercepting and doing battle with just about every Japanese force that attempted to reinforce their garrisons in the central Solomons."[7]

Foster Hailey selected this unit, though, because in his opinion the Cactus Striking Force typified early 1943 naval combat in the South Pacific. He arranged to be placed aboard *O'Bannon*, where, standing on the bridge next to her new skipper or sitting in the mess room with the enlisted, he could study the role of a destroyer in combat. When Hailey first inspected *O'Bannon*'s crew, most looked so young that he thought he was back in high school. As he mingled with the sailors, most of whom had less than a year of naval service, he found that they offered a smorgasbord of backgrounds, coming from farms and cities, from newspaper delivery stations and behind drugstore soda fountains. He occasionally came across the weathered face of a veteran, but he guessed that the average age of the crew could hardly be twenty years.

Hailey witnessed enough to inform home-front readers that the crew of *O'Bannon* and her four mates will "go willingly anywhere they are led by officers in whom they have confidence and fight with all their might when they get there." Despite their youth and inexperience, and armed "with only a tin helmet between them and the Japanese bombs and shells," they were prepared to meet the vaunted Japanese and send them packing.[8] Hailey intended to be there at every stage to relay their exploits to his readers.

The bombardments by day and the patrolling by night from Sleepless Lagoon took a toll on MacDonald's crew, some of whom contended that Halsey considered them expendable. "There seemed to be no relief in sight and daily twenty-four-hour operating was a terrific strain," wrote MacDonald. Night after night, MacDonald and his crew, often accompanied by one or more of their Cactus Striking Force brethren, plied dangerous waters, and while MacDonald was proud of his men, "we had to stand more than men ordinarily can endure." He denied the few requests for transfers to shore duty, and while he tried to maintain his men's morale, "it was most difficult trying to cheer them up without much to offer them except the sacrificing of their life for their country."[9] The Cactus Striking Force had to hold the line, though, for it was one of only a few tools Halsey then had at his disposal.

Standing beside MacDonald on the bridge of *O'Bannon*, Hailey saw it, too. He explained to home-front readers that on their behalf, these sailors went without rest, good food, and all the amenities that people in the United States took for granted. A crewmember of the Cactus Striking Force "must spend long days or weeks or even months at sea doing necessary things like convoying or patrol, in which he must always be on the alert for the enemy plane or ship that may be, so far as he knows, a thousand miles away or just over the horizon. If he let it, the strain could become intolerable." Hailey emphasized that during these long, difficult stretches at sea, the sailors saw the same faces every day, none of which were female. "There probably isn't one of them who wouldn't rather be doing something else, but fighting and killing is now their job, and they're not shirking it."[10]

Because his ship was so often at general quarters while operating in the Guadalcanal area, each day the communications officer aboard *De Haven*, Lieutenant (jg) John J. Rowan, spent anywhere from twelve to eighteen hours on the ship's bridge during these hectic times. Twice in one week he remained at his station for thirty straight hours, standing the whole time, and he described most days in the Guadalcanal area as "continuously busy and with a good chance for contact with the Japanese coming down the slot from Rabaul." He called the experience "exhausting," exacerbated by a lack of air-conditioning. Since *De Haven* was almost always either in Condition One or Condition Two, the tropical sun created insufferable environments inside the sweltering ship, and so baked the decks that men dared not step on them barefooted. "A closed steel ship in the sun is like a bake-oven that gets hot and stays hot," said Rowan.[11]

January 19 typified each day in the first two months of 1943. With Hailey observing their operations from *O'Bannon*, the Cactus Striking Force made four firing runs on Japanese positions near Kokumbona Village, on Guadalcanal's northwest corner. For five hours, into early afternoon, the ships bombarded enemy units dug in on ridges and slopes. Guided by naval and Marine observers aboard each ship who communicated via shortwave radio with spotters ashore, the destroyers' five-inch shells pulverized Japanese in foxholes and bunkers. "At times we were firing only fifty yards ahead of the troops," wrote an impressed Hailey, "who were moving in behind the sea-and-shore barrage before the Japanese could reform their shattered defenses."

Hailey wrote that *O'Bannon* and her companions encountered infrequent opposition, even though they "went in so close you often could see the Japanese running around like mad looking for good deep foxholes in which to hide." Aboard *Nicholas* to observe the bombardment, Army Major General Alexander M. Patch was impressed with the intensity and accuracy of the destroyers' gunfire. *O'Bannon*'s gun crews alone expended almost a thousand rounds at the Japanese, leading one of the destroyer's boatswains to joke with Hailey that they had done their job in utilizing their portion of the metal collected in scrap drives back home.

After a day of blasting enemy shore positions, the squadron returned to Tulagi, where instead of resting, the crew brought additional ammunition aboard and prepared for the next outing. Five hours later they followed

Nicholas out of Sleepless Lagoon to patrol near Rua Dika Island to the northwest, sweeping the waters in search of the Tokyo Express.

Throughout the day lookouts and radarmen tracked every airplane that flew within range, and gun batteries remained trained on each until its identity could be established. Aviators often vexed destroyer crews by failing to respond to identification calls, placing gun crews and officers in the awkward predicament of choosing between shooting at a plane that could be friendly or withholding fire and allowing a Japanese intruder to draw closer. MacDonald and other commanders filed reports complaining about the issue, but the problem persisted.

The majority of days and nights were spent at battle stations. "There was little rest for the weary crews," commented Hailey about MacDonald and his men. They patrolled, investigated sonar contacts for enemy submarines, watched for air attacks, and waited to engage the Tokyo Express. At night "Washing Machine Charlie," the nickname given the solitary Japanese scout plane whose engine noises sounded like a washing machine in operation, interrupted their sleep with flares and engine rumbles. The squadron, Hailey observed, "was the only United States naval group actually around Guadalcanal. If battle were to be joined, it appeared we would be the ones who would start it."[12]

"Bad News for Japs"

Halsey ordered another offensive strike in late January to complement the earlier one conducted against Munda. On the west side of Kula Gulf, two hundred miles northwest of Guadalcanal, stood Kolombangara Island and its two plantations, Vila and Stanmore. The Japanese collected supplies at these locations and ferried them to Munda, thirteen miles across the gulf on New Georgia Island, where workers were constructing an airfield. Halsey wanted to bombard the plantations to hinder that construction and to give him additional time to prepare a more ambitious offensive.

The January 22–23 nighttime bombardment of the plantations differed from the one staged earlier in the month. A full moon would make it simpler for Japanese aircraft to spot the encroaching American ships, and should the force reach the narrow waters of Kula Gulf, they could be easy prey for Japanese aircraft based at Kolombangara and New Georgia. Admiral Ainsworth, again in command, decided to advance partway into the gulf, reverse course, and open fire only as the ships were on their way out. He hoped this tactic would shield him from the enemy until his ships were already exiting the gulf and on their way back to Tulagi.

Ainsworth's four light cruisers and seven destroyers left Espiritu Santo on the morning of January 22. After dark, he divided the ships into two divisions, with the bombardment force of *O'Bannon*, *Nicholas*, *De Haven*, and *Radford* escorting *Nashville* and *Helena*, while the other three destroyers remained to the rear with the cruisers *Honolulu* and *St. Louis* as support.

MacDonald, who had assumed command of *O'Bannon* less than two weeks earlier, believed that his crew would perform more efficiently if the men knew as much as possible before they headed into an operation. He thus began hosting almost nightly informational broadcasts over the ship's loudspeaker, during which he explained as much of the planned mission as possible.

This night's message carried more import. Not only was the crew embarking on their first offensive, but the bombardment was also MacDonald's first offensive operation as skipper. How he conducted himself now and during the action was as crucial to his men as were their actions.

"All hands, this is your captain. Tonight we are going to bombard Vila airdrome on Kolombangara Island," he began. Then he immediately plunged into the most dangerous aspect of the mission. "At the present time the Japs are in possession of all the surrounding land. We may see action tonight but no word has been received regarding surface ships." He ended with words designed to ease their qualms: "All hands will be called to General Quarters at 2130 [9:30 p.m.]. Between now and then obtain as much rest as possible. When you are called to your battle stations, proceed quietly. Do not show any lights. Take as much water as you can carry. That is all."[13]

According to Hailey, the ships "boiled along through the night and the next day" to reach their destination.[14] Men cursed the full moon that bathed the ships, thereby handing the enemy a clearer look. At 1:30 a.m. the ships spotted Visuvisu Point and swung southwest to enter the gulf, with every gun manned and lookouts on the alert. As the cruisers and destroyers increased to flank speed, MacDonald moved *O'Bannon* into the lead spot to scout ahead and learn, by offering himself and his crew as bait, whether the Japanese knew they were coming. MacDonald steamed the entire length of the gulf before reaching the bombardment position off Vila and swinging back to the north.

"This was an extremely hectic night," said MacDonald.[15] As the skipper carefully navigated the ship through the darkness, so close to shore in the narrow gulf that Japanese batteries could hardly miss should they open fire, eighteen-year-old Seaman Whisler tensed in his gun mount, expecting at any moment a salvo of enemy shells to rip into the destroyer. He did not even want to consider that a Japanese surface force might steam out to engage them.

"The night was as silent as a tomb, the water smooth and oily-looking," wrote Hailey, standing beside MacDonald during the tense moment. "Our wake made a neat, geometric pattern across its face. We could see the hills of Kolombangara plainly. In the center was the cone of an extinct volcano. Mist was drifting down the narrow valleys from the hilltops toward the sea."[16] To everyone's elation, MacDonald completed his sweep in the gulf, reported that conditions were favorable, and resumed his station with the other ships.

Ainsworth immediately turned his ships parallel to the coast and, while the destroyers of the Cactus Striking Force screened, opened fire. For twenty-nine minutes *Nashville* and *Helena* poured salvo after salvo at the Japanese installations. As MacDonald watched the spectacle through his glasses, the shells arcing through the sky reminded him of "racing comets." Next to him, Hailey marveled at the bombardment's ferocity, and informed home-front readers that the cruisers sent a stream of fireballs shoreward that "served the Japanese a concentrated hell." He wrote that the "tracers lobbing through the air looked like colored balls from Roman candles and flowed in such a steady stream it was like a spray from a deadly garden hose playing back and forth across the Japanese positions." Ashore, the numerous fires merged "and a great pillar of flame hundreds of feet high rose in the air."[17] The *O'Bannon* deck crew emitted a huge cheer when a salvo from *Helena* struck an ammunition dump and kicked up an enormous ball of fire.

Once the cruisers completed their bombardment, those ships exited the gulf and gave center stage to the four Cactus destroyers. Briscoe's ships moved closer to shore and, over the next hour against minor opposition, pumped 3,500 rounds toward Vila. "It was as audacious and courageously tough a raid as had yet been made in the Pacific," concluded Hailey of the bombardment he had just witnessed from *O'Bannon*'s bridge.[18]

After firing their final shells, the quartet "started to get the hell out of there because it was no place to be," as Ensign Clem C. Williams on the *De Haven* put it. The skippers ordered full speed and commenced a wild race to reach Guadalcanal air cover two hundred miles southeast before Japanese warships and aircraft caught up. Rushing along the shore leading to the gulf's exit, MacDonald and Hailey glanced toward Vila, where "there was over the whole area a ruddy glow silhouetting retiring ships against its fiery backdrop."[19]

Thirty minutes after the destroyers rendezvoused with the cruisers, Japanese planes dropped flares that, according to Ainsworth, "seemed to illuminate all of the Kula Gulf area. We felt very naked indeed."[20] As they left the gulf, the Japanese also dropped float boxes in the water to mark for torpedo and dive-bomber attacks the path taken by Ainsworth. Ainsworth formed his ships into antiaircraft disposition and hoped he could make it to Tulagi and friendly air cover before the Japanese trapped him.

His luck ran out at 3:30 a.m. Over a span of two and a half hours, torpedo bombers intermittently attacked the ships, forcing Ainsworth to seek shelter in a sequence of rain squalls. Stationed with the other three destroyers in a box formation about the cruisers, MacDonald evaded two aircraft that shadowed *O'Bannon* on either side. He maneuvered from squall to squall, so limiting the time the ship remained in the open that the Japanese enjoyed only brief moments to form up for an organized attack. When *Radford* gunners splashed one of the intruders with radar-directed five-inch shells containing preset fuses, they became one of the first crews to accomplish that feat.

Ainsworth successfully hopped from squall to squall until dawn, when the force reached the Russell Islands and its welcome air cover. Four Wildcat fighters from Henderson Field, followed by more than fifty American torpedo planes, dive-bombers, and their fighter escorts on their way to Vila, rose to attack the Japanese. "Look to the sky," announced *O'Bannon*'s executive officer, Lieutenant George Philip Jr. "There goes the might of the United States. The enemy is on the run."[21] Sailors on deck let out a huge cheer at Philip's words.

By a slim margin Ainsworth's ships won the race down the Slot. Admiral Halsey radioed to Ainsworth that his task force "is bad news for Japs. Your second successful bombardment has hammered another nail in the coffin and this time spike size. Well done."[22]

The officers and crews of the newly formed Cactus Striking Force had prowled the southern Solomon waters since the previous October, with brief times in back areas when the ships needed minor repair work. MacDonald longed to give his weary crew a break, but unlike the cruisers that headed south away from Guadalcanal, the destroyers remained in Solomon waters, facing yet more days and nights patrolling and screening. "It was quite a letdown in feeling," said MacDonald, "because we knew that once again we were here until the end, with no relief in sight." In his writing, Hailey had sung their praises for his readers, but he now informed his home-front audience, "There was little rest or liberty at rear bases for the men of the tin-can navy."[23]

Hailey did not rest, either. Having gathered what he wanted aboard *O'Bannon*, he asked to be placed on one of the other Cactus destroyers to gain a different perspective. Commander Charles E. Tolman, skipper of *De Haven*, invited Hailey to join his destroyer, but Hailey opted instead for *Nicholas*, the more experienced ship.

The innocent choice carried life-and-death implications.

"The Japs Were Here for the Kill"

Since arriving in the South Pacific the previous September, *O'Bannon*, *Fletcher*, and *Nicholas*, the trio of ships that would later become the anchors of Destroyer Squadron 21, had carried the load. *De Haven*'s appearance in December boosted the number to four, and five more joined their ranks in January. When USS *Chevalier* arrived shortly afterward, for the first time the squadron's core ten ships operated together.

Three—*Chevalier*, *La Vallette*, and *Taylor*—tangled with the enemy before January ended. The action started when American aerial reconnaissance noticed increased activity at the major Japanese terminals of Rabaul, on New Britain, and Buin, on the island of Bougainville in the Solomons. American intelligence erroneously concluded that this was yet another run by the Tokyo Express.

Halsey combined two operations. While transports removed most of the Marines who had been fighting on the island since August, cruisers and destroyers would lie in wait near the transports and surprise the Japanese surface vessels.

His opponent, Admiral Yamamoto, would not be trapped, however. The man who had planned the successful attack on Pearl Harbor had subsequently seen his navy absorb catastrophic losses at Midway, a reversal in the Coral Sea, and continued pounding in the Solomons. With fuel supplies running low, he could neither mount a vast naval operation nor afford to lose many ships. Instead, Yamamoto organized an aerial attack involving Lieutenant Commander Joji Higai's thirty-two torpedo bombers from Rabaul's airfields.

Halsey scraped the bottom of the South Pacific barrel to collect a unit he could throw into battle. Rear Admiral Robert C. "Ike" Giffen's Task Force 18 consisted of the heavy cruisers *Wichita*, *Chicago*, and *Louisville*, the light cruisers *Montpelier*, *Cleveland*, and *Columbia*, and a screen of six destroyers, including *La Vallette*, *Chevalier*, and *Taylor*. A separate unit of battleships, whose screen included MacDonald's *O'Bannon*, supported Giffen's cruisers.

Ike Giffen was not new to command. He had battled German U-boats in the Atlantic Ocean and operated in North African waters, but he had never seen action in the Pacific, where air assaults on ships at sea were more common than they were in the Atlantic and the Mediterranean. "They were quite inexperienced in fighting the Japs," said MacDonald, "and this, of course, is one of the reasons they ran into so much trouble."[24]

Giffen arrived fifty miles north of Rennell Island, which stands 120 miles southeast of Guadalcanal, late in the afternoon of January 29. Because of his experience operating against German U-boats, Giffen stationed his destroyers in a semicircle two miles ahead of the cruisers. While appropriate for the Atlantic, where air assaults at sea rarely occurred, this formation was ill suited for the Pacific's air attacks. Giffen's disposition exposed his cruisers' after beams and quarters, making them vulnerable to torpedo planes and dive-bombers attacking from behind.

Shortly after twilight, Lieutenant Commander Higai approached with his thirty-two torpedo bombers from Rabaul. Though radar picked up the force, Giffen failed to change course, alert his aircraft, or issue orders to his ships about what they should do in case of attack.

Within twenty minutes Higai and his pilots had descended toward their targets. Lieutenant (jg) Chuck Witten, *La Vallette*'s radar officer, was in the wardroom with other officers when a shrill voice announced over the loudspeaker, "This is no drill. General Quarters. General Quarters. All hands man your battle stations. No shit!" Witten dropped what he was doing and raced to his post on the secondary gun control, fully expecting enemy planes to be closing in, but instead "the planes ignored us and went for the big boys."[25]

On the *Chevalier*, Yeoman R. H. Roupe heard the call to general quarters and thought, "Our baptism of fire had come."[26] The officer of the deck stepped over to Roupe's gun and told the crew that once they received word to open fire, they were to keep the shells going even if they could see no target.

The torpedoes from Higai's first wave missed Giffen's zigzagging ships. Giffen, who assumed the Japanese attack had ended, halted the maneuvering and returned to a steady course, a move that made them easy pickings for

Higa's second wave. "The Japs were out in full force," wrote Seaman 1/c James J. Fahey on the cruiser *Montpelier*; "they were here for the kill."[27]

Japanese scout planes dropped parachutes from which dangled yellow-white flares. As they slowly descended to the ocean, the flares brightly illuminated Giffen's two cruiser columns, perfectly silhouetting them for Higai's aviators. Giffen put out over the TBS what MacDonald described as "a very hectic call" that Japanese aircraft were about to attack and that he required assistance.[28]

All the ships in Giffen's force opened fire as Japanese aircraft charged in from every angle. Bombs propelled towers of water skyward, torpedoes sliced through the waters, and Japanese machine guns sparked streams of ammunition toward the ships. Red tracers and shell bursts further lit the sky, turning the battle arena into a daytime matinee. One torpedo missed *Chicago* by yards. A second smacked into *Louisville* but failed to explode. Higai charged through thick antiaircraft fire until an American shell burst sent his plane plummeting to the Pacific off *Chicago*'s port bow, killing the commander.

The good fortune did not last, however. Minutes after Higai's death, two torpedoes ripped a huge gash on *Chicago*'s starboard side, flooding the forward engine room. *Chicago* floated aimlessly on the surface as Captain Ralph O. Davis and his crew frantically attempted to regain control and save the ship.

After Higai's second wave departed, *Chevalier*'s skipper, Lieutenant Commander Ephraim R. McLean Jr., announced to his men that *Chicago* had been badly hit. McLean promised payback for the deed and told his men to stand easy at their guns. "The loudspeaker hummed and faded" as another cruiser began pulling *Chicago* away at four knots, recalled Roupe. "The captain's cool, steady voice had affected us like a shot in the arm. 'Let the Japs come!' we thought jubilantly. We'd be ready!"[29]

Chicago intended to reach Espiritu Santo, but the cruiser never made it. After receiving orders from Admiral Halsey to return to Efate, Giffen split Task Force 18 during the afternoon of January 30. He took most of the ships with him, leaving only his six destroyers to screen the *Chicago*.

The Japanese air fleet commander at Rabaul, Vice Admiral Jinichi Kusaka, pounced at the opportunity to finish the damaged cruiser and sent a group of Japanese aircraft to pursue *Chicago*. Of the screening destroyers, *La Vallette* stood squarely in the path between the Japanese planes and the cruiser.

"They came at us directly out of the sun," said Lieutenant Witten on the *La Vallette*. "They were going for the crippled *Chicago*. We were a couple of thousand yards abaft her beam, and some of them had to pass over us to get to their primary target." The destroyer's gun crews opened fire at maximum range, but the Japanese charged through the shell bursts and bullets and steadily closed the distance. One plane dropped a torpedo at *La Vallette* and continued directly over the destroyer toward the cruiser, but *La Vallette*'s fire sent the invader toward the sea in flames. "The plane passed so close over our stack, almost hitting it, that I could actually see the pilot's face," said Witten. "Then 'bang' we were hit."

The explosion knocked Witten to the deck, and although he suffered a neck injury, the officer continued to direct his guns. "Mr. Witten," said the lieutenant's talker, who had developed a reputation for bickering over the incessant drills, "if I ever complain about having to have drills again you can kick my ass from the bow to the fantail."[30]

On the port-side depth charge guns, Jack Wilkes, a torpedoman, wished he could do something to help the gunners, but "you cannot shoot depth charges at planes." When the torpedo dropped, he ducked behind the depth charges for protection, but shrapnel injured both legs and pierced his right calf. "I was so scared that I felt no pain. The last thing that I remember was the ship almost coming out of the water and I saw nothing but water coming my way and I was knocked unconscious."[31] Wilkes soon regained consciousness to find that he had been tossed yards from his post. When he tried to rise, jolts of pain shot through both legs, and Wilkes then noticed that blood covered both shoes.

Watertender Second Class M. W. Tollberg was severely burned and blinded by a spurt of live steam that gushed from a damaged pipe. Though in enormous pain from fleshless hands and blackened feet, the dying Tollberg managed to climb topside to reach an oil valve that needed to be closed. Later the ship's medical officer found Tollberg still clutching the oil valve in a heroic attempt to close it.

Lieutenant Eli Roth perished at his post in the forward engine room, but he had so thoroughly trained the ship's repair parties that they prevented the destroyer from sinking. Metalsmith 2/c J. A. Masi, Machinist's Mate 2/c H. M. Marsh, and Machinist's Mate 2/c P. A. Gregory ignored the danger of a weakened bulkhead to race into the damaged fireroom and plug a fourteen-inch hole through which water poured. In the radar room, Seaman 1/c William T. McGee and Seaman 2/c Joseph P. Essick, according to the executive officer, J. A. McGoldbrick, "remained cool and collected" under fire and continued to deliver accurate information to gun control and to the bridge. Lieutenant Commander Harry H. Henderson, *La Vallette*'s skipper, praised Seaman 1/c Albert V. Conte, who, "although young and relatively inexperienced and in his first engagement, handled the wheel throughout like a veteran."[32]

The explosion killed one officer and twenty-one men, flooded the aft fireroom, stopped the engines, temporarily cut off electrical power, and interrupted communications. Within two minutes Henderson had power and was under way until another vessel came alongside and towed the ship to Espiritu Santo.

The tug *Navajo* had come to *Chicago*'s aid, but before the tug could offer help, five torpedoes ripped into the cruiser's starboard side. With the cruiser badly listing and sinking, Captain Davis ordered the ship abandoned. Six officers and fifty-six men went down with the cruiser, while other vessels retrieved 1,049 survivors from the water.

The Japanese government claimed her aircraft sank one American battleship and three cruisers and damaged others. The Japanese had scored a minor victory in sinking *Chicago*, but they lost twelve aircraft and one of their top torpedo bomber commanders with the death of Higai. In addition, because attention had been focused on Giffen's force, the transports were able to land their troops on Guadalcanal without interference.

Admiral Giffen had been so concerned with the threat from Japanese submarines that his ships steamed in poor formation for defense from an air attack. American naval superiors, especially Halsey and the Commander in Chief, Pacific Fleet, Admiral Chester Nimitz, were irate over the loss of *Chicago*, which Halsey described as a devastating blow caused by errors in judgment.

Nimitz at first intended to include a harsh condemnation of Giffen in his official report, but he watered it down to the less strident conclusion that the loss of *Chicago* was regrettable. However, he ordered that the cruiser's sinking be withheld from the public and vowed in a staff meeting that he would discipline any officer who divulged the loss.

La Vallette safely arrived at Espiritu Santo, where a heartwarming sight awaited. "As we were slowly towed through the nets and into the harbor," explained Lieutenant Witten, "we saw that the other ships there, including some of the [squadron] destroyers, were manning their rails and cheering us as we inched along."

The next task, removal of the bodies of their dead shipmates, was not as uplifting. Aided by volunteers from other ships, the crew carefully retrieved the bodies, some little more than mangled chunks of flesh, and placed them in body bags for burial. "After several days in tropic waters the bodies were quite bloated and discolored and the stench was really bad," wrote Witten.[33]

Most of the officers and enlisted men then marched over to the burial grounds for a ceremony, where they buried their shipmates in a common grave. A chaplain from another ship conducted the services, after which a bugler sounded taps.

When the ship entered drydock and Henderson, Witten, and others examined the damage, they wondered how the ship had survived. A hole stretched from the cracked bulkhead in the forward fireroom above the waterline all the way to the keel. Since Espiritu Santo lacked the facilities to correct the damage, Henderson took his patched ship on a slow voyage across the Pacific to Mare Island Navy Yard, near San Francisco.

The actions of *La Vallette* in the South Pacific had been brief but impressive. She was not finished, however. Her squadron mates would see her back in the Solomons by October.

The End of *De Haven*

On New Year's Eve Emperor Hirohito met with Prime Minister Hideki Tojo and top military commanders to consider recent developments on Guadalcanal. The year had started in heady fashion with a victory-marked expansion from the Home Islands, but events in the Coral Sea, at Midway, and now in the Solomons forced them to reexamine a deteriorating situation. After much discussion, they decided to evacuate the remaining troops on Guadalcanal, erect a new defensive line on New Georgia to the north, and wage the battle from there.

In January, in a daring move spread over three nights, their destroyers evacuated the final thirteen thousand troops from Guadalcanal, abandoning the island to the American infantry closing in on them. "It is still one of the miracles of the war to me," wrote Commander Hara, "that this should have remained such a successful secret." He was surprised that the ships had swiped the men out from under the noses of American air superiority, but he was too realistic to get carried away. The six-month struggle had "left 16,800 Japanese bodies strewn in the tropical jungle, and scores of warships sunk with their thousands of sailors around this bitterly contested island. The many pages of reports on the subject all boiled down to one fact: Japan had lost the Battle of Guadalcanal."[34]

Once Halsey realized what had occurred, he knew that the bitter days at Guadalcanal had at last ended. The Japanese Empire had reached its southernmost point and had been turned back. This moment marked the start of a slow but inexorable Japanese retreat that ended in Tokyo Bay. "From here on they retreated at our will," Halsey wrote after the war. "I am immensely proud of the Guadalcanal campaign. It started with a frayed shoestring and little repairs were made to that shoestring during the campaign. The shoestring was tough and it did its job. The Japs were halted in their tracks and thrown from the offensive to the defensive. They never regained the offensive role."[35]

O'Bannon, *Fletcher*, and *Nicholas* were a key part of that shoestring. In the company of the other *Fletcher*-class destroyers that arrived in late 1942 and early 1943, these little-heralded destroyers and their crews would become even more vital to American success in the Solomons.

Japanese land forces might have retreated from Guadalcanal, but the Cactus Striking Force still faced the dangers presented by the Slot. Over the previous three months the original three *Fletcher*-class destroyers—*O'Bannon*, *Fletcher*, and *Nicholas*—had escorted transports, hunted submarines, battled air attacks, and fought in the major November surface engagement without suffering a loss to either ship or crew, an anomaly that most sailors believed was bound to end.

Lieutenant (jg) John J. Rowan aboard *De Haven* hoped the luck would continue. A graduate of the Naval Academy, Rowan already boasted a full war resume. As an ensign he had been aboard the cruiser USS *Vincennes* (CA-44) as part of Lieutenant Colonel James H. Doolittle's audacious April 1942 Tokyo bombing raid. Four months later he floated in the waters off Guadalcanal for five hours when his cruiser was sunk in the Battle of Savo Island. He figured that with the *Vincennes*'s sinking, he had punched that ticket. What were the odds of having two ships shot out from beneath you within six months?

When he joined the destroyer in mid-January, *De Haven* looked to be a good ship manned with a solid crew. Even though this destroyer was his first command, Commander Charles E. Tolman had gained significant experience with the submarine fleet, and his executive officer, Lieutenant Commander John P. Huntley, had served aboard the carrier USS *Yorktown* (CV-5). The ship's doctor, John H. Bates, kept everyone loose with his sharp wit and delightful sense of humor, something that would be especially helpful in the difficult days ahead.

The nagging concern among some of the officers was that, in order to rush the destroyers to the Pacific, the ship's shakedown cruise had been shortened. They needed additional time to drill and train the young crew, but time was at a premium in the South Pacific in late 1942.

They would also have liked to train some of those irritating aviators who failed to identify themselves. Lieutenant Commander Andrew J. Hill Jr., *Nicholas*'s skipper, attended regular conferences with Captain Briscoe, during which Briscoe discussed upcoming operations with his officers. In one of those meetings, the commanders of the first four destroyers shared their disgust at the alarming number of American aircraft that flew dangerously close to their formations without properly identifying themselves. Almost every night, one or more swooped in as if they were inspecting the destroyers, inviting death from itchy gun crews and skippers who had to protect their ships. The tense moments could be eliminated if the pilots identified themselves, as procedure required. The commanders feared that because almost every intruder turned out to be American, air alerts might not be taken seriously and gun crews might relax their vigilance. That could lead to tragic results if enemy aircraft appeared.

On the morning of February 1 transports escorted by *Nicholas* and *De Haven* finished emptying their cargoes and headed north toward Cape Esperance, where they veered east toward Tulagi. In midafternoon an air alert southeast of Savo Island called everyone to stations, but when the alert was canceled five minutes later, gun crews aboard both ships griped that another of those pesky American pilots had forced them to man their posts.

Thirteen minutes later came another air alert. Hill on *Nicholas* ordered top speed and began maneuvering, but he noticed that *De Haven* continued her slower pace. Had Commander Tolman assumed this was another false alert?

Ensign Clem C. Williams, at his station on *De Haven*'s fantail 40mm antiaircraft gun, also wondered why Tolman maintained his speed and course. Anxious gun crews wanted to open fire, but they had to refrain until Tolman gave the assent from the bridge. Lieutenant Archie R. Fields, *De Haven*'s assistant engineering officer, saw that the main batteries were tracking the aircraft, "and we were waiting for permission to commence firing, but the order never came."[36]

On the bridge, Tolman told Seaman 2/c Albert L. Breining to ask lookouts to report to the bridge as soon as they identified the aircraft. When no response arrived, Tolman exclaimed, "Damn, tell them to hurry up!" Breining again relayed Tolman's request, at which one lookout shouted, "They're Japs, we can see the meatballs!"[37]

Six planes peeled away and attacked on the starboard quarter. Lieutenant Fields followed the tracers as they ripped toward the first aircraft, which he thought looked "like a pretty toy" until a descending bomb changed his opinion: "Unfair, why are they using such big ones?!" As the bomb came down, Fields, who thought it was heading toward him, shoved the man next to him into the lookout station and followed behind. "There was a thump and a blast," he said.[38]

Tolman had belatedly ordered top speed and left full rudder to evade the aircraft, but the bomb crashed amidships on the port side in the forward engine room. Men aboard *Nicholas* saw a bomb blow out the port side of the ship, a burst of flame engulf *De Haven*'s midsection, and steam coming from below.

"All hell broke loose at that point," said Ensign Bernard W. Frese Jr., stationed in *De Haven*'s fireroom. A jolt hurled the man to his right, Fire Controlman 3/c Charles N. Biegel, straight into the air, flipped apparatus onto another sailor, and threw Frese into the fire control switchboard, pinning his legs under overturned electronic equipment. "Everything turned pitch black with an acrid smell. All I could hear was a tinkling sound like the glass icicles on the Christmas trees used to make."[39]

Torpedoman 3/c Leonard Elam had been scraping paint on the deck when the alarm came, and he rushed to his station at the torpedo director on the starboard side of the bridge. When the first bomb struck, it demolished the area he had only moments before been scraping.

In rapid succession a second and then a third bomb struck the reeling *De Haven*. The second toppled the forward stack and lifted the five-inch gun director off its foundation, while the third ignited ammunition magazines and covered the ship with thick yellow smoke that billowed three hundred feet into the air. The explosion knocked Elam onto a pile of potatoes, and bounced Lieutenant Fields around as if he were a marble in a cup. He rose to his feet to find that "the ship was a pile of steaming, oil-smeared junk."[40] Hill and Hailey, aboard *Nicholas*, feared that *De Haven* had ruptured in half and would soon sink.

Ensign Williams remained at his fantail 40mm gun, directing his crew, as the Japanese planes neared. Operating at the ship's end, they felt more exposed to the aircraft swooping down than they would have had their gun stood amidships, and Williams saw that the experience unnerved some of his young sailors. He replaced those most rattled and kept his guns firing until he looked behind him and saw that the bridge area had been demolished. "There was no sign of life forward and the bow was sinking rapidly," he recalled.[41]

Williams remained at his station awaiting orders, but none came. Unwilling to linger any longer, Williams told his men to abandon ship, checked to ensure the depth charges had been set on safety so they would not explode on the way down and maim the men in the water, directed the removal of the wounded into two cork nets flung onto the water, and jumped over the side.

With time running out before the ship went under, Ensign Frese struggled to free himself in the fireroom. He pushed against the switchboard to free his wedged head from between the switches, and as the room filled with oil gushing from a ruptured fuel tank, he ripped his pants while unsuccessfully trying to slide from beneath the equipment. When the oil and water reached his neck, Frese unzipped his pants and wriggled out.

"At that point I started praying," Frese said, for *De Haven* was about to go down. In the dark he could hear but not see the men near him, but when someone cried, "She's going down fast!" Frese sloshed through the waist-high water, scrambled onto a deck that "was a shambles of twisted metal," and jumped overboard.[42]

Only Lieutenant Rowan and Quartermaster 2/c Dale W. Beemus survived the destruction of the bridge. A disoriented Rowan sat up to find that his right leg was dislocated at the knee, with the lower half resting on his lap. He felt no pain, thanks to being in shock, but in the acrid air he sensed the ship tilt as if ready to embark on her death plunge. Rowan crawled over debris cluttering the deck to the starboard side and, to protect his leg, dropped headfirst ten feet to the water. Lieutenant Fields almost waited too long but, with the onrushing water swirling two feet away, stepped into the water and swam from the ship to avoid being caught in the suction as she went down.

Ensign Williams, the senior unwounded officer remaining aboard, made a final check for survivors. Convinced that everyone had gone over the side, and with the rapidly rising water engulfing the deck, he joined his shipmates in the water. Thirty seconds later the ship's "stern rose sharply and she went down."[43]

Meanwhile, every gun on the *Nicholas* was repelling its own intruder, with "the red tracers of the 20-millimeters arching up to a converging cone at the nose of the enemy bomber," as Hailey wrote. Despite the bullets and shells, the plane drew closer, at which point an ensign standing on the bridge with Hailey grabbed a tommy gun and opened fire. Flames danced along the plane's wings as the pilot first fired his machine guns and then dropped a bomb. "I had a feeling of detachment," wrote Hailey, "which is not uncommon, others have told me, as I watched it come down. I was sure it was going to hit." That bomb missed Hailey and the *Nicholas*, but in the next few minutes eight more aircraft charged the destroyer, "which was twisting and turning at flank speed" to avoid the bombs that exploded ten yards away.

When the firing stopped, Hailey heard Chief Radio Electrician Hector Constantino "crying like a heart-broken child." A patriotic sailor who made no attempt to hide his love for his new country, Constantino had come from Greece before World War I and proudly served the United States in that war. Constantino cried when he learned of the *Chicago* sinking, and he now cried for two shipmates who had just perished, Sonarman 3/c Robert Lee Moir, telephone talker in secondary control, and Gunner's Mate 2/c Furman Fox, a member of a five-inch gun crew. "It's no pose with Hector," one officer told Hailey. "He cries whenever he hears of one of our ships being lost."

Hailey surveyed the ship, now bloodied from the body parts lying around one of the deck guns. Turning seaward, he focused his glasses to where he thought *De Haven* and the accompanying LCTs (Landing Craft, Tank) were. "The little fellows were all right, circling near where a great cloud of black smoke rose up from the sea to a height of hundreds of feet. I could see no ship at the base of the smoke."

Hill noticed Hailey's quizzical look. "Gone," he told the newsman. "I saw a bomb hit her just forward of the bridge. It must have penetrated to the magazine, for there was a terrific explosion and she broke right in two. I doubt if anyone came off the bridge. The explosion just blew it to pieces."[44]

Hailey's surprise paled in comparison to the emotions felt by the *De Haven* men in the water, who watched their ship slip beneath the waves only ten minutes after they had first sighted their attacker. Ensign Frese flipped over on his back to find the ship's propellers directly above him and the ship ready to embark on her final plunge. "Needless to say," he recalled, "I set a record doing the backstroke and getting out of the way as the ship sank."[45] To make it easier for his shattered leg, Lieutenant Rowan floated on his back and propped his right leg with his left, hoping his life belt would keep him afloat until help arrived.

The LCTs rushed over to pick up the exhausted men. Ensign Herbert Solomon, skipper of one of the LCTs, lowered his vessel's ramp and stood at the edge, leaning out to sea to drag in man after man as the waves splashed about him. Ensign Frese tried to stand when an LCT retrieved him from the water, but he collapsed in a heap. One of the young sailors aboard the LCT held Frese's head in his arms, whispering soothing words to calm the officer, while Ensign Williams administered morphine.

Williams took charge of the *De Haven* men in Solomon's LCT, giving morphine from his meager supply only to the most serious cases. There was little Williams could do for the men with burns but keep them comfortable and out of the sweltering midafternoon sun. Along with the other LCTs, Solomon headed toward Lunga Point when Hill brought *Nicholas* alongside to retrieve the rest of the survivors. There were few for them to rescue, for as Hailey described, "it was live or die on the *De Haven* that day."

Chief Machinist's Mate R. C. Andrews, a muscular man in his forties with a thick black mustache, climbed aboard *Nicholas* with one finger hanging by only a thin piece of skin. "Here, son, cut this off," Andrews barked to a *Nicholas* sailor. When the seaman replied that their doctor might be able to save it, Andrews replied, "Nope, she's too far gone," cut the piece of skin himself, and tossed the finger over the side.[46]

The doctor aboard *Nicholas* treated the seriously wounded. After examining Ensign Frese, he covered the body with a blanket and erroneously declared Frese dead. Frese heard the words and nudged the blanket from his head enough for a sailor near him to alert the doctor.

Lieutenant Rowan, who now had the dubious distinction of twice in five months having been aboard ships that sank, told Williams that "he is getting quite tired of the water around Savo Island."[47] The only moment he later wished to remember was when Lieutenant Commander Robert Montgomery, the famed Hollywood film star now serving as Briscoe's communications officer, came over and asked if he could do anything for Rowan.

Back on Guadalcanal, for the first time the survivors realized the extent of the losses. Shipmates they had known since commissioning were dead or missing. Correspondent Hailey recalled Tolman's invitation to join *De Haven* and was thankful that a snap decision had placed him aboard *Nicholas* instead. Had he boarded *De Haven*, he would have been on the bridge with Tolman and the other men who perished at that spot.

Lieutenant Rowan lay in a field bed underneath a palm tree for two days, each night praying that neither the Japanese bombers attacking Henderson nor the shrapnel plunging to earth from American antiaircraft guns would kill him. On February 3 a plane took him and the other seriously wounded men to Espiritu Santo.

While *De Haven*'s survivors were still being rescued, reports flooded in of a powerful Japanese cruiser-destroyer force barreling southward down the Slot. Halsey ordered Briscoe's destroyers, joined by a handful of PT boats, to halt rescue efforts and steam north to check the enemy. "There was no time to mourn the dead or comfort the living," Hailey wrote. "The squadron and half a dozen PT boats were the only force available to stop them. We had to be about it."

Crew from the *Nicholas* placed the *De Haven* wounded into Higgins boats and turned north. As they left, *De Haven* men cheered the *Nicholas*, telling its crew to get in a few licks on their behalf. Gunner's Mate 3/c Lewis Samuels, a *Nicholas* sailor whose hand had been shattered during the fighting and had to be left behind with the *De Haven* survivors, shouted to his shipmates as *Nicholas* pulled away, "Keep her floating, you guys." Samuels continued to wave with his good hand until his destroyer steamed out of sight.

"It was an emotionally and physically exhausted crew that took the *Nicholas* out west of Savo that night," wrote Hailey. "Few of them had had any sleep for forty-eight hours, since we had been out on patrol all the previous night. They had seen their shipmates killed and wounded and a sister ship destroyed in exactly six minutes. The deck was still slippery with blood in places. There had been no time to clean up. Now they were going out to intercept the Tokyo Express. Three ships against twenty. All other American ships in the area—freighters, tenders, corvettes, and the escorts—had been ordered to leave."[48]

Briscoe in *Fletcher* led the squadron north, followed by *Nicholas* and *Radford*. Briscoe figured his best chance at stopping the superior enemy force was to launch a surprise torpedo attack. When at midnight PT boats spotted the Japanese near Savo Island, they immediately attacked, losing two of their craft to enemy gunfire while sinking a Japanese destroyer with their torpedoes. Dive-bombers from Guadalcanal joined in, treating Hailey to a spectacle as gunfire, explosions, and flares lit the nighttime sky.

Instead of that night's version of the Tokyo Express, the Japanese force arrived to complete the Guadalcanal evacuation. American aircraft and mines sank a few more destroyers, but the rest boarded the final land troops and raced away before Briscoe could advance close enough to launch torpedoes. Briscoe pursued up the Slot but turned back before he came within range of enemy air cover.

Admiral Ainsworth recognized what he had asked of *O'Bannon*, *Fletcher*, and their destroyer companions. "Briscoe's little force really had a grim time of it," Ainsworth concluded in his report, "but these operations marked the first time we had been able to keep a surface force in the area. With the complete defeat of the Japs on Guadalcanal in early February we were now definitely on the offensive in the Solomons."[49]

If MacDonald on *O'Bannon* or Hill on *Nicholas* thought they had been busy, the remainder of the year proved that they had seen nothing yet.

CHAPTER 6

STRUGGLE FOR THE SLOT

Now that the Japanese had withdrawn from Guadalcanal, Halsey focused on the central and northern Solomons. The victory terminated the opening phase of the war, but hard combat, on land and at sea, lay ahead to sweep the enemy out of the Solomons for good.

In the months since he had been named South Pacific commander, by necessity Halsey had to rely on defensive tactics until he gained a lodgment on Guadalcanal and until additional ships and troops filtered into the region. The first two months of 1943 had given him the opportunity to stage limited offensive strikes with the Cactus Striking Force, and as March arrived he intended to expand from those initial forays. Offensive operations, small at first, began replacing his defensive tactics. His first step was to seize the Russell Islands, fifty-five miles northwest of Henderson Field, so that he could move his air arm closer to the enemy airfield at Munda on New Georgia.

Halsey's second step was to reorganize his burgeoning destroyer force into a squadron. On March 10, for the first time in the war, *O'Bannon* and her companion destroyers appeared on the roster of the Pacific Fleet as Destroyer Squadron 21 (Desron 21), under Captain Francis X. McInerney, based initially at Espiritu Santo. McInerney's orders included not merely halting Japanese surface forces cutting southward from Rabaul but also staging offensive thrusts to the north. No longer handcuffed to Guadalcanal waters, Halsey's destroyers would be free to strike deeper into Japanese waters and hit enemy bases and airfields.

In McInerney, Halsey chose wisely. Born in 1899, the native of Cheyenne, Wyoming, graduated from the Naval Academy in 1921. After serving aboard four vessels, two of which were destroyers, McInerney earned a law degree from George Washington University Law School in 1935. Skipper of a destroyer at the time of Pearl Harbor, McInerney participated in strikes in the Solomons and Coral Sea before being handed his new assignment. His years of experience with destroyers made him a good fit to lead the new squadron.

His squadron at first comprised two divisions of four destroyers each, with his flagship attached as a fifth destroyer to one. In Destroyer Division 41 McInerney's flagship *Nicholas* operated with *O'Bannon*, *Chevalier*, *Strong*, and *Taylor*, while *Fletcher*, *Radford*, *Jenkins*, and *La Vallette* constituted Destroyer Division 42. McInerney possessed a good mixture of experienced ships in the original three destroyers, as well as more recent arrivals, the last being *Chevalier* the month before. He split the original three destroyers so that at least one battle-tested ship and crew anchored each division to lend guidance and stability. When at sea, he operated from his flagship, which was most often *Nicholas*, where he commanded the squadron while the skipper ran the ship.

In plying the Slot, a watery vein sixty miles across at its widest that separated the two Solomon island arms leading to Bougainville in the extreme northwest, McInerney faced an imposing task. He often ventured beyond the range of American airpower into waters where he could be attacked by aircraft operating from a string of airfields peppering islands from Bougainville in the northern Solomons all the way south to Munda.

Day after day the crews lived and worked with their shipmates, inevitably creating a special bond with them, but over the course of the next few months, in so freely intermingling with the crews of the other squadron ships, they also developed a sense of pride in the unit. They embarked on nightly runs into the Slot together, docked in Purvis Bay or Espiritu Santo at the same time, drank beer and gambled and fought with those sailors. Their first loyalty would always be to their ship and shipmates, but a second link, forged from the pride each felt in belonging to the unit, fashioned the ships into a squadron. They sometimes operated as an entire unit, while at other times they steamed out on missions alone or with one or two other squadron destroyers, just as various platoons in a company received different assignments, but the men enjoyed the recognition they received from being part of Destroyer Squadron 21, a fighting unit that gained a reputation for being a superb squadron. That squadron pride, forged in 1943, lasted through the war's final day, which saw them leading Halsey's fleet into Tokyo Bay.

In a freewheeling style reminiscent of Civil War blockade runners or sixteenth-century English pirates, for much of 1943 McInerney's destroyers barreled to the north in almost nightly forays, plunging deep into enemy-held waters to stage bombardments, lay minefields, hunt submarines, and counter Japanese actions. After completing their assignments, the destroyers whisked southward to reach the protective umbrella provided by American fighters.

Operations cut from Halsey's playbook, these missions permitted his men to take the initiative instead of passively reacting to Japanese moves. When Halsey visited *Fletcher* during this time, he noticed that the crew wore blue-dyed T-shirts. "You're informal," he said to Cole.

"Admiral, we have a war to fight," was the reply.[1]

Better words could not have been uttered to the old destroyerman.

Commander MacDonald was as pleased as Halsey with the switch to the offensive and was certain that his crew, having been bloodied in the major November engagement and in numerous smaller encounters as part of the Cactus Striking Force, would be up to the challenge. However, two issues gnawed at him. The original three destroyers now operated with inexperienced skippers and crews, and MacDonald hoped his ship and men would not suffer due to those untested arrivals trickling into the South Pacific. He also prayed that senior commanders who took Desron 21 into battle would properly employ destroyers as separate units capable of mounting massed torpedo attacks. He had debated this topic with his compatriots, both during formal meetings at Noumea and over drinks at officers' clubs, and all agreed the destroyers worked more effectively as an independent arm.

Their forays up the Slot during the remainder of the year kept them on the move almost around the clock. Ships returned from one mission only to load up with more ammunition and fuel and head back into the Slot for another. In addition to surface engagements with enemy cruisers and destroyers, they conducted bombardments, hunter-killer missions, and patrols. They rocketed five-inch shells shoreward and antiaircraft fire skyward. They dropped depth charges and eluded enemy fighters.

In commanding the squadron, Captain McInerney juggled his ships, sometimes sending part of his squadron to conduct one assignment while the remainder of the squadron executed other tasks. On June 3, for instance, while *Nicholas*, *Fletcher*, and *Taylor* were at anchor in Espiritu Santo, *La Vallette* was undergoing maintenance work, and the other destroyers escorted ships to and from Guadalcanal.

The nearly yearlong Battle of the Slot offered exhaustion and fear, death and loss, exhilaration and joy. By the time it ended, the Japanese no longer controlled the Solomons.

"The Fightingest Thing Afloat"

"Isn't there some way, some place, where we can win a real victory over the Americans?" asked Emperor Hirohito of his commanders after the military withdrawal from Guadalcanal. He wanted a triumph that would cement the Japanese hold in the Solomons, but military action in the first part of 1943 fell abysmally short of that objective. "The way we're waging war now raises the enemy's morale just as on Guadalcanal," he complained.[2]

One commander stepped to the front. In the same month that Halsey formed Desron 21, Commander Tameichi Hara received command of Destroyer Division 27. His four older destroyers could not match MacDonald's *O'Bannon* in speed or radar, but Hara's skills as a commander compensated for some of the ships' shortcomings. In his flagship, *Shigure*, like her American counterpart *O'Bannon* the only Tokyo Express destroyer to emerge without losing a man, Hara gained acclaim in the South Pacific for his daring and competence. Other commanders called *Shigure* the "Ghost Destroyer" and nicknamed Hara the "Miracle Captain" for the many times he eluded his foe. Even Hara admitted that his time in the South Pacific in 1943 "was indeed the most glorious period of my career."

His initial examination of his destroyer crews revealed that they were undisciplined malcontents who required extensive training before he would be comfortable taking them into battle. Hara repeatedly drilled the crews, telling his officers that if they could not perfect matters in practice, they would certainly perish in battle. Promoted to captain in May, Hara opted to retain command of *Shigure* instead of handing it over to another officer. He believed his squadron required a steady hand in the flagship in the coming months, and that his experience made him the obvious choice.

Like MacDonald and Halsey, Hara loved destroyers. He claimed that they "were the work horses of the Imperial Navy" and that, as the *Fletcher*-class destroyers were doing for Halsey, they capably filled in for the larger warships until those battleships and cruisers were needed. "My happiest duty in the Imperial Navy was in destroyers," he said.[3]

In Hara, MacDonald and his compatriots faced a worthy foe.

Hara's counterpart in the Slot, MacDonald, matched his antagonist skill for skill. He and his crew left Tulagi-Purvis Bay, across Ironbottom Sound from Guadalcanal, and turned northwestward to enter the Slot. Few threats existed along the northern arm, which comprised mainly Santa Isabel and Choiseul

Islands, but the southern arm featured airfields and harbors along its length, especially on Vella Lavella, Kolombangara, and New Georgia Islands. Almost every day the Japanese, often commanded by Hara in *Shigure*, entered the Slot from the northwestern end while MacDonald and his Desron 21 mates approached from the southeastern end, groping for each other in the passageways and channels of the nautical no-man's-land. The two sides engaged in a multilayered struggle that lasted for much of 1943, a clash consisting of hundreds of incidents ranging from antisubmarine patrols to four major surface encounters that brought the destroyers into close combat with each other.

"It was the beginning of a long and violent campaign," described *Time* magazine. "Up & down the lush green coasts and pale, flat waters of the Solomons, the 2,100-ton *O'Bannon* and her sisters steamed with bones in their teeth and a swift hard punch for Japanese ships great or small. She and the other lean, thin-skinned cans, manned by youngsters fresh from colleges and high schools, screened the big ships, fought submarines, covered landings, popped Jap planes out of the coppery skies, blasted shore installations with their 5-in. rifles."[4]

MacDonald and the captains of the Desron 21 destroyers started most operations by conferring with the squadron commander, McInerney. The group discussed the rights and wrongs of previous missions, and McInerney outlined the plans for upcoming missions and shared information from Halsey.

In the Slot during 1943, however, the Japanese did not always allow time to discuss missions. "Get under way and go up the Slot" was the oft-heard command from headquarters; "more later."[5] Fast alerts sent ships scrambling to counter the Tokyo Express.

In groups of three to six, the destroyers embarked on nightly runs up the Slot. Often "we weren't told exactly what was coming," wrote MacDonald.[6] Men aboard the *O'Bannon* figured that whenever Officer's Cook 3/c Rudolph Rivers walked to the bridge with a thermos of coffee for MacDonald, they were about to charge up the Slot, for MacDonald would not need the liquid unless he planned to remain on the bridge all night. Muttering profanities under their breath, the crew prepared for hours standing at stations and waiting for a clash that would inevitably arrive at some point.

"Sleepless and stunned," MacDonald said, "we would come down from battle or bombing, only to refuel, load ammunition and supplies, and turn the prow northward to the shoals of death. . . . Everybody could see what direction we were heading in, but they didn't want to believe what they saw." MacDonald tried to alleviate some of the concern by explaining over the loudspeaker what they might expect. He could not always divulge specifics, because sometimes even MacDonald had little idea of what awaited, but he believed that if the men felt their skipper was honest with them, they would be more conscientious for him when the firing started.

"I just told them in a matter-of-fact way and voice something like this: 'Men, we probably will intercept a light Japanese task force at about 10:30 o'clock tonight. Sleep a little if you can, until the call for battle stations. Whatever you do, don't worry. Leave that to me.'" He found that even a few words produced results beyond what he expected. "Cheerless as these little talks were, I am surprised at what they did for the morale of the crew."

His crew even began joking about their commander's brief messages. One time when he announced, "We may meet a light Japanese task force at 10:30 o'clock," a Swedish machinist's mate said, "*Ja*, light battleships, light heavy cruisers and light barges that make 45 knots an hour."

MacDonald did not realize how much the men appreciated his words until the night he forgot to talk to the crew. His quartermaster later asked about the omission and told MacDonald that the men had been standing around the loudspeakers waiting for him to speak. It was then that MacDonald realized his men "had become almost superstitious about these cannonside chats. Some of them felt that it was a ritual necessary to victory, that without it they might be sunk."[7]

Each trip started in late afternoon so that the ships would arrive in no-man's-land around dark. On the rare occasions when cruisers accompanied them, the destroyers formed an antisubmarine screen and maneuvered into standard night antiaircraft formation after dark, at which time the crews went to general quarters until the next morning.

They became expert at spotting dark-shrouded landforms identifying their location off New Georgia or one of the other islands. They had to be skilled in such matters, for night in the tropics arrived with a suddenness that startled newly arrived sailors, as if the ocean swallowed the orange-red sun and every trace of light in a massive gulp. Faint pinks on the water's surface turned dark in the humid tropical night, with the brilliance of the Southern Cross constellation and other stars twinkling above offering a wondrous contrast to the darkened stage below.

In quieter moments, when he could for a few moments escape the dangers of the battle zone by being alone with his thoughts, Seaman Chesnutt found comfort in observing the beauties of nature that, under more normal circumstances, could have adorned a travel poster highlighting South Pacific attractions. "At night when we were steaming along, I could look at the bow of the ship and as it cut through the waves, phosphor[escence] would cause sparks in the water," he wrote. "It was unusual and pretty. When everything was dark and no lights, we could also see the stars so much better. It looked as if there were millions of them and they were very bright. It was beautiful."[8]

Men also stared into the pitch black, alert to the potential terrors that might be lurking. "We knew it was always possibly dangerous because of submarines or lone bombers," said Machinist's Mate 1/c Willy Rhyne of *O'Bannon*. "You always had something to worry about. They kept us alert. Anything could happen at any time. Going up the Slot, we were at battle stations all night."[9] The enemy seemed to know the ins and outs of every inlet and channel in the Solomons, and even if they did not, flares often aided their efforts by marking the destroyers' courses.

The crew leaned on each other for reassurance. Rhyne gained confidence because of the experienced, disciplined crew around him. He placed his life in their hands, and they in his, and in unison they handed their futures to MacDonald on the bridge. The ship's crew became an intricate organism of its own, depending on each man in the same way a body depends on internal organs. They took pride in being part of what the men called the "Dungaree Navy," a reference to the blue jeans and work shirts the sailors wore and to the lack of rigid decorum that structured life on battleships and cruisers.

"Little has been written of the part that our destroyers are playing in the Pacific War, where they are called upon to fulfill such a variety of missions that they have become multi-purpose ships, engaging in any form of combat," wrote Commander Frederick Bell, skipper of USS *Grayson*, in 1944. "Bantamweights in comparison with the great battlewagons, they pack a punch out of all proportion to their size. They are triple-threat weapons, built to strike at any enemy on or over or under the sea." Bell quoted an admiral's characterization of the destroyers that operated in the Slot "the fightingest thing afloat."[10]

Lacking the occasional specific mission, such as a bombardment, Desron 21 destroyers plied the waters in search of submarines or barges. They returned to Tulagi-Purvis Bay early the next morning, enjoying the pleasant scent of tropical flowers and the cool early morning breezes yet unsullied by the day's glaring sun. Once at anchor, crews brought aboard ammunition to replace whatever had been expended the night before and refueled the ship to be ready for the next night's run up the Slot, catching whenever possible an hour or two of rest in the midday sun.

"We shall never forget the countless, seemingly endless hours we spent at General Quarters while prowling in enemy waters, dodging bombs, shells, mines, and torpedoes," wrote Lieutenant Commander Henry DeLaureal of the *Taylor*. "Someone aptly called the 'Slot' a hellhole. And after we returned to our anchorage at Tulagi, we were visited regularly by Jap snoopers and bombers. How we would have liked to have strangled the Jap who used to come down to Purvis Bay every night, depriving us of rest when it was so badly needed by all!"[11]

The stress of spending what correspondent Foster Hailey termed "another sizzling day" in the tropical heat exacted a toll on everyone. Temperatures in engine rooms often soared beyond 120 degrees. Men showered, only to be covered with sweat before they stepped on deck. One skipper compared it to living inside a heated steel box, where the oppressive warmth nearly suffocated the crew as they performed their tasks. "Even at dusk, when black clouds tumbled across the mountains and the heavens descended in a mighty deluge there was no relief, for moisture condensed within the ship and dripped down the bulkheads or drifted about in wisps of foggy dampness. We could not get dry. We could not keep cool. And there was no rest." The skipper said that operating in the Slot aboard a destroyer was "like going to jail, with the added inconvenience of running the risk of being drowned."[12]

Men abandoned their quarters belowdecks—which, Hailey wrote, "fairly crawled with heat," much as if they lived in "a Turkish bath"—to sleep topside. Sailors plopped mattresses wherever they found space on deck, and hoped they were interrupted only a few times by rain bursts. Hailey said that each morning the crews would awaken "and rise from their sodden bunks to greet the blood-red sun of a new, hot day almost as tired as when they turned in the night before."[13]

Seaman Whisler and his *O'Bannon* shipmates shook off their weariness and trod to their stations as another day and night in the Slot beckoned. "It's what you had to do," said Whisler years later. "You get so tired that you just lay on your life jacket and catch every minute of sleep. When you were at general quarters, you stayed there day and night! I think that's why today I sleep so well. I value sleep. I can fall asleep in five minutes now."[14]

Hailey, who had covered other battles and other units in the war's first year, gained increased admiration for the destroyers of Desron 21 with each day that he accompanied *O'Bannon* and *Nicholas* into the Slot. Surface engagements, however deadly, were typically fleeting moments of intense fighting. Running up the Slot, however, ground on day after day. "There were days and weeks of only hard work," Hailey conveyed to home-front readers. "Most sailors will tell you those were worse to live through then the purple nights when the Tokyo Express was running and Advance Striking Force, Tulagi, was on the prowl."[15]

Attentive to signs among his crew, MacDonald noticed that the tension he observed among the younger sailors the previous fall had now also taken a toll among the veterans. The heaviest worriers, MacDonald thought, were often some of the smartest crewmembers, because they more clearly understood the risks and visualized the dangers.

One night a respected veteran approached MacDonald and, with tears in his eyes, said, "Captain, I can't go back up there. I can't endure it. Don't you see, sir, we're up here until we're dead!'" MacDonald had expected something like that, for "a lot of us had begun to feel that we were up there until we were dead, that we were the sacrifice that must be made until new ships could be built and sent and new men could be trained."

"I know," MacDonald said, trying to console the man. "We all hate it. We all want to go home. We can't quit. You know the enemy. We must stop him."[16] After explaining that he could not order the man stateside, he added comforting words until the veteran regained his composure and returned to his station.

MacDonald could not control his crew's issues with the home front. Some contended with problems, such as learning in a letter that a father or a baby son was ill, or that a girlfriend wanted to break up. While they laughed at the propaganda statements broadcast over the airwaves by Tokyo Rose, such as when she mentioned that a Japanese wrestler could handily defeat Popeye, they fell into melancholy when she played romantic favorites from Frank Sinatra, Bing Crosby, or any of the other popular singers back home. "People back there were having a good time," MacDonald wrote of the home front. "Out here people were dying."[17]

As the weeks passed, MacDonald had no choice but to send some men home. One sailor with twelve years of experience broke under the strain and had to be transferred to a hospital. Lieutenant Malcolm M. Dunham, *O'Bannon*'s doctor, who had been a concern of MacDonald's following the November Naval Battle of Guadalcanal, required a change of scenery to avoid a complete collapse. Dunham left in March for a hospital in New Caledonia, where he capably served for the rest of the war.

One officer who had been awarded a Silver Star for his actions on December 7, 1941, at Pearl Harbor, developed a nervous condition from which "he rapidly wilted physically from the beautiful specimen he was when he first arrived to somewhat of a shadow of his former self. When this became very evident to me," said MacDonald, "it was felt that for his own good we had better transfer him to some other duty."[18] The officer later regained his health and returned to command his own ship.

A chief pharmacist swallowed mercurochrome in an attempt to leave the ship, and MacDonald worried about a young ensign who, because he lacked confidence and knowledge of his duties, failed to gain the respect of the petty officers and crew. On one bombardment run, two men purposely failed to appear at their stations in the lower handling rooms in hopes of being court-martialed and sent out of the fighting zone. MacDonald had another solution in mind: "We're going back up there [the Slot] again tonight and, instead of your being given freedom, when I call for general quarters I'm going to lock you up."

That night MacDonald told the master-at-arms to confine the pair in the paint locker. After one night inside, "they came up on the bridge practically on their hands and knees" and begged to return to their posts. MacDonald agreed, and the pair turned into reliable crewmen. "It just took this type of treatment to get them over what had happened in the past" and divert their attention from the dangers and drudgery of the Slot.[19]

In a strange quirk, the superstitious among the crew supported MacDonald's handling of the incident, for the last thing they wanted was for more men to be transferred off *O'Bannon*. The ship and crew had served in the Solomons since the previous September without sustaining any deaths, and if MacDonald too greatly altered the ship's chemistry by subtracting clusters of men from the roster, the departing sailors might take the ship's good luck with them.

Some turned to their faith as the trips into the Slot piled up. Catholic crew wore scapulars about their necks or placed medals and rosaries in their pockets. After *Chevalier* returned to Tulagi from a run up the Slot, the crew carried shells and powder cans from an ammunition barge to the handling rooms. Near their ship's bow stood a Catholic chaplain giving each man a communion wafer as he walked by. "I guess he didn't think we needed to go to confession after being up the Slot," said engineering officer Lieutenant George Gowen, "and he didn't ask us if we were Protestant, Jewish Hebrew, Muslim, Catholic or whatever—we were all one faith going into battle." Religion helped the men deal with the pressures of daily operating in the Slot, but as MacDonald wrote, "still it was tough, even with humor and religion. It was tough to be out there until you were dead."[20]

Despite the handful he had to transfer, MacDonald—like his fellow Desron 21 skippers—found most men capable and conscientious, even after weeks at their posts. In that way they reminded him of those London citizens who withstood the German storm. He felt certain his men would now do the same.

"These guys were so loyal they were dying on their feet," wrote MacDonald. "They were getting so tired, some of them, really, because it was hot up there. We were pretty close to the equator and we had no awnings, no rugs. It was pretty hard even to rest. People lost weight. They were tired, but, boy, they certainly went to their stations and carried on beautifully when they were called upon."[21]

Ensign Warren H. Gabelman aboard *Nicholas* provided another explanation: "The above experiences would suggest that we lived a hectic life. We did. But human beings adjust to all kinds of stress. It helped to be young."[22]

It also helped to have a skilled commander. *La Vallette* men boasted that in Commander Robert L. Taylor they had the finest skipper around. Fair yet demanding, the dashing officer looked the part, with a cigarette dangling from his lips and hat tilted slightly to one side. Some claimed that if Hollywood made a film about destroyers, they would select the good-looking Taylor to play the role of skipper.

On the other hand, some of the *Fletcher* crew complained about Commander Robert D. McGinnis, who succeeded Lieutenant Commander Johnson in April 1943. Seaman Chesnutt's diary for the last eight months of 1943 is sprinkled with references to McGinnis's inability to run a ship or crew. He cited McGinnis's failure to grasp military tactics and his ineptness at navigation, which resulted in more than a few minor collisions with other vessels as the captain tried to dock the ship. "The Skipper wasn't the guy he should be," Chesnutt wrote on August 28, after McGinnis refused to allow his crew to go aboard a tender the *Fletcher* was tied to and mingle with that crew. "The other skippers would let us." Chesnutt blamed McGinnis for lowering the morale of a battle-tested crew. "Showers on only half hour each day and wash face one hour each day—like a prison."[23] On the other hand, some of his shipmates shrugged off McGinnis's orders as nothing more than a commander exercising his rights.

The steady MacDonald served as the stabilizer for the squadron skippers. He had gained their admiration first for suffering through the London Blitz and then for his roles in the November naval clash and the many skirmishes that followed. MacDonald rarely lost his composure, but when he did, as in the case of the two sailors who failed to report to their posts, the men readily accepted it. *O'Bannon* crew compared him to that rare football quarterback who led his team to win after win.

In between missions, MacDonald would often sit in his chair on the bridge and "while away the hours thinking about theoretical problems of strategy" and crafting solutions to problems he might face in the future.[24] Unlike McGinnis, MacDonald handed his best men increased responsibility, told them what he wanted done, and stepped away to allow them to perform their tasks. He relied on his petty officers, figuring they knew the crew better than anyone because they so closely worked with the men during their daily duties. Following the adage that the way to a man's heart is through his stomach, MacDonald was so insistent that his men receive the best food possible under the circumstances that they boasted they were the best-fed crew in the squadron.

"Dead Japs and Destruction Behind Us"

Munda Airfield, on New Georgia's southern coast, standing 180 miles northwest of Henderson Field, and Vila Airfield, twenty miles farther to the northwest on Kolombangara's southeast side, had long been thorns in Halsey's side, receiving additional reinforcements and aircraft in spite of American aerial attacks. He turned to naval bombardments, usually involving Desron 21 accompanied by other ships, to neutralize these problems.

The task required the destroyers to race north of the Russell Islands up the Slot toward New Georgia, continue to Kula Gulf, and enter the dangerously narrow water bounded by Japanese bases on New Georgia on one side and Kolombangara on the other. The ships left Tulagi in the evening in order to arrive at their destination after dark, conducted their bombardments, and rushed out of the gulf for the speedy dash back to Tulagi.

In the three months following the formation of Desron 21, squadron destroyers bombarded the Vila and Stanmore area in March and May, as well as Vila in early July. Each time he steamed to Kula Gulf, MacDonald expected to encounter opposition, for barreling into Kula Gulf and bombarding Japanese airfields was akin to poking a lion in the eye. He and his crew had avoided harm since the previous October, but their luck, as *De Haven* proved, could not last forever during a period he called "a pretty hectic life."[25] *O'Bannon* and the force had to navigate close to land, through mined waters masking uncharted coral reefs, only to turn into a gulf guarded by enemy land artillery on both sides, backed by Japanese aircraft and submarines or warships.

"This is going to be a very ticklish operation," wrote Seaman 1/c James Fahey, aboard the cruiser *Montpelier* during one of the bombardments into the gulf, "and it is going to take place right in the Japs' living room."[26]

Hailey accompanied *Nicholas* on many of these bombardment runs. The officers and crew hated full or partially full moons because they silhouetted the ships for enemy aircraft and guns. During bombardments, Hailey felt the ship rock back and forth from the gun recoil. Since the ships lacked flashless powder, "the blinding flash of the four destroyers' guns blinded those of us who were watching from the bridge."[27] Hailey learned to count the seconds between salvos and close his eyes moments before the guns fired, then reopen them as the shells raced shoreward.

The ships walked shells up and down the targets, hoping to pockmark the airstrips and make them unusable to the Japanese. Fiery red balls, interspersed with multicolored tracer shells from the different destroyers, arced through the air. Seconds after each muted explosion, sounds rent the sky and rumbles reverberated across the gulf.

MacDonald and the other skippers were especially wary of any plane that approached without quickly identifying itself. *De Haven* had been lost, in part, because her skipper withheld fire while he tried to identify the planes. When similar incidents occurred in an early March bombardment, Lieutenant Commander Johnson of *Fletcher* vented his complaints in his report. "As usual the insatiable curiosity of friendly planes (Black Cats) caused more concern, grey hairs, palpitations of the heart, and pressure-relieving cussing than all the potential and actual Jap counter measures available in the Solomons," he wrote following the bombardment. He explained that the last thing he wanted was to shoot down a friendly plane, but "if they continue to make unnecessary harassing approaches on this ship within gun range, they will be taken under fire when the slightest doubt exists of their true identity."

The pilots' failure to identify themselves "has gone beyond the stage of 'note with concern,'" he added, and called their actions "sheer stupidity." He noted that in the previous six weeks, he had had to deal with twelve separate approaches that were "dangerously threatening in nature," all by friendly PBYs assigned to work with them and who knew in detail the exact ship locations. Johnson pointed out that while his ship twice opened fire, he kept his guns silent the other ten times, mainly because he did not want to divulge his position; "the decision was made to accept possible bombing instead of opening fire."

Most alarming to Johnson, though, was not that his crew might down a friendly plane and kill a pilot but that, if unchecked, the situation would make it impossible for ship commanders to withhold fire on any plane. He stated that he would not accept the "potential destruction of his ship" by delaying out of fear that the aircraft was friendly, "and 325 lives and $8,000,000 of ship will not be sacrificed to save a few friendly planes and crews from their own foolhardiness." He begged that aviators be acquainted with the "facts of life."[28] McInerney responded by telling his skippers that should a similar circumstance arise in the future, they were to shoot first and query second.

Desron 21 skippers on the line, as well as Halsey in headquarters, regarded the Kula Gulf bombardments as successes. "What we did," confided Seaman Fahey to his diary, "was like having some enemy warship go up the Hudson River and bombard New York City and its shipping, then turn around and head for the open sea. We really rubbed it into the Japs, they will never get over this one." He said they struck the Japanese "like a streak of lightning" and hit "troop barracks, ammunition dumps, radio towers, [and] airfield planes"; "broken bodies were everywhere." He concluded that with the bombardments, "we were a very happy group of warships as we made our way out of the Gulf with dead Japs and destruction behind us."[29]

Each of the crews earned praise. Johnson stated that on his destroyer, "all hands cooperated to score another victory for the *Fletcher* combat team," while Halsey complimented Admiral Ainsworth and said the success of his units, including Desron 21, "has become a habit."[30]

"Why Couldn't They Stay at Home at Least One Night?"

Lieutenant Commander William T. Romoser, skipper of the USS *Radford*, had no doubt that he preferred Pacific action to European duty. For most of the past four years he had been the commanding officer of destroyers that operated in the Atlantic, and while that had provided the thirty-nine-year-old Baltimore native useful experience in managing a crew, he saw little of the combat faced by MacDonald's *O'Bannon*. He expected that to change once *Radford* joined the other South Pacific destroyers in January 1943. First as part of the Cactus Striking Force and subsequently as part of Desron 21, with any luck he would find that sea activity.

The promising start boosted his hopes. *Radford* had participated in four separate bombardments, attacked an enemy submarine, and fought off eight air attacks in the brief time since her arrival. Some might hesitate to place such actions in the same category with a major surface engagement, but Romoser and his fellow squadron commanders considered those more frequent actions to be better tests of their crews' proficiency and courage than those few surface engagements in which a ship might be involved.

Minelaying missions lacked the glamour of headline-grabbing naval battles, but the endeavor could be one of the most effective and safe ways to sink Japanese ships without endangering American vessels. During those actions, destroyers watched the sea and sky for the enemy while minelayers planted a string of mines across the entrance to a strait or other path in the Kolombangara–Vella Lavella area frequented by the Tokyo Express.

Typical was the night of May 7–8, when Romoser led three minelayers through Blackett Strait, the southern entrance to Kula Gulf between Kolombangara and New Georgia, to mine one of the main supply routes to Vila and Munda. With *Radford* on guard, the trio of vessels laid a mine every twelve seconds as they steamed across the strait at fifteen knots. Seventeen minutes later, after planting 250 mines in three rows across the entrance, the four ships departed and returned to Tulagi.

Later that day four Japanese destroyers, under the command of Captain Masao Tachibana, entered the strait with supplies bound for Vila. Within half an hour three of his ships struck the mines Romoser's unit had dropped; one sank and the other two were damaged. The next day American aircraft finished the task, sending Tachibana's two cripples to the bottom and damaging the sole survivor.

Romoser avoided an air attack during his mission, but enemy aircraft were a constant source of danger in the Slot. "It is a terrible sensation," wrote Commander MacDonald, "when these planes start coming down on you and you know you are a target."[31] Unlike German bombs, which indiscriminately hit London targets, Japanese fighters and bombers barreled straight toward his ship.

"I don't think a day went by that we didn't have an air raid," wrote Seaman Chesnutt on *Fletcher*. "There were air raids all day and nuisance raids at night. They would come over and drop one or two bombs just to keep everyone awake." During one attack involving the *Nicholas*, Lieutenant Johnny Everett Jr., the torpedo officer, muttered to correspondent Hailey, "Damn them, why couldn't they stay at home at least one night?"[32]

Antiaircraft crews battled frequent Japanese air strikes between January and June 1943; *Nicholas* and *Fletcher* tallied the most, with nine and eight, respectively. Even when Desron 21 destroyers did not have to fend off an actual air attack, multiple alerts sent everyone to quarters, where they remained until the intruders were identified as friendly.

The largest air strike occurred June 16, when 120 Japanese fighters and bombers struck *O'Bannon*, *Nicholas*, and *Strong* off Guadalcanal. Waves of dive-bombers charged in from all directions while American fighters from Henderson rose to intercept, and near misses sprayed waterspouts that drenched their targets. On *Nicholas*, Hailey looked up to see "the red-hot tracers from the 5-inch guns and automatic weapons arching out across the star-studded sky in a beautiful if terrible pattern, reminiscent of some of the fireworks displays at the New York World's Fair." Suddenly two aircraft swooped down, apparently "guided by our foaming white wakes," and dropped two bombs that splashed fifty yards astern and two other near hits that doused Hailey.[33]

Antiaircraft crews on the three destroyers joined the aviators to send 80 percent of the attackers into the sea. "The boys on the machine guns had a great time shooting the planes at close range and then shifting their fire as the planes got out of range or out of sight," wrote MacDonald of his gun crews. Their group produced such a heavy volume of fire that MacDonald warned the American fighters to stay clear of the destroyers: "They are putting up a lot of lead."[34]

They would occasionally encounter downed Japanese pilots floating in the water. After the first few enemy pilots rebuffed the Americans' efforts to rescue them, MacDonald adapted. "So these were the treacherous beasts who had made life almost unbearable?" he wrote. "Well, the men of the *O'Bannon* would see about that. They did. Their hate grew. They trusted no Jap. And the Japs no longer trust them. They swim away when boats try to pick them up."[35]

Threats in the Slot also came from under the surface. Submarines bothered crews more than did enemy aircraft. Lookouts could spot a fighter or bomber coming at them, but submarines operated out of sight, lurking in the depths to rip their ship apart with their deadly Long Lance torpedoes. Japanese submarines usually operated at night after lying on the bottom during daylight near the Russell Islands, New Georgia, or Santa Isabel Island, but Desron 21 crews could never dismiss the threat.

Correspondent Duncan Norton-Taylor, who often accompanied some of those destroyers as they sliced through the Solomons and southward, "was impressed with the terrible efficiency of this rolling, bucking mechanism of destruction." He added, "We were a spear without a shield. Our thin skin would hardly stop a 50-caliber bullet."[36] He feared what a Long Lance could do to those meager hulls.

In hunting submarines, Desron 21 destroyers formed a fifteen-hundred-yard line and swept sections of water at fifteen knots. Sonarmen listened to pings, the electrical impulses emitted by the sonar projector attached to the hull below the waterline. If an impulse struck a solid object, it bounced back with an echo, allowing sonarmen to determine the distance to the object by the length of time it took for the ping to return. The bridge calculated the submarine's course, speed, and depth and planned an attack to bracket the submarine with charges ahead of, behind, and on either side of the boat.

Upon receiving the order, torpedomen fired depth charges one hundred yards out from each side and dropped others off the fantail. When the charges exploded, deep rumbles shook the destroyer as bubbles and foam broke the surface. If the strike was successful, debris and oil from the submarine soon appeared.

The tricky maneuver demanded skill aided with luck. "Imagine you are leaning over the roof of a twenty-story building with a fistful of grenades in your hand," said one destroyer skipper in describing a depth charge attack, "trying to hit an automobile that is cruising around a large parking lot at twenty-five miles an hour."[37]

All nine destroyers frequently encountered false submarine contacts, such as a whale, porpoises cutting through the waves, a floating log, or an underwater coral formation. "The false submarine echoes are as frequent as an antsy hunter sees deer," wrote Watertender Wing, on *Nicholas*, "but there are enough real ones to do a lot of killing."[38]

The most unusual incident involved *O'Bannon*'s April 5 submarine encounter. When MacDonald's radarmen picked up a surface contact at seven thousand yards, MacDonald cautiously maneuvered *O'Bannon* so close to the unsuspecting target that the ship's cook, who was on deck when the attack started, later told MacDonald that he thought he could have thrown potatoes at the boat.

MacDonald simultaneously dropped depth charges and ordered his 40mm and 20mm guns to open fire. Crew on deck saw the submarine rise out of the water and settle by the stern moments before feeling a violent explosion, and when the next day aviators reported a thick oil slick at the location, *O'Bannon* received credit for a probable sinking of the submarine.

The American press soon picked up the story, but printed it as a tale of a destroyer that attacked a submarine by throwing potatoes at surprised Japanese sailors standing on the boat's tower. Potato growers in Maine struck a plaque honoring the occasion, and the tale lingered so long after the war that MacDonald admitted, "I've been trying to drive a stake through this story for years." He agreed that he maneuvered *O'Bannon* close to the submarine, but explained that even the crewmember with the best throwing arm could not have tossed a potato or anything else across the gap. "From that single remark [of the cook] has grown the entire legend of the use of Maine potatoes to sink a Japanese submarine."[39]

Escorting transports to and from Espiritu Santo still occasionally took Desron 21 officers and crews away from the Slot. Skippers hated being yanked from an active combat zone to lumber across the ocean guarding slow-moving transports; they argued that this "sheep dog" duty relegated their offensive capabilities to secondary status.

Halsey disliked removing destroyers from the Slot as well, but felt he had no choice. Those transports brought the supplies and reinforcements he needed, and he could not send them across Torpedo Junction without an escort.

"We were under the enemy's guns, as it were, the moment we stuck our noses out [of Espiritu Santo]," wrote correspondent Norton-Taylor. "Japanese submarines had been active in the Coral Sea in recent weeks and every hour of our progress north brought us closer within the range of the Jap's aircraft."[40]

MacDonald stifled his anger over the inexperience of some transport skippers and of the newer destroyers arriving in the South Pacific. One rattled captain reported five contacts on one trip, each time forcing MacDonald, as convoy commander, to shift course as an evasive measure. After the final time, when *O'Bannon*'s sonarmen again failed to detect anything, "I finally had to shut him up, tell him to keep quiet until I told him when to get worried about submarines in the area."[41]

"Roosevelt's Professional Killers"

The 1943 operations in the Slot handed Desron 21 crews the experience and confidence necessary to execute their tasks. By year's end the neophyte crews of untested civilians had been replaced by self-assured sailors ready to match skills with the Japanese.

"Day by day we were becoming more experienced in the art of warfare against the Japanese and we were beginning to feel like veterans from the old school," pronounced the *Taylor* cruise book about the ship's time running up the Slot. "The whole crew drew predictably closer during these arduous nights up the Slot," said Yeoman R. H. Roupe of his *Chevalier* shipmates. "A spirit of comradeship flourished which has no parallel in civilian life. The constant proximity of sudden and violent death, the danger and excitement and sometimes terror of our precarious existence gave an added stimulus to the strengthening of brotherhood among us."[42]

Roupe explained that *Chevalier*'s crew looked to *O'Bannon* as the model toward which they strove. "The *O'Bannon* was a remarkable little ship," Roupe wrote. "She had been in the South Pacific before our arrival and had been in the thick of the great sea battles off Guadalcanal in those early desperate days when the Japs had hurled their fleet against ours with reckless abandon." She had emerged intact from those perilous days and nights "still jauntily, proudly, unbelievably afloat. Her luck and courage had made her name a legend. It was said that an angel rode upon her foremast." *Time* magazine heralded MacDonald and his ship for being in "almost continuous naval warfare" around Guadalcanal and up the Slot, and Tokyo Rose labeled the ship's crew "Roosevelt's professional killers."[43]

MacDonald sensed the emerging confidence among his men, an attitude that he said combined experience with hatred of the enemy. He explained that the transformation took place "through the awful nights of bombing, the exchange of shots with cowardly ships, the sickening vigil, the breaking strain," and added that because of it, "hate began to emerge: 'What right have they to be doing this to us? They are pounding at this beautiful little ship until they smash it. We will smash them. We are not here until we are dead. They are here until they are dead.'"

His men were better able to match talents with the Japanese when they loosened the shackles binding them to civilian life. "Then the men of the *O'Bannon* really began to fight. They no longer thought of the green hills, the sodas, the pretty girls. They became hunters. They were no longer the hunted. The steel in their hearts was at last tempered."

He saw evidence of this the night that *O'Bannon* received a rare night off from Slot duty. A young sailor walked by and asked MacDonald, "Aren't we going, too?"

"Not tonight," MacDonald replied.

"What's the matter, Captain? Are we slipping?"

MacDonald appreciated the remark, which came from a sailor who in the early days off Guadalcanal had trembled at the sound of explosions. "I knew then the tide had turned. The boys of the *O'Bannon* were jealous of the privilege of fighting the Japs."[44] This was no longer the young crew he had first seen gather at Bath, Maine. Boys then, they had in the intervening months become battle-hardened men.

The *O'Bannon* crew, still without a casualty, agreed that a guardian angel protected them, and other crews called them "the Galloping Ghost of the Solomons Coast" because, as MacDonald said, "it was felt that we had some sort of a protector there. They felt very strongly that someone was looking out for us. I don't think there were any atheists on board, I'll tell you that."[45]

In 1942 and 1943, MacDonald's crew had "reached the point of perfection. All I had to do was say, 'Commence firing!' and they put on a wonderful show. They all knew their job and they did it well. They really had arrived at the peak of fighting form. We really had extreme confidence and only dared the enemy to come out and play with us."[46]

Time magazine summed it up for home-front readers: "Around South Pacific bars, MacDonald's *O'Bannon* became a legend."[47]

Time also printed words indicating that Desron 21's work was far from complete. Military analysts expected that surface engagements would soon embroil the destroyers in decisive battles against skilled enemy warships and crews.

"But as South Pacific fighting went into its second spring," declared *Time* in March 1943, "one paradox grew plain: though the Allied position in the past year had improved infinitely, Japan's position was not correspondingly worse. The fighting had only taken up the slack in battle lines. Now each adversary had a firm foothold. The next blow would be to the other's body."[48]

The ships and crews of Desron 21 would be directly in the middle of those body blows, which together delivered a knockout punch that left the Japanese clinging to their final defense line in the Solomons.

CHAPTER 7

KULA GULF CONFRONTATIONS

Lieutenant Hugh B. Miller was already accustomed to being on the first team, although his prior unit had consisted of eleven football players at the University of Alabama. In 1930 he quarterbacked the squad to an undefeated season and a share with the University of Notre Dame of the national championship. The next year he led his squad to a shutout 24–0 win over Washington State to capture the Rose Bowl.

Gridiron glory had accustomed Miller to the cheers of thousands. But the football star now listened to a different call—the one issued by his country in wartime, a call that would pit not athlete against athlete on football fields but adversary against adversary on the high seas. He had proven his leadership skills during fall football weekends, but as his ship, the destroyer USS *Strong*, wound toward the South Pacific, Miller faced a new arena. When bombs and shells replaced opposing tacklers, would he react with the same coolness?

Since the *Strong*'s January 1943 arrival in the South Pacific, the ship had performed the usual functions of Halsey's destroyers in those 1942–1943 days: escorting convoys, bombarding enemy land installations, hunting submarines, and laying mines across Blackett Strait. But the crew's impatience at missing a surface engagement concerned Miller. He had seen similar impatience during football games, and not once had it helped his team. If it had been up to him, *Strong* would have avoided all such duels with enemy battleships and cruisers. He had scrambled for his life during gridiron contests, and he did not relish being involved in one where bullets instead of linemen came at him.

The former quarterback relied on what he knew best—practice. Like his Alabama coaches, who stressed repetition as the best way to improve, Miller drilled his 20mm gun crews with such proficiency that an impressed skipper,

Commander Joseph H. Wellings, said, "The way he trained and drilled our 20mm gun crews, one would think he was still calling signals for his beloved Alabama football team in a bowl game against the University of Oklahoma."[1]

MacDonald and other Pacific commanders longed to improve destroyer tactics but were stymied by resistance from above. Commander Arleigh A. Burke, a compatriot of MacDonald's who would gain acclaim for his exploits with his own destroyer division, believed promptness in launching torpedoes was crucial to victory. His widely circulated statement that the difference between a successful destroyer officer and a poor one was ten seconds referred to destroyer skippers being hampered by having to wait to launch their torpedoes until the division commander ordered it. That brief interval handed the enemy the opportunity to seize the initiative and launch first. Burke suggested that destroyers strike upon contact with the enemy rather than wait for orders. Rather than learn from earlier surface actions or listen to prescient observations, some senior commanders still declined to use destroyers as intact units. MacDonald and the other destroyer skippers were alarmed at such misuse of their vessels.

In May he submitted a written document outlining his tactics. He advocated placing his destroyers in one unit, split into two parallel columns. After launching torpedoes, the first column would turn away and draw enemy fire to them. The second column would then counter with a torpedo attack from a different direction.

MacDonald hoped that senior commanders would seriously consider Burke's tactics. Maybe the June 1943 appearance of a new manual, *Current Tactical Orders and Doctrine, U.S. Pacific Fleet*, which promoted similar revisions, would prod commanders into change.

The Japanese Long Lance torpedoes were another prominent topic of conversation. Rear Admiral Ainsworth was cautioned about their enhanced range and was advised to open fire as quickly as possible to avoid running into a wave of Long Lances and being knocked out of the fight before he could fire.

Answers would come from four brutal surface engagements that erupted from July to October. Like opposing heavyweight boxing foes, the US and Japanese navies steamed into battle off New Georgia–Kolombangara in a quartet of slugfests. At the end, one foe limped away, in the process yielding control of the Solomons to the victor.

After months of escorting troop transports, bombarding land targets, and the myriad tasks Halsey handed to them, MacDonald and the skippers of Desron 21 soon found themselves trading punches with Japanese warships.

"The Japanese Were Really Stirred Up"

Control of vital New Georgia was the prize of the four battles. If the Japanese retained its hold on the island, including its airfields at Munda, they could halt the American advance up the Solomons and confine Halsey to the Russell Islands–Guadalcanal area. If the United States seized New Georgia, they could restrict the Japanese to the northern Solomons, assert control in the central Solomons, and take a large step toward pushing the Japanese out of the islands for good.

Halsey collected a joint Navy-Marine expedition for the first operation, the New Georgia landings. While Marines rushed ashore at Rice Anchorage, on New Georgia's western coast, the Navy would block Japanese attempts to bring reinforcements from Kolombangara across the Kula Gulf to Munda. Three cruisers escorted by nine destroyers, including *O'Bannon*, *Nicholas*, *Strong*, and *Chevalier* from Desron 21, accompanied seven destroyer-transports ferrying the Marines to Rice Anchorage.

For MacDonald and his crew, it was once more "into the dangerous waters of the Solomons." The week before Independence Day had been particularly hectic, and "we had been going up almost every night for a week and we felt due for a rest. But there we were heading northward."[2]

Correspondent Duncan Norton-Taylor had first thought of joining MacDonald's *O'Bannon* in June. He had heard of the ship's accomplishments, which earned *O'Bannon* praise as one of the "most courageous of the Tin Can Fleet," and MacDonald and his young officers, most of whom had been in the Navy two years or less, impressed him. "A few years before most of them had been peaceful young citizens," he wrote. "Now they were tough veterans." After an initial inquiry, Norton-Taylor concluded that he "already knew the *O'Bannon*'s reputation for sticking her sharp nose into things," and so instead he chose *St. Louis*, "one of Ainsworth's large and more heavily armored and gunned cruisers."[3]

With Norton-Taylor aboard *St. Louis*, the force left for New Georgia at sunset on July 4 and moved up the Slot to Kula Gulf, a narrow body of water standing 180 miles northwest of Guadalcanal. Twenty-five miles long and anywhere from ten to twenty-five miles wide, the gulf separated New Georgia on the east from Kolombangara to its west. The ships would enter the gulf from the north, steam southward along the coast of Kolombangara to bombard Vila at its southern tip, execute a U-turn to blast Bairoko Harbor and Rice Anchorage on New Georgia's western coast, and depart through the gulf's northern exit for the return to Tulagi. The high-risk plan required the ships to steam within range of enemy coastal batteries and operate in waters frequented by Japanese submarines.

Once in the Slot, MacDonald informed the crew that on their nation's birthday they were headed toward New Georgia, where they would help land the Marines and conduct a fireworks celebration of their own. After speaking to them, he made certain that the St. Christopher medal his fiancée had handed him in Boston was safely ensconced in his left breast pocket. MacDonald liked the medal's presence, almost as if Cecilia were with him.

Deck crews donned steel helmets and life jackets, while in the wardroom *O'Bannon*'s doctor laid out instruments he hoped he would never have to utilize. A chief pharmacist's mate checked men posted at an aft station to handle casualties there, then made certain that boxes of dressings and other medical supplies were properly placed at all battle stations. In the coding room, the communications officer stuffed code books and other top-secret documents into a bag, secured it, and weighted it with bricks to ensure that, should the ship sink, the material would not land in Japanese hands. Wooden shores and plugs of various sizes stood belowdecks in case crew needed to patch leaks or cover holes. Repair parties waited at different locations to battle fires and floods should the destroyer be hit.

As the unit neared Kula Gulf that night, Lieutenant Miller aboard *Strong* checked on his men. They were familiar with the area around Guadalcanal, which Miller called "our baby. We knew it and its adjacent waters as we knew our own backyards at home," but once they neared Kula Gulf, they entered unknown waters.[4]

Around midnight his ship and *Nicholas* pulled ahead of the other vessels to search the gulf with their radar and sonar. While they expected a hot greeting, they found only stillness.

The cruisers and destroyers followed, steaming down the east coast of Kolombangara until they arrived at their bombardment stations. Lieutenant Pfeifer, aboard *O'Bannon*, felt as though he could cut the tension with a knife as he and others waited for the Japanese to rain shells their way. "If the Japs had spotted us," he later wrote, "we could expect all hell to break loose from torpedo boats, midget subs, surface craft, planes, shore batteries and mines."[5]

Once at their bombardment stations, the main batteries from *Helena*, *Honolulu*, and *St. Louis* lit the skies with thundering salvos directed at Vila, followed by more from *O'Bannon* and *Chevalier*'s five-inch shells. Observing through a pair of binoculars, Norton-Taylor noticed that the guns bathed the ships in a pinkish glow as they boomed shells shoreward. He wrote that as the shells raced toward their targets, "they look more like Christmas tree balls and it is possible to follow them with the eye until they reach the end of their trajectory, where they simply vanish in the pockets of the darkness with no apparent effect."[6] Thunder from distant explosions rolled across the ships, and flames from shore indicated that their shells had struck.

After blasting Vila, the bombardment force veered east toward New Georgia, turned north along its coast, and bombarded Bairoko Harbor before covering the Marine landings at Rice Anchorage. Aboard *O'Bannon*, Ensign John J. Noonan, a battery officer on a small gun, nearly jumped when the guns broke the stillness. The destroyer lurched, and "a great mass of yellow flame shot out from the guns," leaving him momentarily blinded. As he "watched the trail of light streaking into shore, made by tracer powder," Noonan glanced across the waters toward *Helena* and saw a "perfect arc" streaming from the cruiser to the island, "as though a hose of fire was being played on the target."[7] So numerous were the shells flowing toward the island that one officer thought they looked like snowflakes in a New England snowstorm, and eruptions on Kolombangara outlined the trees against burning barracks and ammunition dumps.

Once assured that the Marines were securely ashore on Rice Anchorage, the force steamed up the New Georgia coast and left the northern entrance. Good fortune had once again blessed the crew of *O'Bannon*, as yet another mission had been completed without a single crew killed or injured.

Then MacDonald's TBS suddenly came alive with a frantic call for help. Moments earlier, aboard *Strong*, Lieutenant James A. Curran, the ship's gunnery officer, had spotted a white phosphorescent wake heading toward the port side amidships. He started to alert the bridge, but an explosion cut him short and knocked men to the deck. *Strong* shook under the impact, lurched to port, and tilted fifteen degrees to starboard. The ship lost power, deck plates buckled from the impact, and water gushed through a gaping hole on the port side. A Long Lance torpedo from a Japanese destroyer an estimated eleven miles away, a distance no one thought possible, had inflicted the damage.

Ainsworth ordered *O'Bannon* and *Chevalier* to assist the stricken *Strong*. Aboard *Chevalier*, Commander Ephraim R. McLean Jr. announced to his crew that they were turning back into the gulf. "We thought that this was going to be rough," said Machinist's Mate 1/c Burt Gorsline of going back to enemy-controlled waters. "The Japanese were really stirred up by now."[8] They returned to Kula Gulf to find *Strong* badly listing in the waters two miles west of Rice Anchorage, in the northern third of the gulf.

Commander Joseph A. Wellings, *Strong*'s skipper, told his officers that when the destroyer's list reached forty-five degrees, they should at that time make preparations to abandon ship, but not actually do it until ordered. He told his officers, though, that they were not to actually relay the order to the men until Wellings gave them the approval. He sent his executive officer, Lieutenant Commander Frederick W. Purdy, to take charge of abandoning the ship from the forecastle, but admonished him not to take any foolhardy risks and to get into the water before the ship sank. "Don't worry about me, Captain," said Purdy as he turned toward the forecastle.[9]

As men aboard *Strong* scurried about the deck, MacDonald and McLean approached the stricken destroyer on opposite sides. MacDonald was inching *O'Bannon* along the starboard side to take off survivors when *Chevalier*, in moving closer to the damaged destroyer, rammed into *Strong*'s stern. The ship immediately listed to fifty degrees, making Wellings fear that the destroyer would break up and sink. Confusion spread about the forecastle, where some of the men appeared ready to leap over the side, but they stopped when Lieutenant (jg) Orivall M. Hackett, the torpedo officer, threatened to shoot anyone who tried to jump without his explicit orders. In the dark no one noticed that Hackett was not carrying a sidearm.

Standing on the main deck, Lieutenant Donald A. Regan heard a tapping sound coming from the Number One engine room. He looked through an emergency hatch to find the room all but flooded. Feet from him stood Electrician's Mate 2/c Willard G. Langley, pinned between a pipe and the main electric board, crying for help as he tried to keep his head above water. Regan held on to a three-foot piece of rope anchored by another man, grabbed Langley, and lifted him up from the hatch to the main deck.

When Japanese land batteries targeted the trio, MacDonald positioned *O'Bannon* between the other two destroyers and the Japanese in an attempt to deflect fire from the damaged *Strong*. This bold move placed his ship within easy range of the enemy's guns, and MacDonald would have to battle it out until *Strong*'s crew was rescued, all the while silhouetted against the bright backdrop provided by the burning *Strong*. Observing from his cruiser, and relieved that he had not earlier selected to travel on the other ship, which now appeared to be ready to sacrifice itself, Norton-Taylor watched shells splash near *O'Bannon*, "a target for Jap batteries, which now opened up with new fury, hoping to get another victim."[10] Neither the London bombings nor the November battle matched the peril MacDonald and his crew now faced.

Near MacDonald, Lieutenant Pfeifer momentarily looked up as shells sang overhead and slammed into the water not more than fifty yards from the destroyer. Explosions hurled shrapnel that punctured holes in the superstructure, forcing MacDonald and others to take cover, and bullets whistled through the rigging. Japanese aircraft soon joined, dropping bombs and further illuminating the ship with flares.

One man standing next to seventeen-year-old Soundman 3/c John H. Artesani mistook the flashes ashore as indicators that *O'Bannon*'s shells had struck their targets. Artesani wanted to tell him those flashes were the Japanese guns shooting at them, but the teenager was so frightened that he was unable to speak. "The Japs were shelling hell out of us," said Ship's Cook 1/c George Peterson. "They lit us up like a Christmas tree and we were sitting there dead in the water."[11]

Deck gun crews maintained a steady rhythm throughout, creating bright orange flashes ashore with their hits. "Never was *O'Bannon* in greater danger," MacDonald wrote. "They gave us the works; we gave it back until their fire diminished."[12]

While MacDonald waged his battle to divert attention from *Strong* and *Chevalier*, men on the latter two ships continued their efforts to transfer the crew from the sinking ship. *Chevalier*'s bow was stuck in *Strong*'s stern, forming a large V that, for the moment, helped keep *Strong* afloat while rescue efforts continued. When *Chevalier* crew dropped cargo nets over the side and rigged two manila lines to *Strong*, Wellings ordered the crew to abandon ship. Lieutenant Hackett grabbed one line and Lieutenant Regan the other, and both held on for dear life while crew began crossing from the destroyer to her rescuer. Waters continued to add to *Strong*'s list as men scrambled to the forecastle to abandon ship. Crew belowdecks rose from hatches, and Wellings and other officers hurriedly checked the ship to make certain every living man was accounted for.

With *Strong* low in the water and in danger of rolling over, McLean shouted across to Wellings, "Gus, I think everyone who was topside is either aboard, or in the water alongside. I better cast off and get out of here in a minute or two, before I am hit and crippled with all your men on board."[13] He started backing up at 1:20 a.m. as Japanese shells splashed near *Chevalier*'s fantail.

McLean erred in assuming every man was off the ship. Lieutenant Commander Purdy joined Hackett and Regan at the forecastle, helping to get men over the side. As Purdy left to check on a wounded shipmate on the main deck, a man near Hackett shouted that the ship was going under. The waters closed about him so rapidly that Hackett did not even have to jump as the ship sank. Purdy never reached *Chevalier* or a life net; survivors found his body washed ashore on Arundel Island three days later.

With the water rising to bridge level, Commander Wellings ordered Chief Quartermaster Maurice Rodrigos over the side, but Rodrigos refused to leave his skipper. Wellings took a last look around to make certain no one remained on the main deck, then told Rodrigos, "Let's get off right now before we're trapped inside when she rolls over."[14] By that time the waters had risen so high that the pair simply had to step into the water and swim away.

Lieutenant (jg) Benjamin F. Jetton, communications officer, and Ensign William C. Hedrick Jr., assistant communications officer, ignored the risks to remain belowdecks in the passageway, placing secret and confidential documents into weighted bags and throwing them over the side, even after Wellings gave the abandon-ship order. The pair continued their task as the ship went down, giving their lives to ensure that no crucial information floated away from the ship into enemy hands.

While men rushed over the side from the forecastle, Alabama's football star, Lieutenant Miller, hurried to the main deck on the port side to help other men abandon ship, hoping with his presence to lend a calming influence. When *Chevalier* pulled away, Miller started to go over the side, but he halted when he spotted two men whose legs were pinned by the lines used to abandon ship. Ignoring the fast-moving waters, Miller moved closer and cut the two loose just as the waters swallowed him, and "the ship sank under our feet."[15]

The suction carried Miller and the two men downward. Miller held his breath as long as he could, shedding every piece of equipment possible, and finally reached the surface along with his companions. Moments later an underwater explosion numbed Miller to the waist. Three additional explosions followed that briefly knocked him senseless, but when he regained consciousness, he was still holding out of the water the heads of the men he had earlier rescued.

In the water, Wellings and Rodrigos had flipped onto their backs to watch their ship as *Strong* broke in half and disappeared. The explosions from the depth charges rushed at the pair, knocking Wellings unconscious, but fortunately for the skipper, his life jacket kept his head above the surface. Aboard *O'Bannon*, MacDonald and others on the bridge were knocked about by the powerful explosion.

Slowly, groups of men in the water gathered at a life net or in the ship's gig. One group reached Kolombangara, and others made it to Arundel Island at the southern exit of Kula Gulf; most struggled in the waters before drowning or being rescued by another vessel. Commander Wellings regained consciousness as Rodrigos helped him to a floater net twenty-five yards away. Using their hands, the men at the net paddled throughout the night to reach Rice Anchorage, but they had difficulty battling through the gulf's currents. Finally, shortly before dawn, the destroyer USS *Gwin* (DD-433) saw a flashlight that Rodrigos had been using to signal their location, and picked up the group.

The sinking *Strong* dragged Lieutenant Hackett under the water, where he fought the suction and held his breath to reach the surface. Upon gulping fresh air, he grabbed an empty powder can attached to a floater net, where he found himself surrounded by men, some crying for help. Hackett was able to lift Miller, suffering internal injuries caused by the depth charge blast, into the net and administer morphine.

After the depth charge explosions, MacDonald concluded that no one then in the water could have survived. Since *Chevalier* had also been damaged, he decided his first duty was to the crews of the two ships afloat and escorted *Chevalier* out of the gulf.

Chevalier rescued 241 men from the *Strong*, with *Ralph Talbot* and *Gwin* plucking a few more from the waters, but forty-five men died and another sixty-one suffered wounds in the brief encounter. Still floating among the debris were groups of survivors, hoping to evade the dual threats posed by the

Japanese and the sharks. Added to the loss of *De Haven*, *Strong* became the second Desron 21 destroyer to rest on the bottom.

"Willing to Lay Down Their Lives"

MacDonald and *O'Bannon* had again avoided harm, but a message indicating that another installment of the Tokyo Express was barreling south toward Kula Gulf returned MacDonald and the force to the scene. *O'Bannon* and *Nicholas*, joined along the way by *Radford* and *Jenkins*, accompanied *Helena*, *Honolulu*, and *St. Louis* to intercept ten Japanese destroyers.

Ainsworth adhered to the battle tactics that frustrated MacDonald and every destroyer commander. Shortly before 2:00 a.m. destroyer radar screens lit up with blips indicating two groups of enemy ships under Rear Admiral Teruo Akiyama bringing 2,600 troops and supplies to New Georgia. Ainsworth formed into the familiar single column, posting *Nicholas* and *O'Bannon* at the van while *Jenkins* and *Radford* trailed behind the three cruisers. He ordered the rear destroyers to join the cruisers and fire at the transport unit while *Nicholas* and *O'Bannon* targeted three screening Japanese destroyers.

Off Kolombangara, Ainsworth waited until he had closed to within seven thousand yards of the Japanese to open fire. Salvos from *Radford* hit *Amagiri* amidships, sinking the flagship, and other shells screamed into *Niizuki*. "If the s.o.b. wants a fight, we'll give him a fight," barked Lieutenant Commander Hill of *Nicholas*.[16]

Akiyama counterpunched with his Long Lance torpedoes. Aboard *St. Louis*, Norton-Taylor watched a torpedo churning directly at the ship; later the correspondent described it as "a thick white finger coming straight at us like a chalk line drawn across a blackboard."[17] A signalman shouted the alarm and everyone braced for the hit, but it proved to be a dud.

In a three-minute span shortly after the firing began, three Long Lance torpedoes smashed into *Helena* and sliced off her bow. As sailors rushed to abandon the flooding vessel, she split in half and began settling, disappearing beneath the surface forty minutes later.

MacDonald's crew had forged tight bonds with *Helena*. Not only had they participated in numerous actions together, but their crews had often associated at Tulagi, Espiritu Santo, and Noumea. *O'Bannon* men proudly wore the nickname "Little *Helena*," bestowed on them by officers and enlisted in the South Pacific, and some of the crew considered the cruiser an honorary member of their squadron. That cruiser's sailors now needed help, and *O'Bannon* men begged MacDonald to be included in the rescue attempt, even though they were by then almost out of ammunition and under orders to return to Tulagi.

"Captain," said a man who approached MacDonald on the bridge, "we want to go back after the men of the *Helena*. They are our buddies. They've always taken care of us." Moved by that and similar pleas, MacDonald spoke to the crew over the loudspeaker, explained the perils of remaining in Japanese-controlled waters, and asked if they were certain they wanted to risk their lives to retrieve *Helena* crew from the water. When the crew shouted its assent, MacDonald signaled Ainsworth: "The officers and men of the *O'Bannon*, with full awareness of the hazard, request permission to return to pick up survivors of the *Helena*." Ainsworth's denial disappointed MacDonald, but he was never more proud of his men than at that moment. "It was a happy moment of my life. Men have to be great to be willing to lay down their lives for their fellow men."[18] Ainsworth handed the rescue efforts to *Nicholas* and *Radford* while *O'Bannon* continued to Tulagi.

When Hill and *Nicholas* arrived at the scene, only *Helena*'s bow protruded from the water. On *Radford*, Commander Romoser carefully maneuvered his destroyer toward the bow, in the process passing close to survivors waving and yelling for help. "In the white light they looked like a school of black fish thrashing around in the phosphorescence," Romoser explained to Norton-Taylor. "They gave us a cheer and I ordered two boats lowered and they began swarming into them. Many of them had knives in their teeth. They were not certain of our identity and they were prepared to fight for their lives if my ship had turned out to be a Jap."[19]

To avoid panic among the survivors, Romoser shouted instructions through a megaphone to remain calm and slowly maneuver toward the ship. Enemy vessels in the gulf twice interrupted the rescue attempt, but each time Romoser returned to pick up additional survivors. He remained in the area until McInerney in *Nicholas* decided to extract the ships before dawn brought swarms of enemy aircraft.

Crews scrubbed the survivors to remove the grime and oil that clung to their faces and clothing, and cooks provided a continuous supply of hot coffee. When *Nicholas* and *Radford* returned to Tulagi, men standing on the decks of anchored ships cheered the two destroyers for their efforts in rescuing eight hundred fellow sailors.

Commander Donald J. MacDonald gained valuable experience in London during the German aerial blitz of that city. He utilized what he learned in commanding the USS *O'Bannon*, earning two Navy Crosses and three Silver Stars for his exemplary leadership. *(National Archives)*

The USS *O'Bannon* (DD-450) became one of the Pacific war's most heralded destroyers. The ship and crew participated in numerous operations from late 1942 until the war's end, miraculously emerging without suffering a single casualty. In honor of their superb work in the Solomons for more than a year, MacDonald and the crew earned a Presidential Unit Citation. She is seen here in July 1943 retrieving a pilot while her squadron sister ship, USS *Chevalier* (DD-451), operates in the background. *(National Archives)*

The USS *Nicholas* (DD-449), here pictured while conducting trials off the coast of Maine in spring 1942, was one of the first *Fletcher*-class destroyers to reach the Solomons. She earned a Presidential Unit Citation in July 1943 for rescuing survivors of the cruiser USS *Helena* (CL-50). *(National Archives)*

The USS *Fletcher* (DD-445), operating with *O'Bannon* and *Nicholas*, helped Admiral William F. Halsey's overtaxed forces hold off the Japanese in the Solomons until help arrived. *(National Archives)*

Admiral William F. Halsey's affection for destroyers lasted his entire career. Deficient in aircraft carriers and battleships, in late 1942 and early 1943 the aggressive commander relied on *O'Bannon*, *Nicholas*, *Fletcher*, and other tin cans to check the Japanese and turn the tide in the Solomons. *(National Archives)*

One of the first promises Halsey (left) made when he assumed command in the South Pacific was to rush ships, including *O'Bannon*, *Nicholas*, and *Fletcher*, and reinforcements to Major General Alexander A. Vandegrift (right), the commander of the Marines battling on Guadalcanal. *(U.S. Naval History and Heritage Command)*

Rear Admiral Daniel J. Callaghan sacrificed his life while commanding *O'Bannon*, *Fletcher*, and other surface units during the momentous Naval Battle of Guadalcanal in mid-November 1942. *(National Archives)*

Captain Francis X. McInerney, the first commodore to lead Destroyer Squadron 21 into action, sits next to Lieutenant Commander Andrew J. Hill of the *Nicholas* on the bridge of that destroyer. *(National Archives)*

Taken from the *Fletcher*, this April 1943 photograph shows ships in Tulagi Harbor across Ironbottom Sound from Guadalcanal, which along with nearby Purvis Bay served as a home base for the ships of Destroyer Squadron 21 in 1943. *(U.S. Naval History and Heritage Command)*

The USS *Fletcher* at anchor in Purvis Bay in March 1943. Combined with Tulagi, the sheltered harbors provided brief respites from the destroyers' frequent runs up the Slot. *(U.S. Naval History and Heritage Command)*

Taken from the *Nicholas*, this August 1943 photograph shows three Desron 21 destroyers—*O'Bannon* in the lead, followed by *Chevalier* and *Taylor*—en route to Tulagi from a run up the Slot. *(U.S. Naval History and Heritage Command)*

The USS *Taylor* (DD-468) arrived in the Solomons in January 1943, after which the ship and crew participated in operations leading to the war's final day in Tokyo Bay. *(U.S. Naval History and Heritage Command)*

Also arriving in the Solomons in January 1943, the USS *Jenkins* (DD-447) remained in the Pacific until striking a mine off Tarakan Island in April 1945. *(U.S. Naval History and Heritage Command)*

Another January 1943 arrival to the Solomons, the USS *Radford* (DD-446) received a Presidential Unit Citation for rescuing survivors of the cruiser USS *Helena* (CL-50) in Kula Gulf in July 1943. She also operated off New Guinea and the Philippines before leaving for the United States after being damaged by a mine off Corregidor in February 1945. *(U.S. Naval History and Heritage Command)*

The final January 1943 arrival in the Solomons, the USS *Strong* (DD-467) mounted numerous missions up the Slot with her squadron mates before being sunk in July 1943. *(National Archives)*

The USS *Chevalier* (DD-451) had only been in the Solomons a brief time when the ship participated in the Battle of Rennell Island. She remained with Desron 21 until October 1943, when a Japanese torpedo sank the ship. *(National Archives)*

The 1943 runs up the Slot placed Desron 21 destroyers in frequent contact with the Japanese. Their missions included antisubmarine patrols, escorting supply and troop ships, antiaircraft engagements, and bombardments of Japanese land positions. This photograph, taken from the USS *Nicholas*, shows U.S. cruisers and destroyers hitting targets at Vila airfield on Kolombangara Island in May 1943. *(National Archives)*

The USS *De Haven* (DD-469) had the briefest time in the Solomons, being sunk by Japanese air attacks less than two months after she arrived. In this photograph, taken the day before she was sunk, the ship is steaming north of Savo Island. *(National Archives)*

Desron 21 destroyers often headed into the Slot together on various missions. This July 1943 photograph, taken from *O'Bannon*, shows *Nicholas* being followed by *Jenkins* and *Radford* as the four destroyers escort the cruisers *St. Louis* (CL-49) and *Honolulu* (CL-48). *(National Archives)*

The *Nicholas* earned a Presidential Unit Citation for rescuing survivors of the USS *Helena* (CL-50) after the July 5–6, 1943, Battle of Kula Gulf. Men from the cruiser, heavily coated with oil, received clothing and food from the *Nicholas* crew. *(National Archives)*

Hugh Miller's outstanding play for the University of Alabama football squad helped lead them to a national title. He is shown here in a photograph taken during his high school days. *(Courtesy of Fitzhugh Miller)*

Lieutenant Hugh Miller poses for a photograph following his lengthy island ordeal. He still sports the beard he grew while stranded on Arundel Island. *(Courtesy of Fitzhugh Miller)*

Eleanor Roosevelt, who was then on a lengthy tour of Pacific bases, congratulates Hugh Miller (middle) after awarding him his Navy Cross. Admiral Halsey looks on. *(Courtesy of Fitzhugh Miller)*

Lieutenant Hugh Miller's odyssey while stranded on a Pacific island with Japanese forces became the subject of a popular postwar comic book. *(From Government Comics Collection, University of Nebraska's Image and Multimedia Collections)*

Seaman 2/c Jacob Thomas Chesnutt Jr. of the *Fletcher* with Yeoman Ray Allen at Fiji in 1943. Chesnutt's diary illuminated much of what the ship and crew experienced in the Solomons and after. *(From the Thomas Chesnutt Collection)*

Crew from the *Nicholas* captured two Japanese survivors, here wearing United States Navy uniforms after their rescue from the light cruiser *Jintsu*, sunk in the July 1943 Battle of Kolombangara. Most Japanese preferred to swim away from American efforts to pluck them from the waters. *(National Archives)*

The major surface engagements in Kula Gulf saw Desron 21 destroyers using their main batteries against Japanese cruisers and destroyers. The *Nicholas* fires her guns in this August 1943 encounter. *(National Archives)*

Commander MacDonald's gray-flecked hair shows the effects of serving for more than one year in the Solomons. One of the most decorated naval heroes of the war, he capably guided *O'Bannon* through many actions. *(National Archives)*

Commander MacDonald (left) shakes the hand of Captain Thomas J. Ryan, Desron 21 Commander, as MacDonald receives a Navy Cross for his actions in the Slot. *(National Archives)*

MacDonald's successor as skipper of *O'Bannon*, Commander R. W. Smith (left), receives congratulations from Rear Admiral Daniel E. Barbey after the *O'Bannon* was awarded a Presidential Unit Citation. *(National Archives)*

Desron 21's operations off the coast of New Guinea mainly centered on supporting the landing waves and support ships during the assault and providing gunfire support to land forces afterward. In this photograph, ships bombard Japanese positions at Humboldt Bay, New Guinea, on April 22, 1944, as landing craft take infantry shoreward. *(National Archives)*

Desron 21's operations in the Philippines mirrored much of what the squadron conducted off New Guinea, but with the added peril of fending off kamikaze aircraft. During the squadron's activities at Mindoro on December 15, 1944, the same day that kamikazes barely missed hitting Doc Ransom's *La Vallette* and Orvill Raines's *Howorth*, other suicide aircraft smashed into LSTs, as pictured here. *(National Archives)*

The January 1945 landings at Lingayen Gulf attracted more kamikazes. In this photo, a suicide plane approaches the cruiser USS *Louisville* (CA-28) with a nearby destroyer providing antiaircraft fire. In the Philippines, Desron 21 crews had to be continuously on watch, as kamikazes could appear at any moment. *(National Archives)*

The USS *Hopewell* (DD-681), which joined Desron 21 in October 1943 as a replacement for the sunken *Strong*, was herself damaged while supporting operations off Corregidor on February 14, 1945. Smoke billows amidships after a hit that day from a Japanese shore battery shell. *(U.S. Naval History and Heritage Command)*

Damage to the USS *Hopewell* (DD-681), caused by a Japanese shore battery shell, is seen in the numerous holes puncturing the destroyer. *(U.S. Naval History and Heritage Command)*

The USS *La Vallette* (DD-448) arrived in the South Pacific in January 1943. After engaging in much action along New Guinea and the Philippines, the ship was damaged by a mine on February 14, 1945, while operating off Corregidor. *(U.S. Naval History and Heritage Command)*

Lieutenant Dow H. "Doc" Ransom Jr., ship's doctor aboard *La Vallette*, was beloved by his shipmates during the war and by his civilian patients afterward. His sense of humor and dedicated care made him one of the most popular members aboard the destroyer. *(From the Dow Ransom Collection)*

Crew from the *La Vallette* dip Doc Ransom into the water as he transfers from one ship to his destroyer via a breeches buoy. Ransom enjoyed the prank pulled on him by the enlisted, who knew the officer would view the moment as the fun event it was meant to be. *(From the Dow Ransom Collection)*

Elmer Charles Bigelow's actions off Corregidor on February 14, 1945, helped save *Fletcher* from sustaining irreparable damage. In sacrificing his life to extinguish fires that threatened to ignite an ammunition magazine explosion, Bigelow was awarded a posthumous Medal of Honor. *(U.S. Naval History and Heritage Command)*

Orvill Raines encountered kamikazes in the Philippines and at Okinawa aboard the USS *Howorth* (DD-592). *(Courtesy of Meredith McComb, Destroyer History Foundation)*

With crew of the *Nicholas* watching from on deck, the Japanese destroyer *Hatsuzakura* brings out naval officers and harbor pilots to conduct Halsey's Third Fleet into Sagami Wan, just outside Tokyo Bay. *(National Archives)*

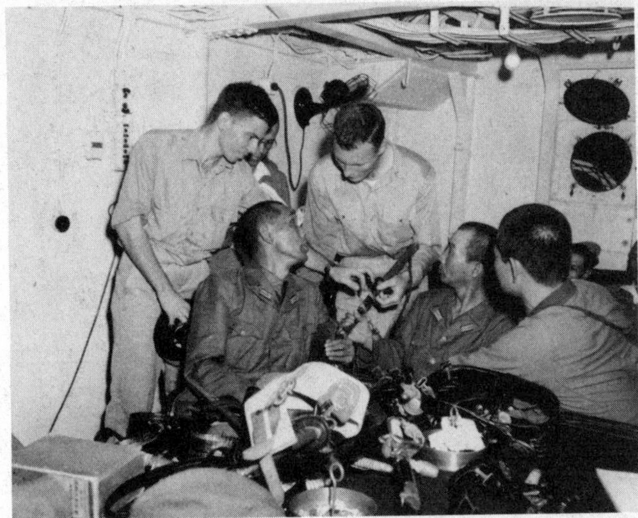

Two *Nicholas* officers confiscate a sword brought aboard the ship by a Japanese naval officer assigned to help pilot the Third Fleet into Sagami Wan. *(National Archives)*

Various ships of Halsey's Third Fleet, including *O'Bannon*, *Nicholas*, and *Taylor*, are anchored in Sagami Wan shortly before the surrender ceremonies. In the background, the sun sets behind Mount Fuji. *(National Archives)*

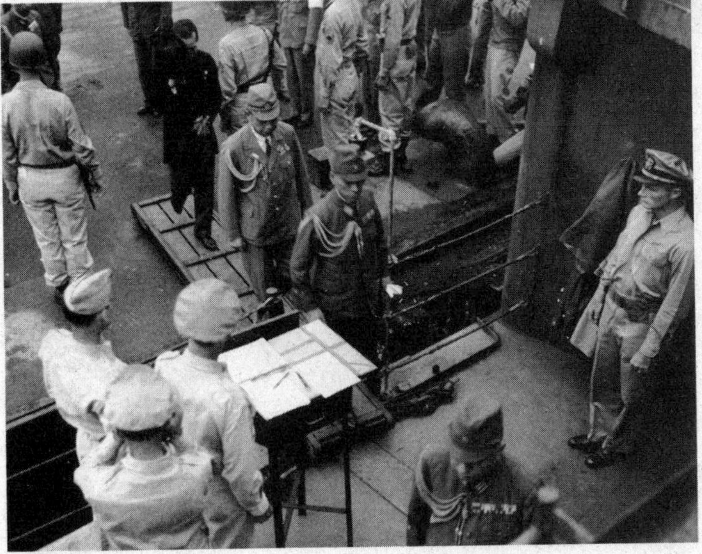

Members of the Japanese delegation come aboard the *Nicholas* prior to the surrender ceremonies. *(National Archives)*

Nicholas officers inspect briefcases brought aboard the destroyer by Japanese officers assigned to the surrender delegation. *(National Archives)*

At age seventeen, Seaman 1/c Robert Whisler was the youngest member of the crew aboard *O'Bannon. (From the Robert Whisler Collection)*

Robert Whisler in 2015, in his Gladwin, Michigan, home enjoying retirement with his wife, Lucille. *(From the Robert Whisler Collection)*

In Kula Gulf, 165 *Helena* survivors drifted to Japanese-held Vella Lavella Island, northwest of Kolombangara. When coastwatchers radioed the news to Guadalcanal that a large group of Americans was hiding in those jungles, Ainsworth arranged a rescue operation. At a conference aboard *Nicholas* attended by MacDonald, Ainsworth ordered one group of destroyer transports and their escorting destroyers, including *Taylor*, to retrieve the men, while four of McInerney's destroyers—*O'Bannon*, *Nicholas*, *Radford*, and *Jenkins*—remained farther out to engage any Japanese warships in the area. "Our job was tough," said MacDonald, "but the *O'Bannon* was willing to do anything to get those boys back."[20]

Late in the afternoon of July 15 the quartet left Tulagi for Vella Lavella. Three hours later, *Taylor* and three destroyers departed with the two destroyer transports. MacDonald chose his words carefully when addressing the crew upon entering the Slot: "Tonight we are going on a mission that might be called dangerous. I hope we will not see any action tonight. This is one night we are not looking for any trouble."[21]

Japanese aircraft descended on the quartet throughout the night. "We had to maneuver nearly all night in a black sea," said MacDonald, "while Japanese airplanes overhead circled us like vultures, dropping bomb after bomb. They are great pyrotechnicians and their flares made us visible again and again." He added, "I think it was the worst night we ever spent, because we couldn't do much about the attack." Despite those risks, his men "stayed through that night like steel."[22]

When they arrived off Vella Lavella, deck lookouts joined radar and sonar crews in searching the waters and beaches for the enemy. The transport group evaded Japanese contact by hugging the Vella Lavella coast, but MacDonald operated farther from shore to draw enemy fire while the transports moved in to rescue the *Helena* survivors. The ploy worked, as the transport group, which included Lieutenant Commander Benjamin J. Katz in *Taylor*, removed the 165 survivors from Vella Lavella's northeast coast.

In the Battle of Kula Gulf, Ainsworth sank two Japanese destroyers but lost a light cruiser and failed to prevent the enemy from landing reinforcements. Ainsworth again shackled the destroyers to his cruisers instead of employing them as an independent force. In a letter to Halsey one week later, Nimitz wondered if Ainsworth's force was too large for proper maneuvering in the tight area, and asked Halsey if the destroyers should be trained to act as a separate unit. "I am convinced that if studied consideration is given to the employment of destroyers by divisions, or better by squadrons, we shall get better results."[23]

For their actions, both *Nicholas* and *Radford* received a Presidential Unit Citation, which is granted when a crew performs above and beyond the norm, and *O'Bannon* added another page to an already sparkling record that would eventually result in a similar citation. Navy Crosses went to Lieutenant Commander Hill of *Nicholas*, Commander Romoser, Lieutenant Commander MacDonald, and Captain McInerney, and posthumous Silver Stars to Lieutenant Jetton and Ensign Hedrick. *Strong* survivors, hoping to keep their ship's name and spirit alive, petitioned the Navy to build another ship bearing the same name and man it with the surviving crew and officers.

Halsey wrote Ainsworth that it was "a grand night's record for an aggressive leader backed by indomitable officers and men. We will miss the *Helena* but she took many times her weight in Jap meat. You paved many miles of the Tokyo Road last night." Turning his attention to McInerney and his Desron 21 destroyers, Halsey wrote that their actions in Kula Gulf had added "further laurels to the combat team which struck thorns in the Jap. Well done." Nimitz jumped in, praising the "high leadership, stout heart, and fine ships."[24]

People in the United States, already aware of *O'Bannon* and the vital work performed in the Solomons by Halsey's destroyers, gained additional appreciation for the nation's tin cans that held the line in the South Pacific. A nationally broadcast radio program called *The First Line* turned the spotlight on Romoser and his *Radford* crew, calling Romoser "the commanding officer of a crew of men who haven't the faintest idea of the meaning of the word 'impossible.'" Terming the sailors "real destroyer men," the program, which included Romoser as a guest, included Romoser's comment, "Old Squadron Two-one has given the Japs the one-two, eh, gentlemen?" After taking listeners through the battle, the radio interview ended with the narrator explaining that the program "has brought you a story of courage and loyalty typical of the men of your Navy as they fight in the First Line."[25]

The drama back in Kula Gulf, however, had not ended.

"A One-Man Army"

Alone in the gulf with the departure of *O'Bannon* and *Chevalier*, the men on Miller's raft and accompanying net took stock of their situation. Only five of the more than twenty survivors were unharmed, and when Miller, the senior officer present, could not at first take over due to his injuries, Lieutenant Hackett stepped up. He figured the best bet to reach friendly forces was to try for Rice Anchorage, but the five made little headway paddling in the gulf. One close call occurred when a Japanese powerboat sped out from Kolombangara and directed fire in their vicinity, but in the darkness the Japanese failed to locate Miller's group. The boat circled the area a few times, concluded the water was free of Americans, and returned to shore.

The next morning Miller was clearheaded enough to take over. When a rubber landing raft floated near, a few able men swam out and retrieved it. Miller told Lieutenant Hackett to take some men and use the bigger boat to reach shore, now about ten miles distant. Hackett's exhausted group succeeded later that afternoon, and they found a small shelter where they rested and cut open coconuts with Hackett's sheath knife.

The men soon began to explore the area, but under the boiling sun they began stripping off all their clothing until, except for shoes, they were completely naked. They devoured a cache of eggs found at a deserted village and eventually, with the help of friendly natives, safely reached the Marines at Rice Anchorage.

The next day Miller ordered a second group shoreward in the remaining raft, hoping that one of the two groups would survive and tell rescue teams about those remaining in the water. Floating in the middle of Kula Gulf, Miller and six other survivors battled an oppressive sun, hunger, and thirst. Pain from the pressure against Miller's diaphragm bolted through his chest with each breath, and several other men in the netting died from similar internal injuries caused by the sinking *Strong*.

Over the next two days Miller's group drifted with the tides. When Miller awoke on the morning of July 8, he found that the net had floated to within one hundred yards of shore. The abler among them paddled with their hands to land the group on a tiny islet off the end of Arundel Island across from Vila. Miller stumbled ashore with five other men, including one officer, Lieutenant Oberg, and there they rested for two days, draining the juice from the few coconuts they could crack open.

On July 10 Lieutenant Oberg succumbed to his injuries. Knowing they could not remain on an island lacking fresh water, Miller and his four companions paddled across the half mile of water separating the little island from Arundel. After two hours, with Miller sitting in the back and kicking to aid the healthier men, the group crawled out of the netting and collapsed on Arundel's shore.

They remained a few more days at an abandoned Japanese lean-to that adjoined freshwater springs and coconut trees. When one of the men died on July 13, only four of the original twenty-three who had made it to the life net and rafts were alive. The next day Miller started bleeding profusely from his internal injuries, and he thought his chances of survival dimmed further.

After almost being discovered by enemy patrols scouting the island, Miller moved the men off the beach. The quartet inched along the southern edge of Hathorn Sound, but after three miles they made camp when Miller, who appeared to be on the verge of collapsing, began passing clotted blood from his rectum. That night, as the other three slept, Miller decided that if he was too weak to continue the next morning, he would order the trio to leave him on the beach and strike out for friendly forces.

When dawn brought no improvement, Miller told the men to save themselves. They objected to leaving their officer behind, but he gave them a direct order and told them to take their equipment with them. Miller kept for himself a small pocketknife with broken blades and a parka, which the three supplemented with some opened coconuts, two Japanese beer bottles filled with fresh water, and extra tins for drinking. Miller, certain he was making his final stand, handed his shoes to one of the barefoot men. "When they finally left me late in the morning, he was crying like a baby," Miller said of the man to whom he gave his shoes. "They felt they were deserting me and hated to go, but they had to obey orders." Once the three left, Miller, thinking he would soon be dead, drank almost the entire supply of water. Somewhat refreshed and at peace with his decision, Miller "lay down there to die."

As the hours passed, the competitiveness to succeed that had made Miller excel at Alabama returned, and he regained the desire to live. Late in the afternoon of July 17, in pain from his injuries, thirsty, and famished, the former quarterback "held a little conversation with the Lord."[26] He promised that if God granted rain and delivered fresh water to him, he would do everything in his power to live. That night the skies opened in a four-hour deluge, enabling Miller to refill the two bottles and drink his fill.

After a decent night's sleep Miller, leaning on a staff and with a blanket draped over his arm, set out for a spring one mile away at the northern tip of Arundel. Hampered by his injuries and in a weakened condition, Miller needed half a day to cover two-thirds of the distance across an open salt flat uncovered by the low tide, much of it consisting of coral rocks that cut deep into his feet. Before Miller reached the spring, an aircraft flew his way, giving him momentary hope for rescue, but bullets from a Japanese fighter dissuaded him of the delusion. Miller was able to extricate from his neck and left wrist the fragments from bullets that shattered against rocks, and then he resumed his trek, which ended later that afternoon at the spring and its welcome waters.

The next morning Miller cracked open a coconut by hammering it against a rock. He gulped the refreshing juice, and for the first time since his ship sank, Miller swallowed solid food, the coconut meat. Bolstered with the abundance of fresh water and coconuts, Miller began regaining his strength.

After a few days of evading Japanese patrols, Miller decided that if he was to survive, he would have to locate a more sheltered hiding spot. Each day for the next five days he ignored the pain from his injured feet to scout the area around the spring. On the fifth day he found a good location deep in the jungle, a spot nestled amid large mangrove trees and shielded on all sides by thickets and branches. Miller fashioned a bunk from palm fronds and shaped a lookout position thirty feet high in the trunk of a mangrove tree. Until he was either captured, killed, or rescued, thought Miller, this camp would be home to him and the collection of lizards that reduced the mosquitoes and red bugs that afflicted Miller.

On July 26 Miller hobbled to the beach when he saw a low-flying American plane. Waving and shouting, Miller enticed the pilot to drop lower and circle several times, during which the pilot "looked me over very carefully, often being so close that I could see the plane crew so well that I could almost identify them if I saw them again."[27] The plane veered away, making an energized Miller believe that a rescue craft might soon follow, but nothing arrived.

Miller continued to operate from his hiding spot, eluding patrols and working on a raft after the Japanese left. He worried that his foot wounds, which had begun to fester, would prevent him from gathering coconuts or running to the beach whenever an American plane flew over, but his greatest fear was being spotted by Japanese soldiers in the troop barges and supply boats that nightly ran down Hathorn Sound from Vila and passed by his camp on their way to Munda.

A week later he heard a craft coming up the channel in a different direction from that normally used by the Japanese. He climbed a tree to see an American PT boat quietly moving along the shore while the troop barges churned toward the boat from the opposite direction. When the Japanese neared the PT boat, the American vessel sprayed the enemy troop barges with its machine guns and killed the soldiers. The boat then turned the guns toward the jungle in case any Japanese lurked there, requiring Miller to seek cover. As the boat left, Miller tried to draw their attention. Rather than shouting that he was an American, which often drew fire because the Japanese had used that ploy to trick Americans into stopping their fire, Miller climbed to the tree lookout post and started singing the Marine Hymn. Unable to hear Miller over the boat's engines, though, the American vessel departed, leaving the officer stranded for a second time.

The next morning Miller ransacked the Japanese bodies and retrieved shoes, socks, a bayonet, two hand grenades, and five tins of beef. Although the meat tasted horrible, Miller consumed one every other day to rebuild his strength. That afternoon he again ran to the beach when an American aircraft flew over. Like the first, this plane circled several times to determine whether the man was American or Japanese before dropping a package with a compress bandage, a small bottle of iodine, and a chocolate ration bar. Miller quickly applied the iodine to his lacerated feet but, just as had happened earlier, no rescue craft came after the plane left.

Before long the Japanese came across the pilfered bodies; the discovery caused them to increase the frequency and strength of their patrols. The next night Miller spied five enemy soldiers moving along the beach toward his hiding spot. He waited until the group was thirty yards away, then rose and, as if he were the quarterback in front of the home crowd at Alabama, "lobbed a nice thirty-yard pass with one of the grenades."[28]

The following morning he retrieved from the bodies official records, photographs, additional hand grenades, uniforms, raincoats, pup tents, haversacks, bayonets, ammunition, five tins of meat, and soap. This time he buried the group and hid the location with plants. Then he used the soap to remove some of the remnants of oil that still covered portions of his body.

Each night after the PT boat attack, the Japanese posted hidden machine gun squads along the Sound in hopes of ambushing any subsequent vessels. Three times Miller crept from his camp until he was within tossing distance and destroyed the machine gun squads by hurling grenades into their midst.

On the morning of August 16, the drone of another American torpedo bomber, piloted by Marine 1st Lieutenant James R. Turner, awakened Miller, who ran to the salt flat and waved a towel at the plane. Turner was prepared to shoot until he spotted Miller's red beard, which he concluded identified the figure as an American. Turner reversed course and flew to Munda to report the sighting to his superior officer.

Given that the earlier two sightings had not resulted in rescue, a dispirited Miller expected more of the same this time. An hour later, however, a seaplane piloted by Major Goodwin R. Luck lifted him out of his doldrums. "My emotions were beyond description," Miller wrote of seeing the rescue plane.

To land near his beach, Luck had to fly within 2,000 yards of Vila on Kolombangara and circle within range of Japanese guns. When Luck landed on Hathorn Sound, Miller started to wade to the plane, but Major Vernon A. Peterson, in charge of the attempt, waved him off. He told Miller to wait until he could inflate a rubber boat and move closer to the weakened officer. While Peterson inflated the boat, Miller returned to camp and collected the Japanese documents, then walked back the short distance to the reef where Peterson waited with the rubber boat. Luck flew Miller to Munda, where doctors inspected the lieutenant and where Miller enjoyed "my first real meal since the night of July 4. I had lost forty pounds during the forty-three days I was missing."[29] The former quarterback remained at Munda for two days before being flown first to Guadalcanal and then to Espiritu Santo before arriving in Noumea.

On September 15 Miller received the Navy's highest honor, the Navy Cross, from none other than the First Lady, Eleanor Roosevelt, who was then in the middle of a lengthy tour of Pacific military installations. While visiting the base hospital, at Admiral Halsey's request Mrs. Roosevelt pinned the Navy Cross and Purple Heart with Gold Star on Miller, whom the *New York Times* identified as "a one-man army who attacked three Japanese machine-gun nests and one patrol, killing at least a dozen Japanese, while marooned for thirty-nine days on Arundel Island, northwest of New Georgia."[30]

The Navy Cross cited Miller's actions while abandoning ship, his freeing two shipmates who had become entangled in lines, his actions in guiding the survivors to land, and his exploits in destroying Japanese machine gun positions after he ordered the healthy men to leave. Newspapers trumpeted his achievements, magazines added to the accolades, and comic books issued accounts of Miller's deeds. The result of the adulation was further notice on the home front for Miller's ship, *Strong*, as well as for *O'Bannon*, *Nicholas*, and the other destroyer crews who had stepped in for the battleships and cruisers and performed so admirably as a crucial ingredient in Admiral Halsey's efforts to stem the Japanese advance. Their comrades in the South Pacific had already recognized their daring exploits; now people back home were taking notice as well.

"A Great Mass of Flames and Explosions"

Over the next four months Desron 21 was involved in three other major surface engagements with the Japanese, all brought about by efforts to halt the Tokyo Express from rushing in more reinforcements. Senior commanders continued to frustrate destroyer skippers by keeping their ships tied closely to the cruisers, but some tactical alterations gave hope that one day destroyers could display the offensive wallop they packed.

On July 12, another sweltering afternoon, *Nicholas*, *O'Bannon*, *Taylor*, *Jenkins*, and *Radford* joined other ships to steam up the Slot and intercept the Japanese. MacDonald's raw crew had earlier been unnerved by the ferocity of surface engagements, "but by this time my boys were getting over the great fear of the battle of Guadalcanal and as I used to tell them not all battles are as terrible as that one."[31]

When the next morning reconnaissance aircraft spotted the Japanese, to MacDonald's dismay Ainsworth formed the usual one-column battle disposition, with his cruisers nestled protectively between two groups of destroyers. Instead of immediately opening with a torpedo launch, he delayed firing until he closed the range to seven thousand yards. Rear Admiral Shunji Izaki, who had swept down from Rabaul with the light cruiser *Jintsu*, five destroyers, and four destroyer-transports, now carried a radar-detecting device that picked up the electric impulses from US radar. He launched his torpedoes at 1:08 a.m., one minute before Ainsworth gave his belated order to attack. Those sixty seconds made all the difference.

Japanese torpedoes hit the Australian cruiser *Leander*, killing twenty-eight and knocking her out of the battle, but American salvos ripped into *Jintsu*, disabling her steering gear, followed by two Desron 21 torpedoes smacking into *Jintsu*'s after engine room and Number Two stack. The cruiser split in half and sent Izaki and most of the 483 officers and men to the bottom.

At that point Ainsworth decided to pursue the fleeing enemy. When radar picked up an unidentified group of ships closing on the area, Ainsworth wasted seven minutes trying to determine whether they were Japanese or part of his destroyer screen. By the time he gave the order to fire, another wave of torpedoes had struck his two cruisers and the destroyer *Gwin*. The cruisers were able to steam away, but *Gwin* had to be scuttled.

Izaki's Japanese destroyer-transports successfully unloaded their reinforcements. In giving his life and losing a cruiser, Izaki succeeded in his main mission and knocked three American cruisers out of the war, one permanently. Combined with Kula Gulf a week earlier, the battle again revealed shortcomings in American surface tactics. In both actions Japanese torpedoes churned toward their targets with Ainsworth's guns still silent.

The Long Lance torpedoes continued to confound Halsey and Nimitz. Fleet intelligence examined a retrieved Long Lance in early 1943 but failed to disseminate the results to Halsey. The commander of the stricken *Helena* warned Ainsworth to draw no closer to his foe than ten thousand yards, a distance that would offer a better chance to evade the weapons, but Ainsworth, believing no torpedo could accurately strike at such long range, disregarded the caution.

MacDonald and other destroyer commanders wondered if they would ever be freed to operate on their own. The next surface engagement proved the validity of their arguments, even though Desron 21 destroyers were not a part of it.

Benefiting from the latest radar and from the development of Wylie's combat information center to collect and evaluate fresh information, Captain Arleigh A. Burke and Commander Frederick Moosbrugger improved night fighting tactics and handed destroyers the methods they needed to operate independently. Hugging the Kolombangara coastline to cloak the movements of his six destroyers, in the August 6 Battle of Vella Gulf Moosbrugger surprised four Japanese destroyers running a thousand reinforcements into Kolombangara. As Burke had suggested, he split his ships into two columns, launched his torpedoes near midnight, and executed a fast turn to the side, from where he directed a cascade of fire that ripped into the enemy. "The havoc caused the enemy by the torpedo attack was terrific," reported Moosbrugger later. "The whole area was a great mass of flames and explosions which continued without interruption under the continuous pounding of our forces until all the enemy except a few survivors had perished."

Within fifteen minutes of commencing the attack, Moosbrugger sank three of the four enemy destroyers, killing nine hundred, while absorbing no casualties. He concluded that "our destroyer doctrine is sound," claimed that "surprise throws the enemy into utter confusion," and recommended that destroyers should operate as independent units.[32]

Halsey disseminated Moosbrugger's report to every commander. Although Desron 21 skippers were absent from the battle, the outcome vindicated their views. Their hope was that other commanders would emulate Burke and Moosbrugger in future contests.

Emperor Hirohito wished the opposite. He expressed his growing dissatisfaction when military advisers informed him of the deteriorating conditions in the Solomons. "When and where on earth are you ever going to put up a good fight?" he asked his military. "And when are you ever going to fight a decisive battle?" When an army general apologized for the turn of events, Hirohito replied, "Well, this time, after suffering all these defeats, why don't you study how *not* to let the Americans keep saying 'We won! We won!'"[33]

Captain Thomas P. Ryan, the commander of Destroyer Division 41 and the officer who would soon succeed Captain McInerney as the commodore of Desron 21, incorporated Moosbrugger's success in the next engagement, the August 18 Battle off Horaniu. A mid-August Marine landing on Vella Lavella returned the squadron to intercept Japanese barges, torpedo boats, and destroyers, including Hara's *Shigure*, and prevent them from bringing in more troops to meet the Marine land advance.

Ryan commanded *O'Bannon*, *Nicholas*, *Taylor*, and *Chevalier*. Hara launched his torpedoes first, and within ten minutes thirty-one Long Lances were speeding toward Ryan. He outmaneuvered each torpedo and ordered his ships to commence fire.

Shells from *O'Bannon* and her three sister ships straddled Hara's *Shigure*, "kicking up pillars of water and spray." When another barrage a few seconds later bracketed Hara's ship, and a third barely missed *Shigure*, sending water into Hara's face, Hara strained into the darkness for the telltale gun flashes that would divulge the American position. "I realized now that we were confronted with the enemy's new flashless powder we had all heard rumored about. That, combined with his radar-controlled guns, presented a formidable opposition."[34]

While the Japanese screen kept the American destroyers occupied, the barges crept toward shore and successfully landed four hundred troops, although Ryan's four Desron 21 destroyers sank two sub chasers, two torpedo boats, and one other craft. Both sides claimed victory, but the destroyers, operating as a separate unit, had accounted themselves well.

October handed Desron 21 its next major surface engagement, the Battle of Vella Lavella, when *O'Bannon*, *Chevalier*, *Taylor*, *La Vallette*, and two other destroyers rushed to the Vella Lavella area to intercept nine enemy destroyers intent on extricating its forces from the island. The American destroyers had just started back to Tulagi from patrolling the Slot throughout the night of October 5–6 when they received orders to return to Vella Lavella. "We were all fairly tired from having been up all night and under the strain that always goes with the anticipation of battle," wrote MacDonald. He delivered his usual talk over the loudspeaker, cautioning the crew that the ship might soon again be in battle against nine Japanese destroyers. "Nine ships against three destroyers," said Yeoman Roupe of the *Chevalier*. "The odds now were more than overwhelming. They were astronomical. If we had any sense, we were the ones to turn tail and run."[35]

The odds improved when three of the Japanese destroyers veered toward shore, leaving six destroyers, including Hara's *Shigure*, to meet the Americans. When the two forces pulled within seven thousand yards of each other, *O'Bannon* and *Chevalier*, joined by *Selfridge*, launched thirteen torpedoes, one of which tore into a Japanese destroyer, and followed half a minute later with salvos from the five-inchers.

The Japanese responded by planting a torpedo into *Chevalier*'s port bow opposite an ammunition magazine. The torpedo ripped off the bow back to the bridge, hurled crew into air, and stunned the skipper, Lieutenant Commander George R. Wilson.

"I looked around to find that the pilothouse was a mass of wreckage," said Yeoman Roupe. "The radio had been blasted off the bulkhead and lay on the deck in twisted ruins. The binnacle was smashed. The navigator's desk hung grotesquely by a single remaining shred of steel. A 20mm gun mount had crashed through the forward bulkhead. Pieces of glass and other unrecognizable debris covered the deck." Roupe left the bridge to look over the side. "The whole forward structure of the ship was gone, clear back to the bridge. Dark whirlpools of water gurgled along the crumpled steel plates below. The bridge itself hung precariously over the water."[36]

The damaged bow caused *Chevalier* to swerve out of control and into a minor collision with the next ship in line, MacDonald's *O'Bannon*, which was partially blinded by her own gunfire smoke. Machinist's Mate 1/c Burt Gorsline of *Chevalier* had just started toward the depth charges when "something made me turn. I saw the USS *O'Bannon* crash head on into our starboard side at the 20mm mounts, just where I had been. She knocked those guns and shield up against the after deckhouse and on top of the after engine room's forward escape hatch on the main deck, jamming it shut. Her overhanging bow wiped out the K-guns on the starboard side as we slid past her."[37]

With a damaged ship wedged into *Chevalier*, MacDonald expected the Japanese to finish what they had begun, either with a Long Lance or with bombs dropped by aircraft that "were just buzzing around us like mad. Why they didn't drop bombs right down our stack, I have no idea."[38]

When MacDonald backed *O'Bannon* off, the action created a whirlpool that sucked some of the men into the water. MacDonald attempted to bring *O'Bannon* alongside once he saw men abandoning *Chevalier*, but *Chevalier*'s warped bow made that operation too risky. MacDonald lowered two of his boats to bring wounded across while uninjured crew jumped over the side and swam to the boats or to *O'Bannon* itself.

Lieutenant Gowen leaped over the port side of *Chevalier* and reached a life raft. When *O'Bannon* picked him up, he received an unexpected greeting from one of the *O'Bannon* crew with whom Gowen had swapped movies. *O'Bannon*'s engineer had asked him for a movie featuring Veronica Lake, a popular Hollywood actress and pinup favorite, and when *O'Bannon* rescued Gowen, "I climbed the Jacob's ladder covered with oil and soaked to the skin, glad to be still alive, and the engineer came running up to me and asked, 'Did you bring the Veronica Lake movie?'"[39]

After he had picked up *Chevalier* survivors, MacDonald hugged the coast to keep *O'Bannon* out of open water and to make his ship a less detectable target for Japanese aircraft. He relied on guts and instinct to guide him by uncharted, submerged reefs and navigate unused channels to reach Tulagi, damaged but whole.

MacDonald's efforts saved 250 of the 301 men aboard *Chevalier*. While MacDonald left with his damaged *O'Bannon*, *La Vallette* remained behind to search for survivors, after which Commander Taylor fired a torpedo into *Chevalier*'s aft magazines and sank her.

Even though Japan claimed a victory after sinking *Chevalier*, her navy could ill afford to lose even the one destroyer sunk by Desron 21's torpedoes. The Japanese were becoming more hard-pressed to find substitutes, which forced them to be more selective in deciding when to send out the fleet.

This battle ended the naval fighting in the Central Solomons and concluded Desron 21's labors in those islands. During the destroyers' tenure, Halsey had forced a Japanese retreat to Bougainville, the northernmost island in the Solomons, and had advanced 250 miles up the chain.

With the final surface action, naval headquarters in Tokyo ordered Japanese forces to withdraw to Bougainville. In the face of an already superior and constantly enlarging US military, the Japanese could only delay the inevitable. In late December, after failing to halt an American landing at Bougainville and after losing control of the waters between New Guinea and New Britain, the Japanese navy withdrew completely from the Solomons and, after more than a year of bitter fighting, yielded control of the South Pacific to Halsey.

"Destroyer Squadron Twenty-One Always Will Be Remembered"

Victory in the Solomons proved to be a critical turning point in the Pacific war. In August 1942 the Japanese had controlled those islands, appeared to be on the cusp of invading Australia, and threatened to sever the crucial supply lines leading from the United States to that continent. Through a combination of Army-Marine landings, airpower, and daring naval actions, Halsey flipped the scenario on its head. Vital to that success was the role of MacDonald's *O'Bannon* and the other destroyers of Desron 21. Lacking the glamour of the sleek aircraft carriers or the power of the imposing battleships, the destroyers darted up the Slot and sliced through Solomons channels, keeping the enemy off guard and its own crews on station.

"Like the infantry, the destroyer crews fight a dogged, determined, unromantic war," wrote Commander W. W. Hollister of the Navy Department in June 1944, "and since steady hard cruising with the constant threat of having to swap punches with adversaries three and four times their size is the rule rather than the exception the war diary of a destroyer is seldom monotonous."[40]

A scan of their war diaries would yield ample evidence of Hollister's assertion. In 1943 alone, Desron 21 destroyers engaged in more than one hundred major actions and countless minor ones, including bombardments, mining operations, antiaircraft duels with fighters and dive-bombers, submarine hunter-killer missions, and major surface engagements. They ranged from the multiple-warship Kula Gulf battles to a handful of vessels mining Blackett Strait, from bombardments at Vila-Stanmore to the rumored *O'Bannon* potato attack against a submarine. Those one hundred actions do not include the innumerable runs Desron 21 destroyers made up the Slot, the escorting of troop transports, the patrolling of harbor entrances to shield anchored ships from enemy submarines, and the other tasks handed to them by Halsey. The intervals between the actions offered little respite, as ship maintenance and resupply swiped additional hours from their already overtaxed schedules.

In recognition of their contributions, in January 1944 Admiral Nimitz paid homage to the Desron 21 crews who had helped force the Japanese from the Solomons. He said their record was "in a sense the record of one entire phase of the Pacific war." Commissioned fewer than eighteen months earlier, the ships and their inexperienced crews had no sooner arrived in the South Pacific than they went toe-to-toe with Japanese warships in November, and the crews "did not get much rest after that."

In January, continued Nimitz, the destroyers had bombarded Munda and Vila-Stanmore plantation. In February the destroyers had been "busy helping derail the 'Tokyo Express,' which was trying desperately to reinforce Guadalcanal," and in March they had returned for more bombardments of Munda and Kolombangara. In between, they had fended off air attacks, escorted ships, and nightly plied the Solomons for signs of enemy activity.

Nimitz mentioned hunter-killer missions in February, air attacks in April, and mining operations in May. He added that the record of the destroyers through June 1943 alone "would have been an impressive one," but it was only enhanced when they again slugged it out with Japanese cruisers and destroyers in Kula Gulf and rescued hundreds of *Helena* survivors in a daring operation.

Nimitz ended his praise with stirring words: "With little time to rest or to overhaul, and with a great variety of missions to accomplish, our destroyers, generally, have performed magnificently, and with little of the publicity which has accompanied the exploits of other units of the Naval Service. Our destroyers have truly been the silent part of our service, but their exploits and their capabilities are well known to those who have to know."[41]

They were so well known, in fact, that three of the ships—*O'Bannon*, *Nicholas*, and *Radford*—received Presidential Unit Citations, awards reserved for only those crews who excelled as a unit. *Nicholas* and *Radford* earned theirs for their roles in rescuing *Helena* survivors, while the Navy honored *O'Bannon* for their entire body of work performed by the officers and crew from September 1942 through October 1943.

After operating in the Solomons for more than a year, the destroyers of Desron 21 finally enjoyed a breather at the end of 1943. *Nicholas*, *Fletcher*, *Radford*, *Jenkins*, *Taylor*, and *La Vallette* participated in the massive November 1943 Central Pacific landings in the Gilbert Islands, where they covered the Marine landings at what became known as "Bloody Tarawa" and where *Radford* was credited with sinking a submarine, and then continued as a unit to the United States for a much-deserved respite from the war.

Damaged during the October surface engagement, *O'Bannon* left Espiritu Santo in November on her way to the Mare Island Navy Yard, near San Francisco, California. MacDonald stepped to the loudspeaker to address his men. This time, however, he did not prepare them for another fight or mission. "I have just received word that we are to proceed, as soon as temporary repairs have been made, to the West Coast," MacDonald told his crew.

After a year of continuous action, he and the ship were returning to the United States, where the destroyer would be overhauled and the men could visit loved ones. They boasted an enviable record since arriving in the Solomons in September 1942, but almost as remarkable was that she had accomplished her tasks without losing a single member of the crew, a record that earned her the appellation "Lucky *O*." When it came time to leave the South Pacific, she departed not because of anything the Japanese had done, but because of a collision that occurred when she rushed to the aid of a squadron mate in distress. As MacDonald took *O'Bannon* out of Tulagi on her way home, one of the crew, accustomed to steaming in the opposite direction toward the enemy, remarked to an officer, "Don't seem right not meeting any Japs tonight, Mr. Pfeifer."[42]

The ships of Desron 21 had earned their break. *O'Bannon*, *Nicholas*, and *Fletcher*, plus the other seven destroyers that constituted first the Cactus Striking Force and then Desron 21, helped reverse the nation's military fortunes with their stirring actions in the Solomons. Operating at a time when the country's battleships had yet to recover from the debacle at Pearl Harbor and before the vaunted fast carrier task forces had been organized, the ten destroyers stepped in, sharing the risks with similar vessels until American shipyards could rebuild the fleet with new battleships, cruisers, and especially the fast carriers that dominated the war's second half. In the crucial moments of late 1942 and throughout 1943, when some at home wondered if the war could be lost, *O'Bannon* and the destroyer crews provided the answer, holding a tenuous line in the South Pacific to give the nation and its military the time they needed to rebound. The majestic aircraft carriers and the sleek cruisers were the glory ships of the Pacific war's latter half, but Desron 21 and other destroyers made their work possible by thwarting the Japanese in the war's initial half.

The squadron lost three ships, emerging from this period bruised and battered but proud. Desron 21 had manned the South Pacific front lines for Halsey, in the process checking the Japanese advance toward Australia as well as reversing the fortunes of war in that vital area.

Admiral Halsey had been scraping the bottom of the military barrel in those trying days in the Solomons, but when he most needed an antidote to the Japanese poison, and when the country's morale begged for good news from the Pacific, Desron 21 stepped in. As the squadron departed the South Pacific, the veteran destroyerman acknowledged his debt to those crews.

"On your detachment from the South Pacific Fighting Forces I wish you Godspeed," Halsey wrote. "Your habit of getting into winning scraps with the Japs made history. Destroyer Squadron Twenty-One always will be remembered when Cactus, Munda, Kula, Vella, and 'the Slot' are mentioned. You may be sure I will welcome you back with open arms anytime, any ocean."[43]

A voyage back to the United States handed the crews a chance to recharge their batteries and prepare for an inevitable return to action. They would need that pause, as a frightening form of warfare involving a single enemy pilot in a single airplane awaited.

PART III

DESRON 21 SWEEPS TO VICTORY

CHAPTER 8

CLIMBING THE NEW GUINEA LADDER

Few in the Navy, officers and enlisted alike, had ever met a man like Lieutenant Dow H. "Doc" Ransom Jr. The ship's doctor aboard *La Vallette*, Ransom displayed amazing intellect at an early age, breezing through high school classes on his way to being accepted into Stanford University's premed program at age sixteen. It seemed natural that he would follow in the footsteps of his father, a highly esteemed physician in Madeira, California, who made house calls at all hours in the California countryside. His father loved his occupation and made a comfortable living with it, but what most appealed to the younger Ransom was that his dad helped people. That powerful aspect was hard to ignore.

Ransom was more than the sum of his talents in the classroom, however. He loved sports, and the good-looking young man was popular with male and female students alike. His piercing brown eyes transfixed classmates, especially girls, and his broad smile and appealing laugh made people gravitate toward him. He certainly had reason to boast, but what most attracted others, in and out of the Navy, was that, despite his many attributes, he avoided praise and attention. He served in a noble profession, to be sure, but once in the Navy he felt that his duties were no more noteworthy than those of the seaman scrubbing the decks or the machinist's mate laboring below. He insisted that everyone call him "Doc" rather than the more formal "Dr. Ransom," whether he was in the wardroom helping his patients or in an officers' club sharing a drink with comrades. His medical skills, concern for the men under his care, and affability led one sailor to write that "'Doc' Ransom was a giant amongst men."[1]

After receiving his medical degree, Ransom entered the Navy and served an internship at Oak Knoll Naval Hospital in Oakland, California. In mid-1943 he headed to sea aboard the *La Vallette* as the ship's doctor, recording his impressions each day in a diary he surreptitiously maintained throughout the war. He received his battle initiation during the tiring days and nights running up the Slot, when his destroyer rarely seemed to enjoy much time off. "Sent out our liberty party and we were ready to go on the beach," he wrote on October 3, 1943, after the ship had pulled into Purvis Bay, "when an emergency signal came through at 1530 [3:30 p.m.] to steam out and again go 'up the Slot' with some other cans." He added, with that quiet sense of humor that quickly made him a favorite aboard the *La Vallette*, "Here we go again!"[2]

Most of Doc Ransom's duties centered on maintaining the crew's general health. Like every Navy doctor, he treated minor cuts and illnesses and performed appendectomies and a few other emergency surgeries. In between, he delivered a series of lectures emphasizing the need for sanitation aboard ship and while on liberty, where the crew was certain to encounter women of questionable morals. Ransom disliked these lectures, which he found repetitious and the men found boring, but like anyone else aboard *La Vallette*, he had to carry out his duties, no matter how distasteful they may be.

"Doc Ransom was a nice fellow, kind," said Quartermaster 2/c Martin Johnson. "He had to be available, and had sick call in the morning for anyone who needed to see him for anything. Guys with infections from shore, etc. He was like an old country doctor, and men saw him when they needed. The guys liked him. We saw him more as a doctor than as an officer."[3]

Ransom's days ran from the mundane to the dangerous. His diary is peppered with thoughts about drills and meals, interspersed with remarks about preparing to engage the Japanese. "One would never know the day of the week or date if it weren't for writing this since every day is alike aboard," he wrote on August 8, 1943. "Have been going through intensive fire, collision, man battle stations, etc. all day. I turn in about 8 p.m. because we are routed out every morning at 0500 [5:00 a.m.] for drills."

Later that month, however, he recorded that he "spent most of the day in Sick Bay wrapping instruments etc. for sterilization" because the skipper announced "that on Sunday we are leaving with a huge task force for operations against the Japs. Everyone is getting a little jittery already." Two days later, he noted that the task force had left for "a destructive (we hope) raid on the Marcus Island which is 900 miles directly East of Tokyo," and that "since we are going through heavily infested sub and mine waters . . . we have been told the chances of returning are against us."[4]

No matter where they were, whether in port or during frightening moments at sea, the crew could count on Doc Ransom to be there for them with his always-present smile and soothing them with his calm demeanor. He countered the war's gravity with humorous limericks that he often broadcast over *La Vallette*'s loudspeaker.

Ransom credited squadron unity for lending stability amid the tribulations of war. Unlike the social gaps that divided students in high school, officers and enlisted were in this endeavor together. They shared the same risks and reveled in the same joys of serving aboard a ship and in a destroyer squadron.

"Arrived at Tulagi (Purvis Bay) at 1300 [1:00 p.m.]," he wrote on October 5. "All the officers of the other cans and ours went over to the 'Des Slot Officer's Club'—a clearing in the jungle along the beach, drank some beer and went swimming. The mosquitoes were terrific. Came back to ship for supper and a movie."

Five days later he wrote about seeing an old friend who was also posted to Desron 21. "Gene Groshart came aboard from the *Nicholas* #449 and we chatted a while. It was sure good seeing someone you knew down here. His ship and mine are in the same squadron so we should see one another often." Later that day, after Groshart had returned to *Nicholas*, Ransom attended the movie shown on the ship's fantail, where his joviality again amused the crew. "Went to another movie tonight. I typed and mimeographed the songs I had written and passed them out to the boys. They get a kick out of singing them on the forecastle before the movie starts."[5]

Six months after joining *La Vallette*, Ransom and the ship became part of the opening Central Pacific assault when the destroyer, along with Desron 21 mates *Fletcher*, *Radford*, *Jenkins*, *Nicholas*, and *Taylor*, lent support to the Marines landing in the Gilbert Islands. The armada of ships stretched wide across the ocean as it inched toward the objective. "A big fleet joined us this morning," he wrote on November 2. "What a sight!" Carriers, battleships, cruisers, and destroyers sliced through the waters in impressive numbers. "Looks like trouble ahead for the Japs."

The next day Ransom watched the force deploy in a battle line, an image of power and splendor that almost brought tears to his eyes. "When you see eight of those 80 million dollar battleships in a line with their guns pointing, it makes you feel damn good to be an American and gives you a lump in your throat."[6]

"The Scourge of the Jap Fleet"

When the squadron's work off the Gilberts was completed, the six ships, including Ransom's *La Vallette*, set a course for Pearl Harbor. Crews looked forward to enjoying a break from the war in one of the most luxurious ports in the world, but surprises awaited.

The first came from the array of ships then in Hawaii. For many, their only previous glimpse of the harbor had been on their way to the South Pacific, when the remnants of the Pacific Fleet lay on the harbor's bottom. Gleaming battleships, cruisers, and destroyers now occupied every inch of water. The desperate days of war, when Desron 21 crews and those of a few other destroyers stood alone in the Solomons, were over. Admiral Nimitz delivered the second surprise with a message welcoming the squadron to Pearl Harbor. "Special greetings to you veterans of the Slot," the admiral gushed. "We are proud to have you with us."[7]

The last, and best, surprise came with the news that instead of remaining in Hawaii, the crews would leave the next day for the United States and a three-week respite. "Land at 1330 [1:30 p.m.] and we docked at 1512 [3:12 p.m.]," Doc Ransom recorded in his diary on December 9. "Just as soon as we pulled alongside the *Fletcher* we heard news we could not believe—that Squadron 21—six of us were leaving tomorrow for Mare Island [near San Francisco]! Shipmates were dancing around, patting each other on the back and yelling their lungs out."[8] The squadron—minus the damaged *O'Bannon* and the three sunken ships, *De Haven*, *Strong*, and *Chevalier*—passed beneath San Francisco's famed Golden Gate Bridge on December 15 to begin their leave in the United States.

The ships berthed not far from their squadron mate *O'Bannon*, which had arrived at Mare Island the month before to repair the damage sustained in the Solomons. Since *O'Bannon* was the first squadron ship home, she had garnered a larger proportion of the praise directed at Desron 21.

For the first time in well over a year, the *O'Bannon* crew could let its guard down. As MacDonald said, "The strain was off, because we had been going up and down that Slot night after night, turned around many times after we were just about ready to go back and told to go back up again." MacDonald explained that a sojourn home "was great relief because then they realized that there was going to be time out for something, whether it was rest and relaxation or something, because we had to be repaired before we could go back."[9]

News of the squadron, and particularly of *O'Bannon*, had preceded their arrival, paving the way for a flurry of adulatory newspaper articles, radio programs, letters, and honors. The Navy started with a December press release that appeared in the *New York Times* and hundreds of newspapers around the country.

"The 'Little *Helena*' is back at a West Coast port" after "more than 14 months of continuous fighting in the South Pacific," stated the release, which hit newsstands as Doc Ransom and the rest of the squadron pulled into San Francisco. During that time, according to the Navy, MacDonald and his crew participated in five major surface actions, conducted numerous bombardments of Japanese land installations, battled air attacks, supported landing operations in the Solomons, and helped sink ten ships, all without suffering a single casualty. They rescued the crews of sunken ships, including "the famous one in which American destroyers stole into Jap-held Vella Lavella and took off survivors of the *Helena*," and took on "so many convoy assignments up the 'Slot' to stop the Tokyo Express that her Commanding Officer had difficulty in counting them."

In the press release, MacDonald told home-front readers, "Seventeen months ago we set out to make our way in the war areas of the then Jap-controlled South Pacific with a crew which was, for the most part, green and untrained in Naval warfare." His men, he added, had no idea of the "hectic—sometimes almost hopeless—year that lay before them; but they quickly learned to blaze the way through the Japs with gunfire and torpedoes." The release included the sentiments of one *O'Bannon* enlisted man who, while he was thrilled to be back home, was eager to return to the South Pacific. "We want to get back there and dish out lots more 'Little *Helena*' hell to those _______ Nips."[10] While the release may have exaggerated certain things, it and the many newspaper articles that flooded the nation conveyed the Navy's esteem not just for *O'Bannon* but for the entire squadron, and showed the nation's appreciation for what Desron 21 had accomplished since October 1942.

"There is something strange and wonderful about the story of the United States destroyer *O'Bannon* and what she did in the Southwest Pacific," wrote correspondent Robert Waithman. "She went out of a navy yard on the East Coast of America in the desperate summer of 1942, a new ship with a crew so green that three in every four of them were putting to sea for the first time. She made her way into waters where a few allied warships were somehow holding back the tide of Japanese conquest. For fifteen months she fought continuously by day and night." Waithman explained that the months in the Solomons were "a hell of flame and noise" that taxed the young crew and their skipper, whose hair "was black not long ago but now is thickly flecked with grey."[11]

Other articles lauded the ship that had been nicknamed by others "Little *Helena*" and by the crew "Little Hellion" or "Lucky Mick," a reference to her Irish name and the good fortune bestowed upon them. "In fact," gushed one article, "the *O'Bannon*'s record reads like a timetable of the South Pacific war. Whenever and wherever something was doing, *O'Bannon* was there," evading bombs and torpedoes with a skill that crafted among the crew "a fatalistic belief in the good luck of their little ship" and faith in their skipper. "By now her name is almost a legend. Through all her adventures she had an Irishman's luck, as had the man, too, after whom she was named."[12]

Comic books and the nation's top newspapers heralded their achievements. *Heroic Comics* featured the destroyer in four pages, concluding that "the hard-hitting *O'Bannon*, with its eight 5-inch guns and AA batteries, won enduring fame in its battle against terrific Jap odds." Not to be outdone by its rival publication, *Real Life Comics* offered six pages calling the ship "*O'Bannon*, the scourge of the Jap fleet" and lauding MacDonald as "the most frequently decorated officer in the United States Navy. But more important than medals is an unsurpassed fighting record, the constant quest for battle which pitted the *O'Bannon* against entire Jap fleet units."[13]

The *New York Times* quoted MacDonald as saying, "I never went into any action that I was not frightened. That's what I told my men when they came to me for encouragement." MacDonald explained that "American boys are not exactly afraid to die, but our boys' greatest desire is to live," and that while much of his crew had come to the ship fresh from training camps, the men proved that Americans were "definitely the best fighters in the world."[14]

One of the nation's most popular columnists, H. I. Phillips, often created poems to mark special occasions. Upon *O'Bannon*'s return, he composed one titled "*O'Bannon* and Mac," part of which proclaims:

> *O'Bannon*, oh baby, oh boy, what a ship!
> In any engagement, oh man, she's a pip!
> MacDonald's her skipper; Oh my, what a pair!—
> A tough "daily double" for Japs anywhere.

O'Bannon-MacDonald . . . their names ring afar;
Wherever there's fighting, well, that's where they are;
This prayer comes from Tokio o'er the seas:
"Keep *O'B* and Mac far away from us, PLEASE!"[15]

Nationally broadcast radio programs lauded *O'Bannon* in January, and in April the popular radio drama *March of Time* profiled MacDonald. Letters poured in for the officer from parents of crew, acquaintances, and the public. Vernice Johnson, the mother of Melvin E. Pitts, a seaman on *O'Bannon*, wrote MacDonald that her son "told me what a fine commander you were, how you prayed for them and how you would ask them to trust in God. I am proud my son served with you and I am proud he served on a destroyer like the *O'Bannon*." She went on, "While you all were in the South Pacific I prayed day and night for God to go with the *O'Bannon* and each member of the crew," and that "I prays [*sic*] that each one of our boys will give Uncle Sam true service to their country. Because we love this land of ours."[16]

The mother of Fireman 1/c Richard J. Hall of *O'Bannon* wrote, "Richard praised you to the skies when he was home at Christmas and I am gratefull [*sic*] that he was under your protection during those trying times in the Pacific." She concluded, "I guess you hold a soft spot in every boy's heart on the *O'Bannon*."[17]

Lieutenant George Philip, who had so ably served as gunnery officer under MacDonald and had left the destroyer a few months earlier, wrote MacDonald, "I am extremely proud I served in her and I am always glad to tell people I came from the *O'Bannon*." Lillian Celmer, a member of the WAVES who had met MacDonald on a December flight, congratulated him after reading news accounts of his ship: "Getting this war over with is the prime purpose of everyone right now and when one small unit can do so much toward that end—it is understandable that the whole country should go a little mad over the thing."[18]

A woman named Betty Keating loved the article about MacDonald and his ship that appeared in *American Magazine*, and felt compelled to write the commander about what their story meant to her: "I am sure it will be a real inspiration to all the readers of the *American Magazine*, and there is no doubt but that all of us are greatly indebted to you fellows in the Navy for holding off the Japs as you did in the early days of the war, with so little help from home. The courage of the 'boys in blue' and the splendid guidance and supervision of men like yourself should make us ever grateful to the U.S. Navy." She wished MacDonald luck, and hoped that "you always stick to your policy of talking to your men and being 'regular' with them."[19]

He even heard from a member of a religious order. "Ever since I read an article written by you for the July *American* about your adventures of war with the good ship *O'Bannon*," said a letter signed by a Dominican nun using the title Sister Superior, "I have wanted to tell you how inspiring that article is and how I wish every American could have the opportunity of reading it."[20]

In being awarded ten decorations, MacDonald received the lion's share of praise for his capable leadership, even though he felt awkward overshadowing what he considered a top-notch crew, a group of young men upon whose efforts the ship built its record and without whom he could never have achieved any success. "On the chest of black-browed MacDonald," wrote *Time* magazine, "whose hair has turned an iron grey, the Navy has pinned the Navy Cross and Gold Star in lieu of a second, the Legion of Merit and a Gold Star, the Silver Star Medal and two Gold Stars."[21] He and his crew received the Presidential Unit Citation for its work, only the fourth such honor bestowed to a Pacific destroyer since Pearl Harbor, not simply for one action, as often happens, but for the body of work he and *O'Bannon* had amassed in the Solomons in sixteen months. In joining *Nicholas* and *Radford* as recipients of the esteemed honor, Desron 21 was the only destroyer squadron in the Pacific to have three ships so recognized.

During his time home, the *O'Bannon* skipper traveled to New York to marry Cecilia. After that happy celebration the Navy, impressed with his work in the Slot, asked MacDonald to join a new destroyer commander school in Norfolk, Virginia, to instruct prospective commanders in how to manage a crew and how to best incorporate the combat lessons MacDonald had absorbed during his time in the Solomons. The Navy hoped that MacDonald could impart his experiences to other officers and make them better prepared to face the trials to come.

"New Guinea and 'Dugout' MacArthur—Oh Joy!"

Doc Ransom would have loved to enjoy more time with family and friends than the three weeks the ship remained in the United States, but the war needed Desron 21 back in the Pacific. After mixing in much fun with business—*La Vallette* practiced landing operations off the California coast around San Clemente Island—on January 6 he and his shipmates again said goodbye. "We shoved off for the Hawaiian Islands at 1830 [6:30 p.m.]—leaving good old USA for how long?" he wrote in his diary upon departure.[22]

The other destroyers gradually filtered out to the war zone, arriving at different times depending upon when their ship's overhauls were complete. Seaman Chesnutt and *Fletcher* left California on January 13, while *O'Bannon* and *Nicholas* left home waters on January 24. Seven days later, *La Vallette* participated in the Marshall Islands assault by bombarding the tiny island of Roi. According to Quartermaster Martin Johnson, the destroyer blasted Japanese defenses "such as gun emplacements, pillboxes, machine gun nests, troop trenches and pits, and buildings. We were inside the 2000-yard line of the beach thus we were the closest DD [destroyer] to bombard that day there." He added, "The whole island was covered with dust, smoke, and debris that it was hidden. How anyone survived this I do not know for it was the heaviest bombardment ever made. Everything moved along favorably. We could see the marines advance and the enemy trying to stop them."[23]

The officers and crews returned to altered roles when they reached the Southwest Pacific. After so gallantly holding the line in the Solomons and giving shipyards and factories time to build the nation's arsenal, they now slipped into a more traditional role for destroyers. Screening for enemy submarines and aircraft while accompanying carriers and cruisers and bombarding landing areas dominated much of their time. The hazards that had earmarked the Slot as dangerous waters followed them to new arenas, but at the same time they were introduced to other forms of warfare. One from the sky, in particular, added a fiery terror that imperiled every crew along the way to Japan.

Back in the Pacific, Doc Ransom's new year began inauspiciously when a Marine with a bowel obstruction was transferred to *La Vallette* for treatment. Ransom operated and removed a perforated appendix, but the Marine failed to respond. "The patient went into a coma 11 hours post op and died one hour later," Ransom recorded in his diary on January 14. "We didn't give him much of a chance as soon as we saw what was up in the abdomen." Upset over the loss of his patient, a glum Ransom "went to bed dead tired. First surgery of 1944 and lost the patient—hope that isn't a bad omen."

His humor returned later that month when he transferred to another ship in the convoy to treat a man with dengue fever. After tending to the patient, Ransom radioed *La Vallette* that he was ready to be transferred back by breeches buoy, a line of ropes connecting the two ships. Ransom quickly suspected the crew had a surprise in mind. "By the time they got the breeches buoy rigged practically the whole crew of our ship was on top side and I knew something was up." As Ransom crossed in the breeches buoy, he spotted one man snapping photographs with his camera, "and when I got half way across in the buoy, they slacked the line from our ship and I slowly lowered into the water up to my hips." As everyone burst into laughter, "they rapidly pulled on the line and I shot up in the air about 20 feet—a wonder it wasn't 200 feet!" The doused physician finally climbed aboard, wet but unharmed, to backslaps and more laughter. "The crew's spirits rose high as a result of the incident and it was pretty funny. Takes a good ship to have a little horseplay when we're only a few days away from Jap islands."[24]

His mention of Japanese islands was a reference to the invasion force headed toward the Marshall Islands, where the six destroyers that had steamed together to the United States—*La Vallette*, *Fletcher*, *Radford*, *Jenkins*, *Nicholas*, and *Taylor*—provided gunfire support for the Marine landing units. Standing two thousand yards offshore, the ships opened fire as the Marines churned toward their objectives in the Marshalls.

"Signal tower blown down, buildings destroyed, crane hit, runway damaged and shore batteries hit," wrote Seaman Chesnutt in his diary about *Fletcher*'s successful bombardment.[25] Japanese shells landed close by and crew spotted a torpedo slicing alongside, but the ship avoided damage.

After the landings, *La Vallette*, accompanied by *Nicholas* and *Taylor*, escorted two aircraft carriers to Pearl Harbor. During the trip Ransom treated a sailor who cut his hand on a can of peanuts, but otherwise sick bay remained quiet. Arrival in the tropical paradise was bittersweet. The crew could enjoy the scenery, but they knew that once in port they would lose their beloved skipper, Commander Robert L. Taylor. On March 10, Commander Wells Thompson boarded *La Vallette* to take over the reins.

"Well today it happened and no one was very happy about it," wrote Ransom. "Captain Taylor was relieved by Captain Thompson. Our old captain gave a swell farewell speech to his officers and crew and with tears in his eyes he had to stop before saying all. He admitted he didn't want to leave the 'Dilly.' As he sailed away in the gig, he kept waving back and never did turn around until he was out of sight." Ransom admitted that "it was a mighty quiet wardroom tonight."[26]

That calm would not long remain. The next month Desron 21, which had operated in the South Pacific with Admiral Halsey for such a crucial portion of the war, entered the Southwest Pacific, where the squadron operated under the supervision of another renowned commander, General Douglas MacArthur. Their time off New Guinea and the Philippines presented different challenges to those they had faced in the Slot, and serving under the imperial MacArthur was certainly a stark contrast to their months with the sailor-friendly Halsey. "This will be our new theater of operations and the rest of Squad 21 will join us next week," Doc Ransom wrote in his diary. "We are leaving the 3rd Fleet command to join with the 7th Fleet."

The physician enjoyed working in the South Pacific for Halsey, an admiral who held every sailor's respect for his aggressive way of fighting and his high regard for the men under his command. MacArthur, however, was another story. Like any American, Doc Ransom followed the general's exploits with admiration; there was no denying MacArthur's courage. But the unassuming physician could not relate to MacArthur's love of the spotlight. Already sailors talked about the general's war communiqués, which usually included only one name for every action—MacArthur's. Officers joked that upon entering the Southwest Pacific and service with MacArthur's Seventh Fleet, they would from that moment on remain anonymous and overshadowed by MacArthur. "New Guinea and 'Dugout' MacArthur—Oh joy!" Ransom scribbled in his diary.[27]

Ransom dismissed those thoughts as *La Vallette* steamed on a course for Cape Sudest in southeastern New Guinea, for he had too many details to handle. He had lectures to deliver on prophylactics and venereal disease, and he had to treat crew sick with fever or banged up from manning the machinery.

He was surprised at the noise a destroyer made at sea. He expected thundering sounds in battle, but even when the ship slowly glided through the Pacific, far from the sites of those Kula Gulf surface engagements, noise seemed everywhere. His squadron mate aboard *Nicholas*, Sonarman Douglas Starr, claimed that even "in a normal sea, a destroyer is a noisy ship. There's always the whine of the wind and the slap and splash of the sea along the hull."[28] The ship's screws smacked the water whenever they broke the surface, and the anchors knocked against the hull with each lift and fall of the bow. Ocean waters swept across the forecastle, and the steady drum of the engines mingled with the barked commands from chiefs to deck crew.

It seemed that the next operation might be another big one, Ransom thought as a collection of military brass boarded *La Vallette* at Cape Sudest. Sixteen high-ranking officers from the Navy, Army, and Marines, plus an Australian general, had selected the ship as their observation post for what Ransom would soon learn would be MacArthur's final steps in securing all of New Guinea and establishing a launching pad for his long-awaited move north to the Philippines. Over the next four months American forces would land at six locations on New Guinea's northern coast, from Aitape in the middle to Sansapor at the western end. The first three landings—at Aitape, Humboldt Bay, and Tanahmerah Bay—would unfold in April, followed by landings at Biak Island off New Guinea's coast in May and Noemfoor Island and Sansapor in July. If all went according to plan, MacArthur would gain control in New Guinea and be ready to take the next step on his way back to the Philippines.

The eight destroyers of Desron 21—Ransom's *La Vallette*, *O'Bannon*, *Jenkins*, *Nicholas*, *Hopewell*, *Howorth*, *Radford*, and *Taylor*—would play key roles in each operation, mainly by escorting the landing craft to the beaches, lending gunfire support as the troops crashed ashore, and keeping enemy submarines and aircraft at a distance. For the April landings, the first six destroyers accompanied the landing teams to Aitape while *Radford* and *Taylor* sailed to Humboldt Bay, a body of water that, along with Tanahmerah Bay, flanked the important port of Hollandia.

The large collection of destroyers and transports, backed by escort carriers and cruisers, rendezvoused northwest of the Admiralty Islands two hundred miles above the objectives on April 20. The next day the flotilla split into groups, with each heading toward its designated landing area. MacArthur, who watched from the cruiser *Nashville*, later wrote of the impressive array, "Just as the branches of a tree spread out from its trunk toward the sky, so did the tentacles of the invasion convoy slither out toward the widely separated beaches in the objective area."[29]

In between the typical demands of sick bay, which currently housed a man with appendicitis, Ransom prepared his surgical instruments and medical supplies in case the ship sustained casualties, and checked to see that his pharmacist's mates were ready. "Continuing 'en mass,'" he wrote on April 21. "Very hot today and we are almost on the equator. Got all medical material ready for instant use. At 1700 [5:00 p.m.] our group turned south and the force will split into 3 invasion groups—ours for Aitape, the others for Humbol[d]t Bay and Hollandia. We strike at 0630 [6:30 a.m.] tomorrow and we will shell the beach from a short distance out. Hope they don't have too big or too many guns firing back! We shall see."[30]

Ransom waited at his station in the ship's wardroom for the naval bombardment from *La Vallette* and the other escorting ships. A ten-minute naval barrage at 6:00 a.m. lifted to allow aircraft to bomb and strafe the beaches, then resumed as the troop-laden landing craft moved toward shore. Nine waves reached the beach against minor opposition from the small Japanese defense detachment.

"It was quite a show and we surprised them all right," Ransom wrote of Aitape. "We, alone, fired 440 rounds of 5 inch into the landing area." After the troops hit the beaches, "we then remained in the water stopped and watched the show and waited for any additional fire support orders—which never came."[31]

While Ransom's day passed without incident, that night another Desron 21 destroyer, *Jenkins*, sighted what they called a "suspicious object in water" while on antisubmarine patrol. When the task group commander ordered the ship to investigate, the skipper, Commander Philip D. Gallery, at first concluded it was a drifting log. To be safe, he ordered the object illuminated and destroyed by his 20mm gun crews, but Gallery and everyone else on deck received a surprise. "Numerous Japs seen to dive off barge or raft, which was repeatedly hit," Gallery explained in his action report. Crew then used their forty-five-caliber pistols to shoot at the Japanese, killing most while forcing the rest to swim toward a nearby island. "Scratch one barge. Killed eight Japs. Resuming patrol," reported Gallery to the task group commander.[32]

"Watched the dive bombers attack the village of Aitape where 1000 Japs still remain," recorded Ransom from his quiet post aboard *La Vallette*. "The *Jenkins* sank a barge of Japs (8) trying to escape last night. Lots of our planes flying around all day and no zeros [Japanese fighter aircraft] in sight. The destroyers will probably return tomorrow for Sudest. Hope so, it's dull here."[33] Unfortunately, on the way back a *La Vallette* sailor fell overboard and, despite a thirty-minute search by the ship, was lost.

Radford and *Taylor* encountered something very similar at Humboldt Bay 150 miles to the west. The destroyers and two cruisers, with MacArthur watching from *Nashville*, covered the unopposed landings before spending the remainder of the day maneuvering offshore to provide fire support for the units moving inland.

"Our World Was the Ship We Were Standing On"

After the rush of action experienced in the Slot and during the Kula Gulf battles, it is not surprising that the crews of Desron 21 found New Guinea's four-month succession of landings and escorting tame by comparison. No one wanted a repeat of those earlier trying times, but the less frenetic pace made the days pass slowly. For a unit that had built a reputation based on nonstop action and combat with the Japanese, New Guinea was both a welcome break and a letdown. They enjoyed the breather, but thought they could do more than merely escort landing forces.

Despite the change of pace, officers tried to maintain the same level of readiness that the Solomons had required. The example of the sunken *Strong*—a key component of the squadron one instant and a battle casualty the next—remained as a cautionary tale that death was never far distant. Even minor operations had to be taken seriously.

To fill the gaps, Doc Ransom added to what had become a favorite tradition aboard *La Vallette*—his humorous recitations over the ship's loudspeaker. Men at their stations looked forward to hearing his voice waft throughout the destroyer, offering a joke, a humorous poem, or a clever characterization of one of his fellow shipmates. Ransom brought a touch of home to a crew already weary of a war that separated them from loved ones.

Submarine hunting occupied some of the hours. Ransom's shipmates in the sonar room sent underwater electronic pings that returned an echo whenever they hit a solid object. While the object usually turned out to be a whale, a school of fish, or an outcropping of rock, the crew still had to man stations in any event.

Ransom preferred submarine hunting to being posted on listening watch, where *La Vallette* stood off a harbor's entrance and scanned the depths with her sonar to prevent submarines from sneaking by and attacking the ships inside, or to conducting one of the many gun drills. Antiaircraft crews had to be sharp, but Ransom expressed surprise that gunnery practices often expended $25,000 worth of ammunition.

The few breaks while in Humboldt Bay gave the men from different squadron ships the chance to mingle. Tied up to tenders, crews walked back and forth to other ships, where a sailor could socialize or find a welcome at a poker game or craps. The downtime helped cement squadron unity, and even though their main loyalty was to their individual ships, the sailors boasted that they served in the top Pacific squadron. "We were all part of the same squadron and had pride in both it and in our ship," said Ensign Gabelman.[34]

Unlike the talks to crew about social diseases, Doc Ransom enjoyed the first-aid lectures, in which he showed the men how to apply the battle dressings and use the morphine syrettes that were stored in boxes at each gun station and other strategic posts. He provided additional training to Chief Pharmacist's Mate J. R. Cloward, and taught the four pharmacist's mates how to organize the aft dressing station and how to direct stretcher bearers. He emphasized medical education because he recognized that in the heat of battle, a prepared pharmacist's mate could save lives that poorly trained ones might lose, and a medically knowledgeable gunner or torpedoman could keep the man next to him alive until Doc Ransom or one of the pharmacist's mates arrived.

Battle wounds sometimes came from unexpected places. On May 2, Ransom treated an Army infantryman rushed to the destroyer when another soldier's rifle accidentally discharged and hit him in the face. "Removed several pieces of fragments from forehead and eyelids," Ransom wrote on May 2. "One eyeball was lacerated and the choroid hanging out in shreds. Dressed him up and transferred him after we returned to Humbol[d]t Bay at 1600 [4:00 p.m.]."[35]

No one enjoyed much rest or privacy while on a destroyer at sea. When Ransom and his shipmates donned the naval uniform, they handed over any expectations they had for privacy. "You learned that your days of privacy were over while you were in the Navy and they would not return until you were back in civilian life again," wrote Seaman 1/c James Fahey, of his ship, the USS *Montpelier*, a cruiser almost twice as long as Ransom's *La Vallette*. "When you ate, slept, took a shower, etc., you were always part of the crowd, you were never alone."[36]

If that was true for Fahey aboard a cruiser, it was even more so for Doc Ransom and anyone else stationed on one of the Desron 21 destroyers. As Sonarman Starr of *Nicholas* put it, "Our world was the ship we were standing on—a block long and a street wide."[37]

Privacy and trust became a bigger issue when a crew suffered under the hands of an unpopular skipper. Seaman Tom Chesnutt on *Fletcher*, like everyone else aboard that destroyer, valued the skilled combination offered by Lieutenant Commanders Cole and Wylie and their immediate successors, but in some eyes the current skipper, Commander John L. Foster, failed to measure up. Chesnutt and a few shipmates applied the label "GQ John" to their new commander, who called an inordinate number of general quarters and drills throughout the day, something many skippers minimized when in the war zone. "Under Cole, when GQ was called, we manned it in less than a minute," said Chesnutt. "Under 'GQ John,' who wanted to be a career Navy guy and called many GQs, it took us five to six minutes."[38]

Chesnutt's diary contained numerous references to the incessant drills and restrictions imposed by the skipper. "Hot as heck, no cool area," he wrote on June 25, 1944. "This crew is getting in a bad way. This Ole Man is fast losing a fighting ship. His drills, inspection and no rest is driving them NUTS. A few days in a cool, civilized world could do wonders."

In August they steamed into one harbor, but Foster refused to give the men a respite. "Not one Jap plane or ship has been spotted anywhere near here in weeks," Chesnutt complained in his diary. "This damn Ole Man says this ship needs more drill and GQ and no liberty or recreation. I'd hate to see a ship with a crew any lower in feeling."

Later that month Foster removed the coffeepot Chesnutt and the others had placed in the radar shack, and imposed a ban on reading and writing letters while at that station. "This life is hard enough without his screwy ideas. I have heard many of the fellows wish for this ship to get hit, so as to return for repairs. I'll take my chances and sometimes I think death would be better than continuing this way. A fellow needs a rest once in awhile."

When one of the decoder wheels used in the typing machine to decode top-secret messages disappeared, Chesnutt's predicament worsened. The decoder was similar to a typewriter, but with the proper decoder wheel, when the clerk typed the groups of letters received in a coded message, the decoder wheel spun out the letters in readable order. Foster was so incensed at the disappearance that he stopped his crew's mail from leaving the ship and banned anyone from leaving the *Fletcher*, even just to cross onto ships tied alongside, until the wheel was located.

"No one seems to be making any progress on the wheel matter," Chesnutt wrote after two weeks of the restrictions. "This ship has really fallen from the top of the list as a good fighting ship. No one cares what happens. The Skipper isn't for the men or at least, he doesn't show it. Morale of crew is way down. They need a rest. One of the boys in our gang got a letter his father died and for two weeks now he has been unable to write his mother."[39]

The contrast between Foster and other skippers emphasized the value of a skilled captain. MacDonald employed frequent chats over the loudspeaker to keep his men informed and bring some levity into their days. He was a stickler for drilling as much as anyone, but when he entered the war zone, MacDonald kept it to a minimum, figuring the men were at their posts long enough as it was. The men appreciated his thoughtfulness and responded in kind.

MacDonald created a happy crew, one that continued with his successor, Commander R. W. Smith. Seaman Whisler and some buddies secreted beer in the bilge below the carpenter shop, and from time to time they had a sample. "Captain Smith found out and made us carry the beer up to the foc'sle," said Whisler years later, "and he said we were going to throw away the beer. All the guys were ready to cry! He didn't though."[40]

Ransom enjoyed life aboard *La Vallette*. He received plenty of mail from home (ten letters on May 8 was his record), the ship's library offered a diverse collection ranging from Shakespeare and Dickens to Wild West stories and magazines, and whenever possible he and the crew gathered on the fantail to watch Hollywood films, which were swapped between crews when ships were in port. The *La Vallette* was not large enough to stage baseball games, but boxing or wrestling matches vied with fantail entertainment as popular attractions.

The few stops in back ports such as Espiritu Santo or Noumea offered at least a semblance of a vacation. Whisler and his buddies guzzled the two bottles of beer handed to each man and cheered their team in the baseball contests pitting crews from different ships in highly wagered affairs, while Ransom headed to the officers' club for a stronger beverage and small talk with fellow lieutenants and ensigns.

Even for those aboard a good ship, time at sea eventually weighed on them. With nothing but water stretching to the horizon on every side, the ocean became little more than a repetition of never-ending waves, rain squalls, and steaming equatorial heat.

"This is monotonous and time drags," Ransom wrote in the midst of the New Guinea operations on May 3. "Surely hope this [escorting] duty isn't permanent with L.S.T.'s," he wrote in June, adding he "thought we had graduated from that league!"[41] Escorting convoys and providing fire support were fine, but bloody battles remained to be fought before he could return to his family and home. As far as Ransom was concerned, they might as well get right to them.

"Another Day's Work Done for MacArthur"

They did just that at the end of May when *La Vallette*, *Fletcher*, *Radford*, and *Jenkins* crossed Geelvink Bay on New Guinea's northwest coast to complete the operations at Biak, Noemfoor, and Sansapor. These moves would give

MacArthur control of airfields along the western edge of New Guinea, while an added landing at Morotai to the northwest would provide air bases and logistical support for the leap north to the Philippines. "Maybe now we can see a little action instead of sitting around," wrote Seaman Chesnutt in June.[42]

Like the first three, these four operations unfolded without complications. The entry Quartermaster Johnson made about Sansapor, "No bombardment was necessary. Leaving in the evening," could have been repeated for each mission.[43]

A moment of excitement marked the Biak landing when on the night of June 8–9 *La Vallette* and three other squadron destroyers pursued enemy ships attempting to bring in reinforcements. "Everyone was excited that we were finally getting a chance to hit some Japanese ships," said Quartermaster Johnson, who was at the wheel of *La Vallette*.[44]

With his medical instruments and supplies laid out in the wardroom below, and with *La Vallette* second in the column behind *Fletcher*, Ransom had a front-row seat on deck as the chase ensued. For six hours the destroyers pursued their quarry, once narrowing the distance enough to open fire with their main batteries. Japanese torpedoes twice passed by the column, and shells dunked into the water fifty yards off *Fletcher*'s bow, but no ship was hit.

Shortly before 2:30 a.m. the destroyers slowed and reversed course. They had been ordered to break off the chase if by that time they had not already formed for an attack, as continued pursuit would place them dangerously close to enemy bases. Ransom returned to the wardroom after "one of the most exciting nights we have ever spent," but he was "very disgusted to think the Japs were able to get away" despite his ship having traveled 140 miles.[45]

At Noemfoor on July 2, one of the *La Vallette*'s 20mm guns exploded during firing and sprayed shrapnel into the gun crew. Deck hands rushed four men to the wardroom, where Doc Ransom treated one with multiple fragment lacerations to both thighs, one with superficial wounds to his face and left shoulder, a third with wounds to his abdomen, and a fourth with his face covered with blood. A fifth sailor on another 20mm gun was bowled over by the blast from a nearby five-inch battery, and although the man coughed up blood for a time, Ransom nursed him back to health. "All of the above men were treated and are recovering satisfactorily," wrote their skipper, Wells Thompson, in praising his ship's doctor.[46]

During the final landings at Morotai, when *La Vallette* received orders to join *Fletcher* and pursue three enemy ships reported to the north, Ransom reacted jubilantly. "We were happy and excited for such an assignment, but after speeding up there at 25 knots we couldn't find a thing! Very disappointed and we turned back."[47]

By comparison to the Slot, New Guinea offered a sedate routine. Ransom handled minor medical mishaps, such as treating a man suffering from appendicitis and another who sprained his ankle from a fall off a scaffold. He sat up all night keeping tabs on a sailor in shock after being rescued from falling overboard, and whenever the ship anchored at a rear base he accompanied small groups of men to a hospital ship for dental work. Most days were similar to September 29, when he recorded, "Routine day. Gave typhoid shots to the crew."[48]

They did not consider routine the Japanese twin-engine bomber off Biak that was hit by antiaircraft fire. As it descended, the pilot swerved his plane in an attempt to crash into a destroyer. He smashed into the water barely short of the ship, but the spectacle of a man purposely flying his plane into a target instead of trying to save himself made an indelible imprint on those who witnessed it.

"At 1800 the *Jenkins* and three others of us formed up with eight empty L.S.T.'s and began our returns to Hollandia," wrote Doc Ransom off Noemfoor. "Another day's work done for MacArthur in which he will claim the credit."[49] Ransom hoped that the next phase, the invasion of the Philippines, would bring more rewarding work.

CHAPTER 9

THE PHILIPPINE WHIRLWIND

From ports near and far, naval units converged off the Philippines for MacArthur's planned October 20 landings. Knowing how valuable possession of the islands was to the Japanese, who feared being severed from valuable natural resources in the Philippines and Indochina, few expected to again encounter the relatively light opposition they had met along New Guinea. After landing in Leyte Gulf, MacArthur planned to move north through the Philippines and, in a subsequent series of assaults, drive the enemy from that land.

Desron 21 would again play a supporting role, but attacking the enemy in the Philippines, with their entrenched defenses and with the possibility of a powerful surface force challenging the United States Fleet, carried deeper risks than New Guinea. "Got underway at 0400 [4:00 a.m.] for rehearsal for the coming operation," Doc Ransom wrote on October 9. "We're going to be screening large troop transports this time—guess we have graduated from the L.S.T. stuff—we hope." Five days later he added, "We are off on the invasion of the island of Leyte in the Central Philippines—should be quite a show."[1]

Within four days every major naval unit involved was steaming toward Leyte Gulf and the October 20 landings. The fleet from Hollandia impressed Ransom with its size and power, but he figured that as they approached the Philippines, the crew would have been called to general quarters at least a handful of times. So far, though, no enemy aircraft had been sighted.

On *O'Bannon*, Captain Smith shared Ransom's concerns. He had informed his men that in escorting a convoy of sixty-eight ships into Leyte Gulf, they should expect enemy PT boats, midget submarines, and air attacks day and night. The destroyer had drawn within one day of the landings without incurring opposition. It seemed too easy.

Radioman 2/c Walter A. Lee of *O'Bannon* believed that Halsey's aircraft carriers "have taken care of the major opposition. We have enough ships and planes to subdue the Japs for a while anyway. Any kind of attack by the Japs will be on a small scale, in view of the plans and power dedicated to success." Even Doc Ransom started to think this first Philippine landing might be simple when, one day before the scheduled landings, they had passed within range of forty enemy airfields without being attacked. "Still no Japs attacked us so I guess Halsey is really knocking them down."[2]

Men dismissed as braggadocio the broadcasts from Tokyo Rose that promised doom. "Jap propaganda programs come in all times of the day," Seaman Chesnutt aboard *Fletcher* wrote on October 18, "telling of the defeat of the American forces and tonight they said a landing on the Philippines was impossible. If one were to be tried, it would be repulsed with heavy loss to the US. Couple days shall tell."[3]

Doc Ransom and Seaman Chesnutt had their answer when floating mines impeded their progress as the ships turned into Leyte Gulf's waters in the early morning hours of October 19. *Taylor* and *Jenkins* sank six mines with rifle and machine gun fire, but not before a seventh struck the destroyer USS *Ross* (DD-563) and forced her to limp away for repairs.

The armada slowly moved up the gulf toward the beaches. As troop-laden landing craft churned toward shore, Japanese mortars ripped into the formation, sinking or damaging nine landing craft. Enemy aircraft joined in, cutting through *Fletcher*'s fire while attacking a nearby destroyer. Another crossed *La Vallette*'s stern while on its way to strafing a destroyer, while a third plane dropped a bomb that smashed into the cruiser *Australia*, killing one and badly injuring her captain.

La Vallette patrolled along the beaches throughout the day, maintaining contact with infantry units to provide gunfire support. Both the ship and the infantry to which *La Vallette* was assigned carried the same charts, and when an Army officer radioed the coordinates, *La Vallette*'s guns turned toward that sector and opened fire. Doc Ransom was called to his station only once, to treat a sailor on a 40mm antiaircraft gun who sustained blast burns when a five-inch gun opened fire.

Around noon of landing day, several large canoes manned by Filipinos approached *La Vallette*, shouting "thank you" and "victory" in broken English. One Filipino, helped in translation by the destroyer's cook, a native of the Philippines, reported that one hundred Japanese soldiers were hiding in caves on a nearby point.

Their obvious jubilation over the arrival of the Americans delighted the crew. "The smile on their face of gratefulness and being free after 3 years was a sight to behold and the lump in your throat was as big as your fist," Ransom wrote on October 20. "That sight was well worth any risk to us." Ransom and other men handed cigarettes and candy to the Filipinos, who returned the favor later that afternoon by bringing out coconuts, bananas, and two live chickens. "There is no doubt that Filipinos are pro-American!" Ransom wrote.[4] Other Filipinos delivered a rooster to Chesnutt's *Fletcher*; the men sarcastically nicknamed the creature "GQ" and allowed it to roam about the destroyer as their mascot. The rooster loved perching along the railings behind the bridge, where it was sheltered from the stronger winds, and thrived on the frequent petting provided by the sailors. GQ added a much-appreciated touch of levity, and a bit of home to those from farms, by crowing into the loudspeaker.

Late on October 21 *La Vallette* and the escorting ships formed around sixteen LSTs and two cargo ships for the trip back to Hollandia. While they were leaving the gulf, reports flooded in telling of a Japanese surface force bound for the Philippines. The commander of *La Vallette*'s task force informed all ships on October 24 that the enemy could be expected to appear during the night, as numerous units had already been sighted approaching Surigao Strait to the south. A few hours later gun flashes thirty miles away indicated that fighting had begun in the strait. Ninety minutes later the task force commander ordered six destroyers, including four from Desron 21, to patrol the entrance to San Pedro Bay, at the northwest end of Leyte Gulf, where US ships berthed, and intercept any Japanese vessels that broke through the fighting. *Taylor* and *Jenkins* each repelled three aircraft, with *Jenkins* laying a protective smoke screen around the destroyer USS *Grant* (DD-649), damaged in the Surigao Strait action, and then shooting down a Japanese Zero that tried to finish off the crippled *Grant*.

Upon reaching Hollandia with *La Vallette*, Ransom heard additional reports of another surface engagement to Leyte Gulf's north, off the island of Samar. "Looks like the Japs are going to fight for the Philippines," he wrote. "Heard that one of our C.V.E.'s [escort carriers] was sunk and several cans [destroyers] damaged. Fueled at sea, so if ordered, we could return to Leyte immediately."[5]

Everything leading up to late October was mere prelude to what occurred next, as on October 25 the Japanese introduced one of the most feared weapons to appear in the war: the organized kamikaze assault. While there had been earlier instances of Japanese pilots diving into ships, they had been sporadic and unorganized, more the case of an aviator swerving his damaged aircraft into the closest target of opportunity. This sudden appearance of a planned kamikaze attack, however, was destruction on a magnified scale.

The first kamikazes came in low, hugging the water's surface to avoid American radar before climbing to 6,000 feet and dropping toward their targets. One kamikaze crashed into the port catwalk of the escort carrier USS *Kitkun Bay* (CVE-71), while a second immolated against the flight deck of the USS *St. Lo* (CVE-63). Other kamikazes slammed into the USS *Kalinin Bay* (CVE-68), damaged the USS *White Plains* (CVE-66), struck the USS *Fanshaw Bay* (CVE-70), and sank the USS *Gambier Bay* (CVE-73).

Doc Ransom and every sailor in the Philippines reacted with revulsion. The attacks had been sudden and fast, and they inflicted harm out of proportion to the forces committed. At the cost of one plane, the Japanese could damage or sink an escort carrier. Ransom, who devoted his life to saving men, could not understand men who purposely flew to their deaths. The actions were alien to everything he believed, and if one plane could inflict such harm to an escort carrier, what might a similar plane do to the smaller *La Vallette*? He hoped these attacks were a one-time occurrence, but his ship was due to operate in Philippine waters in the coming months, and he feared that more instances would occur.

He and others in Desron 21 did not have to wait long for the next kamikaze encounter. Ten days after kamikazes made their dramatic entrance, Seaman Chesnutt referred to "the suicide dives the Japs made on our ship. Since the beginning of the Philippine operation they have been taking a heavy toll on our ships this way." He later recorded that so many ships were being damaged by kamikazes that sailors labeled Surigao Strait "Suicide Strait."[6]

"Suicide dive bombers observed going down on TG 77.2 [Task Group 77.2]," Commander Nicholas J. Frank Sr., *Taylor*'s skipper, reported on November 29. "Large explosion and flames observed on starboard bow of *Maryland*." Six minutes later "*Saufley* reported via TBS to CTU 77.2.7 [Commander Task Unit 77.2.7] that she had been attacked by suicide dive-bombers. One had crashed into the ship causing superficial structural damage and two had landed in the water nearby. Also reported that *Aulick* had been hit by a bomb in the bridge structure." More worrisome, as far as Doc Ransom was concerned, was that *Aulick*'s medical officer was among those killed. No one was safe from a kamikaze, whether he was a sailor laboring in a gun mount or a physician treating casualties in sick bay.

Destroyer skippers alerted headquarters that it was now more crucial that American aircraft use their IFF (Identification, Friend or Foe) to radio ships below as to their identity. As a necessary precaution, Commander Frank informed his men that the frequent appearances of kamikazes, combined with numerous friendly aircraft in the area, made it difficult to keep track of every plane, "especially when friendlies are non-combatant planes with indifferent IFF performance. Therefore," he emphasized, "suspect them all. Eternal vigilance is still the price of safety!"[7]

Desron 21 destroyers may have been absent from the main portions of the monumental October 25 Battle of Leyte Gulf, but they provided crucial assistance both at that time and in the battle's aftermath. They shepherded transports to and from the landing areas, patrolled the entrance to Leyte Gulf, fought off air attacks, exploded floating mines, and rescued downed American aviators. The crews were so busy that Ransom recorded fourteen times *La Vallette* men went to general quarters on November 24.

"It's a Miracle That We Have Survived"

In December and January, Desron 21 destroyers participated in MacArthur's three-pronged advance up the Philippines' western side to gain airfields and staging areas for larger assaults on the way to Tokyo. First the military would transport and land Army units at Ormoc Bay, on Leyte's northwest side; then they would use airfields and facilities seized at Ormoc to organize and support landings at Mindoro, off Luzon's southwest coast, and employ facilities at Mindoro to support the third, and largest, assault at Lingayen Gulf, 120 miles above Manila.

Desron 21 ships faced the same tasks at each assault—escort ships to the landing areas, screen for enemy submarines and aircraft, and provide gunfire support for the troops ashore. Most planners expected the fighting to intensify as the American units moved northward during the three phases, as the Japanese were desperate to retain control of the Philippines and their vital natural resources. Complicating matters was that Desron 21 and every other ship had to operate in narrow channels and wind through hundreds of islands, always within range of enemy airfields. As a result, they would have less maneuverability against kamikaze attacks. "Things might be hot for a while," Doc Ransom wrote in his diary on December 3, a few days before the Ormoc invasion occurred.[8]

Ransom understated matters. Two days later, as *La Vallette* patrolled the southern end of Leyte Gulf, Japanese aircraft attacked a convoy entering Surigao Strait. Commander Thompson immediately turned *La Vallette* in their direction to offer assistance, but before he arrived, kamikazes smashed into two transports and one destroyer.

As *La Vallette* neared, a fourth kamikaze charged toward that vessel. Thompson ordered hard left rudder to avoid the kamikaze as shells from the ship's antiaircraft guns kicked up water geysers on all sides of the low-flying plane. At the wheel, Quartermaster Johnson thought the plane was attempting to hit the bridge, and as it drew nearer, he tried to squeeze down between the wheel and the ship's compass while still keeping a hand on the wheel. "I wanted to get out of there, but I stuck with it."[9]

"We opened fire with everything we had," wrote Doc Ransom, "and still he headed down at us." Ransom watched shells bounce off the water, much like those rocks he had skipped across a pond as a child. He felt helpless as he stood there, seeing the plane and its suicidal pilot draw closer through the fire. Finally the kamikaze exploded and crashed fifty feet off *La Vallette*'s port quarter. "The stern was covered with plane parts and parts of the Jap's body—two teeth, a forearm and part of the mandible. No damage or personnel casualties!—by the grace of God. We are sure he was hit before he crashed. Hope we don't have another day like this again." When kamikazes struck more American ships over the next three days, Ransom added, "Japs are raising hell with destroyers with these suicide planes."[10]

On December 9 *La Vallette*, joined by *O'Bannon*, Desron 21 newcomers *Howorth* and *Hopewell*, and three other destroyers, rendezvoused in San Pedro Bay and proceeded toward Ormoc for MacArthur's first step up the islands. *La Vallette* was assigned to bombard a cluster of buildings thought to be Japanese barracks, while the other destroyers focused on targets nearby.

Due to the heightened threat from kamikazes, the crew remained at stations all night. With so many enemy airfields close by, Doc Ransom was certain that sooner or later his ship would be attacked. "They were really scary," said Seaman Robert Whisler on *O'Bannon*. "There was nothing you could do but hope they got shot down."[11]

At dawn, Thompson moved *La Vallette* closer to the landing beaches to begin her bombardment. At the prearranged time, *La Vallette*'s main batteries hurled shells in the midst of the barracks before pulling back to patrol offshore. Again, Doc Ransom treated only one minor casualty when, during the bombardment, a sailor dropped a shell that fell on and broke one toe and badly cut another. The ships returned to Leyte Gulf the same day, happy to have avoided injury. Aboard *O'Bannon*, Radioman Lee entered in his diary, "Seems like the *O'Bannon* just misses everything. It is a lucky ship."[12]

They felt more fortunate when they anchored in San Pedro Bay and saw grim evidence of the destructiveness inflicted in the dangerous waters off the Philippines' western coast. They had already heard of the torpedo that on December 3 tore into the USS *Cooper* (DD-695), sinking the ship in less than one minute and taking 191 of the crew to their deaths. Now, right beside them, floated what remained of the damaged destroyer USS *Hughes* (DD-410), with twisted metal and squashed gun mounts where *Hughes*'s midsection used to be. Sailors had mingled with some of the *Cooper* and *Hughes* crews during the infrequent downtimes, making the image of the ruined destroyer more powerful. "It's a miracle that we have survived," wrote Radioman Lee after gazing at the *Hughes*, "but I don't want to speak too soon. We could get ours in the next few minutes."[13]

If kamikazes were to hit *La Vallette* during the next operation, the landing at Mindoro, they would have to punch through more than one hundred cruisers, destroyers, and transports. An immense armada of 110 ships traversed the waters, with *La Vallette* and other destroyers ringing the formation seven thousand yards from its center and powerful cruisers posted inside at each corner. A unit of escort carriers and their fighter aircraft steamed not far away, ready to supply air cover should the need arise.

MacArthur needed Mindoro so that he could establish airfields and staging areas closer to Luzon, which would be the final step of his Philippines campaign. The operation would again require Desron 21 destroyers to skirt enemy airfields and pass through narrow straits—perfect ambush sites for Japanese submarines—along much of the route. Hanson Baldwin, the respected military correspondent for the *New York Times*, warned his readers, "We may have to accept large ship losses. For the first time we have sent our shipping into the narrow waters west of the Philippines, waters that are the 'happy hunting grounds' of Japanese submarines and torpedo craft, and into areas where Japanese planes can converge upon us from many directions."[14]

December 13 passed uneventfully until midafternoon, when a Japanese plane raced five hundred feet above *La Vallette*'s bow, passed behind

O'Bannon, banked to the right, and dived into *Nashville*'s port side, causing a huge explosion and fires between the stacks. Already assigned to a recovery unit intended to aid disabled ships, Commander Thompson turned *La Vallette* toward the stricken cruiser.

Additional enemy aircraft appeared two hours later. *La Vallette* guns deflected one bomber toward American fighters, which quickly splashed the intruder, while the other planes dropped errant bombs and disappeared. Three hours later a kamikaze charged through thick fire in a dive on *Hopewell*, which had joined Desron 21 in October 1943 as a replacement for the lost *Strong*, but 150 yards off the port beam, the plane's left wing dipped sharply and scraped the water's surface, and the aircraft spun into the sea only forty yards from the destroyer. An hour later two more kamikazes approached the formation but were shot down two thousand yards off *Fletcher*'s starboard quarter. Except for *Nashville*, the force had escaped harm, but the enemy had been alerted to their presence. The next day, landing day, figured to be tougher than the Americans had hoped.

Just before daylight on December 15 *La Vallette*, *Hopewell*, and *O'Bannon* followed *Fletcher* to their fire support areas off Mindoro, later spreading out along a line that paralleled their assigned sectors. Thompson was prepared to bombard the beaches off the town of San Augustin when he spotted natives casually walking near the shore with their flocks of animals. When *O'Bannon* and *Fletcher* also reported natives and cattle in their sectors, all three skippers fired warning shots to drive the Filipinos inward and out of harm's way.

With the bombardment complete, the invasion forces headed toward shore. An hour after the first troops landed, two kamikazes plunged into LSMs (Landing Ship, Medium). While *Hopewell* rushed to their aid, another kamikaze dived toward *La Vallette*. "We fired every kind of gun aboard and we shot him down about 6,000 yards from us," wrote Ransom, "tense moments those! Luckily, he was flying so low he didn't have far to go to hit the water."[15]

Two other kamikazes raced toward *Howorth* "with unmistakable suicide intent," according to the ship's skipper, Commander Edward S. Burns.[16] Burns turned left full rudder and upped speed to twenty knots while gun crews zeroed in. They struck one kamikaze at five hundred yards, causing the plane to spiral out of control; it passed only ten feet over a five-inch gun before crashing into the water twenty feet off the starboard side. The impact hurled parts of the plane onto *Howorth*'s forecastle and spread sections of the plane and pieces of the pilot aft of the bridge. Just as the first kamikaze hit the water, Burns called for full right rudder, and thirty seconds later the second kamikaze's undercarriage scraped into the air search radar antenna, which split the plane's gasoline tanks and sprayed gas onto the deck. The right wing glanced off the port bow seconds before the kamikaze crashed in the water, dousing the men on deck with a column of water.

By 6:00 p.m. the surviving landing craft had emptied their holds and were ready to depart. *La Vallette* and her companion destroyers formed a protective screen to escort the ships out of the area toward Leyte Gulf. Doc Ransom observed in his diary: "After that things quieted down and we're all very tired again tonight."[17]

In their action reports, commanders listed suggestions about how to combat the kamikazes. Wells Thompson of *La Vallette* urged low-flying fighter patrols, radical ship maneuvering at high speed, heavy gunfire from the ship's own guns, and "eternal vigilance of personnel." Commander Burns mentioned the same, and cited "kindly Providence" as a reason his ship had so far avoided harm.[18]

The reference to Providence proved apt. With the latter half of December upon them, the destroyer crews planned Christmas celebrations that, they hoped, would provide moments of peace and calm between the actions they were likely to face in the future.

While they were at anchor Ransom crossed over to *O'Bannon* to visit an old friend, and then at sundown joined others for a picnic organized by men from *O'Bannon* and *Howorth*. As Christmas approached, the *O'Bannon* crew placed a withered Christmas tree on the ship's bow, and men on all ships listened to carols played on the radio and thought of family back home. On Christmas morning *La Vallette*'s crew gathered for a service on the forecastle, after which they enjoyed a turkey dinner with all the trimmings, including dressing, mashed potatoes and gravy, apple pie, and cigars. The printed menu contained sixteen dinner items, plus a special Christmas message from Commander Thompson. "Christmas is ordinarily a time when our footsteps turn to home and friends, to be with our loved ones," Thompson told his crew. "Unfortunately war has changed this, and made it necessary that we make our own 'home and fireside' this year right here on the ship. We have had a strenuous year, and recently have gone through some critical times together. Here we are, safe and sound, 'carrying on' as a stout ship does, and 'ready for anything." He ended his message by saying, "I wish to extend to each of you my sincere wish that your Christmas today will be a happy one."[19]

Like his predecessor, Commander Smith of *O'Bannon* recognized the toll that the holidays would take on his men. With additional strenuous days ahead, and without the prospect of leaving the combat zone for a break, he arranged what he called "fishing trips" for the crew. Each day during the holiday season a different section of the crew, with each man clutching two bottles of beer, entered the destroyer's boats for leisurely cruises about San Pedro Bay. The boats never strayed far from *O'Bannon*, but the outings gave the men a chance to relax, enjoy their beer, and return to the destroyer a bit refreshed. After six days of these outings, on Christmas Eve the War Diary cited a boost to the crew's morale and claimed that there had been "a big improvement in this otherwise non-recreational area that we have operated in for over six weeks."[20]

With luck, this would be the final Christmas away from loved ones.

Their assignments for the Lingayen Gulf invasion were carbon copies of those for Ormoc and Mindoro—screen for ships and provide fire support for the forces ashore during and after the landings. The route to Lingayen Gulf, one hundred miles northwest of Manila, again took the destroyers through narrow channels and close to Japanese airfields on Luzon, Formosa, and Okinawa.

The armada of 164 ships left San Pedro Bay for Lingayen Gulf, 1,100 miles distant. They exited Leyte Gulf and entered Surigao Strait before navigating the Mindanao Sea, where they listened to a Japanese radio broadcast promising a warm welcome wherever they tried to land.

"Going across Mindanao Sea all day," Doc Ransom wrote on January 5. "Since this is where the *Nashville* was hit last time we came up, we kept a very alert watch today. At about 1400 [2:00 p.m.] the cruisers ahead of us about 10 miles were attacked by a sub and although two torpedoes were fired no one was hit. Tense moments from now on, it looks like."[21]

La Vallette's squadron mate, *Taylor*, eliminated the submarine threat to which Ransom alluded. While searching the narrow waters between Negros and Mindanao from which the two torpedoes had been fired, *Taylor* crew spotted a midget submarine surfacing dead astern. The skipper, Commander N. J. Frank Jr., ordered right full rudder and emergency flank speed, and rammed the tiny boat as it tried to submerge. He followed with six depth charges set to ignite at a shallow depth. The explosions jarred all hands, and sailors in the ammunition magazines and engineering spaces below heard scraping noises along their hull. Oil and debris floating to the surface indicated that the sixty-foot submarine had disintegrated.

Two days later enemy aircraft dropped a bomb one thousand yards from *Taylor*. "Bogies [enemy aircraft] were around the formation most of the night," Commander Frank stated in his action report for the night of January

7–8.[22] At dawn the planes came again, but their attempts to barge through the thick antiaircraft screen were futile. Later that day, a kamikaze evaded antiaircraft fire and damaged the port side of the escort carrier *Kitkun Bay*.

"At 1800 [6:00 p.m.] the whole convoy turned east as we are nearing Lingayen Gulf," wrote Doc Ransom. "At sunset, although we could not see land, we could hear the battleships bombarding within the Gulf. Tomorrow morning at 0930 [9:30 a.m.] our troops are to land at Lingayen and it should be a busy day for all."[23]

Shortly after midnight the formation entered Lingayen Gulf, at which time *La Vallette* and the screen moved closer to the transports. Lookouts posted on deck spotted several mines floating within one hundred yards, which Thompson easily evaded. Near dawn an enemy plane dived at *La Vallette*, but the pilot turned away in the face of the antiaircraft curtain put up by *La Vallette* gunners.

Two hours later Ransom's ship arrived in position off her assigned beach and commenced a twenty-five-minute bombardment. The Japanese response sent enemy shells splashing among the formation, with one coming so close that Ransom heard it swish as it passed over and hit the *Jenkins* only a thousand yards away. The shell struck one of *Jenkins*'s gun mounts, punctured the rear of the gun shield, and burst upon hitting the starboard bulkhead, blowing out the door and throwing fragments throughout the gun chamber. Three men died from their wounds and another ten were wounded, but the ship's captain, Commander Philip D. Gallery, credited the foresight of his medical officer, Lieutenant James Pullman Jr., with saving lives. As Ransom had done aboard *La Vallette*, Pullman had instructed his crew in basic first-aid techniques, such as how to apply a tourniquet and administer morphine.

In midafternoon shells again fell among the destroyers. The first struck ahead of *La Vallette*, and each of the next three landed in the water successively closer to the destroyer. Thompson increased speed and turned his main batteries toward the Japanese gun flashes; joined by the fire from *Jenkins*, he silenced the enemy guns.

When by sundown the transports had completed unloading the infantry and supplies, the Desron 21 ships formed their familiar protective screen and escorted the ships back to Leyte Gulf. This time one of their own, *Jenkins*, had been hit, and the squadron had lost crewmembers. The longer they remained in enemy waters, many thought, the more likely it was that they would fall prey to enemy shells, torpedoes, or kamikazes.

Mail from home was the best antidote to those risks, but for reasons Commander Frank of the *Taylor* could not fathom, his crew had failed to receive any mail since November 1—two months of risking their lives without communication with family and friends back home. He considered the matter so important that he included special comments in his action report for the Lingayen operation. "Only small amounts of mail have reached this vessel during the last three months in spite of repeated requests to Commander Naval Base at Hollandia and Manus. It is believed that extra efforts should be made by planning agencies to insure delivery of mail prior to commencement of extended operations. Mail is extremely necessary for maintenance of morale, especially after a ship has been at sea for one year or more."[24] He hoped that would settle the issue.

Morale would be a more vital factor in the coming weeks, as two Desron 21 destroyers would learn in the waters off Corregidor.

"What Kept Us from Blowing Sky High, No One Knows"

The island of Corregidor was not just another tiny plot of soil in the Pacific with an unfamiliar name. Beginning in December 1941 and continuing into the first months of 1942, Corregidor and the nearby Bataan Peninsula dominated the nation's headlines. Each day weary, outnumbered American soldiers and their Filipino allies had battled Japanese infantry intent on sweeping them out of the Philippines, and each day the nation followed their progress, bolstered by their stirring fight against overwhelming odds. The Japanese had gradually forced MacArthur to retreat into the Bataan Peninsula, northwest of Manila, and onto the island of Corregidor, an island bastion guarding the entrance to Manila Bay. The Americans and Filipinos had continued their inspiring defense until, running out of matériel and food, and without any chance of rescue, their commander, Major General Jonathan M. Wainwright, who had succeeded Douglas MacArthur when President Roosevelt ordered him off the island, was forced to capitulate to his opponent.

As the war continued and the defenders languished in Japanese prison camps, Americans in and out of the military embraced the names of Bataan and Corregidor as emblematic of all that was noble about their military. MacArthur had promised to return to the islands, and now, in February 1945, it appeared his forces were about to restore Bataan and Corregidor to American control.

Desron 21 destroyers again played their familiar supporting role. The ships were to conduct bombardments; provide gunfire support in the assaults of Corregidor, southern Bataan, and three tiny islands protecting the entrance to Manila Bay; and cover minesweepers tasked with clearing the waters about Corregidor and Manila Bay of mines.

"Cruisers and cans all got underway at dawn for Corregidor and Bataan where we bombarded and protected the mine-sweeps during their mine-sweeping of Manila Bay," Doc Ransom recorded on February 13. "Corregidor is really a bastion and we watched the planes hit it time and again. We threw 120 rounds into Bataan."[25]

Each morning during the operation the destroyers left their base in Subic Bay, two hours north of Manila Bay, to arrive off Corregidor for the scheduled bombardment and minesweeping operations. They began on February 13 with bombardments of targets on both Bataan and Corregidor. At the same time men on deck with rifles swept the waters to destroy any mines that floated in their vicinity.

Operations off the Philippines were more hazardous than similar assignments along New Guinea, mainly because of the kamikaze threat. However, Japanese gun batteries in Corregidor's caves and Manila Bay mines caused damage on Valentine's Day of 1945.

Chesnutt's *Fletcher* was first. In an effort to locate and eliminate enemy gun batteries before American troops landed on the island, the destroyers moved closer to Corregidor and sat dead in the water as bait to entice the Japanese into firing, at which point waiting gun crews would zero in on the enemy's flashes and puffs of dust. On one occasion Commander Foster waited for the telltale flashes, returned fire, and reversed course, but not before an enemy shell smacked against the ship's forward five-inch gun mount. Seaman Chesnutt had been watching the action with a shipmate on deck when he left to go below. Before he reached his bunk, a shell hit where Chesnutt had been a few seconds earlier, killing the sailor with whom he had been standing and opening a hole in the deck before exploding seven feet above Chesnutt's bunk. "Holes everyplace," Chesnutt confided to his diary later that day, "I can see sky, water and below. My bunk wet from burst water lines and holes all in it. What kept us from blowing sky high, no one knows."[26] *Fletcher*'s batteries silenced the offending enemy gun, but the shell's shrapnel killed three men and wounded six.

While in his action report Foster censured his ammunition magazine crew, who he contended left their posts too hastily, he praised Watertender

2/c Elmer C. Bigelow. A member of one of the repair parties, Bigelow ignored the risks and rushed into the blinding smoke and searing fires to prevent the magazines from igniting. Bigelow, who declined wasting precious seconds to don protective clothing and gas mask, used two fire extinguishers to douse the threat. As he battled the flames, acrid, burning smoke seared Bigelow's lungs, but he extinguished the fires and cooled the ammunition to prevent it from exploding. Had the fire ignited those magazines, *Fletcher* and most of her crew would have been sent to the bottom by her own shells. His valiant effort saved his shipmates but cost Bigelow his life, as the next day he succumbed to the effects of inhaling the toxic gases and smoke. For his efforts, Bigelow was awarded a posthumous Medal of Honor.

The crew had hardly shaken off the effects when Foster received orders to assist another Desron 21 destroyer, *Hopewell*, in rescuing men from a sinking minesweeper, *YMS-48*. *Hopewell* had already raced over to assist the stricken minesweeper, but thick enemy gunfire kicked up water and sprayed the decks. One shell passed so close that the ship's gunnery officer, Lieutenant Claude N. Sapp, said he thought he could have reached out and grabbed it.

As *Hopewell* picked up the first survivors, the destroyer, according to a Navy Department press release, "lurched violently from several Jap hits. Splashes in the water were dangerously close to the survivors swimming frantically toward the *Hopewell*."[27] The ship sustained hits in four places, including the diesel generator room and the deck house, while losing seven dead and twelve wounded.

Now *Fletcher* was asked to move into the same area and help fellow sailors, a move that required her to operate under the same guns that had knocked out two ships. As Foster nudged *Fletcher* closer to the minesweeper, turning his destroyer into a more enticing target, an American pilot swept low to shield the destroyer with a plume of smoke, and then spotted as *Fletcher*'s batteries located and destroyed the offending guns. "The courage and endurance of our badly wounded lying maimed on the bloody decks with the ship shaking from rapid continuous counter battery fire cannot be too highly spoken of," wrote Foster after the incident.[28]

The carnage Chesnutt saw on the fellow squadron ship was horrific. After months of meeting the enemy without sustaining casualties, he and the *Fletcher* crew now witnessed enough, on his ship and on *Hopewell*, to last the war. As *Fletcher* neared *Hopewell*, Chesnutt saw men whose torsos had been ripped apart, dead bodies hanging over rails, "and the deck was red with blood." On *Fletcher*, a young sailor who had been aboard the battleship

USS *West Virginia* (BB-48) and survived the attack at Pearl Harbor, now lay at Gun Number One in a bloody heap. "His legs were almost entirely blown off between knee and feet," wrote Chesnutt, "he died later. His name was Wilhelm, and he was always smiling and always had a cheerful word." A sixteen-year-old sailor from Alabama who had lied about his age had the "top of head blown off and other parts blown open. I had talked to him a short time before and it doesn't seem true. One boy I had left 5 minutes before he was hit in the head."[29]

Later that afternoon *Fletcher* and *Hopewell* were ordered back to Subic Bay, but Doc Ransom and *La Vallette* were next into the enemy's lair.

"A Horrible Experience and Night"

Valentine's Day for *La Vallette* started like almost every other day in the Southwest Pacific—an early morning departure to another station for patrolling, escorting, or bombarding. There was no reason to think that this day's assignment—blasting targets on Bataan and Corregidor—would be any more difficult than similar prior missions. Doc Ransom would be ready with his medical instruments in the wardroom, but it was just as likely the *La Vallette* would carry out her tasks and return to Subic Bay without mishap.

Commander Wells Thompson took *La Vallette*, again joined by *Radford* and the cruiser *Montpelier*, out of Subic Bay at 5:30 a.m., veered south, and headed for Manila Bay. Three hours later the trio stood off Manila Bay's entrance, where they patrolled the waters south of Corregidor to clear the way for the minesweepers that would follow.

That afternoon the two destroyers moved closer to Mariveles to screen for the minesweepers, with *La Vallette* astern of the last minesweeper and *Radford* following behind. *Radford*'s skipper, Commander Jack E. Mansfield, alerted Thompson by TBS that mines had been sighted dead ahead, and when Thompson spotted a cluster five hundred yards out, he stopped *La Vallette* and ordered a 40mm gun crew, aided by men with rifles and a machine gun, to destroy the mines. "I was a good shot as a kid," said Quartermaster Johnson. "The mines were popping up, and I got a rifle to see if I could hit any."[30] Ransom thought he saw at least seven of the enemy devices, but his ship withdrew after the three closest had been dispatched so that minesweepers could enter the harbor.

Ransom walked back to the wardroom to check on his pharmacist's mates and to listen to the radio. He had just sat down when a huge explosion tossed him onto the deck and toppled a stack of phonograph records onto him. On the bridge, Thompson felt the ship lift twice. Others near him were thrown to the deck as a torrent of water engulfed them, and the man at the wheel was swept into the adjoining charthouse. One sailor was tossed several feet into the air before falling onto the radio antenna, and the engineering officer, Lieutenant G. W. Soete, had been walking on the main deck when a torrent of water washed him over the side. He broke surface fifty yards from the ship, swam to a powder can floating in the water, and used it to keep him buoyant until a whaleboat from the *Radford* rescued him.

The ship's executive officer, Lieutenant M. P. Myers III, hurried to the main deck to find it littered with loose life nets, lines, a radar antenna, and other items. He started down the fireroom hatch to help a man struggling to move, but was kept away by the rush of hot steam coming from below. Watertender 1/c Robert H. Redman donned an asbestos suit, disappeared down the hatch into the Number One fireroom, and dragged a severely scalded fireman to the hatch, where Myers and another man lifted their shipmate to the deck. Electrician's Mate 2/c Theodore F. Mackert and Electrician's Mate 3/c Coy R. Wilson raced into the flooded communications room to pull out several shipmates, saving their lives in the process.

As *La Vallette*'s bow continue to settle lower in the water, Commander Thompson took quick action. He ordered every man topside in case he needed to abandon ship, sent aft as many as he could to lighten the load on the bow section, and had sailors throw overboard the starboard anchor, ammunition in two handling rooms, spare gun barrels, and other loose items, to reduce the strain on the ship's forward section.

The men from two ammunition magazines below, surrounded by explosives, evacuated, but in their haste forgot to shut the watertight hatches as they emerged. Six compartments flooded because of the oversight. When Thompson later investigated, he learned that each man had assumed others trailing behind would close the hatches. Thompson declined to censure his men, and placed the onus on himself for not training them as well as he could.

Two minutes after the explosion rattled *La Vallette* and blew men overboard, Commander Mansfield hoisted a flag asking Thompson if he needed assistance. When Thompson replied in the affirmative, Mansfield lowered his whaleboat to rescue *La Vallette* sailors and moved his ship closer to *La Vallette* to take her in tow.

Radford was only one hundred yards out when she struck a second mine. The explosion knocked out all bridge instruments on *Radford*, impaired her steering, and tossed Doc Ransom's counterpart in *Radford* one hundred feet into the water, where the ship's whaleboat rescued the unconscious officer. *Radford* lost three dead and four injured in the explosion.

"What an explosion," wrote Seaman Fahey aboard *Montpelier* after *La Vallette* was damaged. "A large geyser of water went high into the air, covering a very large section of the Bay. When everything had cleared, I could see that part of the bow had been blown off." He watched as *Radford* rushed to *La Vallette*'s aid, only to erupt from a second mine. "The water surrounding the two ill-fated destroyers was cluttered with toilet paper, supplies and life rafts. Both ships were dead in the water."[31]

The squadron known throughout the Pacific for its good luck—*O'Bannon*, *Fletcher*, and *Nicholas* until now had fought the Japanese for more than two years without a scratch—had suddenly lost four destroyers in five hours.

Upon hearing groans and shouting, Doc Ransom ran out of *La Vallette*'s wardroom onto the main deck, "where there was fuel oil all over everything and steam coming out of the forward fire room hatch." When someone yelled that casualties littered the bridge, he rushed up to find a signalman with a bloodied face, "lying across two radio antennas where he had been blown by the blast."[32] Ransom checked the sailor, treated him for minor wounds, pulled him out onto the main deck, and looked around for the next casualty.

Ransom noticed that his pharmacist's mates were already at their stations with first-aid kits, tending to the bleeding and dazed men. He checked each casualty to determine the seriousness, gave his pharmacist's mates instructions about treating the minor injuries, and then handled the more serious cases himself. Quartermaster Johnson was in the wardroom tending to a friend suffering from severe burns when Ransom came by. "We removed his shoes, and skin came away with them. Ransom gave him a shot of morphine. Ransom was all over the place, trying to be everywhere to treat the wounded," recalled Johnson.[33] Ransom could do nothing but try to make the sailor, a teenager from Iowa, comfortable before he succumbed a few hours later.

For thirty uninterrupted hours Ransom patched up the more grievously wounded, actions for which he was awarded a Bronze Star. His five pharmacist's mates worked either at the aft or forward dressing stations or at a temporary one set up on the forecastle, mending the sailors brought to them or stumbling in for treatment. Those training sessions Ransom had conducted, not only with his assistants but with the entire crew as well, now reaped dividends. Ransom concluded that he had been able to treat what might ordinarily have been an overwhelming number of casualties only "due to previous planning and instruction periods," and recommended that his quintet be commended. He stated in his report that they had performed "wonderful and remarkable work," and that "several patients' lives were saved by their splendid assistance."[34]

Seeing that the ship was settling by the bow, and uncertain whether the destroyer would remain afloat, Ransom checked that every casualty wore a life jacket. He hurried to the wardroom, now so filled with casualties that it looked like a hospital emergency room after a major catastrophe. "One boy, who had been dragged out of the fire room alive, was in bad shape," wrote Ransom of a sailor who suffered from second- and third-degree burns over his entire body. Another patient lay in a coma from a compound skull fracture, a third bore a ten-inch abdominal laceration and suffered from a fractured nose, and another "had a deep laceration of the scrotum and perineum," while one sailor "had a puncture wound of the knee joint."[35] Ransom kept the men with minor injuries aboard ship and transferred the more serious cases, such as Ensign Edward A. Christofferson Jr., with lacerated head and face, to the cruiser *Denver* or to the hospital ship *Hope*.

For the first time in the war, Ransom treated men he knew would not survive. The doctor did what he could to make comfortable Fireman 1/c Donald W. Mai, who had been in the Number One fireroom, but with second- and third-degree burns covering his entire body, Mai could not last more than twenty-four hours. Ransom transferred Mai to *Denver*, where he succumbed the next day.

After treating every case in the wardroom, Ransom returned to the main deck. At least seven men were unable to move because of severe back injuries, which worried Ransom. What would these men do if Commander Thompson ordered abandon ship? The back injuries "caused much concern," he wrote. "The main thought in caring for these back injuries was to have all of them ready to be evacuated in case we had to abandon ship, and the possibility of sinking was ever present in my mind throughout the night."[36]

In his diary, Ransom listed seven men who had either been killed outright or later died from their wounds, and many injured, including "nine fractures, 46 lacerations, 10 brain concussions, 14 severe contusions, and one 3rd degree burn and acute pneumonia."[37] Within the first few hours, Ransom transferred eight of the most serious cases to the cruiser *Denver*, which had come alongside to assist, or to the hospital ship *Hope*. The bodies of four dead crew remained in the ravaged fireroom below for two days, until repair parties could finally extract their lifeless forms.

"It was a horrible experience and night," Ransom concluded of the explosion's aftermath. As the exhausted physician tended the wounded who lay in his wardroom and on the main deck, shipmates cast admiring glances at the man everyone preferred to call "Doc" rather than the more formal "Doctor." He had won their admiration for his many humorous announcements over the ship's loudspeaker and for the meticulous care he gave the crew, in and out of battle. Doc Ransom was the military version of the country doctor who made house calls to ailing families, much as his father had done during his medical career. "He had the respect of the entire crew long before we hit the mine, when he really showed his stuff," wrote Jack Bell, a sailor aboard *La Vallette*.[38]

Commander Thompson had to move his damaged ship out of the harbor and away from the Japanese land batteries, but with his steering ability hampered and with the loss of one engine, he faced a testy exit through those nasty mines that seemed to pop out of nowhere. Finally, by early evening, he cleared the bay and reached open waters. Five hours later a tug arrived to tow *La Vallette*, one of the few destroyers in the war to carry the dubious distinction of being both torpedoed and mined, to Subic Bay, where the pair arrived the next morning.

"The ship is a mess with fuel oil everyplace," Ransom entered in his diary. "The mine hit on the port side just aft of the wardroom and really tore up the ship. The bow is about four feet out of the water and we came mighty close to losing her."[39] Thompson docked *La Vallette* alongside the submarine tender *Griffin* as repairs began.

The ship remained in Subic Bay for the next five days, during which time repair parties assessed the damage, removed the four bodies from below, pumped out flooded compartments, and patched up a sixteen-foot hole in *La Vallette*'s hull. Similar work was done aboard *Radford*, which had also returned to the bay after being damaged by the mine.

While *La Vallette* was being repaired, the other Desron 21 destroyers focused on Corregidor. *O'Bannon*, *Taylor*, and two cruisers steamed to the north side of the island, and *Hopewell*, *Nicholas*, and one cruiser flanked to the south to provide cover for the February 15 assaults against Corregidor and the Bataan

Peninsula. As paratroopers descended on the island and infantry landed on Bataan, the ships blasted targets along the Mariveles shore and the enemy guns concealed in the caves that pockmarked Corregidor's cliffs.

"We bombarded Corregidor as long as it was daylight," wrote Sonarman Starr aboard *Nicholas*. "For two days, the *Nicholas* and others steamed close to the cliffsides, point-blank-range close, to draw Japanese fire from the tunnel openings. The idea was to find the guns and silence them. But we had to give the Japanese first shot."

Starr and his shipmates had to endure the thought that, to obtain a fix on their targets, their skipper had to move *Nicholas* in close to the island and act as bait for enemy batteries. For two days *Nicholas* and the other destroyers operated at point-blank range, taunting the enemy into firing by slowing their speed and waiting for the telltale blast from shore to indicate their target.

The exhausting work continued until sunset, when the unit returned north to Subic Bay. Despite arriving near midnight, the crews could not rest, for they had to refuel and restock the ammunition they had expended during the day in order to be ready for the next day's action. "As a result," wrote Starr, "we hit the sack about 0100 [1:00 a.m.] for an all-too-brief two- to three-hour sleep."

Back the next morning, the crews remained at battle stations throughout the long daylight hours. They ate breakfast and supper during the trips to and from Corregidor, and snacked when they could at stations. "I don't remember showering during those four days," recalled Starr. "I didn't want to give up my sleep time. Besides, who cared what we smelled like. We always smelled of sweat and diesel fuel smoke anyway."[40]

Crews enjoyed a front-row seat to one of the war's most exciting spectacles when, forty-five minutes after a February 15 pre-invasion bombardment, paratroopers dropped on Corregidor from Army transport planes. Soldiers dangled from white chutes, while red, green, and black canopies gently bore equipment to the ground. A short distance away, awestruck *Nicholas* and *Fletcher* crew watched the multicolored display, which was more reminiscent of a balloon-filled festival sky than of a bloody battleground.

"Paratroopers began landing for one hour at 8:30 AM, then small landing crafts went in at 1030," Seaman Chesnutt wrote in his diary. "Heavy firing met them. More paratroopers after noon. We went in to 2,000 yards firing, some near misses on us and no hits. We silenced a few shore batteries." As the Army advanced across the island, *Fletcher* and her companions swept for mines, exploding more than one hundred. "One mine exploded between

Jenkins and us in close to the beach of Corregidor late this afternoon," noted Chesnutt.[41]

When winds blew some of the paratroopers off track and into the bay, PT boats helped the destroyers retrieve the soldiers. Most, however, successfully dropped onto the island and overwhelmed the Japanese garrison, making men on the decks of *Fletcher* and *Nicholas* proud to again see Old Glory fluttering over an island that meant so much to the United States.

Over the ensuing ten days the destroyers provided support as Army units seized three other islands in Manila Bay. By mid-March, once Caballo, El Fraile, and Carabao had been secured, the bay was firmly in MacArthur's hands, and Allied attention could be shifted north of the Philippines. The *Nicholas* crew celebrated the progress by staging a beer and swimming liberty on an island off the mouth of Subic Bay.

Doc Ransom and *La Vallette* would not be a part of that. After nearly three months undergoing repairs, on May 2 the destroyer left Subic Bay for what the men hoped would be the long journey home. "Departed from Subic Bay at 1130 [11:30 a.m.] for Pearl Harbor (!) via Guam and the Marshall Islands," wrote Doc Ransom. "Been waiting for this day a very long time." Three weeks later his ship, still showing signs of the mine's explosion, arrived at Pearl Harbor, where Ransom and his shipmates anchored to an emotional reception. "Arrived at P.H. at 0800 [8:00 a.m.] and they gave us a five gun salute from the shore guns," wrote Ransom on May 22. "CinCPac [Admiral Nimitz] sent us a message as we entered saying 'Welcome to Pearl. The battle record of the *La Vallette* is an inspiration to all hands. Hearty Congratulations.'" Ransom's fears that the ship might be repaired in Hawaii and quickly returned to the fighting were allayed with the news that they would remain at Pearl Harbor only two days before heading home.

"Underway at 0930 [9:30 a.m.] for San Francisco!!" he added on May 24, not even trying to hide his excitement. "Left Pearl with our homeward bound pennant flying and our whistle and siren screeching. We will arrive in San Francisco on May 30th."

Six days later, after a crew accustomed to tropical heat slowly adjusted to the surprisingly cold temperatures, the coast of California appeared on the horizon, bringing with it welcome leave with family for the crew while their ship received further repairs. "Passed under Golden Gate Bridge at 0840 [8:40 a.m.]," wrote Doc Ransom. "Left with the agriculture inspector and went to San Jose by train. Home Sweet Home!!" Quartermaster Johnson wrote his mother, "This has been a great day—one that we have waited for quite some time—one that we have often dreamed and thought about. Yes today was the day that we returned back to the U.S.A."[42]

Doc Ransom had come back to home and family, at least until *La Vallette* was again ready for battle, but the remaining ships of Desron 21, now a severely depleted unit, continued to fight in the Pacific. Of the twelve destroyers that were members of Desron 21 throughout the war, only half remained, including the original trio of *O'Bannon*, *Fletcher*, and *Nicholas*. Three had been sunk in the Solomons, while *La Vallette*, *Radford*, and *Hopewell* had been knocked out of action in the Philippines.

While Ransom and his shipmates reunited with loved ones, their compatriots in the Southwest Pacific enjoyed no such respite. Islands named Iwo Jima and Okinawa, filled with Japanese soldiers imbued with the desire to halt what so far had been an inexorable American drive toward the Home Islands, awaited.

Orvill Raines and the *Howorth* were about to find out just how determined those enemy defenders were.

CHAPTER 10

KAMIKAZE CARNAGE

It was hard not to like Orvill Raines. The *Howorth* yeoman loved a good joke, and it did not bother him that his shipmates teased him because of the long letters he wrote to his wife, Ray Ellen, or the lipstick imprints she left on her letters to him. His love for her was open and deep, and shipmates joshed him not because they despised the man but because they knew how real his passion was for his wife.

Born in Oklahoma on September 6, 1918, James Orvill Raines was the youngest of seven children. His father died before Orvill was out of high school, and when his mother remarried and moved to Arkansas, Raines chose instead to live with his sisters in Dallas. He settled into a job at the *Dallas Morning News*, quickly rising to reporter status.

He met Ray Ellen on a blind date in April 1939 and knew right away he had found the perfect match. "I stuck my head inside an automobile and saw something wonderful, fresh and beautiful that smiled," he wrote in one of his many letters to Ray Ellen, later to be collected in a volume and beautifully edited by Professor William McBride. "I was smitten in the solar plexus and a curious funny ache has been there ever since."[1] The pair dated for a year before marrying in June 1940.

The war disrupted their life together. He enlisted in the Naval Reserve in November 1942, was assigned to the new destroyer *Howorth*, and left for the Pacific in August 1944. Before departing, he and Ray Ellen agreed to continue the practice they had started shortly after marrying. Each night the couple gave each other what they called their "official good night," usually a passionate kiss, but sometimes a bit more. Orvill vowed to continue the practice no matter where *Howorth* went, timing his imaginary kiss to coincide with her nighttime in Dallas. Far away in the South Pacific, he often had to mutter his good night in midday, frequently in the mess hall.

As a yeoman, Raines had a station on the bridge, where he recorded events that involved the skipper and other officers. The ship stopped first at Pearl Harbor and Guadalcanal before reaching Humboldt Bay, New Guinea, in September. "We get closer to battle each day," he wrote Ray Ellen on September 12. "And as we approach, the men are withdrawing more to themselves. Conversation goes on as before but it is conversation between touchy men."[2]

Raines was happy, at least, to see an old friend. Torpedoman 3/c Glenn Murray had been with *O'Bannon* through the November 1942 battles off Guadalcanal, the countless runs up the Slot, and the major surface engagements in and around Kula Gulf. Raines enjoyed sharing thoughts with Murray whenever the two ships were anchored together, and he was surprised when Murray complained that he missed his former skipper, Commander MacDonald, and that MacDonald's replacement, Commander R. W. Smith, failed to measure up. Raines wanted to experience combat before he formed a final opinion of his skipper, Commander Edward S. Burns.

Those experiences arrived rapidly once *Howorth* joined Desron 21 for the Philippine campaign, where kamikazes and shore bombardments were common. "Darling, the 'West Side' [of Leyte Island] is beautiful," he wrote Ray Ellen on December 9 while involved with the Mindoro landings. "We weave through the numerous small islands, continually changing course. Always uncertain what lies beyond the next point." When kamikazes attacked nearby ships, as they did so often in the restricted waters off Leyte Island, Raines and his shipmates encouraged other crews with shouts: "Kill the bastards" and "Come on you guys, hit 'em."[3]

Raines was at his station early one morning when a shadow loomed off the starboard side. He looked out as a destroyer limped into port, her superstructure a twisted mass of metal from absorbing kamikaze blows. Raines could only imagine the fear that must have engulfed that crew as the pilot barreled toward them at high speed with the sole intent of killing them. Those men served on the same size ship as Raines and completed the same tasks, held similar hopes for survival and nurtured the common dream of reuniting with loved ones as he did; yet for some, at least, those hopes and dreams had ended in an instant of fiery destruction. It was hard for Raines not to wonder about the fate of the man at the same duty station Raines held. He assumed *Howorth* might face a similar ordeal, but also remembered the experience of

O'Bannon, a destroyer that since late 1942 had survived the worst the enemy could throw at her. Maybe his luck would match that of his buddy Glenn Murray.

Raines's first encounter with kamikazes occurred on December 15, landing day at Mindoro, when three aircraft attacked his destroyer. Gunfire enveloped the first kamikaze in flames but, according to *Howorth*'s ship history, "two 'Zekes' consecutively dived at this ship through heavy anti-aircraft fire."[4]

Seaman 1/c Russell Bramble stood near the captain that day as the port wing lookout. After entering the Navy in the fall of 1943, the native of Hastings, Nebraska, had helped put the ship in commission eight months earlier, and he now faced the most trying moments of his young military career. Bramble knew that the kamikaze pilots did not just attempt to hit his ship but, more precisely, tried to smash into the bridge, right where he happened to be posted. "What the pilots wanted to do was aim for the bridge where all the controls were," he said years later. "It happened so fast that we had no chance to be scared" at the time, but he realized that he operated at the center of the enemy's bull's-eye. "The kamikazes came in real low, where the radar couldn't pick them up so good. We were closer to land and the captain was maneuvering the ship, but they came in so fast and just blew up."[5]

Commander Burns ordered hard left and right rudders to avoid the oncoming kamikazes, which, according to Raines, "came in like a hornet." One barely missed the aft smokestack and splashed in the water on the starboard side so close to Raines that parts of the wing and fuselage flew near him. As the second charged toward the bridge, the officer of the deck and another officer stood halfway outside the bridge so they could shout the range and probable direction.

"As he flew closer and closer, bearing down right at them, I never saw such fear on anyone's face," Orvill wrote Ray Ellen of the men around him. The officers shouted "duck" only three seconds before the plane crashed feet from the destroyer, hurling a torrent of water right near Raines, "and the ship gave a mighty heave and groan, twisting and staggering like a bull clouted with a hammer." Raines looked down to find a piece of the Japanese aircraft near his feet. When shells from *Howorth* ruptured the third kamikaze's gas tank, it sprayed "the entire ship top to bottom, bow to stern." The plane smashed forward and bounced off the port side of the forecastle, scattering wreckage all over, including "a piece of the Jap's cheekbone picked up by the medical officer."

Raines now had evidence of his skipper's skills. During the attack Burns stood on the bridge, shouting his orders to ensure that everyone around him heard his commands, and weaved the ship to port and starboard to avoid taking a direct hit. It was comforting to know that the ship had a capable commander, one whose talents could increase the crew's odds for survival, but some of those damaged and sunken vessels had had gifted captains as well. Luck would also have to be on his side.

Raines wrote Ray Ellen, "I will admit that after it was over, little Orvill was nervous as hell" because "I know those devils were aiming at me personally." He continued, "Honey, they turned right at us and to every man on the ship, it looked like they were after them personally. The feeling of chance and uncertainty was almost unbearable." A combination of good fortune and Burns's talents saved *Howorth*, but two LSTs near them were sunk. *O'Bannon*, with his buddy Glenn Murray, operated close by, her antiaircraft gun crews joining those of *Howorth* to prevent the planes from hitting either ship. "It seems his ship is always nearby. Almost every move we've made, he has been right with us."[6]

The crews returned from the Mindoro operation without suffering serious casualties, but they were worn down. "As a result of the operations of the past twelve days, the crew is tired; not so much physically as mentally, from repeated strain," stated *O'Bannon*'s war diary on December 18.[7] They had avoided serious harm, and for a brief interlude the active phase of their fighting was over, but the torments and anxieties associated with combat accompanied them day after day. The enemy's guns and the kamikazes might have faded for the moment, but the fears remained.

A third assault in January 1945 took Raines north of Manila for the landings in Lingayen Gulf. According to Raines, the grueling Philippine operations, which followed on the heels of *Howorth*'s work off New Guinea, made even some of the roughest characters aboard homesick. The absence of mail for almost a month deepened their melancholy.

Home would have to wait. The Japanese first needed to be overcome at a series of Pacific locations, each undoubtedly offering fierce resistance, before the Americans could launch the invasion everyone feared—the final assault of the Home Islands. Two of those locations, Iwo Jima and Okinawa, now beckoned.

"We Never Got Much Sleep"

Raines and his shipmates would not miss the Philippines, where, according to the ship's history, "much of that time had been spent at general quarters repelling air attacks."[8] They had seen enough of kamikazes and bombardments, but they gloomily concluded that their next objective, Iwo Jima, would undoubtedly offer more of the same.

In early February the *Howorth* was temporarily assigned to the Fifth Fleet to be part of the naval element supporting the Marine landings at Iwo Jima, a place ever since associated with the flag raising atop Mount Suribachi. As soon as Commander Burns took *Howorth* out of Saipan on February 16 to escort the troop transports to the island, he announced to the crew their destination. "You never knew where you were going until you had left your port," said Seaman Bramble. "When the captain said, 'Iwo Jima,' we said, 'Where's that?'"[9]

Admiral Nimitz needed Iwo Jima, located in the Volcano Islands seven hundred miles northwest of Saipan, as an air base for operations against the Japanese. Airstrips there could offer an emergency landing field for B-29 bombers on their return trips to Saipan after hitting Japan, a place to house the fighters that escorted those bombers, and a base from which to strike the next target, Okinawa.

Early in the morning of February 19, after sweeping for submarines west of Mount Suribachi, *Howorth* took station seven miles out from the island while battleships and cruisers blasted Japanese positions in the heaviest pre-invasion bombardment of the war. Grabbing a pair of binoculars, Raines watched mammoth sixteen-inch battleship batteries hurl projectiles that rose in an arc before descending on the Japanese. American fighter aircraft so dotted the sky that he feared some might collide, and when he gazed northward, he saw shells mercilessly pounding Mount Suribachi.

A few hours later, landing craft began ferrying in the first of what by nightfall would be thirty thousand Marines. *Howorth*'s work then began in earnest, and would last twenty-three days. That time was described in the ship's history as a taxing period, "without anchoring or mooring, being underway continuously."[10]

Their daily missions never varied. They patrolled the sea about Iwo Jima for enemy surface craft or submarines, and moved closer to the beaches to provide gunfire support for Marines advancing on enemy positions. "We bombarded Iwo Jima for sixteen days," said Seaman Bramble. "During the day we fired at Japanese positions, and at night we shot starshells for the Marines so they could see the enemy. We never got much sleep as we were going day and night."[11]

Raines, Bramble, and the crew expected kamikazes to again attack their ship, possibly in larger numbers than the Philippine onslaught, but few aerial threats interrupted their operations. "I was surprised that there were no kamikazes," said Seaman Bramble. "At night you could see a lot of action farther out at sea where the fleet was keeping the kamikazes away." While a handful of planes sneaked in to damage two ships and sink one escort carrier, earlier American air strikes against Japanese airfields on Honshu drastically reduced their overall impact.

During *Howorth*'s sojourn off Iwo Jima, the ship conducted eight bombardments that lasted twenty-four hours apiece, each within range of enemy gunfire, as well as briefer shellings on other days. Through his binoculars, Bramble watched Marine units and tanks engaging the enemy, turning to flamethrowers and artillery to gouge the defenders from their pillboxes and nests. "I saw one Jap gun emplacement get plastered. Tracers were going right into it and it just blew up."[12] Bramble said the ship moved so close to Iwo Jima's shore that the enemy once fired a thirty-caliber weapon at them.

Shooting starshells at night to illuminate Japanese positions prevented an already stressed crew from getting much sleep, but delivered an impressive display. "It was interesting watching the shells float downward through a thick white cloud," Raines wrote Ray Ellen three days after the landings. "They would burst in the midst of the cloud and cause it to glow like snow and then drift downward through the layers and finally through the bottom and light up the whole island."

Firing shells, Burns worked in coordination with the shore fire control party, which consisted of a Marine with a walkie-talkie on Iwo Jima calling out grid locations of targets to the destroyer. *Howorth*'s five-inch guns turned to those locations, fired a few salvos, and then waited until they received another request from the Marine. One time Raines heard the Marine shout, "Look at those bastards run!" and knew that his ship's batteries had hit their mark; another time the Marine said, "It might interest you to know your shooting is very good. The results are very gratifying."

On another occasion the Marine contact called in grid coordinates for a gun that the Japanese rolled in and out of a cave. The Marine told Burns that when he shouted, the ship should immediately commence firing on that spot. The Marine waited until he saw the Japanese begin to roll out the gun, then shouted over his walkie-talkie, "Open fire immediately." *Howorth*'s guns boomed fifteen shells directly on the location and silenced the offending gun.

"I'm glad, in spite of the sacrifice I feel that you and I are making, that I had something to do with killing some of them," Raines gushed to Ray Ellen about their work off Iwo Jima. "I really feel grand about it. I get a special kick out of killing them. I only wish I were in close enough to see their bodies and parts of bodies go sky high when our shells hit."[13]

He had second thoughts on those occasions when they moved toward the beaches to provide close-in gunfire support. According to a Navy press release, "Heavy shells from Jap shore batteries dropped all around her, and machine gun bullets chewed into her skin and superstructure spasmodically."[14]

Howorth escaped harm, but the kamikazes off the Philippines and those bullets made him realize that their good fortune could change in an instant. He wrote Ray Ellen after one close encounter off Iwo Jima, "It just occurred to me that a guy could very easily get killed out here and consequently consider that all the chances we've taken and still remain unscratched as far as personnel injuries are concerned, we are pretty lucky."

On March 14, almost one month after leaving for Iwo Jima and just after watching a group of B-29s land on the hastily patched airfield, Burns received orders to return to Saipan. Two days later *Howorth* entered Saipan's harbor, where the crew spotted three American nurses standing on a hospital ship. Raines waved to them from the bridge, and when the nurses waved back, "the whole ship started waving and whistling. The poor girls' arms ached I guess by the time we passed."[15]

After the trying experiences with kamikazes and mines off the Philippines, in comparison Iwo Jima had been a relatively calm experience. No Japanese aircraft attacked *Howorth*, and daily patrols and bombardments often kept them a safe distance from land. Some wondered whether the Japanese had reached the end of their resources.

Okinawa would provide an alarming answer.

"Enemy Planes Were All Around"

More than twelve hundred ships, including *Howorth*, *O'Bannon*, *Nicholas*, *Taylor*, and two hundred other destroyers, gathered to seize Okinawa. Under the command of Admiral Raymond A. Spruance, the hero of Midway, and Vice Admiral Richmond Kelly Turner, the massive naval units rivaled those that had assembled off the coast of Normandy the previous year for D-Day. Once Okinawa was in their hands, the Americans intended to use airfields there as bases for the waves of bombers and fighters set to attack the Home Islands, and the rest of the island as a staging area for the final assault against Japan proper.

"The Ryukyu invasion would in a sense mark the end of the road in the vast 'ocean' phase of the war against Japan," explained an article in the *New York Times* on April 1. "The road began at Guadalcanal almost three years ago."[16] During the intervening years, the nation's military had pushed the Japanese back three thousand miles, retaken most of their conquests, and cut their supply routes to precious natural resources in Southeast Asia and the Philippines.

A key part of that progress was Desron 21. Two and a half years after the original trio arrived off Guadalcanal in the fall of 1942, four of those squadron destroyers participated in the Okinawa invasion, including two of the original three vessels. The Japanese would fight to the last man to retain the island, which stood 350 miles south of Kyushu, as an American assault on Okinawa, which was considered a part of Japan, would be akin to attacking Tokyo. Should Okinawa fall, little remained to stop the Americans from invading the Home Islands, something that had never come to pass in Japan's long history. "We figured we might get hit by more kamikazes because we were moving closer to Japan," said Seaman Bramble, "but you never know."[17]

At a March 29 meeting with his military, Hirohito urged them to consider every option, including kamikazes, as the fight for Okinawa "will decide the fate of our Empire."[18] Imperial General Headquarters concluded that in such a desperate situation, there was no longer any alternative to using kamikazes on a scale not previously seen in the war. The plan, named Ten Go (Heavenly Operation), called for a series of *kikusui* (floating chrysanthemums), colossal air raids involving anywhere from fifty to three hundred aircraft, to assault American ships off Okinawa. Except for the newest aircraft and most experienced pilots, which would be retained in the homeland to defend Japan's shores, every available aircraft, including seaplanes, outdated fighters, training planes, and scout planes, would be used to repel the invaders.

Tokyo radio broadcasts cautioned the Japanese people that "the war situation continues to grow more serious with each added second" and that the decisive battle on Okinawa would determine their war fortune. The broadcast emphasized the importance of defeating the Americans on Okinawa, as a defeat meant that much of southern Japan, including Tokyo and other large cities, "will come within the flying radius of the enemy B-24s." The Tokyo newspaper *Yomiuri Hochi* admitted in an editorial that losing Okinawa would leave Japan "no hope of turning the course of the war" and that "the loss of Okinawa will mean the collapse of the vanguards of Japan."[19]

Kamikaze pilots were an enigma to Raines and every other American sailor in the Pacific. They knew that an attack could inflict grievous harm on a ship, maybe even sink it, at the cost of one plane and one pilot, but the idea that a man would willingly fly an aircraft into a ship remained incomprehensible to them. Admiral Halsey contended that kamikaze pilots could not be understood by Americans: "The psychology behind it was too alien to ours; Americans, who fight to live, find it hard to realize that another people will fight to die."[20]

Most kamikaze pilots sacrificed their lives out of a sense of duty and honor, and hoped with their deaths to help their nation avoid defeat. They followed the code of *bushido*, observed by the ancient samurai warriors and revered for centuries in Japan, which emphasized honor, courage, and loyalty to the emperor. Voluntary death was preferable to living in shame. The highest honor, granted to most kamikaze pilots, was to be enshrined at Yasukuni, a special shrine visited twice a year by the emperor.

Before leaving for their final flight, each pilot wrote a farewell letter to his parents. "I have been given a splendid opportunity to die. This is my last day," wrote Flying Petty Officer First Class Isao Matsuo of the 701st Air Group to his parents on October 28, 1944. "The destiny of our homeland hinges on the decisive battle in the seas to the south where I shall fall like a blossom from a radiant cherry tree." Matsuo thanked his parents for their years of nurturing and hoped that his sacrifice "will in some small way repay what you have done for me. Think well of me and know that your Isao died for our country."[21]

Ensign Ichizo Hayashi, a graduate of the Imperial University at Kyoto, wrote his mother, "I am going to score a direct hit on an enemy ship without fail. When war results are announced you may be sure that one of the successes was scored by me. I am determined to keep calm and do a perfect job to the last, knowing that you will be watching over me and praying for my success. There will be no clouds of doubt or fear when I make the final plunge." He added, "It is gratifying to live in this world, but living has a spirit of futility about it now. It is time to die. I do not seek reasons for dying. My only search is for an enemy target against which to dive."[22]

Japanese radio broadcasts placed so much faith in kamikaze attacks that they called them "sure-hit and sure-kill" aircraft.[23]

Dating back to their runs up the Slot in the Solomons more than two years earlier, Desron 21 ships were accustomed to facing tight predicaments, but fending off swarms of kamikazes was a specter of another level. "Okinawa," Raines wrote to Ray Ellen in late March. "Just looking at it on the map breaks us out in a cold sweat." He added that "Okinawa spells Kamikaze Corps to us," and admitted that the crew was particularly worried. "Somebody's gotta get it and we may be lucky or unlucky."[24]

Howorth's crew tried to distract themselves by watching movies on the ship's fantail. On March 29 men gathered for the 1942 Academy Award–winning film *Mrs. Miniver*, the story of a courageous British family withstanding Hitler's air blitz of London. They admired the husband and wife, played by Walter Pidgeon and Greer Garson, but walked away at the film's end more unsettled than they had expected. Was this a foreshadow of coming events?

Early in the morning of April 1, Easter Sunday, Commander Burns took *Howorth* between the troop transports and the landing beaches at Okinawa to sweep the area of mines. He then moved out to sea to patrol while landing craft ferried in the first waves of Marines toward the island. *Howorth* was not alone, as a ring of ships screened Okinawa, prepared to intercept enemy submarines, suicide boats, torpedo craft, and aircraft. Raines thought that, for such a huge assault against a major island, the ship enjoyed a relatively calm day, but kamikazes struck four other vessels. Prior to their appearance, gun crews had considered themselves successful if they shot down 80 to 90 percent of enemy attackers, but now they had to destroy every single plane to avoid serious harm. Defensive tactics were improvised at best and mostly fell to the skipper, who had to change speed and course at an instant's notice.

The calm ended the next day, when before daylight three aircraft flew near the ship, twice drawing fire from *Howorth*'s antiaircraft guns. One swerved away, a second veered toward the landing beaches, and the third, according to *Howorth*'s war diary, "without warning . . . passed close aboard down the port side, flying low."[25] The enemy plane appeared so suddenly that the ship's gun crews never had a chance to open fire before it departed.

A nearby American destroyer's five-inch shells provided more of a threat when, because of incorrect fuse settings, they hit close to *Howorth*. Raines watched each succeeding shell splash two hundred feet closer to his destroyer, "and after six rounds we were really worried. It got to the point that the very next shell (we felt certain) would hit the ship." Suddenly the splashes stopped, and although Raines concluded, "I think the *Howorth* bears a charmed life," he recognized how close everyone had come to death. "I could just feel that shell ripping into our superstructure."[26]

After patrolling off Okinawa for two days, on April 4 Raines and the crew near him watched as the escort carrier USS *Wake Island*, "having been damaged by enemy suicide planes, passed through patrol stations with escort."[27] The carrier was another reminder that death and destruction could materialize in seconds.

"Be sweet Mommie and remember that I love you with everything I've got," Raines wrote to his wife. "No sleep last night due to Bogies but things are squared away now. Bye darling. More later."[28]

April 6 promised to be more of the same. The ship patrolled off Okinawa's west coast until late in the afternoon, when, according to a Navy press release, "all hell broke loose."[29] The swarm of kamikazes marked the first *kikusui* of Japan's massive Ten Go operation.

"There was not much going on for the first few days," said Seaman Bramble. *Howorth* had been posted to picket duty at one of the sixteen stations about Okinawa, placed there to intercept kamikazes and to provide an early warning system to alert the ships closer to shore that the enemy was on their way. Few crews looked forward to the duty, as those destroyers would be the first to absorb the attacks. "We were on picket duty, and I was on the bridge when we heard over the radio that twenty kamikazes were coming in from one direction and another twenty from a different direction." We figured, 'Here it comes.'"[30]

While the combat air patrol splashed the majority of the aircraft, some battled through in the north to sink the USS *Bush* (DD-529) and the USS *Colhoun* (DD-801). Kamikazes dived into targets off southern Okinawa and off the east coast, sinking three destroyers, one LST, and two ammunition ships. Burns later wrote in his action report, "It was soon obvious that the combat air patrol was putting up a great fight, but that the enemy was beginning to sift through because of overwhelming numbers."[31]

Seaman Bramble, the port wing lookout, nicknamed "Radar" because of his keen eyesight, spotted two groups of enemy aircraft coming in on the starboard quarter. Combat air patrol splashed some of the invaders, but others charged through to strike the destroyer *Mullany* (DD-528) and dive toward *Howorth*. Burns radioed to the central fighter director over TBS that they were "under heavy attack," while a nearby ship stated there were at least forty kamikazes in the area.[32]

Antiaircraft fire from both *Howorth* and the cruiser *St. Louis* downed one plane, briefly boosting the spirits of some, but those feelings quickly dissipated. "We shot down that first plane and everyone on the bridge yelled like we had just scored a touchdown," said Seaman Bramble. "Then things got itchy."[33]

Several more kamikazes barreled toward the destroyer. The first of them emerged from clouds sixteen thousand yards out and glided toward *Howorth*. Every deck gun joined in, and in seventy seconds they fired seventy-six 5-inch, four hundred 40mm, and five hundred 20mm rounds at the kamikaze. Even though the plane started smoking from hits, it continued toward the ship. It passed between the stacks, flipped over in a roll, and severed with its left wing all radio antennas and wires before splashing into the water just off the ship's starboard side.

On the bridge, Raines tried to focus on his duties, but it was difficult to block out the sounds and images. Radar screens showed several groups of kamikazes approaching, but Raines was more concerned with four planes on their starboard bow, which split into two groups and commenced a coordinated attack on his ship.

Burns called for top speed and began maneuvering to bring all his guns into play. The five-inch guns fired first, joined by the 40mm guns when another kamikaze drew within four thousand yards of the destroyer. Raines and Bramble wondered how anything could weave through that curtain of steel, but the plane continued directly toward the middle of the ship—his station. Fortunately, *Howorth* shells knocked down that kamikaze, which fishtailed into the water two hundred yards from *Howorth*.

The next kamikaze, hoping to sneak in while *Howorth*'s guns were focused on another target, attacked at the same time. Deck guns swerved toward it as soon as they had splashed the previous one, directing streams of shells toward the latest kamikaze. Now emitting smoke, the plane droned onward and passed between one of the five-inch guns and the fantail 20mm battery, scraping the deck and clipping lifelines before smashing into the water. "The captain was maneuvering to get the guns in position to fire at the plane and everyone was shouting as one came between the stacks," said Seaman Bramble. "The captain was good at maneuvering the ship."[34]

Yet another kamikaze attempted to sneak in, but Burns swerved the ship in time to bring his 40mm and 20mm guns into play. Those guns fired so rapidly that, even though repair parties and torpedomen helped break out additional ammunition, they had difficulty keeping the guns supplied. The plane went out of control and crashed 250 yards out. "It was now obvious that the ship had its hands full," wrote Burns. "Enemy planes were all around."[35]

With *Howorth*'s gun crews focused on that plane, one more kamikaze started a high, fast glide on the disengaged bow to try to come in dead ahead, giving Burns, Raines, and most of the men in the bridge a clear view of the oncoming plane approaching from the starboard side. "Just before we got hit, the navigator on the bridge told me I had better get off my chair," said Seaman Bramble. "He also shouted, 'Target, angle zero!' meaning the kamikaze was coming right at us. When you see everyone else hitting the deck, you know something's about to happen. I hit the deck just before the plane hit right above us. I might have died had I still been in that chair."[36] Five-inch shells from the forward battery ripped into the plane, but the kamikaze smashed directly into the bridge, igniting fires, killing men, and hurling Raines into the water. The final plane made a run on the port side, but 40mm gun crews shot him down five hundred yards astern of the ship.

Those final five kamikazes attacked in less than eight minutes. During that interval, *Howorth*'s gun crews fired 332 five-inch shells and more than 3,600 40mm and 20mm rounds. Four men were dead and fourteen wounded, with another five, which included Raines, listed as missing. "Once again 'Lady Luck' was on board ship," wrote Burns. "The plane that crashed could have caused considerably more damage. The contributing factors in stopping these suicide planes proved to be high speed, a large volume of accurate fire, good battery discipline, and radical maneuvers."[37]

Lady Luck accompanied Seaman Bramble into the water. He was standing only feet from Orvill Raines when the plane hit, tumbling Raines over the side and setting Bramble's clothes on fire. "I couldn't get out through the gangway," said Bramble, "because it was all on fire, so I jumped over the port side while the ship was doing about thirty knots. I hit head first in the water, and could have broken my neck because I was still wearing my helmet."[38]

Bramble removed his shoes, helmet, and binoculars, then looked around to see if anybody else from the ship, already hastening from the area, was nearby. "Radar, Radar, help me, help me!" he heard someone cry from not far away. When he spotted Raines struggling in the water without a life jacket, Bramble swam over to his shipmate and put his arms around him to help Raines keep his head above the surface. Bramble needed only a quick glance to see that Raines was badly burned, but he hoped he could help his buddy survive until a ship picked them up. "I held him up as long as I could," said Bramble, "but I could see he was in bad shape. Raines threw up, jerked a couple of times, and muttered through clenched teeth, 'This is a hell of a way to die.'" Moments later Raines's head slumped, and the letter writer succumbed. "I had to let him go," explained Bramble, upset that he had to part with his shipmate.[39] He had no choice, though, but to let Raines's body float away so he could focus on saving himself.

A minesweeper soon plucked Bramble, suffering from burns on both hands and his legs, from the water. After a week of treatment aboard ship, plus a few days in a Guam hospital, Bramble, still listed as missing in action, got word to his ship that he had survived.

Kamikazes sank six ships and damaged another fifteen during their April 6 *kikusui* onslaught. Repair parties aboard *Howorth* quickly extinguished the fires, and with steering restored, Burns took the destroyer to Hagushi Harbor for temporary repairs before leaving three days later for Saipan. On April 15, the crew gathered to conduct a nondenominational service to honor the memory of their fallen shipmates as well as that of President Roosevelt, who had died three days earlier from a cerebral hemorrhage. One day later the ship departed for Pearl Harbor, where the surviving crew enjoyed the good news: "Proceeding independently to Navy Yard, Mare Island, California, U.S.A."[40]

The ship arrived at Mare Island six days later to great acclaim. A Navy press release called her the "Haughty *Howorth*" and described her as a ship that "has plowed through thousands of miles of the western Pacific during the past nine months, and has participated in virtually every type duty assigned to destroyers. She has escorted convoys, covered landing assaults, bombarded shore installations and briefly traveled with fast carrier task forces."[41]

For *Howorth* and her crew, the war was over. For Ray Ellen, though, it continued. She figured that Orvill was all right and that she would soon receive another of his letters, but newspaper accounts describing the recent fighting off Okinawa as having "attained an intensity seldom rivaled before in the Pacific war" could not have eased her concerns.[42]

Ray Ellen learned nothing until Commander Burns's letter of sympathy arrived. Because of the heavy number of Okinawa casualties swamping the Navy Department, she had not yet received an official telegram stating that Orvill was missing, but Burns provided some information. He wrote Ray

Ellen that her husband was missing "following an enemy air attack upon this ship" on April 6. He informed her that several men, including Orvill, either had been blown overboard or jumped into the sea, and that "it is possible that one of the several ships close by picked him up."[43] On June 1, 1945, the couple's fifth wedding anniversary, Ray Ellen received official word from the Navy Department that Orvill was listed as killed in action.

Russell Bramble contacted Ray Ellen to inform her that her husband had not died alone. In a May 27 letter, which Bramble said "was a very hard letter for me to write," he admitted that he had debated sending the note but felt that she would want to know about Orvill's final moments. He explained that after he went overboard during the action, he swam to help Orvill, but that her husband was so badly burned that there was little he could do. "I'm sorry to say that James passed away in my arms," he told her, and wanted Ray Ellen to know "that I stayed with him until the very last."[44]

The most wrenching letter Ray Ellen received came from Orvill himself. The year before, he had written a letter for his wife, mailed it to her father, and asked him to deliver it to Ray Ellen if something happened to him. In that letter, dated July 30, 1944, Orvill told Ray Ellen, "I hope that you never read this letter. I have asked Pop to give it to you only in the event of my death." He mentioned that leaving her in San Francisco to go to the Pacific "was the hardest job I ever undertook, Baby. Just walking away from you, maybe forever." He said that he had cried so hard that men and women in the hotel lobby noticed it. "I haven't cried since but my soul has been disintegrating within me. I live only to get back to you. You will know by this letter that I'll never be back. That my life span has been completed, however brief, and our four wonderful years together will have to do us."

He wrote, "However I get it My Darling, remember that my last breath was drawn in an effort to get back to you." He told her to remarry. "These are the hardest words I could ever write or say to you," he acknowledged, but "somewhere there IS a man who can make you happy and cause you to forget." Even in such an emotional letter, Orvill inserted a touch of humor: "I just ask that you be SURE I am gone before taking any steps." Before signing, "Your devoted husband, Orvill," he included a final farewell: "Good bye, My Darling Baby. As I've said before, you gave me enough happiness during our four years together to justify any one man's lifetime."[45]

The correspondence of Orvill Raines conveys the emotions not only of Raines but of thousands of other sailors in the Pacific. Most never wrote such powerful letters, but they lived through the same tribulations and heartbreak as their gifted colleague. Desron 21 had one Orvill Raines, but the squadron contained hundreds of young men who left family and homes to fight for their nation. Many failed to return, and they and their families shed the same tears and felt the same pain of separation Raines so movingly described.

The crews of *O'Bannon*, *Nicholas*, and *Taylor* had far less tumultuous times off Okinawa, where they escorted a task group of escort carriers conducting air strikes from eighty-five miles out. The three saw no signs of kamikazes, and besides *Taylor* rescuing a downed Navy aviator, nothing unusual marked their ten days near Okinawa. Tarakan provided more of a challenge.

"Persuasion Is in the Form of a Tommy Gun"

The crews of the *Fletcher*, *O'Bannon*, *Nicholas*, *Jenkins*, and *Taylor* were not as worried about kamikazes for their next operation. The planned seizure of Tarakan, an island off Borneo's eastern coast, took them southwest of the Philippines instead of northward toward the kamikaze hunting grounds. Few if any of the suicide planes were expected to show up at Tarakan, an island that would give the Allies airfields to support subsequent landings and oil for their ships.

The five destroyers left Subic Bay on April 24 to provide the usual bombardment and fire support for the assault troops ordered to take that oil-rich island from the Japanese. Two days out, the unit came upon a group of rafts containing Japanese soldiers who were apparently attempting to flee the southern Philippines and reach friendly forces in Borneo. When *Nicholas* pulled closer to a pair of rafts holding two Japanese each, hoping to pick up and interrogate some of the prisoners, they were instead greeted with puffs of smoke from the hand grenades the soldiers used to commit suicide.

Taylor enjoyed better luck, capturing five Japanese who surrendered after a show of force by the ship's new skipper, Commander Henry H. DeLaureal. Although DeLaureal found nothing of significance, he wrote in his action report that they grabbed the five "after receiving encouragement by means of the Bull Horn and a rifle shot over their heads. In spite of leaving five rifles and at least two dozen hand grenades in their raft, the prisoners very reluctantly but most assuredly swam one by one away from their armory to the side of the ship. None of the five appeared to have the stomach for even as much as a display of fight." DeLaureal added, with much satisfaction, that "with persuasion, the enemy will surrender without qualms, particularly when the persuasion is in the form of a tommy gun."[46]

On the final day of April the Desron 21 destroyers followed the pattern that had often been repeated in the Philippines. They screened for minesweepers, conducted a pre-invasion bombardment of the beaches, and remained offshore to lend fire support for the infantry ashore. When the landing troops encountered no opposition, Commander Philip D. Gallery, the ship's skipper, took *Jenkins* from the bombardment area, but struck a mine as he exited. Men in the mess hall had just begun eating their sandwiches when the explosion rent the destroyer's port side. With the waters rushing in, the final man exited only moments before the compartment was flooded.

One man was killed and two wounded in the mishap, and *Jenkins* absorbed significant damage to her port side. All electrical power forward of the forward engine room was lost, the sonar gear no longer operated, and five compartments were flooded. Gallery noted that three of the compartments flooded after men failed to close hatches in their haste to reach the main deck and safety, and he urged the Navy to more strongly emphasize the matter during training and in drills.

The crew pumped water out of the flooded compartments to help keep the destroyer afloat, and the next morning the cruiser *Phoenix* came alongside to take some of the men aboard, give them the opportunity to shower to remove the oil clotting their skin, and provide them with fresh clothes.

After receiving temporary repairs at Subic Bay, the *Jenkins* started for the United States for more repairs. "When we tied up at the pier in Long Beach [California]," recalled Torpedoman's Mate 3/c Paul E. Mahan of their July arrival, "several men jumped off the *Jenkins* and kissed the ground."[47]

When on May 13 *Fletcher* left for the United States and an overhaul, only three Desron 21 destroyers—*O'Bannon*, *Nicholas*, and *Taylor*—remained in the Pacific. Those ships would take the fight directly into Tokyo Bay.

CHAPTER 11

EYEWITNESS TO VICTORY

A unit that had originated almost three years earlier with the trio of *O'Bannon*, *Fletcher*, and *Nicholas* again stood at three, with *Taylor* joining the old stalwarts *O'Bannon* and *Nicholas* to finish the war. The three operated off the Japanese coast screening for the units that had replaced them as the Navy's main tool—the fast carrier task forces. Destroyers had borne the load in the South Pacific when Nimitz and Halsey had few other surface vessels with which to check the Japanese, but in 1944 powerful carrier forces, sent to the Pacific by the home-front factories, assumed that mantle. *O'Bannon* and *Nicholas* had been in the Pacific since the beginning of their nation's comeback. It was apt that those two were now present at the end, reunited with Admiral Halsey to enjoy the fruits of their efforts.

Not that the crew wanted to be there. "Since we fully realized the menace and damaging effectiveness of the suicide plane tactics, this operation seemed to promise more excitement and danger than any of us really wanted," wrote *O'Bannon* Seaman 1/c George R. Thompson to his parents at the time.[1] Their sister ship *Howorth* had experienced the fury of kamikazes off Okinawa, and most military commanders expected that to be a pale preview of what Japan would unleash to protect the homeland. The apocalyptic battle to reach Japanese soil would overshadow in blood and destructiveness those earlier desperate encounters in the Solomons.

"Was the Killing Really Over?"

For most of July and into early August, the three screened for the fast carriers as they launched air strikes against Honshu and Hokkaido. Steaming anywhere from fifty to three hundred miles out, three carrier task groups operated at will off Japan's coast, strafing and bombing airfields and industrial targets. "Our planes would strike inland; our big guns would bombard coastal targets," stated Halsey, and "together they would literally bring the war home to the average Japanese citizen."[2] Each bomb became payback for what the Japanese had done, not just to their nation at places such as Pearl Harbor and Bataan but also to their Desron 21 ships and crews that were not present at the end, especially those of the sunken *De Haven*, *Strong*, and *Chevalier*. The only part Halsey could not understand was Nimitz's stern order to avoid bombing certain cities, including one named Hiroshima, but with a multitude of targets at hand, the ban seemed a minor issue.

Halsey selected Japan's most important centers for his first raids. From July 13 to July 15 Halsey's Third Fleet carriers, with *O'Bannon* screening, veered north to attack a major concentration of kamikaze aircraft, as well as airfields, shipping, and transportation in Hokkaido and northern Honshu, areas that until then had been beyond range of the Army's B-29 bombers and so had escaped American attack. While his aviators centered on the kamikazes, fourteen ships moved close to the Japanese shore to conduct a bombardment against a steel plant on Honshu. Halsey called the event "a magnificent spectacle," one he had wanted to observe since the Japanese attacked his United States Navy at Pearl Harbor.[3] With American ships operating so freely offshore and the carrier aircraft blasting inland targets, the Japanese Empire would soon be in ashes.

Desron 21 crews hoped that the war would soon end, as the frequent operations taxed their energy and consumed their food supply. *Nicholas* had been at sea for more than fifty days, a stretch requiring the crew to rely on dry stores such as flour, beans, rice, coffee, and canned meat. "For two weeks," said Sonarman 3/c Douglas Starr, "we had been eating nothing but weevily bread, beans, and rice, and moldy beef."[4]

The home front welcomed news that destroyers such as *Nicholas* and carrier aircraft were bringing the war directly to the enemy's shores, led again, as *Nicholas* had been in the Solomons, by Halsey. "The Third Fleet that swung up & down the east coast of Japan was the mightiest the world had ever seen," boasted *Time* magazine, led by "the tough, stubby seadog whom the Japanese mortally hate & fear. 'Bull' Halsey was on the prowl." Calling Halsey "the Annapolis-trained Dead End Kid" and "the calculating, chance-taking seaman," the magazine stated that the raids proved the end of the war was near.[5]

Listeners on the home front enjoyed Halsey's comments about the raids when the Navy broadcast his remarks in an effort to raise support for war bonds. Halsey's blunt assessment promised that the devastating raids would be repeated until Japan lay in ruins. "What is left of the Japanese Navy is helpless, but just for luck we're going to hunt them out of their holes," he vowed. "The Third Fleet's job is to hit the Empire hard and often. We are doing just that, and my only regret is that our ships don't have wheels, so that when we drive the Japs from the coast, we can chase them inland."[6]

One matter Sonarman Starr preferred to avoid was the invasion of the Home Islands. Monitoring the seas while carriers launched aircraft carried risks, but nothing like those that awaited once American forces landed on Japanese soil. While the Fifth Fleet under Spruance supported the landings on Kyushu, Halsey's Third Fleet, including the three Desron 21 destroyers, would operate with the United States Eighth Army in its assault on the Tokyo plains.

Every crew awaited the final call to assault Japan, which Starr wrote was "an operation the 300 officers and crew knew would be their toughest fight of the Pacific war." Starr heard that "the Japanese people would repel to the death any invasion of their sacred soil," and that Nimitz and Halsey predicted American casualties would approach one million. "All in all, we were a salty crew who had been through sixteen battles and invasions and countless convoy runs from Guadalcanal to Okinawa. None of us was eager about it, but we figured we could handle the Japanese home island, too."

Starr's hopes of survival rose dramatically on August 6, when word arrived that an American bomber had, with a single weapon, devastated Hiroshima. When a second bomber followed with a similar attack against Nagasaki three days later, it seemed that peace might any day be proclaimed. "Nobody cheered," wrote Starr, "but we all knew that, for all practical purposes, the Pacific war was over."[7]

Crews operated in a limbo between full-scale war and prospects for peace. They had to follow orders, but with war's end in sight, no one wanted to take unnecessary risks. "During the five days of negotiation, which terminated in the war's end, the atmosphere seemed charged with tense expectancy and suppressed excitement," George Thompson wrote his parents. "Moods alternated from soaring optimism to impatient pessimism as all hands eagerly awaited developments." When Halsey continued the air strikes on August 13–14, "our spirits sagged."[8]

In the early morning of August 15 carriers launched their strike groups for another round of attacks against airfields and factories in the Tokyo plains. Shortly after planes in the first two waves reached their targets, however,

Halsey abruptly canceled the operation when President Harry Truman announced that Japan had accepted peace terms. Ensign John C. McCarthy, aboard *Taylor* ninety miles off the coast, heard a fellow officer shout, "The war is over!" Aboard *O'Bannon* "there was a little cheering, backslapping, and handclasping," wrote Thompson, "but most of the men received the news with a sense of calm relief, sober and undemonstrative. The war was over, a job had been well done."[9]

Men gathered around radios to listen to Halsey's fifteen-minute announcement to the Third Fleet about the termination of hostilities. "You have brought an implacable, treacherous, and barbaric foe to his knees in abject surrender. This is the first time in the recorded history of the misbegotten Japanese race that they as a nation have been forced to submit to this humiliation." Then, thinking of all the officers and enlisted who had served under him, including Desron 21, he continued, "Your names are writ in golden letters on the pages of history—your fame is and shall be immortal. . . . Whether in the early days, when fighting with a very frayed shoestring, or at the finish, when fighting with the mightiest combined fleet the world has ever seen, the results have been the same—victory has crowned your efforts. The forces of righteousness and decency have triumphed."[10]

Although sailors aboard the three Desron 21 ships smiled at Halsey's directive that his aviators were to "investigate and shoot down all snoopers—not vindictively, but in a friendly sort of way," no wild celebration marked the occasion. "There was no cheering, no clapping or back slapping," wrote McCarthy of the reaction aboard *Taylor*. "No hand shaking. Just stunned silence. Then one voice spoke for all: 'I can't believe it. But if it's true, what's next? Do we go home now?'"

The emotions of the moment engulfed McCarthy. He wanted to be alone to process the news that the long, grueling war, one that had so often placed him and Desron 21 in tight predicaments, had at last ended. "Instead, I unexpectedly sank to my knees by my bunk to thank God—something I had seldom done before in the Navy," he wrote. "Was the killing really over? Nobody knew for sure. But there was an overwhelming feeling of relief that there would be no invasion of Japan."[11]

Nicholas's final war-related action of that day was to retrieve a downed aviator, Ensign Olen D. Glaize, who upon returning from the canceled air strikes crashed in the water alongside the carrier USS *Shangri-La* (CV-38). On a day that saw hostilities cease, the *Nicholas* crew appropriately saved a life instead of taking one.

Commander James A. Pridmore requested permission for his *O'Bannon* to display the ship's Presidential Unit Citation. Thompson wrote his parents that when Halsey replied, "Affirmative. Pat her on the cheek for me," Pridmore ordered the pennant hoisted from the foremast.

Crews still went to general quarters at sunrise and sunset in case a disgruntled Japanese aviator staged an attack. Even though eight planes were shot down in the hours after Halsey's announcements, conditions gradually calmed. Sporadic calls to man stations interrupted routine ship maintenance, but officers and enlisted operated more like a peacetime crew. "Most of us spent hours topside during this period nearly awestruck by the tremendous strength displayed by this mighty fleet," wrote Thompson. "As far as the eye could see were our first line carriers, battleships, heavy, light and antiaircraft cruisers, screened by some seventy destroyers."[12]

The *O'Bannon* crew again had the opportunity to see the admiral with whom Desron 21 had been linked since those dark days off Guadalcanal when, on August 19, Admiral Halsey boarded to be taken to HMS *Duke of York* preparatory to the surrender proceedings. Halsey's bulldog approach to war perfectly matched the disposition of destroyer crews, and Halsey did not disappoint. "The 'Bull' lived up to his reputation as a gruff congenial seadog with a good sense of humor," George Thompson wrote to his parents. "It's a great day, isn't it, lad?" Halsey said to Seaman Whisler, who was at the helm when Halsey boarded. All the young sailor could think of was, "Yes, sir."[13]

Men strained their necks to catch a glimpse of the admiral, whose love of destroyers shone in the comfortable way he moved about *O'Bannon*'s decks. "Having aboard, even for such a short period, Admiral Halsey and his staff, was a real pleasure," recorded the ship's war diary. "Since this crew had served immediately under Admiral Halsey in the days of Guadalcanal and the 'Slot' in 1942, they felt keen pleasure and sincere pride in having him aboard for the second time."[14]

In Halsey, the enlisted had not simply a skilled leader but a man they considered a friend. No one could imagine walking up to Douglas MacArthur to say hello, but they could visualize such a scene with Halsey, maybe even share a beer with the weathered leader. "He was a great guy," said Seaman Whisler, who remained at the helm while Halsey sat on the wing of the bridge. "Everyone admired Halsey because he was a front line admiral, right there, not always back at headquarters."[15] The crew's esteem for Halsey deepened when men learned that as *O'Bannon* and *Nicholas* pulled alongside his flagship, *Missouri*, to pick up the admiral, Halsey announced to the battleship's crew that if they wanted to get a look at a pair of fighting ships, all they needed to do was glance over the side at *O'Bannon* and *Nicholas*.

On August 27 the two destroyers, accompanied by *Taylor*, became the first American surface ships to enter Japanese waters since before the war when the Third Fleet anchored in Sagami Wan, a body of water adjoining the entrance to Tokyo Bay. According to instructions, the Japanese were to have trained their coastal batteries inland, opened the gun breeches, and removed all gun crews, but aboard *Taylor*, Lieutenant Commander DeLaureal took no chances. He asked Ensign McCarthy to survey the coast with his binoculars and alert him if he saw anything suspicious. The *Taylor* crew had been through enough, and the last thing DeLaureal wanted was to be harmed by a surprise bombardment. As *Taylor* and the group of ships slowly steamed along the coastline toward Sagami Wan, McCarthy scrutinized the shore, but he detected nothing alarming. Navy fighter aircraft confirmed his assessment by reporting over voice radio that the shore batteries were, as instructed, trained away from the ships.

McCarthy kept his attention shoreward anyway. When majestic Mount Fuji appeared in the background McCarthy, an avid stamp collector as a child, was pleased that it looked just like the images on his Japanese postage stamps. McCarthy's delight increased when an aviator radioed that he had just passed over a building whose rooftop announced in huge white letters, "Pappy is here!" Gregory "Pappy" Boyington, the top Marine ace of the war, had been shot down in the South Pacific in early 1944. Until that point no one had been certain whether he had survived the action, but the good news that Pappy was alive shot through the fleet.

Shortly after 7:00 a.m. *Nicholas* lookouts spotted the Japanese destroyer *Hatsuzakura* coming over the horizon. As previously ordered, *Nicholas* moved out ahead of the formation to meet the ship, closed to within two hundred yards, and lowered a boat containing a group of men led by Lieutenant (jg) Ernest G. Fanning and interpreter Lieutenant (jg) Donald K. Anderson. They were to pick up two Japanese naval officers—Captain Takasaki Yoshihito from the Yokosuka Naval Base and Captain Inaho Ontani of the Tokyo Navy Department—thirteen pilots, and six interpreters who would help the Third Fleet navigate home waters. The Desron 21 officers and sailors had been combating the Japanese for three years, and other than a few floating bodies or failed rescue attempts of enemy aviators, they had not seen their enemy up close. Now the young officers and their men were about to be in the same whaleboat with foes who had been trying to kill them. Both officers figured the transfer of the Japanese from *Hatsuzakura* to Halsey's *Missouri* and other ships would progress peacefully, but they took no unnecessary risks. When the whaleboat brought the Japanese to *Nicholas* the skipper, Commander Dennis C. Lyndon, had his men at general quarters, and sailors with sidearms escorted the group to the wardroom, where the Japanese were relieved of their swords and searched for weapons.

Every hand on *O'Bannon* packed the ship's superstructure to get a look at *Hatsuzakura*. Some were shocked at the dilapidated condition of the enemy destroyer, which lacked the martial splendor of the Japanese vessels *O'Bannon* had so bitterly fought in the Solomons.

While *Nicholas* transferred her guests to Halsey, *O'Bannon* and *Taylor* steamed to their anchorage in Sagami Wan. In the early evening, after an exciting day, they dropped anchor about one mile offshore. "The entry was uneventful," stated the war diary, "but very interesting and most gratifying."[16]

Halsey's assent to lighting up the ships at night concerned some aboard. Crews had become so accustomed to darkened conditions that the illumination made them uneasy during those first nights, when they could not be certain every Japanese pilot had followed orders to surrender. "Nothing untoward happened," wrote Starr. "Emperor Hirohito—God, to the Japanese—had told all Japanese people that the war was over, and that they should treat Americans as visitors, not as enemy."[17]

George Thompson and his buddies discussed what the day's events meant for a crew whose experiences could have been the template for the Navy's role in the Pacific war. They had witnessed the bombings and the island landings and the kamikazes, but now their silent guns were mute testimony to the triumph *O'Bannon* and her Desron 21 companions had helped fashion.

"The *O'Bannon* had fought the Japs from Guadalcanal through New Guinea and the Philippines to the threshold of the 'unconquerable invincible' Japanese homeland," Thompson wrote his parents, "and now a dream long cherished by all who had served on her would soon become a reality when the ship steamed victoriously into Nipponese waters."[18]

They celebrated the next evening. Commander Pridmore posted sentries to guard against suicide boats or swimmers, while the rest of the crew gathered topside to enjoy a movie. It was not the same as strolling into the Rialto or Summit Theater back home with a girlfriend, but under the circumstances, it was not a bad way to spend an evening in the Pacific.

"We Have Fought a Long Time for It"

No sailor present in Tokyo Bay on August 29 had ever witnessed such a spectacle. Any task force with which they had served during the war, however immense, shrank before the vast assemblage of almost four hundred warships—victory ensigns fluttering from their highest mast—that entered the bay that morning. The collection represented the naval might assembled by the United States to defeat Japan. Majestic carriers lingered at sea, their air squadrons ready to pounce should diehards decide to mount a last, desperate attack. Massive battleships and sleek cruisers, their powerful guns gleaming in the daylight, dwarfed the nimble destroyers that sliced through the waters.

"Admiral William F. Halsey triumphantly entered Tokyo Bay today aboard his flagship, the mighty battleship *Missouri*, as thousands of American and British bluejackets and marines stood by to make the first seaborne occupation of prostrate Japan," wrote the *New York Times*.[19] Halsey had his choice of any ship to lead in that impressive collection. His flagship, *Missouri*, or any of the battleships resurrected from Pearl Harbor to rejoin the fleet would have been apt selections, just as would any of those cruisers that had so frequently pulverized Japanese possessions during the many island assaults. One of the aircraft carriers that Nimitz and Halsey had relied on in the war's latter half to vanquish the Japanese could have been given the honor. Instead, without hesitation, Halsey turned to Desron 21, the destroyer crews that had held a frayed line off Guadalcanal when battleships and cruisers were lacking, moved from the Solomons to support New Guinea and Philippine landings, helped return revered Corregidor to US hands, and battled kamikazes as they approached Japan.

Nicholas, *O'Bannon*, and *Taylor* led the way, a trio of destroyers that, along with their absent Desron 21 comrades, were the smaller, faithful companions to the sleek aircraft carriers and the lumbering battleships, operating in the shadows while their larger brethren garnered much of the home front's attention. They represented the sacrifices made by the thousands of sailors to make this day possible, while in their van steamed the formidable collection sent to the battle areas by a nation united.

Once the ships anchored in Tokyo Bay, they tended to routine matters until September 2 and the surrender ceremony. *O'Bannon* transferred a prize crew and interpreter from the Yokosuka Naval Base to a surrendered Japanese submarine in Sagami Wan, and *Nicholas* took aboard eighty-six officers and enlisted for eventual transfer to the United States.

The only remaining vessels of Desron 21 operating in those waters shrank by one when, on the final day of August, Halsey designated *O'Bannon* to be the first to return. The ship and crew of the most honored destroyer of the war had earned that right, gained from accumulating a Presidential Unit Citation and seventeen battle stars, each star denoting meritorious service in battle. Commander Pridmore announced that the men had a choice of either remaining for the surrender ceremony or immediately heading home. "The crew," according to Seaman Whisler, "one hundred percent said United States." The next afternoon, one day before the surrender ceremony, Pridmore gave the order to lift anchor and took the ship out of Tokyo Bay, and, as George Thompson related, "we set sail for the good old U.S."[20]

Thirteen days later, with her decks jammed with excited officers and sailors who had not seen their homeland since early in 1944, *O'Bannon* arrived in California. People lined the Golden Gate Bridge as the fabled destroyer passed beneath. Ships in the harbor sounded their whistles, and crews lined their decks to honor the arrival of a warship that had so honorably served the nation for almost the entire Pacific conflict. "Passed under the Golden Gate Bridge," stated *O'Bannon*'s war diary, "and stood into San Francisco Bay, a thrill anticipated for twenty months."[21]

Only two destroyers from Desron 21 remained in Japan. Their crews would have loved to join *O'Bannon* for the trip home, but they took comfort that they could at least be part of the surrender ceremony, a once-in-a-lifetime event. Shortly after dawn on September 2, a Japanese delegation crossed *Nicholas*'s deck and boarded another ship to be taken to *Missouri*, followed by eighty-eight Allied notables that Commander Dennis C. Lyndon would transport to the battleship. *Nicholas* crew were thrilled to see Lieutenant General James "Jimmy" Doolittle, the Army officer who had commanded the bombers in the daring 1942 air attack on Tokyo; Lieutenant General J. W. Wainwright, who had languished in Japanese prison camps since his surrender at Corregidor early in the war; and the other renowned military figures from the United States and seven other nations.

Taylor ferried 238 war correspondents to the scene, including Richard Tregaskis, whose account of the Solomons fighting, *Guadalcanal Diary*, became a best-selling book as well as a popular film. As a military band played from a Yokohama dock, trucks and automobiles, displaying signs of wear from the long war, brought the reporters from their quarters to *Taylor*. According to William L. Worden, a *Saturday Evening Post* writer covering the surrender, "The destroyer *Taylor*, alongside the quay, had its crew in whites, and in its wardroom mess stewards struggled to provide coffee for 200 newspapermen who had been without it for a week." When Worden and the others stepped aboard, one of *Taylor*'s officers explained that "we've never been mentioned in print, for all the battles we've seen. You spell the name *T-a-y-l-o-r*."[22]

Taylor also boarded four Japanese reporters permitted to cover the proceedings. While the crew treated them with cautious respect, *Taylor*'s mascot, Subic, a small yellowish dog the men had picked up in the Philippines, gave one reporter a rude greeting. Shipboard scuttlebutt held that Subic had been badly abused by the Japanese, and Ensign John McCarthy, assigned to shepherd the Japanese during their time on the ship, watched as "Subic leaped forward and clamped his jaws on the lower leg of one of my charges." McCarthy pulled Subic off, expecting to be bitten by the snarling little dog, but instead the dog "looked at me with a pained expression," as if wondering why McCarthy had blocked his attempt at revenge. Worden observed the incident and wrote that Subic's bite "may well have been the last really overt act in the most terrible war in history."[23]

Nicholas and *Taylor* delivered their passengers to *Missouri* an hour before the scheduled 9:00 a.m. ceremony, and then anchored close enough to observe the surrender. Crew marveled at the ships that blanketed Tokyo Bay and at the nonstop stream of aircraft assigned to intercept any Japanese pilot who might try to interrupt the proceedings by smashing his plane into the battleship. When MacArthur arrived, he stepped over to Halsey and, with *Nicholas* and *Taylor* alongside, said that "it was grand to see so many of Bill Halsey's old South Pacific fighting scoundrels in at the kill." Halsey agreed, adding, "God what a great day this is. We have fought a long time for it."[24]

The two crews lingered on deck while MacArthur conducted the ceremony. After everyone had affixed their signatures to the surrender documents, MacArthur walked to Halsey and whispered, "Start 'em now!" At Halsey's signal, five hundred carrier aircraft and Army bombers droned above as an apt exclamation point to the war. Masuo Kato, one of the Japanese reporters, recalled Captain Hiraide's boast earlier in the war that a victorious Japan would one day hold a naval review in New York Harbor, and noted that instead "Japan had bowed to a conqueror in her own home waters"; had there been any doubts, "hundreds of American planes in beautiful formation roared overhead as a final reminder of the power that had destroyed an Empire."[25]

After the ceremony, *Nicholas* and *Taylor* returned the dignitaries to Yokohama. As the reporters and military personnel passed by Ensign McCarthy on their way off the ship, Masuo Kato extended his right hand to shake the ensign's. McCarthy briefly paused as if unsure what to do, then grasped Kato's hand in a friendly handshake. Kato bowed, thanked McCarthy, and stepped off the *Taylor*.

Once the guests had departed, DeLaureal gathered his officers in the wardroom to thank them for their help in what had been a hectic and emotional morning. He mentioned, however, that one of the military dignitaries, General Carl Spaatz, had told DeLaureal that he observed one of his ship's officers shaking hands with the enemy. Spaatz wanted the man disciplined for the action.

McCarthy knew that DeLaureal was referring to him, and he waited for his punishment. As the room fell silent, DeLaureal added, "I looked into the incident. It took place after the formal surrender. The war is over. The Japanese was a non-combatant newsman. Now we have to make the peace work. And as Captain of this ship I do not take orders from passengers, even if he is a General of the United States Army Air Corps." DeLaureal turned to McCarthy, reached across the table, and shook his hand. "You did a fine job today, Mac. Now let's all have some dinner and write a letter home or see a movie on the fo'c'sle. Then get a good night's sleep for a change."[26]

Nicholas and *Taylor* remained in Japan for another month. In mid-September they helped transport 250 Allied prisoners of war from various camps to a hospital ship. When along the way the former captives shared their experiences during those trying years of incarceration, the sailors were both thankful that they had avoided those terrible circumstances and angry over the Japanese cruelty to their countrymen.

Sonarman Starr wrote that the prisoners were "skeletons, some too weak to walk unaided." Starr added that nobody, crew or former prisoner of war, slept that night while *Nicholas* returned to Tokyo. "The POWs were too excited to sleep. They asked us questions, such as 'Who won the World Series?'" Starr hoped to learn about their ordeals in prison camp, "but they didn't talk much about that."

The next morning, crew had to help the POWs to the mess hall, because walking along the rolling deck and maneuvering the ladders was too difficult a task for men who had gone without sustenance for so long. "The cooks served the All-American breakfast, pancakes, butter, and syrup. The POWs' eyes were a lot bigger than their stomachs. They could have all they wanted, so they took 8, 10, 12, whatever pancakes. They ate one or two bites and couldn't eat any more because the food was too rich. They weren't used to eating so much at one time."

The crews enjoyed liberties ashore, where they walked among the ruins of what used to be part of Tokyo. They were surprised by the friendliness of the Japanese civilians, who, once their emperor advised them to accept the surrender, switched from military to civilian mode. Starr wrote, "When we got liberty, which we did in Tokyo, Yokohama, and, later, Sendai, we were treated as tourists, walking about, looking, shopping, talking with people who could speak English, settling down for lunch, that sort of thing."

Some ships, such as *Nicholas*, hired Japanese civilians to do the dishwashing and disposing of the garbage. "Normally we threw away our uneaten food," wrote Starr. "But the Japanese were hungry; they took that food home, reheated it, and fed their families and neighbors." The image of impoverished Japanese civilians hoarding scraps of food reminded Starr of the Depression era back home, when out-of-work men and their families, including his, had waited in breadlines. "My own family had stood in welfare lines for a pound of beans and a pound of rice," he wrote, "so seeing the Japanese taking our discards home to eat did not seem unusual or out of the ordinary. Hungry people ate whatever they could find." After observing the sad state of the civilians, Starr was convinced that if the atom bombs had not put an end to the war, hunger "almost certainly would have, and fairly soon."[27]

Both ships hoisted their homeward-bound pennants in October. *Nicholas* arrived in Seattle on October 19, "a great day" according to the ship's cruise book. The executive officer, Lieutenant Commander R. Townshend Jr., told the crew, "In looking back over the period of World War II and the record of the '*Nick*,' it is my earnest hope that you feel as proud as I do to be able to say, 'I was a *Nicholas* man.'"[28]

Three more Desron 21 destroyers returned to the United States in November, joining the four—*La Vallette*, *Radford*, *Fletcher*, and *Jenkins*—already in home waters for repairs. *Taylor* arrived on November 1, followed the next week by *Hopewell*. *Howorth*, which had been repaired from her kamikaze attack and was on her way back to the Pacific when the war ended, was the final squadron ship to return when she steamed beneath the Golden Gate Bridge on November 28.

EPILOGUE

Once hostilities ended, Commander MacDonald enjoyed a distinguished naval career during which he attained the rank of rear admiral. After leaving *O'Bannon*, he helped organize a school in the United States to instruct prospective commanding officers of destroyers before joining Allied forces in Europe, where he served as operations and plans officer and was reunited with his former London boss, Admiral Ghormley. Following the war, he commanded the presidential yacht, *Williamsburg*, during President Truman's tenure. Upon retirement from the Navy, MacDonald became a military consultant for various industries and a stockbroker. He died in 1997 at the age of eighty-eight.

Doc Ransom returned to California, where for more than forty-five years he tended civilian patients in San Jose with the same care he had given his *La Vallette* sailors. Doc Ransom performed numerous surgeries and delivered hundreds of babies, becoming a respected member of the community. The proud father of four children also loved Stanford University, never failing to attend the football team's home games and often accompanying them to away contests. In a sign of the esteem in which the San Jose area held Doc Ransom, the wake following his death from cancer on July 17, 1992, was heavily attended by his former patients and by many of the parents of the babies he had delivered.

Seaman Chesnutt returned to his hometown, Hope Hull, Alabama, where he and Betty, his wife of seventy years, enjoy a happy retirement. The explosions and noise from those battles of seven decades ago have receded, but the effects linger. Tom Chesnutt lost nearly half his hearing, making it difficult for him to discern softer sounds, such as crickets in the field or grandchildren at play. He deflects praise over what he and his squadron achieved so long ago, contending in 2016, "It was just a job we had to do."[1]

Ray Ellen followed Orvill Raines's wish that she remarry, but his memory never faded. In 1994, family granted permission to William M. McBride to edit and publish Orvill's powerful letters in the moving book *Good Night Officially: The Pacific War Letters of a Destroyer Sailor*.

Russell Bramble still thinks of the shipmate he held in his arms as they floated in the water. "He's on my mind quite often," said Bramble in 2016 from his home in Hastings, Nebraska, where he has lived his entire life. That Bramble stood not far from Raines on the bridge—a brief distance that resulted in Raines succumbing and Bramble surviving—has not been lost on him, but he tries to put life in perspective. "Every day's a holiday with me," said Bramble, who with his wife, Joan, recently celebrated their sixty-seventh wedding anniversary. Nonetheless, the memory of Orvill Raines is never far from his thoughts.[2]

Seaman Robert Whisler returned to Gladwin, Michigan, where in 1950 he "married the prettiest girl around," Lucille Koontz. He retired after a long career with Dow Chemical, and, as of this writing, enjoys a good life with Lucille and "lots of trout streams, golfing, and bowling." One constant in his life remains the now dulled silver dollar given him before the war by his grandmother, which he believes helped pull him through. "I carried it all through the war," he said. "It was always in my pocket. I had a guardian angel. I still have it. I still carry it in my pocket every day. I feel it is a part of me."[3]

The war altered Quartermaster Martin Johnson of *La Vallette* in a positive way. He said in 2016 that the ship's officers, who because of their college degrees held more important posts, inspired him to continue his education. "I saw the officers, who looked barely older than me, and they were officers because they had the education and I was a sailor because I didn't."[4] After the war Johnson earned a degree in optometry and spent the rest of his life in that field. He is now retired and living in New Mexico with Frances, his wife of fifty-nine years, and proud of their three children, seven grandchildren, and one great-grandchild.

Seaman 1/c Jack O'Neill of *Nicholas* chooses not to forget his experiences or the people with whom he served. Most shipmates are now gone, but his membership in a veterans group in Connecticut helps keep their memories vibrant. "We do military funerals," he explained in 2015. "That's what keeps you going." A sign in O'Neill's home adorning the entrance to one room, filled with *Nicholas* memorabilia, reads, "USS *Nicholas* (DD-449) Crew's

Quarters," and the former sailor proudly drives about town in a car bearing the license tag USS NIC.[5]

Tameichi Hara's exploits in the war, from the conflict's opening days in December 1941 until his nation's collapse in 1945, gained the officer great prestige and acclaim. One of the few Japanese destroyer captains to survive such extensive service, Hara returned to his wife, raised three children, and wrote an extraordinary memoir of his wartime experiences before he died in 1980. He could justifiably claim that, due to his many contributions to his nation during the war and because of his daring as a destroyer captain, he had obeyed his samurai grandfather, Moichiro, who admonished his grandson to live as a samurai, be prepared to die, and restore military honor to the family.

It would take pages and pages more to completely detail the record of Desron 21. Suffice it to say that ships of the squadron served in both theaters and in every major US offensive of the Pacific war save for the Mariana and Palau campaigns. In the Pacific, they began at Guadalcanal in 1942, swept up the Solomons and on to the Gilberts and Marshalls, moved along the New Guinea coast to the Philippines, and advanced north to Iwo Jima and Okinawa before being honored participants in the Tokyo Bay surrender. The twelve destroyers that served in the squadron earned more battle stars than any other unit, including seventeen for MacDonald's *O'Bannon*, sixteen for *Nicholas*, and fifteen each for *Fletcher* and *Taylor*.

Ships from the squadron fought in the Naval Battle of Guadalcanal and the Battle of Tassafaronga in November 1942, exchanged quick salvos in the furious fighting in the Slot and in the jarring 1943 Kula Gulf clashes, and evaded shells off Corregidor and mines in the Philippine waters. They held their breath as kamikazes swooped toward them in the Philippines and Okinawa, and again when they led Halsey's ships into Tokyo Bay.

They did not always participate in those headline-snaring surface engagements in which battleships and cruisers slugged it out with the Japanese, nor did they glide across the waters in grand style as did the fast carriers and their air squadrons. Theirs was more often the grunt work—the bombardments, the escorting assignments, and the harbor screenings—that, while less glamorous and not as exciting for home-front readers, chipped away at the Japanese military foundation as steadily as waves erode a shore. That work was equally as vital as those titanic sea clashes, and Desron 21 excelled in these areas.

Most important, the fast carrier task forces never would have been able to dominate Pacific waters in 1944–1945 without the courageous deeds of

Desron 21 and other destroyer crews in 1942–1943. When the nation needed time to expand its arsenal, those officers and enlisted helped stall the Japanese advance in the Solomons and begin the turnaround that led to victory. Their sacrifices in the war's first half helped enable the nation's armed forces to overwhelm a Japanese military plagued by depleted resources as the United States added to theirs.

Let one of the squadron officers argue the case. "The ships of Desron 21 achieved a remarkable record, sharing in the sinking of a Japanese battleship, several cruisers, a half dozen destroyers and dozens of aircraft," wrote Ensign McCarthy of the *Taylor*. "They were credited with sinking ten submarines, three by the *Taylor*." He said the unit "participated in countless shore bombardments, rescued 1,800 sailors and downed airmen," and earned a record number of battle stars during the war.[6] The initial trio of *O'Bannon*, *Fletcher*, and *Nicholas* each steamed more than 230,000 miles during the war, equal to nine times around the world at the equator.

Besides engaging the enemy, Desron 21 made other significant contributions to the war. Admiral Halsey's belief that Desron 21 was a key factor in holding the line in the Solomons until help arrived, an achievement of the admiral's that may have saved the Pacific war, led to Halsey selecting the final three destroyers from the squadron to lead his armada into Tokyo Bay. Cole and Wylie of *Fletcher* promoted the benefits of radar and helped develop the combat information center, which numerous commanders cited as a significant enhancement in their ability to wage surface combat. MacDonald and fellow skippers pushed for a reform of destroyer tactics, which blossomed under the guidance of Arleigh Burke.

It came with a cost, however. Three ships—*De Haven*, *Strong*, and *Chevalier*—were sunk, either from aerial bombs or by torpedoes. Five sustained heavy damage, including Doc Ransom's *La Vallette*, Orvill Raines's *Howorth*, *Radford*, *Fletcher*, and *Jenkins*. Almost four hundred men perished. Remarkably, while some destroyers were sunk, *O'Bannon* sustained little damage and its crew absorbed not a single battle casualty.

Nicholas, too, was fortunate. "We were a lucky ship," wrote Ensign Gabelman. "When the *De Haven* was sunk by six dive bombers, eight more had gone after the *Nicholas*. We lost two men (our only two of the war) to a near miss. On at least two different occasions, we saw torpedoes passing our ship but missing. We were only 400 yards ahead of the *Strong* the night she was sunk by a torpedo fired from eleven miles away. Later in the war, a kamikaze tried to crash our ship. It barely missed the bridge but it did clip part of the yardarm high up on the mast. It took lots more than skill to remain afloat."[7]

Service with Desron 21 affected the crews in different ways. Sonarman 3/c Douglas Starr packed a lifetime of experiences into just a few years. "I was one month over 18 years old and a sonarman 3/c when I joined USS *Nicholas* (DD 449) at Mare Island Naval Shipyard in mid-December 1943," Starr wrote after the war. "Twenty-one months later, *Nicholas* and I had fought in 11 battles and island landings and sunk two Japanese submarines, and I was not yet 20 years old. All in all, it was a grand adventure; I would not have missed it for the world."[8]

Commander MacDonald was proud to watch his crew coalesce before his eyes. The lessons he learned in London, where he worked side by side with English citizens as they stood resolute, united by Winston Churchill in their defiance of the Nazi threat, helped mold the skipper who so capably commanded in the Pacific. Like those brave London residents, his crew withstood everything the Japanese offered and emerged triumphant. "The *O'Bannon* is a great ship but the crews cannot be overlooked as they are what has made her so," MacDonald wrote in 1964. "From the start of her life it seemed that someone above was looking out for us. We called it luck but it was more than that. The crew learned to fight together."[9]

As far as Lieutenant George Gowen, *Chevalier*'s engineering officer, was concerned, the war prepared him and others to face future tribulations, for if they could emerge from the chaos that was the Pacific war, they could deal with anything. "I'm sure that you will all agree that our service in *Chevalier* affected our whole lives. Those who came through looked deep into their own hearts and souls and characters and they have marched forward through all their trials and tests with pride and confidence."[10]

Soldiers and sailors returning from the war typically put those experiences behind them to concentrate on building families and careers. Reflection on what they did comes later, when an event or action jars the memory. One occurred in 1983 with a letter from Alvin Brooks, formerly of the cruiser *Northampton*, to *Fletcher* sailor Olon Henderson. After the *Northampton* sank in the November 1942 Battle of Tassafaronga, Brooks had been struggling to stay above the surface of the water when *Fletcher*'s crew came to his rescue. Forty-one years later he wished to thank those men for saving his life and for giving him years to fashion home and family that otherwise could have been denied him.

"I was one of those oily Gobs that you and your buddies pulled from the Pacific Ocean on Nov. 30–Dec. 1, 1942. I'm sure glad your shipmates were on the ball that fateful night because I was tired of swimming," he wrote. "I sincerely owe my life to the USS *Fletcher* and her crackerjack crew." He added that he wanted Henderson and every other member of *Fletcher* to know "how grateful I and my *Northampton* shipmates are that the *Fletcher* came to the rescue."

Brooks wrote a poem titled "The USS *Fletcher* DD-445" to express his gratefulness for *Fletcher*'s actions of four decades earlier. Here are three of the stanzas:

> Oh! What a wonderful sight it was
> Her beacon lighting up the swell
> To me she was an angel of mercy
> Pulling me from the grips of hell.
>
> *Fletcher* didn't know the meaning of fear
> And remained within harm's way
> She plucked us from the oily sea
> To fight another day.
>
> Yes, I hate to get hung up on numbers
> But there's lucky ones of every size
> And on November 30th, 1942
> My lucky one was 445 [*Fletcher*'s hull number].[11]

Thomas Chesnutt, one of the *Fletcher* crew honored by Brooks's poem, considered that, except for his marriage, his time in the Navy was the noblest period of his life. His pride in his ship and his shipmates, who banded together to help defeat the Japanese, and his love for the Navy, which was such a large part of that victory, still shine. "'Anchors Aweigh' still makes shivers run up and down my back," he wrote. "I guess I will always be a United States Navy man at heart!"[12]

So, too, is Machinist's Mate 1/c Willy Rhyne of *O'Bannon*, who continues to attend his ship's reunions even though many of his buddies are no longer with him. The years have taken a toll, but the spirit of his destroyer, instilled by Commander MacDonald, continues to resonate. He is proud of the ship and of the officers and men with whom he served.

Rhyne is glad as well that they have not been forgotten. In 2015 he and a handful of World War II shipmates, as part of that year's reunion, attended a San Diego Padres baseball game. "We were guests at the Padres game and had VIP seats," said Rhyne. "They mentioned on the big screen that *O'Bannon* heroes were here, and we got an ovation."[13]

Al Grimes of the *Strong* honors the memories of his shipmates, especially those who perished after the ship went down, but claims that victory was possible only because of the combined efforts of everybody who served. His words encapsulate the key ingredient to victory in the Pacific and the common thread that ran throughout the destroyers of Desron 21: "Each old sailor cherishes his own private inner shrine that is filled with the memories of those great old guys he knew so long ago. They did what was needed when it was needed, regardless of the hours and risk—and it was no big deal. Each of us knew many like this; they were everywhere. That's the way it was on *Strong*."[14]

That's the way it was, too, in Destroyer Squadron 21. A career Navy officer, a civilian seaman, a gridiron hero, a doctor, and a romantic yeoman, backed by far-thinking officers and shipmates willing to sacrifice the utmost, melded to form the most honored destroyer squadron of the Pacific war. Together, they bested Hara and the Japanese in the Solomons and helped take the war to the waters of Tokyo Bay.

They were the heroic men and ships of the Navy's most decorated destroyer squadron.

CHRONOLOGY

1942

September: *O'Bannon*, *Nicholas*, and *Fletcher* arrive in the South Pacific
November: North Africa landings
November 12–15: Naval Battle of Guadalcanal
November 12, 1942–January 19, 1943: Seizure of Guadalcanal
November 30–December 1: Battle of Tassafaronga
December: *De Haven* arrives in the South Pacific

1943

January: *Taylor*, *Jenkins*, *Radford*, *La Vallette*, and *Strong* arrive in the South Pacific
January: The Cactus Striking Force is formed
January 29–30: Battle of Rennell Island
February: *Chevalier* arrives in the South Pacific
February 1: *De Haven* is sunk
March 10: Destroyer Squadron 21 is formed
July 5–6: Battle of Kula Gulf
July 5: *Strong* is sunk
July 5–August 16: Lieutenant Hugh B. Miller wages his one-man battle with the Japanese
July 12–13: Battle of Kolombangara
August 6: Battle of Vella Gulf
August 15–16: Battle off Horaniu
August 31: Marcus Island raid
October: *Hopewell* arrives in the South Pacific
October 6: Battle of Vella Lavella
October 6: *Chevalier* is sunk
November: Operations off the Gilbert Islands

1944

January–March: Operations off the Marshall Islands
April 22: Landings at Aitape
May–June: Operations off Biak
July 2: Landings at Noemfoor
July 27: Landings at Sansapor
August: *Howorth* arrives in the South Pacific
September 15: Landings at Morotai
October: Operations at Leyte Gulf
December 6–9: Landings at Ormoc
December 12–15: Landings at Mindoro

1945

January 8–9: Landings at Lingayen Gulf
February 13–15: Operations at Corregidor
February 14: *La Vallette* and *Radford* are damaged off Corregidor
February–March: Operations off Iwo Jima
April–May: Operations off Borneo
April–June: Operations off Okinawa
April 6: *Howorth* is damaged by kamikazes
June 18: *Jenkins* is damaged
July–August: Operations off Japan
August 27: Desron 21 destroyers lead Halsey's fleet into Tokyo Bay
September 2: Desron 21 destroyers participate in the surrender ceremonies

APPENDIX I
BATTLE STARS AWARDED

BATTLE STARS

O'Bannon	*17*
Nicholas	*16*
Fletcher	*15*
Taylor	*15*
Jenkins	*13*
Radford	*12*
La Vallette	*10*
Hopewell	*9*
Howorth	*5*
Chevalier	*3*
Strong	*2*
De Haven	*1*

CAMPAIGNS EARNING THE BATTLE STARS

USS O'Bannon

1942

Naval Battle of Guadalcanal, November 12–15, 1942
Seizure of Guadalcanal, November 12, 1942–January 19, 1943

1943

Rennell Island, January 29–30, 1943
Actions in the southern Solomons, March–June 1943

Antisubmarine actions, April 4, 1943
New Georgia operations, including the Battles of Kula Gulf, July–October 1943

1944

Hollandia operations, April–May 1944
Escort and antisubmarine operations with Task Group 30.4, May–June 1944
Western New Guinea landings, June–September 1944
Leyte operations, October–December 1944
Luzon operations, December 1944–January 1945

1945

Antisubmarine actions, January 31, 1945
Operations in the southern Philippines, February–March 1945
Manila Bay operations, April 1945
Borneo operations, April–May 1945
Okinawa operations, May–June 1945
Operations off Japan, July–August 1945

USS Nicholas

1942

Seizure of Guadalcanal, November 12, 1942–January 19, 1943

1943

Actions in the southern Solomons, March–June 1943
New Georgia operations, including the Battles of Kula Gulf, July–October 1943
Gilbert Islands assault, November 1943

1944

Antisubmarine actions, February 17, 1944
Hollandia operations, April–May 1944
Escort and antisubmarine operations with Task Group 30.4, May–June 1944
Western New Guinea landings, June–September 1944
Leyte operations, October–December 1944
Antisubmarine actions, November 12, 1944

1945

Luzon operations, December 1944–January 1945
Corregidor-Bataan assault, February 14–28, 1945

Operations in the southern Philippines, February–March 1945
Borneo operations, April–May 1945
Okinawa operations, May–June 1945
Operations off Japan, July–August 1945

USS Fletcher

1942

Naval Battle of Guadalcanal, November 12–15, 1942
Seizure of Guadalcanal, November 12, 1942–January 19, 1943
Battle of Tassafaronga, November 30–December 1, 1942

1943

Antisubmarine actions, February 11, 1943
Actions in the southern Solomons, March–June 1943
Gilbert Islands assault, November 1943

1944

Marshall Islands assault, January–March 1944
Hollandia operations, April–May 1944
Escort and antisubmarine operations with Task Group 30.4, May–June 1944
Western New Guinea landings, June–September 1944
Leyte operations, October–December 1944
Luzon operations, December 1944–January 1945

1945

Corregidor-Bataan assault, February 14–28, 1945
Operations in the southern Philippines, February–March 1945
Borneo operations, April–May 1945

USS De Haven

1942

Seizure of Guadalcanal, November 12, 1942–January 19, 1943

USS Taylor

1943

Rennell Island, January 29–30, 1943
Actions in the southern Solomons, March–June 1943
Antisubmarine actions, July 11, 1943

New Georgia operations, including the Battles of Kula Gulf, July–October 1943
Gilbert Islands assault, November 1943

1944

Hollandia operations, April–May 1944
Escort and antisubmarine operations with Task Group 30.4, May–June 1944
Antisubmarine actions, July 10, 1944
Western New Guinea landings, June–September 1944
Leyte operations, October–December 1944
Luzon operations, December 1944–January 1945

1945

Corregidor-Bataan assault, February 14–28, 1945
Operations in the southern Philippines, February–March 1945
Borneo operations, April–May 1945
Okinawa operations, May–June 1945

USS Jenkins

1942

North Africa landings, November 1942

1943

Actions in the southern Solomons, March–June 1943
New Georgia operations, including the Battles of Kula Gulf, July–October 1943
Gilbert Islands assault, November 1943

1944

Marshall Islands assault, January–March 1944
Hollandia operations, April–May 1944
Escort and antisubmarine operations with Task Group 30.4, May–June 1944
Western New Guinea landings, June–September 1944
Leyte operations, October–December 1944
Luzon operations, December 1944–January 1945

1945

Antisubmarine actions, January 31, 1945
Corregidor-Bataan assault, February 14–28, 1945

Operations in the southern Philippines, February–March 1945
Borneo operations, April–May 1945

USS Radford

1943

Seizure of Guadalcanal, November 12, 1942–January 19, 1943
Actions in the southern Solomons, March–June 1943
Antisubmarine actions, June 1, 1943
New Georgia operations, including the Battles of Kula Gulf, July–October 1943
Gilbert Islands assault, November 1943
Antisubmarine actions, November 25, 1943

1944

Marshall Islands assault, January–March 1944
Hollandia operations, April–May 1944
Escort and antisubmarine operations with Task Group 30.4, May–June 1944
Western New Guinea landings, June–September 1944
Luzon operations, December 1944–January 1945

1945

Corregidor-Bataan assault, February 14–28, 1945

USS La Vallette

1943

Rennell Island, January 29–30, 1943
Marcus Island raid, August 31, 1943
Gilbert Islands assault, November 1943

1944

Marshall Islands assault, January–March 1944
Hollandia operations, April–May 1944
Escort and antisubmarine operations with Task Group 30.4, May–June 1944
Western New Guinea landings, June–September 1944
Leyte operations, October–December 1944
Luzon operations, December 1944–January 1945

1945

Corregidor-Bataan assault, February 14–28, 1945

USS Strong

1943

Actions in the southern Solomons, March–June 1943

New Georgia operations, including the Battles of Kula Gulf, July–October 1943

USS Chevalier

1943

Rennell Island, January 29–30, 1943

Actions in the southern Solomons, March–June 1943

New Georgia operations, including the Battles of Kula Gulf, July–October 1943

USS Hopewell

1944

Marshall Islands assault, January–March 1944

Hollandia operations, April–May 1944

Escort and antisubmarine operations with Task Group 30.4, May–June 1944

Seizure of the northern Solomons, June–August 1944

Western New Guinea landings, June–September 1944

Leyte operations, October–December 1944

Luzon operations, December 1944–January 1945

1945

Corregidor-Bataan assault, February 14–28, 1945

Operations off Japan, July–August 1945

USS Howorth

1944

Western New Guinea landings, June–September 1944

Leyte operations, October–December 1944

Luzon operations, December 1944–January 1945

1945

Assault of Iwo Jima, February–March 1945

Okinawa operations, May–June 1945

APPENDIX II

LOCATION OF SHIPS AT WAR'S END

O'Bannon	Tokyo Bay
Nicholas	Tokyo Bay
Taylor	Tokyo Bay

Elsewhere

Hopewell	Sailing from Guam
Howorth	Returning to Pacific after repairs

Sunk

De Haven	February 1, 1943: aerial bombs sink her off Savo
Strong	July 5, 1943: torpedo sinks her
Chevalier	October 6, 1943: torpedo sinks her

In United States from Damage

La Vallette	February 14, 1945, to United States after mine damage
Radford	February 1945, to United States after mine damage
Fletcher	May 13, 1945, to United States for overhaul
Jenkins	June 18, 1945, to United States after mine damage

NOTES

PROLOGUE

1. William F. Halsey and J. Bryan III, *Admiral Halsey's Story* (New York: McGraw-Hill, 1947), 275, 277.

2. Destroyer Squadron 21, "World War II in Quotes," found at http://destroyerhistory.org/fletcherclass/index.asp?r=4210&pid=4213, accessed June 30, 2015. This and subsequent quotes from this website are used courtesy of Meredith McComb, widow of Dave McComb, Destroyer History Foundation.

3. James D. Horan, *Action Tonight: The Story of the American Destroyer* O'Bannon *in the Pacific* (New York: G. P. Putnam's Sons, 1945), vii.

CHAPTER 1: THE DESTROYERS GO TO WAR

1. "Reminiscences of Rear Admiral Donald J. MacDonald, U.S. Navy (Retired)," United States Naval Institute, Annapolis, Maryland, Interview Number 1, May 22, 1974 (hereafter "MacDonald Reminiscences, May 22, 1974"), 2–3, 9.

2. Ibid., 13–14.

3. Ibid., 17, 35–37.

4. Ibid., 47, 54, 58–59, 67.

5. "Reminiscences of Rear Admiral Donald J. MacDonald, U.S. Navy (Retired)," United States Naval Institute, Annapolis, Maryland, Interview Number 2, July 23, 1974 (hereafter "MacDonald Reminiscences, July 23, 1974"), 126, 157.

6. Letter from Donald MacDonald to Dad and Family, February 25, 1941, in Papers of Donald J. MacDonald, Box 1, Folder 7, "Correspondence, 1930, 1936–1942," Naval Historical Foundation Collection, Manuscript Division, Library of Congress.

7. Frederick J. Bell, *Condition Red: Destroyer Action in the South Pacific* (New York: Longmans Green, 1944), 176.

8. Bernard Brodie, *A Guide to Naval Strategy* (Princeton: Princeton University Press, 1944), 65–66.

9. "Recollections of Rear Admiral MacDonald," Papers of Donald J. MacDonald, Box 5, Folder 7, "Historical Material, Writings by MacDonald, Unidentified Draft [Written First Half of 1944]," Naval Historical Foundation Collection, Manuscript Division, Library of Congress (hereafter "MacDonald Recollections").

10. Ibid., 2.

11. Diary of Virgil Wing, USS *Nicholas*, June 4, 1942, found at http://destroyerhistory.org/fletcherclass/index.asp?r=44905&pid=44932, accessed July 7, 2015 (hereafter "Wing Diary").

12. "Reminiscences of Rear Admiral Donald J. MacDonald, U.S. Navy (Retired)," United States Naval Institute, Annapolis, Maryland, Interview Number 3, August 6, 1974 (hereafter "MacDonald Reminiscences, August 6, 1974"), 188; Donald J. MacDonald, "They Went to Hell and Back with Me," *American Magazine*, July 1944, 24.

13. MacDonald, "Hell and Back," 25.

14. "Oral History of Rear Admiral Joseph C. Wylie, USN (Ret.)," Naval War College, Oral History Program, interview conducted by Dr. Evelyn M. Cherpak on December 17, 1985 (hereafter "Wylie Oral History"), 60.

15. MacDonald Recollections, 3; MacDonald Reminiscences, August 6, 1974, 189.

16. Author's interview with James Setter, July 21, 2015.

17. MacDonald Recollections, 3–4.

18. "Command Summary of Fleet Admiral Chester W. Nimitz, 7 December 1941–31 August 1945," September 10, 1942 (hereafter "Greybook").

19. Fred Gressard, "Reminiscences," found at http://destroyerhistory.org/fletcherclass/ussfletcher/index.asp?r=44500&pid=44504, accessed December 4, 2014.

20. Wylie Oral History, 65.

21. MacDonald Reminiscences, August 6, 1974, 200.

22. C. Raymond Calhoun, *Tin Can Sailor: Life Aboard the USS* Sterett, *1939–1945* (Annapolis, MD: Naval Institute Press, 1993), 62.

23. MacDonald Recollections, 6.

24. MacDonald Reminiscences, August 6, 1974, 204.

25. Wing Diary, September 11, 1942.

26. Ibid., September 19, 1942.

27. Greybook, October 1, 1942.

28. Charles Hurd, "Jungle Island Becomes the Heart of Great Battle for the Pacific," *New York Times*, October 18, 1942.

29. Hanson W. Baldwin, "Solomons Action Develops into Battle for South Pacific," *New York Times*, September 27, 1942; Hanson W. Baldwin, "South Pacific War Develops on a Vast Scale," *New York Times*, October 4, 1942.

30. Masuo Kato, *The Lost War: A Japanese Reporter's Inside Story* (New York: Alfred A. Knopf, 1946), 82.

31. Matome Ugaki, *Fading Victory: The Diary of Admiral Matome Ugaki, 1941–1945* (Pittsburgh: University of Pittsburgh Press, 1991), 177.

32. MacDonald Recollections, 6.

CHAPTER 2: INITIATION AT GUADALCANAL

1. Wing Diary, October 1, 1942.

2. Quote found at http://destroyerhistory.org/fletcherclass/desron21/index.asp?r=4210&pid=4213, accessed September 23, 2015.

3. Charles Hurd, "Ships Sunk by Foe," *New York Times*, October 22, 1942; Hanson W. Baldwin, "Fighting for Outposts in Pacific Is Prelude to Greater Struggle," *New York Times*, October 11, 1942, E4.

4. A. A. Vandegrift, *Once a Marine* (New York: W. W. Norton, 1964), 181.

5. Ibid., 175.

6. Ibid., 177–178.

7. Matome Ugaki, *Fading Victory: The Diary of Admiral Matome Ugaki, 1941–1945* (Pittsburgh: University of Pittsburgh Press, 1991), 232.

8. Ibid., 240; Samuel Eliot Morison, *History of United States Naval Operations in World War II*, volume V, *The Struggle for Guadalcanal, August 1942–February 1943* (Boston: Little, Brown, 1949), 287.

9. "Reminiscences of Hanson Weightman Baldwin, U.S. Navy (Ret.)," interview by John T. Mason, United States Naval Institute, Annapolis, Maryland, 1976, 345.

10. E. B. Potter, *Nimitz* (Annapolis, MD: Naval Institute Press, 1976), 192.

11. William F. Halsey, "Life of Admiral W. F. Halsey," undated typewritten memoirs dictated by Halsey after the war (copies distributed by the Virginia Historical Society), 367 (hereafter Halsey, "Life"); William F. Halsey and J. Bryan III, *Admiral Halsey's Story* (New York: McGraw-Hill, 1947), 109.

12. Robert Trumbull, "All Out with Halsey!" *New York Times*, December 6, 1942, 14, 35.

13. Gilbert Cant, *America's Navy in World War II* (New York: John Day, 1943), 359.

14. *Los Angeles Times*, October 26, 1942; *New York Times*, October 25, 1942.

15. "Patch of Destiny," *Time*, November 2, 1942, 29–31.

16. Foster Hailey, "Halsey Defends Battleship's Role," *New York Times*, November 19, 1942, 8; Halsey, "Life," 403.

17. "Third Fleet Operation Highlights, 1943–1945," Third Fleet War Diary, in the Admiral William F. Halsey Collection, Naval Historical Foundation Collection, Manuscript Division, Library of Congress, Washington, D.C.

18. "Face to Face," *Time*, November 9, 1942, 17.

19. C. Raymond Calhoun, *Tin Can Sailor: Life Aboard the USS* Sterett, *1939–1945* (Annapolis, MD: Naval Institute Press, 1993), 65.

20. Author's interview with Robert Whisler, October 15, 2015.

21. Herbert P. Bix, *Hirohito and the Making of Modern Japan* (New York: Harper Collins, 2000), 458.

22. Author's interviews with Robert Whisler, July 10, 2015, and July 22, 2015.

23. MacDonald Recollections, 7.

24. Wing Diary, October 24, 1942.

25. Ibid., October 25, 1942.

26. Ugaki, *Fading Victory*, 255; Dan Kurzman, *Left to Die: The Tragedy of the USS* Juneau (New York: Pocket Books, 1994), 88.

27. Ugaki, *Fading Victory*, 261.

28. Tameichi Hara with Fred Saito and Roger Pineau, *Japanese Destroyer Captain* (Annapolis, MD: Naval Institute Press, 1967), 3.

29. Greybook, November 3–8, 1942.

30. Ibid., November 9, 1942.

31. Halsey and Bryan, *Admiral Halsey's Story*, 125.

32. Halsey, "Life," 383, 389.

33. Whisler interview, October 15, 2015.

34. Author's interview with Donald Holmes, October 14, 2015.

35. Wylie Oral History, December 17, 1985, 67, 69–70.

36. Hanson W. Baldwin, "Showdown in Solomons," *New York Times*, November 16, 1942.

37. Donald J. MacDonald, "They Went to Hell and Back with Me," *American Magazine*, July 1944, 25; MacDonald Recollections, 7a.

38. Carl F. Pfeifer and Jack S. McDowell, "Lucky Mike Plays for Keeps," *True, the Man's Magazine*, May 1944, 26.

39. MacDonald Reminiscences, August 6, 1974, 208; MacDonald Recollections, 7a.

40. Pfeifer and McDowell, "Lucky Mike," 27.

41. Executive Officer to Commanding Officer, "Report of Action," November 15, 1942. This and all other vessel action reports are at the National Archives and Records Administration, College Park, MD.

42. USS *O'Bannon* War Diary, November 12, 1942.

43. Pfeifer and McDowell, "Lucky Mike," 28.

44. MacDonald Reminiscences, August 6, 1974, 209–210; MacDonald, "Hell and Back," 25.

45. Commanding Officer to Commander in Chief, United States Fleet, "Report of Engagement with Japanese Units on Morning of November 13, 1942," November 17, 1942 (hereafter "Wilkinson Action report, November 17, 1942").

46. Author's interview with Donald Holmes, October 22, 2015.

47. MacDonald Reminiscences, August 6, 1974, 211; MacDonald, "Hell and Back," 25.

CHAPTER 3: NAVAL SLUGFEST OFF GUADALCANAL

1. Tameichi Hara with Fred Saito and Roger Pineau, *Japanese Destroyer Captain* (Annapolis, MD: Naval Institute Press, 1967), 130.

2. Samuel Eliot Morison, *History of United States Naval Operations in World War II*, volume V, *The Struggle for Guadalcanal, August 1942–February 1943* (Boston: Little, Brown, 1949), 244; Hara, *Japanese Destroyer Captain*, 126.

3. Hara, *Japanese Destroyer Captain*, 131.

4. MacDonald Reminiscences, August 6, 1974, 211.

5. C. Raymond Calhoun, *Tin Can Sailor: Life Aboard the USS* Sterett, *1939–1945* (Annapolis, MD: Naval Institute Press, 1993), 77.

6. Donald J. MacDonald, "They Went to Hell and Back with Me," *American Magazine*, July 1944, 25, 89.

7. Hara, *Japanese Destroyer Captain*, 133.

8. MacDonald Reminiscences, August 6, 1974, 213.

9. MacDonald, "Hell and Back," 89; MacDonald Reminiscences, August 6, 1974, 213.

10. Executive Officer to Commanding Officer, "Report of Personal Impressions and Recollection of the Night Action with Japanese Units in Guadalcanal–Florida Island Area, November 13, 1942," November 16, 1942, 2 (hereafter "MacDonald Action Report, November 16, 1942").

11. "How Pounds Won the Battle," *U.S.S. O'Bannon Shipmates Association Newsletter*, June 1980, found in the Papers of Donald J. MacDonald, Box 5, Folder 4, "O'Bannon, Historical Material, Newsletters," Naval Historical Foundation Collection, Manuscript Division, Library of Congress.

12. Whit Richardson, "Maine-Made USS *O'Bannon* 'Led the Way' at Guadalcanal," Portland, Maine, *Press Herald*, November 15, 2014.

13. Whisler interview, October 15, 2015.

14. Carl F. Pfeifer and Jack S. McDowell, "Lucky Mike Plays for Keeps," *True, the Man's Magazine*, May 1944, 28.

15. Author's interview with Willy Rhyne, October 20, 2015.

16. A. A. Vandegrift, *Once a Marine* (New York: W. W. Norton, 1964), 198–199.

17. Ira Wolfert, "Solomons Battle a Fiery Spectacle," *New York Times*, November 28, 1942.

18. MacDonald, "Hell and Back," 89.

19. MacDonald Action Report, November 16, 1942, 5.

20. Rhyne interview, October 20, 2015.
21. Pfeifer and McDowell, "Lucky Mike," 29.
22. MacDonald Reminiscences, August 6, 1974, 213.
23. Wylie Oral History, December 17, 1985, 72.
24. Author's interview with Thomas Chesnutt, March 3, 2016.
25. Commanding Officer to Commander, Task Force 67, "Report of Action," November 15, 1942, 3 (hereafter "Cole Action Report, November 15, 1942").
26. Author's interview with Thomas Chesnutt, March 7, 2016.
27. Wylie Oral History, December 17, 1985, 72.
28. Holmes interview, October 14, 2015.
29. Wylie Oral History, December 17, 1985, 72.
30. Ibid.
31. Ibid., 74.
32. Fred Gressard, "Reminiscences," found at http://destroyerhistory.org/fletcherclass/ussfletcher/index.asp?r=44500&pid=44504, accessed December 4, 2014.
33. Hara, *Japanese Destroyer Captain*, 126, 134, 137–140.
34. MacDonald Recollections, 12.
35. Wylie Oral History, December 17, 1985, 79.
36. Diary of Jacob Thomas Chesnutt Jr., November 13, 1942, in the J. Thomas Chesnutt Collection (AFC/2001/001/58477), Veterans History Project, American Folklife Center, Library of Congress, found at http://lcweb2.loc.gov/natlib/afc2001001/service/58477/pd0001.pdf, accessed October 13, 2015 (hereafter "Chesnutt Diary").
37. Greybook, November 13, 1942.
38. William F. Halsey and J. Bryan III, *Admiral Halsey's Story* (New York: McGraw-Hill, 1947), 130.
39. Ibid., 131–132.
40. Ibid., 132.
41. MacDonald Reminiscences, August 6, 1974, 213.
42. Wilkinson Action Report, November 17, 1942.
43. Cole Action Report, November 15, 1942.
44. MacDonald Recollections, 32.
45. Chesnutt interview, March 3, 2016.
46. Halsey, "Life," 381.
47. Hara, *Japanese Destroyer Captain*, 144.
48. "Japanese Victory Claimed by Tokyo," *New York Times*, November 17, 1942.
49. United States Strategic Bombing Survey, *Interrogations of Japanese Officials*, Volume II, No. 467, "Interrogation of Capt. Toshikazu Ohmae, Chief of Staff, Southeastern Fleet at Rabaul," November 20, 1945 (Washington, D.C.: Naval Analysis Division, 1946), 471.
50. "Victory off Guadalcanal," *Time*, November 23, 1942, 28.
51. "Hit Hard, Hit Fast, Hit Often," *Time*, November 30, 1942, 28–31.

52. Charles Hurd, "Solomons Sea Victory Staggers to Japanese," *New York Times*, November 22, 1942.

53. Message from General Vandegrift to Admiral Halsey, November 16, 1942, in "General Correspondence, November 1943–March 1944," in Admiral William F. Halsey Collection, Naval Historical Foundation Collection, Manuscript Division, Library of Congress, Washington, D.C.

54. Halsey and Bryan, *Admiral Halsey's Story*, 132.

CHAPTER 4: BLUNTING THE TOKYO EXPRESS

1. Letter from Lieutenant Gerard St. George Walker to Commander Donald MacDonald, April 26, 1944, Papers of Donald J. MacDonald, Box 1, "Correspondence, 1944 Jan–June," Naval Historical Foundation Collection, Manuscript Division, Library of Congress.

2. Letter from Admiral William Halsey to Admiral Chester Nimitz, December 11, 1942, in "Halsey-Nimitz Letters, 1942–1943," in Admiral William F. Halsey Collection, Naval Historical Foundation Collection, Manuscript Division, Library of Congress, Washington, D.C. (hereafter "Halsey-Nimitz Correspondence").

3. Halsey to Nimitz, November 29, 1942, Halsey-Nimitz Correspondence.

4. Halsey to Nimitz, December 11, 1942, Halsey-Nimitz Correspondence.

5. Donald J. MacDonald, "They Went to Hell and Back with Me," *American Magazine*, July 1944, 91.

6. Chesnutt Diary, November 16–20, 1942.

7. Carl F. Pfeifer and Jack S. McDowell, "Lucky Mike Plays for Keeps," *True, the Man's Magazine*, May 1944, 29.

8. Frederick J. Bell, *Condition Red: Destroyer Action in the South Pacific* (New York: Longmans Green, 1944), 83.

9. Wylie Oral History, December 17, 1985, 83.

10. Tameichi Hara with Fred Saito and Roger Pineau, *Japanese Destroyer Captain* (Annapolis, MD: Naval Institute Press, 1967), 149–150.

11. Zenji Orita with Joseph D. Harrington, *I-Boat Captain: How Japan's Submarines Almost Defeated the U.S. Navy in the Pacific* (Canoga Park, CA: Major Books, 1976), 131.

12. Hara, *Japanese Destroyer Captain*, 94, 156.

13. Matome Ugaki, *Fading Victory: The Diary of Admiral Matome Ugaki, 1941–1945* (Pittsburgh: University of Pittsburgh Press, 1991), 177.

14. Wylie Oral History, December 17, 1985, 86.

15. Chesnutt Diary, November 30, 1942.

16. Wylie Oral History, December 17, 1985, 90.

17. Chesnutt Diary, November 30, 1942; Chesnutt interview, March 7, 2016.

18. Halsey to Nimitz, January 1, 1943, Halsey-Nimitz Correspondence.

19. Nimitz to Halsey, December 18, 1942, Halsey-Nimitz Correspondence.

20. Samuel Eliot Morison, *History of United States Naval Operations in World War II*, volume V, *The Struggle for Guadalcanal, August 1942–February 1943* (Boston: Little, Brown, 1949), 315.

21. MacDonald Recollections, 13.

22. Ugaki, *Fading Victory*, 317, 319.

23. Morison, *Struggle for Guadalcanal*, 317.

24. Greybook, December 30, 1942.

25. Hanson W. Baldwin, "Ominous Lull on War Fronts," *New York Times*, December 17, 1942.

26. Chesnutt Diary, November 30, 1942.

27. William F. Halsey and J. Bryan III, *Admiral Halsey's Story* (New York: McGraw-Hill, 1947), 143; J. Norman Lodge, "Halsey Predicts Victory This Year," *New York Times*, January 3, 1943, 14.

28. Halsey and Bryan, *Admiral Halsey's Story*, 142.

29. John G. Norris, "What Comes Next in the South Pacific?" *Washington Post*, January 10, 1943, B5.

30. Halsey to Nimitz, December 11, 1942, Halsey-Nimitz Correspondence.

31. Walden L. Ainsworth, "Cruiser-Destroyer Task Forces, Solomons Campaign," January 17, 1946, 1–2 (hereafter "Ainsworth, 'Cruiser-Destroyer Task Forces'").

32. MacDonald Reminiscences, August 6, 1974, 236.

33. Executive Officer to Commanding Officer, "Action Report," January 6, 1943.

34. "Munda Hit by Big Blasts," *New York Times*, January 12, 1943.

35. MacDonald Reminiscences, August 6, 1974, 237–238.

36. Commanding Officer to Commander in Chief, United States Pacific Fleet, "Action Report—Munda Bombardment," January 6, 1943, 3–4; Commanding Officer to Commander, Task Force 67, "Bombardment of Munda Point, New Georgia Island, Solomon Group, Early Morning January 5, 1943," January 7, 1943, 3.

37. "Oral History of Rear Admiral Joseph C. Wylie, USN (Ret.)," Naval War College, Oral History Program, interview conducted by Dr. Evelyn M. Cherpak on January 15, 1986, 113.

38. R. H. Roupe, "Hell and High Water," found at http://destroyerhistory.org/fletcherclass/index.asp?r=45109&pid=45113, accessed March 20, 2015.

39. MacDonald Reminiscences, August 6, 1974, 216.

CHAPTER 5: BIRTH OF A SQUADRON

1. Foster Hailey, *Pacific Battle Line* (New York: Macmillan, 1944), 286.

2. Ibid., 285–286.

3. Halsey to Nimitz, January 11, 1943, Halsey-Nimitz Correspondence.

4. MacDonald Recollections, 14.

5. E. B. Potter, *Nimitz* (Annapolis, MD: Naval Institute Press, 1976), 220.

6. Ensign Clem C. Williams Jr., "Sinking of the USS *De Haven* in the South Pacific," June 3, 1944, Office of Naval Records and Library (hereafter "Williams, 'Sinking'").

7. C. Raymond Calhoun, *Tin Can Sailor: Life Aboard the USS* Sterett, *1939–1945* (Annapolis, MD: Naval Institute Press, 1993), 116.

8. Foster Hailey, "Their Morale Is All Right . . . How's Yours?" *New York Times*, November 8, 1942, 6.

9. MacDonald Recollections, 15; Donald J. MacDonald, "They Went to Hell and Back with Me," *American Magazine*, July 1944, 91.

10. Hailey, "Morale," 6, 27.

11. Letter from Captain John J. Rowan, USN (Ret.), to Commander E. Andrew Wilde Jr. USNR (Ret.), November 20, 1995, in E. Andrew Wilde Jr., ed., *The U.S.S.* De Haven *(DD-469) in World War II: Documents, Recollections and Photographs* (Needham, MA: Privately published, 2001), used with the permission of Meredith McComb, widow of Dave McComb, Destroyer History Foundation.

12. Hailey, *Pacific Battle Line*, 287, 300–301.

13. James D. Horan, *Action Tonight: The Story of the American Destroyer* O'Bannon *in the Pacific* (New York: G. P. Putnam's Sons, 1945), 60.

14. Hailey, *Pacific Battle Line*, 288–289.

15. MacDonald Recollections, 15.

16. Hailey, *Pacific Battle Line*, 289.

17. Horan, *Action Tonight*, 63; Foster Hailey, "Task Force Fools the Japanese, Then Batters a Base Near Munda," *New York Times*, February 6, 1943.

18. Hailey, "Task Force."

19. Williams, "Sinking"; Hailey, "Task Force."

20. Ainsworth, "Cruiser-Destroyer Task Forces," 4.

21. Hailey, *Pacific Battle Line*, 292.

22. Walden L. Ainsworth, "Activities of Task Forces Under the Command of Rear Admiral Walden L. Ainsworth, U.S. Navy, Solomon Island Campaigns, 10 December 1942 to 4 June 1944," 57 (hereafter cited as "Ainsworth, 'Solomon Island Campaigns'").

23. MacDonald Recollections, 15; Hailey, *Pacific Battle Line*, 293.

24. MacDonald Reminiscences, August 6, 1974, 231.

25. Chuck Witten, "The Battle of Rennell Island," found at http://destroyerhistory.org/fletcherclass/index.asp?r=44805&pid=44814, accessed March 13, 2015.

26. R. H. Roupe, "Hell and High Water," found at http://destroyerhistory.org/fletcherclass/index.asp?r=45109&pid=45113, accessed March 20, 2015.

27. James J. Fahey, *Pacific War Diary, 1942–1945* (Boston: Houghton Mifflin, 1963), 17.

28. MacDonald Reminiscences, August 6, 1974, 232.

29. Roupe, "Hell and High Water."

30. Witten, "Battle of Rennell Island."

31. Jack Wilkes, "The Battle of Rennell Island," found at http://destroyerhistory.org/fletcherclass/index.asp?r=44805&pid=44815, accessed March 13, 2015.

32. Executive Officer to Commanding Officer, "Battle Report of Action with Enemy Aircraft off Koliula Point, Guadalcanal, on January 29, 1943," February 6, 1943.

33. Witten, "Battle of Rennell Island."

34. Tameichi Hara with Fred Saito and Roger Pineau, *Japanese Destroyer Captain* (Annapolis, MD: Naval Institute Press, 1967), 161, 173.

35. Halsey, "Life," 393.

36. Letter from Commander Archie R. Fields, USN (Ret.), to Commander E. A. Wilde Jr., USNR (Ret.), November 14, 1995, in E. Andrew Wilde Jr., ed., *The U.S.S.* De Haven *(DD-469) in World War II: Documents, Recollections and Photographs* (Needham, MA: Privately published, 2001), used with the permission of Meredith McComb, widow of Dave McComb, Destroyer History Foundation.

37. Al Breining, "Bye-Bye DD!," found at http://destroyerhistory.org/fletcherclass/index.asp?r=46905&pid=46910, accessed March 23, 2015.

38. Letter from Fields to Wilde, November 14, 1995.

39. Letter from Captain Bernard W. Frese Jr., USN (Ret.), to Commander E. A. Wilde Jr., USNR (Ret.), May 2, 1996, in E. Andrew Wilde Jr., ed., *The U.S.S.* De Haven *(DD-469) in World War II: Documents, Recollections and Photographs* (Needham, MA: Privately published, 2001), used with the permission of Meredith McComb, widow of Dave McComb, Destroyer History Foundation.

40. Letter from Fields to Wilde, November 14, 1995.

41. Ensign Clem C. Williams Jr., "Amplifying Report of the Senior Unwounded Survivor on Loss of the U.S.S. *De Haven* on February 1, 1943," June 5, 1943 (hereafter cited as Williams, "Amplifying Report").

42. Letter from Frese to Wilde, May 2, 1996.

43. Williams, "Amplifying Report."

44. Hailey, *Pacific Battle Line*, 311–312, 315.

45. Letter from Frese to Wilde, May 2, 1996.

46. Hailey, *Pacific Battle Line*, 313.

47. Williams, "Sinking."

48. Hailey, *Pacific Battle Line*, 314–315.

49. Ainsworth, "Cruiser-Destroyer Task Forces," 5.

CHAPTER 6: STRUGGLE FOR THE SLOT

1. Chesnutt interview, March 3, 2016.

2. Herbert P. Bix, *Hirohito and the Making of Modern Japan* (New York: Harper Collins, 2000), 464.

3. Tameichi Hara with Fred Saito and Roger Pineau, *Japanese Destroyer Captain* (Annapolis, MD: Naval Institute Press, 1967), xi, xii, 94, 160.

4. "Glory for a Tin Can," *Time*, April 17, 1944, 65–66.

5. Benjamin Katz, "Highlights of Events and Interesting Occurrences," July 1981, found at http://destroyerhistory.org/fletcherclass/index.asp?r=46804&pid=46816, accessed March 22, 2015.

6. MacDonald Reminiscences, August 6, 1974, 229.

7. Donald J. MacDonald, "They Went to Hell and Back with Me," *American Magazine*, July 1944, 91.

8. Chesnutt diary, information added in January 2001.

9. Rhyne interview, October 20, 2015.

10. Frederick J. Bell, *Condition Red: Destroyer Action in the South Pacific* (New York: Longmans Green, 1944), ix–x.

11. Henry DeLaureal, "From Guadalcanal to Tokyo," found at http://destroyer history.org/fletcherclass/index.asp?r=46804&pid=46817, accessed March 22, 2015.

12. Foster Hailey, *Pacific Battle Line* (New York: Macmillan, 1944), 294; Bell, *Condition Red*, 29, 89.

13. Hailey, *Pacific Battle Line*, 296.

14. Whisler interview, July 22, 2015.

15. Foster Hailey, "Heroes on a Tin Can," *New York Times*, July 15, 1945.

16. MacDonald, "Hell and Back," 91.

17. Ibid., 25.

18. MacDonald Recollections, 28.

19. MacDonald Reminiscences, August 6, 1974, 249.

20. George Gowen, "Various Reminiscences," found at http://destroyerhistory .org/fletcherclass/usschevalier/index.asp?r=45109&pid=45110, accessed March 20, 2015; MacDonald, "Hell and Back," 91.

21. MacDonald Reminiscences, August 6, 1974, 250–251.

22. Warren H. Gabelman, "She Was My Yacht," found at http://destroyerhistory .org/fletcherclass/index.asp?r=44905&pid=44935, accessed March 10, 2015.

23. Chesnutt Diary, August 28, September 3, and October 11, 1942.

24. MacDonald, "Hell and Back," 92.

25. MacDonald Reminiscences, August 6, 1974, 228.

26. James J. Fahey, *Pacific War Diary, 1942–1945* (Boston: Houghton Mifflin, 1963), 26.

27. Hailey, *Pacific Battle Line*, 324.

28. Commanding Officer to Commander in Chief, United States Pacific Fleet, "Action Report—Munda Bombardment," March 8, 1943 (hereafter cited as "Action Report—Munda Bombardment."

29. Fahey, *Pacific War Diary*, 27–28.

30. "Action Report—Munda Bombardment"; Ainsworth, "Solomon Island Campaigns," 61.

31. MacDonald Recollections, 18.

32. Chesnutt Diary, January 26–30, 1943; Hailey, *Pacific Battle Line*, 297.

33. Hailey, *Pacific Battle Line*, 298–299.

34. MacDonald Recollections, 18.

35. MacDonald, "Hell and Back," 91–92.

36. Duncan Norton-Taylor, *With My Heart in My Mouth* (New York: Coward-McCann, 1944), 66.

37. Bell, *Condition Red*, 39.

38. Wing Diary, January 13, 1943.

39. John Sherwood, "The Legend of the Deadly Potatoes," *Washington Times*, April 17, 1974.

40. Norton-Taylor, *Heart*, 61.

41. MacDonald Reminiscences, August 6, 1974, 242.

42. USS *Taylor* Cruise Book, December 1945, 23; Roupe, "Hell and High Water."

43. Roupe, "Hell and High Water"; "Glory for a Tin Can," 65–66; "WWII Shipmates Visiting," *Fredericksburg* (TX) *Standard-Radio Post*, September 22, 1993.

44. MacDonald, "Hell and Back," 91.

45. MacDonald Reminiscences, August 6, 1974, 248.

46. MacDonald Recollections, 24.

47. "Glory for a Tin Can," 66.

48. "A Letter to Tojo," *Time*, March 29, 1943, 16–17.

CHAPTER 7: KULA GULF CONFRONTATIONS

1. Rear Admiral Joseph H. Wellings, USN (Ret.), "The Night Strong Was Sunk," *Shipmate*, July–August 1977, 1, found in E. Andrew Wilde Jr., ed., *The U.S.S.* Strong *(DD-467) in World War II: Documents, Recollections and Photographs* (Needham, MA: Privately published, 2001), used with the permission of Meredith McComb, widow of Dave McComb, Destroyer History Foundation.

2. Donald J. MacDonald, "They Went to Hell and Back with Me," *American Magazine*, July 1944, 93.

3. Duncan Norton-Taylor, "The *O'Bannon* and the Battle of Kula Gulf," *Four Star Final*, May–June 1944, 6.

4. Hugh Barr Miller Jr., as told to Frank Tremaine, "The Cast Away of Arundel Island," in *The 100 Best True Stories of World War II* (New York: Wm. H. Wise, 1945), 219; first appeared in *Life*, November 1943.

5. Carl F. Pfeifer and Jack S. McDowell, "Lucky Mike Plays for Keeps," *True, the Man's Magazine*, May 1944, 29.

6. Duncan Norton-Taylor, *With My Heart in My Mouth* (New York: Coward-McCann, 1944), 141.

7. Pfeifer and McDowell, "Lucky Mike," 29.

8. Burt Gorsline, "Loss of Strong," found at http://destroyerhistory.org/fletcherclass/index.asp?r=45111&pid=45130, accessed March 20, 2015.

9. Wellings, "Night," 4.

10. Norton-Taylor, "The *O'Bannon*," 6.

11. Pfeifer and McDowell, "Lucky Mike," 66.

12. MacDonald, "Hell and Back," 93.

13. Wellings, "Night," 4.

14. Ibid.

15. Hugh Barr Miller Jr. to Destroyers Representative, "Report of Activities While Missing," August 24, 1943, 1, found in E. Andrew Wilde Jr., ed., *The U.S.S.* Strong *(DD-467) in World War II: Documents, Recollections and Photographs* (Needham, MA: Privately published, 2001), used with the permission of Meredith McComb, widow of Dave McComb, Destroyer History Foundation.

16. Samuel Eliot Morison, *History of United States Naval Operations in World War II*, Volume VI, *Breaking the Bismarcks Barrier, 22 July 1942–1 May 1944* (Boston: Little, Brown, 1950), 174.

17. Norton-Taylor, *Heart*, 148.

18. MacDonald, "Hell and Back," 93–94.

19. Norton-Taylor, *Heart*, 152.

20. MacDonald, "Hell and Back," 94.

21. James D. Horan, *Action Tonight: The Story of the American Destroyer* O'Bannon *in the Pacific* (New York: G. P. Putnam's Sons, 1945), 123.

22. MacDonald, "Hell and Back," 94.

23. Halsey to Nimitz, July 13, 1943, Halsey-Nimitz Correspondence.

24. Halsey to Ainsworth, July 5, 1943; Halsey to McInerney, July 6, 1943; and Nimitz to Ainsworth, July 6, 1943, in Ainsworth, "Solomon Island Campaigns," 62–64.

25. Radio script, *The First Line*, Episode #126, June 29, 1944, found in the William K. Romoser Papers, Box 15, Naval Historical Foundation Collection, Manuscript Division, Library of Congress, Washington, D.C.

26. Miller, "Cast Away," 219–220.

27. Miller, "Report of Activities While Missing," 4.

28. Miller, "Cast Away," 223.

29. Ibid., 225.

30. "First Lady Presents Navy Cross to Hero," *New York Times*, September 22, 1943.

31. MacDonald Recollections, 21.

32. Frederick Moosbrugger, Commander, Destroyer Division 12, to Commander in Chief, United States Pacific Fleet, "Action Report for Night of August 6–7,

1943—Battle of Vella Gulf," August 16, 1943, 12–13; South Pacific War Diary, 1942–1944, entry for August 6–7, 1943, in the Admiral William F. Halsey Collection, Naval Historical Foundation Collection, Manuscript Division, Library of Congress, Washington, D.C.

33. Herbert P. Bix, *Hirohito and the Making of Modern Japan* (New York: Harper Collins, 2000), 466.

34. Tameichi Hara with Fred Saito and Roger Pineau, *Japanese Destroyer Captain* (Annapolis, MD: Naval Institute Press, 1967), 188.

35. MacDonald Recollections, 25; R. H. Roupe, "Hell and High Water," found at http://destroyerhistory.org/fletcherclass/index.asp?r=45109&pid=45113, accessed March 20, 2015.

36. Roupe, "Hell and High Water."

37. Burt Gorsline, "Loss of *Chevalier*," found at http://destroyerhistory.org/fletcherclass/index.asp?r=45111&pid=45131, accessed March 20, 2015.

38. "Reminiscences of Rear Admiral Donald J. MacDonald, U.S. Navy (Retired)," United States Naval Institute, Annapolis, Maryland, Interview Number 4, September 10, 1974, 257 (hereafter "MacDonald Reminiscences, September 10, 1974").

39. George Gowen, "Various Reminiscences," found at http://destroyerhistory.org/fletcherclass/usschevalier/index.asp?r=45109&pid=45110, accessed March 20, 2015.

40. Review of *American Magazine* article about *O'Bannon* done by Commander W. W. Hollister, USN, Navy Department, June 1, 1944, found in Box 1, Folder, "Correspondence, 1944 Jan–June," Papers of Donald J. MacDonald, Naval Historical Foundation Collection, Manuscript Division, Library of Congress.

41. "Presentation of Presidential Unit Citation to the USS *Nicholas* by Admiral Nimitz," found at http://destroyerhistory.org/fletcherclass/index.asp?r=44904&pid=44923, accessed February 2, 2015.

42. Horan, *Action Tonight*, 157–158.

43. Message from Admiral William Halsey to Destroyer Squadron 21, October 29, 1943, found in Ainsworth, "Solomon Island Campaigns," 70.

CHAPTER 8: CLIMBING THE NEW GUINEA LADDER

1. Jack Bell, "Introduction to 'Doc' Ransom's Diary," found at http://destroyerhistory.org/fletcherclass/index.asp?r=44805&pid=44816, accessed March 4, 2016.

2. Doc Ransom Diary, October 3, 1943. Access to the full diary granted by Dow Ransom's son, Dow Ransom Jr.

3. Author's interview with Martin Johnson, May 16, 2016.

4. Doc Ransom Diary, August 8, August 20, and August 22, 1943.

5. Ibid., October 5 and October 10, 1943.

6. Ibid., November 2–3, 1943.

7. Henry DeLaureal, "From Guadalcanal to Tokyo," found at http://destroyerhistory.org/fletcherclass/index.asp?r=46804&pid=46817, accessed March 22, 2015.

8. Doc Ransom Diary, December 9, 1943.

9. MacDonald Reminiscences, September 10, 1974, 263–264.

10. Navy Department Press Release, December 18, 1943; "U.S. Destroyer *O'Bannon* Returns Home; Helped to Sink Battleship and 3 Cruisers," *New York Times*, December 19, 1943.

11. Robert Waithman, "The U.S.S. *O'Bannon*," typewritten copy of an article enclosed in a letter from Lieutenant Gerard St. George Walker to Commander Donald MacDonald, April 26, 1944, in Papers of Donald J. MacDonald, Box 1, Folder 7, "Correspondence, 1944 Jan–June," Naval Historical Foundation Collection, Manuscript Division, Library of Congress.

12. Richard Shafter, "What's in a Name?" *Our Navy*, Mid-June 1944, 24–25, in Papers of Donald J. MacDonald, Box 4, Folder 17, "Military Service, Historical Material," Naval Historical Foundation Collection, Manuscript Division, Library of Congress.

13. "Hero Ship *O'Bannon*," *Heroic Comics*, March 1945, and "Commander Donald J. MacDonald," *Real Life Comics*, March 1945, in Papers of Donald J. MacDonald, Box 4, Folders 14–15, "O'Bannon Historical Material, Comic Books," Naval Historical Foundation Collection, Manuscript Division, Library of Congress.

14. "Navy's Most Decorated Hero Scared by War," *New York Times*, April 7, 1944.

15. H. I. Phillips, "O'Bannon and Mac," *New York Sun Dial*, April 7, 1944, in Papers of Donald J. MacDonald, Box 5, Folder 1, "O'Bannon Historical Material, Poems, 1943–1944," Naval Historical Foundation Collection, Manuscript Division, Library of Congress.

16. Letter from Vernice Johnson to Donald MacDonald, February 16, 1944, in Papers of Donald J. MacDonald, Box 1, Folder 7, "Correspondence, 1944 Jan–June," Naval Historical Foundation Collection, Manuscript Division, Library of Congress.

17. Letter from Mrs. Richard Hall to Commander Donald MacDonald, April 5, 1944, in Papers of Donald J. MacDonald, Box 1, Folder 7, "Correspondence, 1944 Jan–June," Naval Historical Foundation Collection, Manuscript Division, Library of Congress.

18. Letter from George Philip Jr. to Donald MacDonald, December 5, 1943, in Papers of Donald J. MacDonald, Box 1, Folder, "Correspondence, 1930, 1936–1942"; letter from Lillian Celmer to Commander Donald MacDonald, April 7, 1944, in the Papers of Donald J. MacDonald, Box 1, Folder 7, "Correspondence, 1944 Jan–June," both in Naval Historical Foundation Collection, Manuscript Division, Library of Congress.

19. Letter from Betty Keating to Commander Donald J. MacDonald, June 5, 1944, in Papers of Donald J. MacDonald, Box 1, Folder 7, "Correspondence, 1944

Jan–June," Naval Historical Foundation Collection, Manuscript Division, Library of Congress.

20. Letter from Sister Superior to Commander Donald J. McDonald, August 20, 1944, in Papers of Donald J. MacDonald, Box 1, Folder 7, "Correspondence, 1944, July–December," Naval Historical Foundation Collection, Manuscript Division, Library of Congress.

21. "Glory for a Tin Can," *Time*, April 17, 1944, 65–66.

22. Doc Ransom Diary, January 6, 1944.

23. Martin Johnson Diary of World War II, February 1, 1944, courtesy of Martin Johnson (hereafter "Johnson Diary").

24. Doc Ransom Diary, January 14 and January 26, 1944.

25. Chesnutt Diary, January 30, 1944.

26. Doc Ransom Diary, March 10, 1944.

27. Ibid., March 30 and June 2, 1944.

28. Douglas Perret Starr, "I Would Not Have Missed It for the World," found at http://destroyerhistory.org/fletcherclass/index.asp?r=44905&pid=44937, accessed December 4, 2014.

29. Douglas MacArthur, *Reminiscences* (New York: McGraw-Hill, 1964), 190.

30. Doc Ransom Diary, April 21, 1944.

31. Ibid., April 22, 1944.

32. Commanding Officer to Commander in Chief, United States Fleet, "Action Report 22–23 April 1944—Aitape Beach, Territory of New Guinea," April 25, 1944.

33. Doc Ransom Diary, April 23, 1944.

34. Author's interview with Warren Gabelman, June 10, 2015.

35. Doc Ransom Diary, May 2, 1944.

36. James J. Fahey, *Pacific War Diary, 1942–1945* (Boston: Houghton Mifflin, 1963), 5; author's interview with Douglas Starr, June 18, 2015.

37. Starr interview, June 18, 2015.

38. Chesnutt interview, March 3, 2016.

39. Chesnutt Diary, June 25, July 18, August 11, August 31.

40. Whisler interview, July 22, 2015.

41. Doc Ransom Diary, May 3, June 15, and June 17, 1944.

42. Chesnutt Diary, June 7, 1944.

43. Johnson Diary, July 30, 1944.

44. Johnson interview, May 16, 2016.

45. Doc Ransom Diary, June 8 and September 15, 1944.

46. Commanding Officer to Commander in Chief, United States Fleet, "Action Report—Support of Landing at Noemfoor Island, New Guinea, July 2, 1944," July 13, 1944.

47. Doc Ransom Diary, September 15, 1944.

48. Ibid., September 29, 1944.
49. Ibid., July 2, 1944.

CHAPTER 9: THE PHILIPPINE WHIRLWIND

1. Doc Ransom Diary, October 9 and October 14, 1944.
2. Walter Allen Lee, *One of the Crew: USS* O'Bannon, *World War II* (Victoria, BC: Trafford, 2007), entry for October 19, 1944; Doc Ransom Diary, October 19, 1944.
3. Chesnutt Diary, October 18, 1944.
4. Doc Ransom Diary, October 20, 1944.
5. Ibid., October 25, 1944.
6. Chesnutt Diary, November 4, 1944, and March 13, 1945.
7. Commanding Officer to Commander in Chief, United States Fleet, "Action Report—Operation in Leyte Gulf, 16–29 November 1944," November 29, 1944.
8. Doc Ransom Diary, December 3, 1944.
9. Johnson interview, May 16, 2016.
10. Doc Ransom Diary, December 5 and December 8, 1944.
11. Author's interview with Robert Whisler, May 12, 2016.
12. Lee, *One of the Crew*, entry for December 10, 1944.
13. Ibid.
14. Hanson W. Baldwin, "Blow at Luzon Indicated," *New York Times*, December 16, 1944.
15. Doc Ransom Diary, December 15, 1944.
16. Commanding Officer to Commander in Chief, United States Fleet, "Special Action Report (Anti-Aircraft Action by Surface Ships), Submission Of," December 15, 1944 (hereafter cited as "Howorth, 'Special Action Report'").
17. Doc Ransom Diary, December 15, 1944.
18. Commanding Officer to Commander in Chief, United States Fleet, "Action Report—Invasion of Southwest Mindoro, P. I., December 12–15, 1944," December 29, 1944; Howorth, "Special Action Report."
19. Christmas menu and message from the Martin Johnson Collection.
20. USS *O'Bannon* War Diary, December 24, 1944.
21. Doc Ransom Diary, January 5, 1945.
22. Commanding Officer to Commander in Chief, United States Fleet, "Action Report—Operations in Support of Seizure and Occupation Luzon Island, P.I. 4 January to 31 January 1945," February 1, 1945 (hereafter cited as "Taylor Action Report").
23. Doc Ransom Diary, January 8, 1945.
24. Taylor Action Report.

25. Doc Ransom Diary, February 13, 1945.

26. Chesnutt Diary, February 14, 1945.

27. "Destroyer USS *Hopewell* Trades Blows with Japanese Shore Batteries on Corregidor," Navy Department Press Release, August 23, 1945.

28. Commanding Officer to Commander in Chief, United States Fleet, "Action Report—Manila Bay Operations, 13 February Through 17 February, 1945, Inclusive," February 22, 1945.

29. Chesnutt Diary, February 14, 1945.

30. Johnson interview, May 16, 2016.

31. James J. Fahey, *Pacific War Diary, 1942–1945* (Boston: Houghton Mifflin, 1963), 284.

32. Doc Ransom Diary, February 14, 1945.

33. Johnson interview, May 16, 2016.

34. Medical Officer to Commanding Officer, "Medical Report of Action, 14 February 1945 of the U.S.S. *La Vallette* (DD-448)," February 21, 1945 (hereafter cited as "Ransom Report").

35. Doc Ransom Diary, February 14, 1945.

36. Ransom Report.

37. Doc Ransom Diary, February 14, 1945.

38. Ibid.; Jack Bell, "Introduction to 'Doc' Ransom's Diary," found at http://destroyerhistory.org/fletcherclass/index.asp?r=44805&pid=44816, accessed March 4, 2016.

39. Doc Ransom Diary, February 15, 1945.

40. Douglas Perret Starr, "Taking Corregidor, Manila Bay, 13–16 February 1945," found at http://destroyerhistory.org/fletcherclass/index.asp?r=44937&pid=44974, accessed December 4, 2014.

41. Chesnutt Diary, February 16, 1945.

42. Doc Ransom Diary, May 2, May 22, May 30, 1945; Martin Johnson letter to his mother, May 30, 1945, in Martin Johnson Collection.

CHAPTER 10: KAMIKAZE CARNAGE

1. Orvill Raines letter to Ray Ellen, July 30, 1944, in William M. McBride, ed., *Good Night Officially: The Pacific War Letters of a Destroyer Sailor* (Boulder, CO: Westview Press, 1994), 289.

2. Orvill Raines letter to Ray Ellen, September 12, 1944, in *Good Night Officially*, 72.

3. Orvill Raines letter to Ray Ellen, December 9, 1944, in *Good Night Officially*, 159, 161.

4. USS *Howorth* Ship's History, October 20, 1945, 1.

5. Author's interview with Russell Bramble, June 14, 2016.

6. Orvill Raines letters to Ray Ellen, December 16 and December 20, 1944, in *Good Night Officially*, 167–170.

7. USS *O'Bannon* War Diary, December 18, 1944.

8. USS *Howorth* Ship's History, 1.

9. Bramble interview, June 14, 2016.

10. USS *Howorth* Ship's History, 1.

11. Bramble interview, June 14, 2016.

12. Ibid.

13. Orvill Raines letters to Ray Ellen, February 22, 1945, in *Good Night Officially*, 238–239, 242.

14. United States Pacific Fleet Press Release included with USS *Howorth* Ship's History.

15. Orvill Raines letter to Ray Ellen, March 17, 1945, in *Good Night Officially*, 258.

16. "Japan's Doorstep," *New York Times*, April 1, 1945.

17. Bramble interview, June 14, 2016.

18. George Feifer, *Tennozan: The Battle of Okinawa and the Atomic Bomb* (New York: Ticknor & Fields, 1992), 8.

19. "Japan May Fall, Tokyo Radio Tells People," *New York Times*, April 3, 1945.

20. William F. Halsey and J. Bryan III, *Admiral Halsey's Story* (New York: McGraw-Hill, 1947), 229.

21. Rikihei Inoguchi and Tadashi Nakajima, with Roger Pineau, *The Divine Wind: Japan's Kamikaze Force in World War II* (New York: Bantam Books, 1958), 189.

22. Ibid., 193–194.

23. W. H. Lawrence, "Our Okinawa Guns Down 118 Planes," *New York Times*, April 13, 1945.

24. Orvill Raines letter to Ray Ellen, March 27, 1945, in *Good Night Officially*, 262.

25. USS *Howorth* War Diary, April 2, 1945.

26. Orvill Raines letter to Ray Ellen, April 2, 1945, in *Good Night Officially*, 272.

27. USS *Howorth* War Diary, April 4, 1945.

28. Orvill Raines letter to Ray Ellen, April 6, 1945, in *Good Night Officially*, 276.

29. United States Pacific Fleet Press Release included in USS *Howorth* Ship's History.

30. Bramble interview, June 14, 2016.

31. Commanding Officer to Commander in Chief, United States Fleet, "Special Action Report (Anti-Aircraft Action by Surface Ship), on 6 April 1945, Submission of," April 10, 1945 (hereafter cited as "Burns Action Report").

32. Walter Karig with Russell L. Harris and Frank A. Manson, *Battle Report: Victory in the Pacific* (New York: Rinehart, 1949), 384.

33. Bramble interview, June 14, 2016.

34. Ibid.

35. Burns Action Report.

36. Bramble interview, June 14, 2016.

37. Burns Action Report.

38. Bramble interview, June 14, 2016; Sara Kirkley, "Sunday Salute: Russell Bramble," KHGI-TV interview, Kearney, Nebraska, December 7, 2015.

39. Bramble interview, June 14, 2016.

40. USS *Howorth* War Diary, April 26, 1945.

41. United States Pacific Fleet Press Release included with USS *Howorth* Ship's History.

42. George E. Jones, "Enemy Fliers Hit Troops on Okinawa," *New York Times*, April 8, 1945.

43. Commander Edward S. Burns letter to Ray Ellen, April 7, 1945, in *Good Night Officially*, 278.

44. Bramble interview, June 14, 2016; Russell Bramble letter to Ray Ellen, May 27, 1945, in *Good Night Officially*, 279.

45. Raines letter to Ray Ellen, July 30, 1944, in *Good Night Officially*, 286, 289, 291–292.

46. Commanding Officer to Commander in Chief, United States Fleet, "Action Report—Operations in Support of the Seizure of Tarakan Island, Dutch Borneo, 24 April to 5 May 1945," May 5, 1945.

47. Paul E. Mahan, "Saving Jenkins," found at http://destroyerhistory.org/fletcherclass/ussjenkins/index.asp?r=44700&pid=44704, accessed March 12, 2015.

CHAPTER 11: EYEWITNESS TO VICTORY

1. Letter from George R. Thompson to his parents, undated, with the Third Fleet off Japan, *U.S.S. O'Bannon Shipmates Association Newsletter*, June 1986.

2. William F. Halsey and J. Bryan III, *Admiral Halsey's Story* (New York: McGraw-Hill, 1947), 257.

3. Ibid., 260.

4. Douglas Starr email to author, May 16, 2016.

5. "Bull's Eye," *Time*, July 23, 1945, 27–28.

6. Halsey and Bryan, *Admiral Halsey's Story*, 266.

7. Starr email to author, May 16, 2016.

8. Thompson letter to his parents.

9. John C. McCarthy, "The Handshake," April 9, 2004, found at http://destroyerhistory.org/fletcherclass/index.asp?r=46804&pid=46823, accessed March 23, 2015; Thompson letter to his parents.

10. Admiral Halsey's Victory Speech, as broadcast to the Third Fleet, August 15, 1945, found in "Speeches 1939–45," William F. Halsey Collection, Library of Congress; Halsey, "Life," 592–593.

11. Halsey and Bryan, *Admiral Halsey's Story*, 272; McCarthy, "Handshake."

12. Thompson letter to his parents.

13. Thompson letter to his parents; Whisler interview, May 12, 2016.

14. USS *O'Bannon* War Diary, August 19, 1945.

15. Whisler interview, October 15, 2015.

16. USS *O'Bannon* War Diary, August 27, 1945.

17. Starr email to author, May 16, 2016.

18. Thompson letter to his parents.

19. "Flagship *Missouri* Steams to Site of the Surrender," *New York Times*, August 29, 1945.

20. Whisler interview, May 12, 2016; Thompson letter to his parents.

21. USS *O'Bannon* War Diary, September 14, 1945.

22. William L. Worden, "The Japs' Last Bite," *Saturday Evening Post*, October 27, 1945, 128.

23. McCarthy, "Handshake"; Worden, "Japs' Last Bite," 128.

24. Halsey, "Life," 608–609.

25. Halsey and Bryan, *Admiral Halsey's Story*, 283; Masuo Kato, *The Lost War: A Japanese Reporter's Inside Story* (New York: Alfred A. Knopf, 1946), 264.

26. McCarthy, "Handshake."

27. Starr email to author, May 16, 2016.

28. USS *Nicholas* Cruise Book, 5, 17.

EPILOGUE

1. Author's interview with Thomas Chesnutt, May 31, 2016.

2. Bramble interview, June 14, 2016.

3. Whisler interviews, October 15, 2015, and May 12, 2016.

4. Johnson interview, May 16, 2016.

5. Author's interview with Jack O'Neill, August 11, 2015.

6. John C. McCarthy, "The Handshake," April 9, 2004, found at http://destroyerhistory.org/fletcherclass/index.asp?r=46804&pid=46823, accessed March 23, 2015.

7. Warren H. Gabelman, "She Was My Yacht," found at http://destroyerhistory.org/fletcherclass/index.asp?r=44905&pid=44935, accessed March 10, 2015.

8. Douglas Perret Starr, "I Would Not Have Missed It for the World," found at http://destroyerhistory.org/fletcherclass/index.asp?r=44905&pid=44937, accessed December 4, 2014.

9. Letter from Donald MacDonald to Captain T. F. Utegaard, December 19, 1964, in Papers of Donald J. MacDonald, Box 1, "Correspondence, 1955–1964," Naval Historical Foundation Collection, Manuscript Division, Library of Congress.

10. "Reminiscences of George Gowen," found at http://destroyerhistory.org/fletcherclass/usschevalier/index.asp?r=45100&pid=45109, accessed May 6, 2016.

11. Letter from Alvin R. Brooks to Olon Henderson, 1983, included in Chesnutt Diary.

12. Chesnutt Diary.

13. Rhyne interview, October 20, 2015.

14. "Recollection of Al Grimes," found at http://destroyerhistory.org/fletcherclass/desron21/index.asp?r=4210&pid=4213, accessed May 6, 2016.

BIBLIOGRAPHY

ACTION REPORTS AND WAR DIARIES

All vessel action reports and war diaries are archived at the National Archives and Records Administration, College Park, Maryland.

USS O'Bannon *(DD-450)*

War Diary

Monthly War Diary, June 1942 to October 1945.

Action Reports: Actions Around Guadalcanal, November–December 1942

Commanding Officer to Commander in Chief, United States Fleet, "Report of Anti-Submarine Action," November 12, 1942.

Commanding Officer to Commander in Chief, United States Fleet, "Report of Anti-Aircraft Action," November 12, 1942.

Commanding Officer to Commander in Chief, United States Fleet, "Report of Engagement with Japanese Units on Morning of November 13, 1942," November 17, 1942.

Executive Officer to Commanding Officer. "Report of Personal Impressions and Recollection of the Night Action with Japanese Units in Guadalcanal-Florida Island Area, November 13, 1942," November 16, 1942.

Commander, South Pacific Area and South Pacific Force, to Commander in Chief, United States Pacific Fleet, "Report of Engagement with Japanese Units on Morning of November 13, 1942," November 17, 1942.

Task Force 62, Operation Plan No. A24–42, November 27, 1942.

Task Force 62.4.7, Operation Plan No. 3–42, November 27, 1942.

"Antisubmarine Action by Surface Ship," December 4, 1942.

"Antisubmarine Action by Surface Ship," December 5, 1942.

Commanding Officer to Chief of the Bureau of Ships, "War Damage Report," December 9, 1942.

Action Reports: In the Solomons, January–March 1943

Gunnery Officer to Commanding Officer, "Bombardment of Enemy Shore Installations at Munda Point During Early Hours of January 5, 1943, Report Of," January 6, 1943.

Commanding Officer to Commander Task Force 67, "Bombardment of Munda Point, New Georgia Island, Solomon Group, Early Morning January 5, 1943," January 7, 1943.

Action Reports: Desron 21 in the Solomons, March–July 1943

Commanding Officer to Commander in Chief, United States Pacific Fleet, "War Action Report—Bombardment of Vila and Stanmore Plantations, Kolambungara [*sic*] Island and Munda Aerodrome, New Georgia Island," March 7, 1943.

Commander, Task Group 68.3, to Commander in Chief, United States Pacific Fleet, "U.S.S. *O'Bannon* (DD-450)—Action Report—Shore Bombardment—Forwarding Report Of," March 8, 1943.

Action Reports: To the Philippines

Commanding Officer to Commander in Chief, United States Fleet, "Action Report," April 27, 1944.

Commanding Officer to Commander in Chief, United States Fleet, "Leyte Operation, 18 Oct., 1944, to 30 Oct., 1944, Inclusive, Report Of," November 2, 1944.

Commanding Officer to Commander Seventh Fleet, "Mindoro Operation, Report Of," December 29, 1944.

Commanding Officer to Commander in Chief, United States Fleet, "Shore Bombardment of Bataan Peninsula, Corregidor, Ternate Village—Action Report On," February 19, 1945.

Action Reports: To War's End

Commanding Officer to Commander in Chief, United States Fleet, "Offensive Carrier Air Strikes against Honshu and Hokkaido, Japanese Empire, July and August, 1945, Action Report On," September 1, 1945.

USS Fletcher *(DD-445)*

War Diary

Monthly War Diary, June 1942 to October 1945.

Action Reports: Actions around Guadalcanal, November–December 1942

Commanding Officer to Commander, Task Force 67, "Report of Action," November 15, 1942.

Executive Officer to Commanding Officer, "Report of Action," November 15, 1942.

Captain Gilbert C. Hoover, USN, Ex–Commanding Officer, USS *Helena*, to Commander in Chief, United States Pacific Fleet, "Loss of *Juneau*, Circumstances Of," November 28, 1942.

Commanding Officer to Commander, Task Force 67, "Action Report," December 3, 1942.

Executive Officer to Commanding Officer, "Action Report," December 3, 1942.

Action Reports: In the Solomons, January–March 1943

Commanding Officer to Commander in Chief, United States Pacific Fleet, "Action Report," January 6, 1943.

Commanding Officer to Commander in Chief, United States Pacific Fleet, "Action Report—Munda Bombardment," January 6, 1943.

Executive Officer to Commanding Officer, "Action Report," January 6, 1943.

Commanding Officer to Commander in Chief, United States Pacific Fleet, "Action Against and Sinking of Enemy Submarine," February 12, 1943.

Commanding Officer to Commander in Chief, United States Pacific Fleet, "Action Report—Munda Bombardment," March 8, 1943.

Action Reports: Desron 21 in the Solomons, March–July 1943

CIC Handbook for Destroyers Pacific Fleet, June 24, 1943.

Action Reports: Desron 21 in the Kula Gulf Battles, July–October 1943

Commanding Officer to Commander in Chief, United States Pacific Fleet, "Action Report," July 7, 1945.

Action Reports: Desron 21 in the Gilberts and Marshalls

Commanding Officer to Commander in Chief, United States Pacific Fleet, "Action Report," November 26, 1943.

Action Reports: To the Philippines

Commanding Officer to Commander in Chief, United States Fleet, "Action Report," June 10, 1944.

Commanding Officer to Commander in Chief, United States Pacific Fleet, "Action Report," July 9, 1944.

Commanding Officer to Commander in Chief, United States Fleet, "Action Report—Morotai Bombardment," September 19, 1944.
Commanding Officer to Commander in Chief, United States Fleet, "Action Report—Destroyer Sweep of Ormoc Bay, Leyte Island, Philippine Islands," December 20, 1944.
Commanding Officer to Commander in Chief, United States Fleet, "Action Report—Mindoro Operation," December 24, 1944.
Commanding Officer to Commander in Chief, United States Fleet, "Action Report—Covering Participation in Landings at San Antonio and Subic Bay, Luzon Island, Philippine Islands, Period 28 January Through 30 January 1945," February 2, 1945.
Commanding Officer to Commander in Chief, United States Fleet, "Special A.A. Action Reports for Lingayen Operation—Period from 1 January Through 31 January 1945," February 3, 1945.
Commanding Officer to Commander in Chief, United States Fleet, "Action Report—Manila Bay Operations, 13 February Through 17 February 1945, Inclusive," February 22, 1945.
Medical Officer to Chief of the Bureau of Medicine and Surgery, Navy Department, Washington, D.C., "Report of Casualties," February 15, 1945.
Commanding Officer to Commander in Chief, United States Fleet, "Action Report, Tarakan Operation, 24 April–3 May 1945 Inclusive," May 4, 1945.

USS Nicholas *(DD-449)*

War Diary

Monthly War Diary, June 1942 to October 1945.

Action Reports: In the Solomons, January–March 1943

Commanding Officer to Commander in Chief, United States Pacific Fleet, "Action Report—January 5, 1943—Southern Solomon Islands," January 7, 1943.
Executive Officer to Commanding Officer, "Executive Officer's Report, Action of January 5, 1943, in Southern Solomon Islands Area," January 7, 1943.
Commanding Officer to Commander in Chief, United States Pacific Fleet, "Action Report," February 3, 1943.
Commanding Officer to Commander in Chief, United States Pacific Fleet, "Action Report—Bombardment," March 6, 1943.

Action Reports: Desron 21 in the Solomons, March–July 1943

Commanding Officer to Commander in Chief, United States Pacific Fleet, "Action Report—Shore Bombardment," March 17, 1943.

Action Reports: To the Philippines

Commanding Officer to Commander in Chief, United States Fleet, "Action Report—Aitape, New Guinea—Occupation of April 22, 1944," April 24, 1944.

Commanding Officer to Commander in Chief, United States Pacific Fleet, "Action Report—Philippine Island Occupation—Report Of," November 3, 1944.

Commanding Officer to Commander in Chief, United States Fleet, "Anti-Aircraft Action 29 November 1944—Report Of," November 30, 1944.

Commanding Officer to Commander in Chief, United States Fleet, "Action Report—Occupation of Luzon Island, Philippine Islands," February 6, 1945.

Commanding Officer to Commander in Chief, United States Fleet, "Action Report—Bombardment and Occupation of Mariveles Harbor and Corregidor, 13–16 February 1945," February 21, 1945.

Commanding Officer to Commander in Chief, United States Fleet, "Action Report—Seizure and Occupation of Tarakan Island, Dutch Borneo, 24 April–5 May 1945," May 5, 1945.

Action Reports: To War's End

Commanding Officer to Commander in Chief, United States Fleet, "Action Report—Occupation of Sagami Wan and Entrance into Tokyo Bay Terminating in Surrender Ceremonies, 16 August to 2 September 1945," September 10, 1945.

USS De Haven *(DD-469)*

War Diary

Monthly War Diary, October 1942 to February 1943.

Action Reports: In the Solomons, January–March 1943

"Report of Action, Bombardment of Vila-Stanmore Plantation, Kolombangara Island, Morning of January 24th, 1943," January 25, 1943.

Senior Unwounded Survivor, USS *De Haven* (DD-469), to Secretary of the Navy, "U.S.S. *De Haven* (DD469)—Loss of," February 5, 1943.

Ensign Clem C. Williams Jr., "Sinking of the USS *De Haven* in the South Pacific," June 3, 1944, Office of Naval Records and Library.

Ensign Clem C. Williams Jr., "Amplifying Report of the Senior Unwounded Survivor on Loss of the U.S.S. *De Haven* on February 1, 1943," June 5, 1943.

USS Jenkins *(DD-447)*

War Diary

Monthly War Diary, November 1942 to June 1945.

Action Reports: To the Philippines

Commanding Officer to Commander in Chief, United States Fleet, "Action Report 22–23 April 1944—Aitape Beach, Territory of New Guinea," April 25, 1944.

Commanding Officer to Commander in Chief, United States Fleet, "Action Report Night of 8–9 June 1944, North of Biak Island, New Guinea," June 11, 1944.

Commanding Officer to Commander in Chief, United States Fleet, "Action Report of Bombardment of Noemfoor Island, New Guinea, 2 July 1944," July 16, 1944.

Commanding Officer to Commander in Chief, United States Fleet, "Action Report for Morotai Operation 15 September 1944," September 16, 1944.

Commanding Officer to Commander in Chief, United States Fleet, "Action Report: Reinforcement of Sopi Point, Morotai Island, 21–22 September 1944," September 23, 1944.

Commanding Officer to Commander in Chief, United States Fleet, "Action Report; Leyte Gulf, Philippine Islands, 20 October 1944 to 4 November 1944," November 10, 1944.

Commanding Officer to Commander in Chief, United States Pacific Fleet, "Action Report 9 January 1945, Lingayen Gulf, Luzon, Philippine Islands," January 11, 1945.

Commanding Officer to Commander in Chief, United States Fleet, "Action Report U.S.S. *Jenkins*, 13–17 February 1945, Corregidor, P.I.," February 19, 1945.

Commanding Officer to Commander in Chief, United States Fleet, "Action Report, U.S.S. *Jenkins* (DD-447), Tarakan Island, 27–30 April 1945," May 2, 1945.

Other

Commanding Officer to Secretary of the Navy, "War Record—Forwarding Of," October 5, 1945.

USS La Vallette *(DD-448)*

War Diary

Monthly War Diary, November 1942 to February 1945.

Action Reports: In the Solomons, January–March 1943

Commanding Officer to Commander in Chief, United States Fleet, "Action Report—U.S.S. *La Vallette*," February 6, 1943.

Executive Officer to Commanding Officer, "Battle Report of Action with Enemy Aircraft off Koliula Point, Guadalcanal, on January 29, 1943," February 6, 1943.

Commanding Officer to Commander in Chief, United States Fleet, "Action Report—U.S.S. *La Vallette*," February 8, 1943.

Executive Officer to Commanding Officer, "Battle Report of Action with Enemy Aircraft off Rennell Island on January 30, 1943," February 8, 1943.

Action Reports: To the Philippines

Commanding Officer to Commander in Chief, United States Fleet, "Action Report—Landing Operation at Aitape, New Guinea, 22 April 1944," May 7, 1944.

Commanding Officer to Commander in Chief, United States Fleet, "Action Report—Night Engagement with Enemy Destroyer Force Northwest of Biak, New Guinea, 8–9 June 1944," June 12, 1944.

Commanding Officer to Commander in Chief, United States Fleet, "Action Report—Support of Landing at Noemfoor Island, New Guinea, July 2, 1944," July 13, 1944.

Commanding Officer to Commander in Chief, United States Fleet, "Action Report—Operation Against Morotai Island, September 15, 1944," September 18, 1944.

Commanding Officer to Commander in Chief, United States Fleet, "Action Report—Leyte Island Landing Operation," October 24, 1944.

Commanding Officer to Commander in Chief, United States Fleet, "Action Report—Bombardment of Enemy Installations, Ormoc Bay, Leyte Island, Philippine Islands, on Night of 6–7 December 1944," December 10, 1944.

Commanding Officer to Commander in Chief, United States Fleet, "Action Report—Bombardment of Camp Downes, Vicinity of Ormoc City, Leyte Island, Philippine Islands, 9 December 1944," December 11, 1944.

Commanding Officer to Commander in Chief, United States Fleet, "Report of Camotes Sea Sweep and Bombardment of Coast Lines between Pangtail Point and Calunangan Point, Leyte Island on, 7 December 1944," December 7, 1944.

Commanding Officer to Commander in Chief, United States Fleet, "Action Report—Invasion of Southwest Mindoro, P. I., December 12–15, 1944," December 29, 1944.

Executive Officer to Commanding Officer, "Casualty 2/14/45 as a Result of Underwater Explosion in Mariveles Bay, P. I.," February 17, 1945.

Engineering Officer to Commanding Officer, "Report of Personal Observations, Performance of Duty, and Recommendations Concerning Recent Action and Battle Damage of U.S.S. *La Vallette* (DD-448)," February 17, 1945.

Assistant Engineering Officer to Commanding Officer, "Report and Personal Observations of Action, 14 February 1945 of the U.S.S. *La Vallette* (DD-448)," February 20, 1945.

Medical Officer to Chief of the Bureau of Medicine and Surgery, "Report of Casualties," February 21, 1945.

Medical Officer to Commanding Officer, "Medical Report of Action, 14 February 1945 of the U.S.S. *La Vallette* (DD-448)," February 21, 1945.

Commanding Officer to Commander in Chief, United States Fleet, "Action Report, U.S.S. *La Vallette* (DD-448), Period 13 and 14 February 1945, Mariveles Bay and Corregidor Island Operations," February 23, 1945.

USS Radford *(DD-446)*

War Diary

Monthly War Diary, November 1942 to February 1945.

Action Reports: In the Solomons, January–March 1943

Commanding Officer to Commander in Chief, United States Pacific Fleet, "Bombardment of Munda Airfield and Installation on New Georgia Island on 5–6 March 1943; Action Report," March 6, 1943.

Action Reports: Desron 21 in the Solomons, March–July 1943

Commanding Officer to Commander in Chief, United States Pacific Fleet, "Bombardment of Troop Concentrations in Vila-Stanmore Area, Kolombangara Island, During Night of 15–16 March 1943; Action Report of," March 16, 1943.

Action Reports: To the Philippines

Commanding Officer to Commander in Chief, United States Fleet, "Action Report," June 12, 1944.

Commanding Officer to Commander in Chief, United States Fleet, "Action Report," July 22, 1944.

Commanding Officer to Commander in Chief, United States Fleet, "Action Report," August 3, 1944.

Commanding Officer to Commander in Chief, United States Fleet, "Corregidor-Bataan Occupation, 13–14 February 1945," February 21, 1945.

Navy Department Press Release, August 23, 1945, "Destroyer USS *Hopewell* Trades Blows with Japanese Shore Batteries on Corregidor."

USS Strong *(DD-467)*

War Diary

Monthly War Diary, November 1942 to July 1943.

Action Reports: Desron 21 in the Solomons, March–July 1943

Commanding Officer, USS *Strong*, to Commander in Chief, United States Pacific Fleet, "Action Report," March 21, 1943.

Commanding Officer, USS *Strong*, to Commander in Chief, United States Pacific Fleet, "Action Report of Submarine Attack by U.S.S. *Strong*, 7 April 1943," April 12, 1943.

Executive Officer to Commanding Officer, "Action Report," April 12, 1943.

USS Taylor *(DD-468)*

War Diary

Monthly War Diary, November 1942 to October 1945.

Action Reports: Desron 21 in the Solomons, March–July 1943

Commanding Officer to Commander in Chief, United States Pacific Fleet, "Action Report for Night of March 15–16, 1943," March 16, 1943.

Action Reports: To the Philippines

Commanding Officer to Commander in Chief, United States Fleet, "Action Report—Morotai Operation," October 4, 1944.

Commanding Officer to Commander in Chief, United States Fleet, "Action Report—Leyte Operation," November 1, 1944.

Commanding Officer to Commander in Chief, United States Fleet, "Action Report—Operation in Leyte Gulf, 16–29 November 1944," November 29, 1944.

Commanding Officer to Commander in Chief, United States Fleet, "Action Report—Ramming and Sinking of a Japanese Midget Submarine, 5 January 1945," January 5, 1945.

Commanding Officer to Commander in Chief, United States Fleet, "Action Report—Operations in Support of Seizure and Occupation Luzon Island, P.I. 4 January to 31 January 1945," February 1, 1945.

Commanding Officer to Commander in Chief, United States Fleet, "Action Report—Fire Support Missions Executed During the Occupation of Mariveles and Corregidor, 13–18 February 1945," February 22, 1945.

Commanding Officer to Commander in Chief, United States Fleet, "Action Report—Operations in Support of the Seizure of Tarakan Island, Dutch Borneo, 24 April to 5 May 1945," May 5, 1945.

Action Reports: To War's End

Commanding Officer to Commander in Chief, United States Fleet, "Action Report—Occupation in Support of Task Force Thirty-Eight Strikes on Japan, 8 July–15 August 1945," August 15, 1945.

Commanding Officer to Commander in Chief, United States Fleet, "Action Report—Operation from Cessation of Hostilities to Surrender Ceremonies, 16 August to 2 September 1945," September 4, 1945.

Other

Commanding Officer to Secretary of the Navy, "Submission of War Record," September 25, 1945.

USS Chevalier *(DD-451)*

War Diary

Monthly War Diary, December 1942 to October 1943.

Action Reports: The Kula Gulf Battles, July–October 1943

Commanding Officer to Commander in Chief, United States Pacific Fleet, "Action Report—Shore Bombardment Kula Gulf Area, Night of July 4–5, 1943," July 8, 1943.

Executive Officer to Commanding Officer, "Action Report of Enemy Engagement Night of 6 October 1943," October 14, 1943.

Commanding Officer to Commander in Chief, United States Fleet, "Report of Enemy Action Resulting in Loss of Vessel," October 15, 1943.

USS Hopewell *(DD-681)*

War Diary

Monthly War Diary, August 1943 to October 1945.

Action Reports: To the Philippines

Commanding Officer to Commander in Chief, United States Fleet, "Action Report of Shore Bombardment in Support of Initial Landings at Aitape Bay Area, Mandated New Guinea," April 24, 1944.

Commanding Officer to Commander in Chief, United States Fleet, "Action Report of Morotai Operation from D-4 to D Plus 7 Day Inclusive," September 22, 1944.

Commanding Officer to Commander in Chief, United States Fleet, "Action Report of U.S.S. *Hopewell* in Mindoro Island Operation from U-3 to U+2 Day Inclusive," December 18, 1944.

Commanding Officer to Commander in Chief, United States Fleet, "Action Report of the U.S.S. *Hopewell* in the Mariveles-Corregidor Island Operation from 13–18 February 1945," February 21, 1945.

USS Howorth *(DD-592)*

War Diary

Monthly War Diary, June 1944 to October 1945.

Action Reports: Desron 21 in the Solomons, March–July 1943

Commanding Officer to Commander in Chief, United States Pacific Fleet, "Action Report for Night of March 15–16, 1943," March 16, 1943.

Action Reports: To the Philippines

Commanding Officer to Commander in Chief, United States Fleet, "Action Report, Morotai Operation," October 15, 1944.

Commanding Officer to Commander in Chief, United States Fleet, "Action Report, Leyte Operation—9–31 October 1944," October 31, 1944.

Commanding Officer to Commander in Chief, United States Fleet, "Action Report of U.S.S. *Hopewell* in Leyte Island Operation from A-2 to A-12 Day inclusive," November 1, 1944.

Commanding Officer to Commander in Chief, United States Fleet, "Special Action Report (Anti-Aircraft Action by Surface Ships), Submission Of," November 24, 1944.

Commanding Officer to Commander in Chief, United States Fleet, "Special Action Report (Anti-Aircraft Action by Surface Ships), Submission Of," December 2, 1944.

Commanding Officer to Commander in Chief, United States Fleet, "Special Action Report (Anti-Aircraft Action by Surface Ships), Submission Of," December 13, 1944.

Commanding Officer to Commander in Chief, United States Fleet, "Shore Bombardment of Caminawit Peninsula, Mindoro Island, P.I., by USS *Howorth*, Report Of," December 15, 1944.

Commanding Officer to Commander in Chief, United States Fleet, "Special Action Report (Anti-Aircraft Action by Surface Ships), Submission Of," December 15, 1944.

Commanding Officer to Commander in Chief, United States Fleet, "Special Action Report (Anti-Aircraft Action by Surface Ships), Submission Of," December 17, 1944.

Commanding Officer to Commander in Chief, United States Fleet, "Special Action Report (Anti-Aircraft Action by Surface Ships), Submission Of," December 20, 1944.

Commanding Officer to Commander in Chief, United States Fleet, "Action Report—Invasion of Southwest Mindoro, P. I., December 12–15, 1944," December 29, 1944.

Commanding Officer to Commander in Chief, United States Fleet, "Special Action Report (Anti-Aircraft Action by Surface Ships), Submission Of," January 15, 1945.

Commanding Officer to Commander in Chief, United States Fleet, "Shore Bombardments in Support of Land Forces to West of Rosario, Luzon, Philippine Islands on 14 and 15 January 1945, Report Of," January 20, 1945.

Commanding Officer to Commander in Chief, United States Fleet, "Action Report of U.S.S. *Hopewell* in Luzon Island Operation from 1–31 January 1945," February 1, 1945.

Action Reports: Okinawa

Commanding Officer to Commander in Chief, United States Fleet, "Special Action Report (Anti-Aircraft Action by Surface Ship), on 6 April 1945, Submission Of," April 10, 1945.

Other

Commanding Officer to Secretary of the Navy, "Submission of War Record," September 25, 1945.

Ship's History, USS *Howorth* (DD-592), October 20, 1945.

Desron 21

War Diaries

Monthly War Diary, March 1943–September 1945.

Action Reports: Desron 21 in the Kula Gulf Battles, July–October 1943

Commander, Destroyer Squadron 21, to Commander in Chief, United States Pacific Fleet, "Night Action North of Vella Lavella by Desdiv 41 (Task Unit 31.2) August 17–18, 1943," September 2, 1943.

Commander, Destroyer Squadron 21, to Commander in Chief, First Fleet, "Action Against Enemy Barges and Gunboat Night of October 3–4, 1943, in Kolombangara-Vella Lavella Area—Report Of," October 11, 1943.

Commander, Destroyer Squadron 21, to Commander in Chief, First Fleet, "Japanese Landing Craft Operations Between Kolombangara and Choiseul,

Solomon Islands Nights of Sept. 30, Oct. 1, Oct. 1–2, and Oct. 3–4, 1943—Report On," October 28, 1943.

Action Reports: Desron 21 in the Gilberts and Marshalls

Commander, Destroyer Squadron 21, to Commander in Chief, United States Pacific Fleet, "Operations During Galvanic Movement and Action Report of December 4, 1943," December 9, 1943.

Action Reports: Desron 21 in New Guinea

Commander, Destroyer Squadron 21, to Commander in Chief, United States Fleet, "Action Report on Aitape, New Guinea Operation," May 6, 1944.

Commander, Destroyer Squadron 21, to Commander in Chief, United States Fleet, "Comments on Bombardment of Medina Plantation Area of New Ireland, Night of 28–29 May 1944," June 6, 1944.

Action Reports: To the Philippines

Commander, Destroyer Squadron 21, to Commander in Chief, United States Fleet, "Camotes Sea Sweep and Bombardment Vicinity Ormoc, Report On," December 13, 1945.

Commander, Destroyer Squadron 21, to Commander in Chief, United States Fleet, "Action Report—1 January Through 31 January 1945—Including Luzon Operation," February 10, 1945.

Action Reports: Borneo

Commander, Destroyer Squadron 21, to Commander in Chief, United States Fleet, "Action Report—Seizure and Occupation of Tarakan Island, Dutch Borneo—24 April–5 May 1945," May 9, 1945.

Action Reports: To War's End

Commander, Destroyer Squadron 21, to Commander in Chief, United States Fleet, "Action Report (First Period, 28 May to 1 July 1945, Inclusive)—Neutralization of Airfields in the Sakishima Gunto—17 June to 23 June 1945," July 1, 1945.

Commander, Destroyer Squadron 21, to Commander in Chief, United States Fleet, "Action Report for Period from Cessation of Hostilities (16 August 1945) to Final Surrender of Japan (2 September 1945)," September 22, 1945.

Other

Commander, Destroyer Squadron 21, to Chief of Naval Operations, "Command History," January 11, 1964.

Other

War Diaries

Command Summary of Fleet Admiral Chester W. Nimitz, 7 December 1941–31 August 1945.

South Pacific War Diary, 1942–1944, in the Admiral William F. Halsey Collection, Naval Historical Foundation Collection, Manuscript Division, Library of Congress, Washington, D.C.

Third Fleet War Diary, in the Admiral William F. Halsey Collection, Naval Historical Foundation Collection, Manuscript Division, Library of Congress, Washington, D.C.

Action Reports: In the Solomons, January–March 1943

Commander, Destroyer Squadron 5, to Commander in Chief, United States Pacific Fleet, "Action Report—Bombardment Point Munda—Night of January 4–5, 1943," January 6, 1943.

Commander, Destroyer Squadron 5, to Commander in Chief, United States Pacific Fleet, "Action Report—Munda Bombardment," January 8, 1943.

Commander, Task Group 67.5, to Commander, South Pacific Force, "Report of Operations—January 16, 1943 to February 2, 1943," February 6, 1943.

Action Reports: The Kula Gulf Battles, July–October 1943

Frederick Moosbrugger, Commander, Destroyer Division 12, to Commander in Chief, United States Pacific Fleet, "Action Report for Night of August 6–7, 1943—Battle of Vella Gulf," August 16, 1943.

Rear Admiral Walden L. Ainsworth, "Activities of Task Forces Under the Command of Rear Admiral Walden L. Ainsworth, U.S. Navy, Solomon Island Campaigns, 10 December 1942 to 4 June 1944."

Rear Admiral Walden L. Ainsworth, "Cruiser-Destroyer Task Forces, Solomons Campaign," January 17, 1946.

COLLECTIONS

Admiral William F. Halsey Collection, Naval Historical Foundation Collection, Manuscript Division, Library of Congress, Washington, D.C.

The Dow Ransom Collection

The Martin Johnson Collection

The Papers of Donald J. MacDonald, Naval Historical Foundation Collection, Manuscript Division, Library of Congress, Washington, D.C.

The Personal Papers of Vice Admiral Walden L. Ainsworth, Naval Historical Center, Washington Navy Yard, Washington, D.C.

The Robert Whisler Collection
The Thomas Chesnutt Collection
William K. Romoser Papers, Naval Historical Foundation Collection, Manuscript Division, Library of Congress, Washington, D.C.

INTERVIEWS AND ORAL HISTORIES

Interviews Conducted by the Author

Russell Bramble, USS *Howorth*: Telephone interview on June 14, 2016.
Thomas Chesnutt, USS *Fletcher*: Telephone interviews on March 1, 2016, March 3, 2016, March 7, 2016, and May 31, 2016.
Warren Gabelman, USS *Nicholas*: Telephone interviews on June 8, 2015, and June 10, 2015.
Donald Holmes, USS *Fletcher*: Telephone interviews on October 14, 2015, and October 22, 2015.
Martin Johnson, USS *La Vallette*: Telephone interviews on May 16, 2016, and May 19, 2016.
Jack O'Neill, USS *Nicholas*: Telephone interview on August 11, 2015.
Willy Rhyne, USS *O'Bannon*: Telephone interview on October 20, 2015.
James Setter, USS *Fletcher*: Telephone interview on July 21, 2015.
Douglas Starr, USS *Nicholas*: Telephone interviews on May 4, 2015, June 9, 2015, and June 18, 2015; email to author, May 16, 2016.
Robert Whisler, USS *O'Bannon*: Personal interview on July 22, 2015; telephone interviews on July 10, 2015, October 15, 2015, and May 12, 2016.

Oral Histories

Diary of Jacob Thomas Chesnutt Jr., November 13, 1942, in the J. Thomas Chesnutt Collection (AFC/2001/001/58477), Veterans History Project, American Folklife Center, Library of Congress. Found at http://lcweb2.loc.gov/natlib/afc2001001/service/58477/pd0001.pdf. Accessed October 13, 2015.
Doc Ransom Diary, courtesy of Dow Ransom Jr.
Interview with Fred G. Lampe (USS *La Vallette*). Veterans History Project. Found at http://memory.loc.gov/diglib/vhp/story/loc.natlib.afc2001001.56486/transcript?ID=sr0001. Accessed March 13, 2015.
Martin Johnson's Diary of World War II, courtesy of Martin Johnson.
"Oral History of Rear Admiral Joseph C. Wylie, USN (Ret.)," Naval War College, Oral History Program, interviews conducted by Dr. Evelyn M. Cherpak on November 21, 1985, December 17, 1985, January 15, 1986, January 22, 1986, and February 5, 1986.

"The Reminiscences of Hanson Weightman Baldwin, U.S. Navy (Ret.)," interview by John T. Mason, United States Naval Institute, Annapolis, Maryland, 1976.

"The Reminiscences of Rear Admiral Donald J. MacDonald, U.S. Navy (Retired)," interview by John T. Mason, United States Naval Institute, Annapolis, Maryland, December 1986.

"The Reminiscences of Rear Admiral Joseph C. Wylie, Jr., U.S. Navy (Retired)," interview by Paul Stilwell, United States Naval Institute, Annapolis, Maryland, 2003.

"The Reminiscences of Robert Bostwick Carney," 1964, 342–343, in the Oral History Collection of Columbia University.

"The Reminiscences of Vice Admiral Robert Taylor Scott Keith, U.S. Navy (Retired)," interview by Paul Stilwell, United States Naval Institute, Annapolis, Maryland, April 1996.

BOOKS

Barbey, Daniel E. *MacArthur's Amphibious Navy: Seventh Amphibious Force Operations, 1943–1945*. Annapolis, MD: United States Naval Institute, 1969.

The Battle of Tassafaronga, 30 November 1942. Office of Naval Intelligence, United States Navy, 1944.

Becton, F. Julian, with Joseph Morschauser III. *The Ship That Would Not Die*. Englewood Cliffs, NJ: Prentice-Hall, 1980.

Bell, Frederick J. *Condition Red: Destroyer Action in the South Pacific*. New York: Longmans Green, 1944.

Bix, Herbert P. *Hirohito and the Making of Modern Japan*. New York: HarperCollins, 2000.

Brodie, Bernard. *A Guide to Naval Strategy*. Princeton: Princeton University Press, 1944.

Calhoun, C. Raymond. *Tin Can Sailor: Life Aboard the USS* Sterett, *1939–1945*. Annapolis, MD: Naval Institute Press, 1993.

Cant, Gilbert. *America's Navy in World War II*. New York: John Day, 1943.

Crenshaw, Russell Sydnor, Jr. *South Pacific Destroyer: The Battle for the Solomons from Savo Island to Vella Gulf*. Annapolis, MD: Naval Institute Press, 1998.

Davies, Robert B. *Baldwin of the* Times: *Hanson W. Baldwin, a Military Journalist's Life, 1903–1991*. Annapolis, MD: Naval Institute Press, 2011.

Fahey, James J. *Pacific War Diary, 1942–1945*. Boston: Houghton Mifflin, 1963.

Feifer, George. *Tennozan: The Battle of Okinawa and the Atomic Bomb*. New York: Ticknor and Fields, 1992.

Frank, Richard B. *Guadalcanal: The Definitive Account of the Landmark Battle*. New York: Penguin Books, 1990.

Friedman, Norman. *U.S. Destroyers: An Illustrated Design History*. Annapolis, MD: Naval Institute Press, 1982.

Gow, Ian. *Okinawa 1945: Gateway to Japan*. Garden City, NY: Doubleday, 1985.

Hailey, Foster. *Pacific Battle Line*. New York: Macmillan, 1944.

Halsey, William F., and J. Bryan III. *Admiral Halsey's Story*. New York: McGraw-Hill, 1947.

Halsey, William F. "Life of Admiral W. F. Halsey," undated typewritten memoirs dictated by Halsey after the war. Copies distributed by Virginia Historical Society.

Hara, Tameichi, with Fred Saito and Roger Pineau. *Japanese Destroyer Captain*. Annapolis, MD: Naval Institute Press, 1967.

Horan, James D. *Action Tonight: The Story of the American Destroyer* O'Bannon *in the Pacific*. New York: G. P. Putnam's Sons, 1945.

Hornfischer, James D. *Neptune's Inferno: The U.S. Navy at Guadalcanal*. New York: Bantam Books, 2011.

Inoguchi, Rikihei, and Tadashi Nakajima, with Roger Pineau. *The Divine Wind: Japan's Kamikaze Force in World War II*. New York: Bantam Books, 1958.

Jones, Ken. *Destroyer Squadron 23*. Annapolis, MD: Naval Institute Press, 1997.

Karig, Walter, with Russell L. Harris and Frank A. Manson. *Battle Report: Victory in the Pacific*. New York: Rinehart, 1949.

Kato, Masuo. *The Lost War: A Japanese Reporter's Inside Story*. New York: Alfred A. Knopf, 1946.

Kurzman, Dan. *Left to Die: The Tragedy of the USS* Juneau. New York: Pocket Books, 1994.

Lee, Walter Allen. *One of the Crew: USS O'Bannon, World War II*. Victoria, BC: Trafford, 2007.

Lundstrom, John B. *The First Team and the Guadalcanal Campaign*. Annapolis, MD: Naval Institute Press, 1994.

MacArthur, Douglas. *Reminiscences*. New York: McGraw-Hill, 1964.

Manchester, William. *American Caesar: Douglas MacArthur, 1880–1964*. Boston: Little, Brown, 1978.

McBride, William M., ed. *Good Night Officially: The Pacific War Letters of a Destroyer Sailor*. Boulder, CO: Westview Press, 1994.

Miller, Landon C. G. *Lt. "Rose Bowl" Miller: The U.S. Navy's One Man Army*. Privately published, 2010.

Morison, Samuel Eliot. *History of United States Naval Operations in World War II,* Volume V, *The Struggle for Guadalcanal, August 1942–February 1943*. Boston: Little, Brown, 1949.

———. *History of United States Naval Operations in World War II,* Volume VI, *Breaking the Bismarcks Barrier, 22 July 1942–1 May 1944*. Boston: Little, Brown, 1950.

———. *History of United States Naval Operations in World War II,* Volume VII, *Aleutians, Gilberts and Marshalls, June 1942–April 1944*. Boston: Little, Brown, 1960.

———. *History of United States Naval Operations in World War II,* Volume VIII, *New Guinea and the Marianas, March 1944–August 1944*. Boston: Little, Brown, 1964.

———. *History of United States Naval Operations in World War II,* Volume XII, *Leyte, June 1944–January 1945*. Boston: Little, Brown, 1958.

———. *History of United States Naval Operations in World War II,* Volume XIII, *The Liberation of the Philippines, Luzon, Mindanao, the Visayas, 1944–1945*. Boston: Little, Brown, 1959.

———. *History of United States Naval Operations in World War II,* Volume XIV, *Victory in the Pacific 1945*. Boston: Little, Brown, 1960.

Norton-Taylor, Duncan. *With My Heart in My Mouth*. New York: Coward-McCann, 1944.

The 100 Best True Stories of World War II. New York: Wm. H. Wise, 1945.

Orita, Zenji, with Joseph D. Harrington. *I-Boat Captain: How Japan's Submarines Almost Defeated the U.S. Navy in the Pacific*. Canoga Park, CA: Major Books, 1976.

Potter, E. B. *Nimitz*. Annapolis, MD: Naval Institute Press, 1976.

———. *Admiral Arleigh Burke*. New York: Random House, 1990.

Prados, John. *Islands of Destiny: The Solomons Campaign and the Eclipse of the Rising Sun*. New York: NAL Caliber, 2012.

Roscoe, Theodore. *United States Destroyer Operations in World War II*. Annapolis, MD: United States Naval Institute, 1953.

Sears, David. *At War with the Wind*. New York: Citadel Press, 2008.

Solomon Islands Campaign: VI, Battle of Guadalcanal, 11–15 November 1942. Office of Naval Intelligence, United States Navy, 1944.

Stille, Mark. *USN Destroyer vs. IJN Destroyer: The Pacific, 1943*. Long Island, NY: Osprey Publishing, 2012.

Ugaki, Matome. *Fading Victory: The Diary of Admiral Matome Ugaki, 1941–1945*. Pittsburgh: University of Pittsburgh Press, 1991.

United States Strategic Bombing Survey. *Interrogations of Japanese Officials, Volume II,* No. 467, "Interrogation of Capt. Toshikazu Ohmae, Chief of Staff, Southeastern Fleet at Rabaul," November 20, 1945. Washington, D.C.: Naval Analysis Division, 1946.

U.S.S. Howorth *Ship's History*, October 20, 1945.

U.S.S. Nicholas *Cruise Book*, December 1945.

U.S.S. Taylor *Cruise Book*, December 1945.

Vandegrift, A. A. *Once a Marine*. New York: W. W. Norton, 1964.

Wheeler, Gerald E. *Kinkaid of the Seventh Fleet*. Annapolis, MD: Naval Institute Press, 1995.

Wooldridge, E. T., ed. *Carrier Warfare in the Pacific: An Oral History Collection*. Washington, D.C.: Smithsonian Institution Press, 1993.

ARTICLES

"Action in Solomons." *New York Times*, December 14, 1942, 1–2.

Adler, Julius Ochs. "Big Fleet in Sagami Bay." *New York Times*, August 28, 1945.

"Admiral Takes Big Chances to Gain Big Victories." *Washington Post*, November 17, 1942, 1, 8.

"Aggressive Spirit." *Washington Post*, November 22, 1942, B6.

"A Letter to Tojo." *Time*, March 29, 1943, 16–17.

"Americans Trained at Midway and Pearl Harbor Claim Hundreds of Japanese Planes—And the Enemy Stays Away." *New York Times*, December 30, 1942.

Andrews, Marshall. "Halsey Replaces Ghormley." *Washington Post*, October 25, 1942, 1–2.

Baldwin, Hanson W. "Blow at Luzon Indicated." *New York Times*, December 16, 1944.

———. "Divided Command in Pacific War Gives Australia a Secondary Role." *New York Times*, October 26, 1942, 1, 5.

———. "Fighting for Outposts in Pacific Is Prelude to Greater Struggle." *New York Times*, October 11, 1942, E4.

———. "Lessons of the Solomons Campaign." *New York Times*, October 24, 1942, 3.

———. "Naval Superiority Is Goal in Solomons." *New York Times*, October 30, 1942, 3.

———. "Okinawa's Fate Sealed." *New York Times*, April 9, 1945.

———. "Ominous Lull on War Fronts." *New York Times*, December 17, 1942.

———. "The Pacific Campaign—III." *New York Times*, December 24, 1942.

———. "Plane Superiority Won in the Pacific." *New York Times*, October 27, 1942, 7.

———. "Showdown in Solomons." *New York Times*, November 16, 1942.

———. "Solomons Action Develops into Battle for South Pacific." *New York Times*, September 27, 1942, 1, 42.

———. "Solomons Operation a Magnet for Navies." *New York Times*, October 25, 1942, E5.

———. "South Pacific War Develops on a Vast Scale." *New York Times*, October 4, 1942.

———. "Three Isles in Solomons Devastated Before Landing by U.S. Marines." *New York Times*, September 28, 1942, 4.

———. "U.S. Marines' Song Used Against Them." *New York Times*, September 29, 1942, 10.

———. "U.S. Navy Is Using Big Army Bombers." *New York Times*, October 28, 1942, 6.

———. "Victory in First Phase." *New York Times*, November 18, 1942.

"Battle Probably off Esperance." *New York Times*, December 14, 1942.

Brooks, Alvin R. "A USS *Northampton* Survivor's Thanks to *Fletcher*." Found at http://ussfletcher.org/stories/survivor.html. Accessed March 11, 2015.

"Bull's Eye." *Time*, July 23, 1945.

"By Air and Sea." *New York Times*, October 9, 1942.

"Commander Donald J. MacDonald." *Real Life Comics*, March 1945.

"Destroyer USS *Hopewell* Trades Blows with Japanese Shore Batteries on Corregidor." Navy Department Press Release, August 23, 1945.

"Die, but Do Not Retreat." *Time*, January 4, 1943, 21–24.

Durdin, F. Tillman. "Hard Struggle Forecast." *New York Times*, November 28, 1942.

Eliot, George Fielding. "New South Pacific Chief Aggressive Commander." *Los Angeles Times*, October 26, 1942, 2.

"Enemy Aid to Guadalcanal Blocked by Munda Raids." *New York Times*, December 21, 1942.

Eubanks, Steve. "Former Alabama QB Miller Remembered on Veterans Day." Foxsports.com, November 11, 2013. Found at http://www.foxsports.com/south/story/former-alabama-qb-miller-remembered-on-veterans-day-111113. Accessed March 21, 2015.

"Face to Face." *Time*, November 9, 1942.

"Fight Coming Up?" *Time*, January 18, 1943, 26–29.

"First Lady Presents Navy Cross to Hero." *New York Times*, September 22, 1943.

"Flagship *Missouri* Steams to Site of the Surrender." *New York Times*, August 29, 1945.

"Foe Rallies Fleet for Solomons Blow." *New York Times*, November 3, 1942.

"401 Allied Vessels Poised off Japan." *New York Times*, August 28, 1945.

"Fourth Raid on Munda." *New York Times*, December 15, 1942.

"Glory for a Tin Can." *Time*, April 17, 1944, 65–66.

"Guadalcanal Grip Aided by Landings." *New York Times*, November 18, 1942.

Hailey, Foster. "Halsey Defends Battleship's Role." *New York Times*, November 19, 1942, 1, 8.

———. "Halsey Is Known as a Fighting Man." *New York Times*, October 25, 1942, 41.

———. "Heroes on a Tin Can." *New York Times*, July 15, 1945.

———. "Task Force Fools the Japanese, Then Batters a Base Near Munda." *New York Times*, February 6, 1943.

———. "Their Morale Is All Right . . . How's Yours?" *New York Times*, November 8, 1942, 6, 27.

"Halsey Minimizes Foe." *New York Times*, January 7, 1943, 4.

"Halsey Named Full Admiral by Roosevelt." *Washington Post*, November 21, 1942, 2.

"Halsey Takes Command." *New York Times*, October 26, 1942, 14.

"Hawaii Is Cautious on Pacific Picture." *New York Times*, November 18, 1942.

"Hero Ship *O'Bannon*." *Heroic Comics*, March 1945.

"Hit Hard, Hit Fast, Hit Often." *Time*, November 30, 1942, 28–31.

"How Pounds Won the Battle." U.S.S. *O'Bannon* Shipmates Association Newsletter, June 1980, found in the Papers of Donald J. MacDonald, Naval Historical Foundation Collection, Manuscript Division, Library of Congress.

Huggard, Doug. "Luckiest Ship." Found at http://ussfletcher.org/stories/luckiest.html. Accessed March 11, 2015.

Hurd, Charles. "Batters Japanese." *New York Times*, November 14, 1942, 1, 7.

———. "Foe Lands Troops on Guadalcanal East of Our Force." *New York Times*, November 4, 1942.

———. "Foe Hits from Air." *New York Times*, October 16, 1942.

———. "Foe's Navy Routed." *New York Times*, November 17, 1942, 1, 4.

———. "Guadalcanal Firm." *New York Times*, October 31, 1942.

———. "Japanese May Try Soon for Decision in Pacific." *New York Times*, November 15, 1942.

———. "Joy at Sea Victory." *New York Times*, November 18, 1942, 1, 8.

———. "Jungle Island Becomes the Heart of Great Battle for the Pacific." *New York Times*, October 18, 1942.

———. "Major Pacific Campaign Lies Ahead." *New York Times*, December 20, 1942.

———. "Navies Manoeuvre for Big Stakes in Solomons." *New York Times*, November 1, 1942.

———. "New Pacific Clash Awaited." *New York Times*, November 8, 1942.

———. "Our Bombers Pound Foe's Munda Field." *New York Times*, December 16, 1942.

———. "Our Navy in Action." *New York Times*, November 15, 1942, 1, 34.

———. "Raids on Guadalcanal." *New York Times*, November 13, 1942.

———. "Ships Sunk by Foe." *New York Times*, October 22, 1942.

———. "Solomons Sea Victory Staggers to Japanese." *New York Times*, November 22, 1942.

"Japan May Fall, Tokyo Radio Tells People." *New York Times*, April 3, 1945.

"Japanese Reported Starving." *New York Times*, December 30, 1942.

"Japanese Victory Claimed by Tokyo." *New York Times*, November 17, 1942.

"Japan's Doorstep." *New York Times*, April 1, 1945.

Jensen, John V. "A Collection of Stories from WWII." Found at http://ussfletcher.org/stories/wwii.html. Accessed March 11, 2015.

Jones, George E. "Enemy Fliers Hit Troops on Okinawa." *New York Times*, April 8, 1945.

JVJ. "USS *Fletcher*, Lucky Thirteen." Found at https://app.box.com/s/mfwkwzctfngz2a0hhqdw/1/614749664/5840815304/1. Accessed March 11, 2015.

Kirkley, Sara. "Sunday Salute: Russell Bramble." KHGI-TV interview, Kearney, Nebraska, December 7, 2015.

Lawrence, W. H. "Our Okinawa Guns Down 118 Planes." *New York Times*, April 13, 1945.

———. "Okinawa Looms as Giant Air Base." *New York Times*, April 30, 1945.

Lindley, Ernest. "Needs in the Pacific." *Washington Post*, March 19, 1943, 13.

Lodge J. Norman. "Halsey Predicts Victory This Year." *New York Times*, January 3, 1943, 14.

MacDonald, Donald J. "They Went to Hell and Back with Me." *American Magazine*, July 1944, 24–25, 89–94.

"Macnimsey's Show." *Time*, July 12, 1943.

McCormick, Anne O'Hare. "Optimism at the End of the First Year." *New York Times*, December 5, 1942.

Miller, Hugh Barr, Jr., as told to Frank Tremaine. "The Cast Away of Arundel Island." In *The 100 Best True Stories of World War II*. New York: Wm. H. Wise, 1945. First appeared in *Life*, November 1943.

"'Most Decorated Officer' and Ship Win High Honor." *New York Times*, April 4, 1944.

"Munda Hit by Big Blasts." *New York Times*, January 12, 1943.

"Navy's Most Decorated Hero Scared by War." *New York Times*, April 7, 1944.

"New Bases on New Georgia." *Time*, January 11, 1943.

Norris, John G. "Admiral Halsey, Unorthodox Fighter, Takes Over Navy's Toughest Command." *Washington Post*, November 1, 1942, B2.

———. "What Comes Next in the South Pacific?" *Washington Post*, January 10, 1943, B5.

Norton-Taylor, Duncan. "The *O'Bannon* and the Battle of Kula Gulf." *Four Star Final*, May–June, 1944, 6

"Our Men, Materiel Sparkle in Pacific." *New York Times*, November 15, 1942.

"Pacific Honor Won by U.S.S. *O'Bannon.*" *New York Times*, September 9, 1944.

"Patch of Destiny." *Time*, November 2, 1942, 29–31.

Pfeifer, Carl F., and Jack S. McDowell. "Lucky Mike Plays for Keeps." *True, the Man's Magazine*, May 1944, 26–29, 65–67.

Phillips, H. I. "*O'Bannon* and Mac." *New York Sun Dial*, April 7, 1944.

"Report on the Pacific." *New York Times*, October 31, 1942, 14.

Richardson, Whit. "Maine-Made USS *O'Bannon* 'Led the Way' at Guadalcanal." *Press Herald* (Portland, Maine), November 15, 2014. Found at www.pressherald.com/2014/11/15/obannon-led-the-way-at-guadalcanal. Accessed March 9, 2015.

"'Round 3' Held Won at Guadalcanal." *New York Times*, December 5, 1942.

"Sea Fight by Night." *New York Times*, December 4, 1942.

Shafter, Richard. "What's in a Name?" *Our Navy*, Mid-June, 1944, 24–25.

Sherwood, John. "The Legend of the Deadly Potatoes." *Washington Times*, April 17, 1974.

"Strongest Jap Attempt Frustrated, Nimitz Says." *Washington Post*, November 17, 1942, 2.

"That Heavy Rumbling." *Time*, January 11, 1943, 28.

"The Five Battles of the Solomons." *Time*, November 30, 1942, 30.

"Time of Hirohito Short, Says Halsey." *Los Angeles Times*, January 3, 1943, 1.

"Tokyo Says Navy Has Big Additions." *New York Times*, December 8, 1942.

Tregaskis, Richard. "Halsey Sees 'Absolute Defeat' For Axis Forces This Year." *Washington Post*, January 3, 1943, 1–2.

Trumbull, Robert. "All Out With Halsey!" *New York Times*, December 6, 1942, 14.

———. "Nimitz Confident After Pacific Trip." *New York Times*, October 15, 1942, 6.

———. "Nimitz Is Elated." *New York Times*, November 17, 1942, 1, 6.

"U.S. Destroyer *O'Bannon* Returns Home; Helped to Sink Battleship and 3 Cruisers." *New York Times*, December 19, 1943.

"U.S. Planes Make 4th Raid on Munda." *New York Times*, December 15, 1942.

"Victory off Guadalcanal." *Time*, November 23, 1942, 28.

"War's End." *Time*, August 16, 1943.

Wellings, Joseph H. "The Night *Strong* Was Sunk." *Shipmate*, July–August 1977, 1–6. Found in E. Andrew Wilde Jr., ed., "The U.S.S. *Strong* (DD-467) in World War II: Documents, Recollections and Photographs." Privately published, Needham, MA, 2001.

Wolfert, Ira. "Solomons Battle a Fiery Spectacle." *New York Times*, November 28, 1942.

Worden, William L. "The Japs' Last Bite." *Saturday Evening Post*, October 27, 1945, 23, 128.

"WWII Shipmates Visiting." *Fredericksburg* (TX) *Standard-Radio Post*, September 22, 1993.

Wylie, J. C. "Letter to Bentley Jessee." Found at https://app.box.com/s/mfwkwzctfngz2a0hhqdw/1/614749862/5840830592/1. Accessed March 11, 2015.

ARTICLES FROM HTTP://DESTROYERHISTORY.ORG/FLETCHERCLASS

Destroyer Squadron 21

"World War II in Quotes." Found at http://destroyerhistory.org/fletcherclass/index.asp?r=4210&pid=4213. Accessed June 30, 2015.

USS Chevalier *(DD-451)*

Gorsline, MM1/c Burt. "Loss of *Chevalier*." Found at http://destroyerhistory.org/fletcherclass/index.asp?r=45111&pid=45131. Accessed March 20, 2015.

———. "Loss of *Strong*." Found at http://destroyerhistory.org/fletcherclass/index.asp?r=45111&pid=45130. Accessed March 20, 2015.

Gowen, Lt. George. "Reminiscences of George Gowen." Found at http://destroyerhistory.org/fletcherclass/usschevalier/index.asp?r=45100&pid=45109. Accessed May 6, 2016.

———. "Various Reminiscences." Found at http://destroyerhistory.org/fletcherclass/usschevalier/index.asp?r=45109&pid=45110. Accessed March 20, 2015.

Kley, "Doc." "Personal Recollection of Events Prior to and after the Sinking of the USS *Chevalier*, October 6–7, 1943, 2300 Hours." Found at http://destroyerhistory.org/fletcherclass/index.asp?r=45109&pid=45112. Accessed March 20, 2015.

Roupe, Yeoman R. H. "A *Chevalier* Memoir." Found at http://destroyerhistory.org/fletcherclass/index.asp?r=45100&pid=45114. Accessed March 20, 2015.

———. "Hell and High Water." Found at http://destroyerhistory.org/fletcherclass/index.asp?r=45109&pid=45113. Accessed March 20, 2015.

USS De Haven *(DD-469)*

Breining, Al. "Bye-bye DD!" Found at http://destroyerhistory.org/fletcherclass/index.asp?r=46905&pid=46910. Accessed March 23, 2015.

Elam, Leonard. "Loss of *De Haven*." Found at http://destroyerhistory.org/fletcher class/index.asp?r=46905&pid=46911. Accessed March 23, 2015.

Herr, Ernest A. "Horror at Guadalcanal." Destroyer History Foundation website. Found at http://destroyerhistory.org/fletcherclass/index.asp?r=45007&pid =45018. Accessed February 22, 2015.

———. "The Last Day of the *De Haven*." Found at http://destroyerhistory.org /fletcherclass/index.asp?r=46900&pid=46906. Accessed March 23, 2015.

USS Fletcher *(DD-445)*

Gressard, Fred. "Reminiscences." Found at http://destroyerhistory.org/fletcher class/ussfletcher/index.asp?r=44500&pid=44504. Accessed December 4, 2014.

USS Jenkins *(DD-447)*

Mahan, TM3/c Paul E. "Saving *Jenkins*." Found at http://destroyerhistory.org /fletcherclass/ussjenkins/index.asp?r=44700&pid=44704. Accessed March 12, 2015.

USS La Vallette *(DD-448)*

Bell, Jack. "Introduction to 'Doc' Ransom's Diary." Found at http://destroyer history.org/fletcherclass/index.asp?r=44805&pid=44816. Accessed March 4, 2016.

Eisenberg, George. "Sinking the *Chevalier*." Found at http://destroyerhistory.org /fletcherclass/index.asp?r=44805&pid=44817. Accessed March 13, 2015.

"War Record of the U.S.S. *La Vallette* DD-448." Found at http://destroyer history.org/fletcherclass/usslavallette/index.asp?r=44800&pid=44802. Accessed April 21, 2015.

Wilkes, Jack. "The Battle of Rennell Island." Found at http://destroyerhistory .org/fletcherclass/index.asp?r=44805&pid=44815. Accessed March 13, 2015.

Witten, Chuck. "The Battle of Rennell Island." Found at http://destroyerhistory .org/fletcherclass/index.asp?r=44805&pid=44814. Accessed March 13, 2015.

USS Nicholas *(DD-449)*

Gabelman, Warren H. "She Was My Yacht." Found at http://destroyer history.org/fletcherclass/index.asp?r=44905&pid=44935. Accessed March 10, 2015.

Keith, Robert Taylor Scott. "I Had A Wonderful Crew on There." Found at http://destroyerhistory.org/fletcherclass/index.asp?r=44905&pid=44936. Accessed March 10, 2015.

Moll, Joe. "Rescue at Kula Gulf." Found at http://destroyerhistory.org/fletcherclass/index.asp?r=44905&pid=44934. Accessed March 10, 2015.

"Presentation of Presidential Unit Citation to the USS *Nicholas* by Admiral Nimitz." Found at http://destroyerhistory.org/fletcherclass/index.asp?r=44904&pid=44923. Accessed February 2, 2015.

Starr, Douglas Perret. "I Would Not Have Missed It for the World." Found at http://destroyerhistory.org/fletcherclass/index.asp?r=44905&pid=44937. Accessed March 10, 2015.

———. "Taking Corregidor, Manila Bay, 13–16 February 1945." Found at http://destroyerhistory.org/fletcherclass/index.asp?r=44937&pid=44974. Accessed March 10, 2015.

Turpen, Doug. "Navigating the 'Nick.'" Found at http://destroyerhistory.org/fletcherclass/index.asp?r=44905&pid=44938. Accessed March 10, 2015.

Wing, Virgil. "Destroyer Sailor." Found at http://destroyerhistory.org/fletcherclass/index.asp?r=44905&pid=44932. Accessed July 7, 2015.

Young, Ralph. "Letter from Tokyo Bay." Found at http://destroyerhistory.org/fletcherclass/index.asp?r=44905&pid=44939. Accessed March 10, 2015.

USS O'Bannon *(DD-450)*

Herr, Ernest A. "Horror at Guadalcanal." Found at http://destroyerhistory.org/fletcherclass/index.asp?r=45007&pid=45018. Accessed June 21, 2016.

USS Strong *(DD-467)*

Grimes, Al. "Recollection of Al Grimes." Found at http://destroyerhistory.org/fletcherclass/desron21/index.asp?r=4210&pid=4213. Accessed May 6, 2016.

———. "Stories of USS *Strong*." June 1, 1989. Found at http://destroyerhistory.org/fletcherclass/ussstrong/index.asp?r=46703&pid=46706. Accessed March 21, 2015.

"Lt. Frederick Warren Purdy." Found at http://destroyerhistory.org/sumner-gearingclass/ns_purdy. Accessed March 21, 2015.

USS Taylor *(DD-468)*

DeLaureal, Henry. "From Guadalcanal to Tokyo." Found at http://destroyerhistory.org/fletcherclass/index.asp?r=46804&pid=46817. Accessed March 22, 2015.

Katz, Benjamin. "Highlights of Events and Interesting Occurrences." July 1981. Found at http://destroyerhistory.org/fletcherclass/index.asp?r=46804&pid=46816. Accessed March 22, 2015.

McCarthy, John C. "The Handshake." April 9, 2004. Found at http://destroyerhistory.org/fletcherclass/index.asp?r=46804&pid=46823. Accessed March 23, 2015.

———. "Pearl Harbor Epilogue." Found at http://destroyerhistory.org/fletcherclass/index.asp?r=46804&pid=46818. Accessed March 22, 2015.

WEBSITES

http://destroyerhistory.org

The website of the Destroyer History Foundation, assembled by the late Dave McComb

http://www.projectuss-strongdd467.com/index.html

The website of the USS *Strong* (DD-467), assembled by Tammi Hedrick Johnson

INDEX

Aaron Ward, 45, 56
Abe, Koki, 48–50, 51–53, 54, 57, 61, 68
Achilles, 88
Ainsworth, Walden L. ("Pug")
  advance of, 98–99
  battle tactics of, 145, 154
  crew trained by, 86
  Halsey on, 129
  open fire by, 100
  reports by, 114–115
  rescue ordered by, 147
  shelter sought by, 101
  on Tokyo Express, 85–89
aircraft carriers, 12, 25, 28, 31–32, 159, 185
Akiyama, Teruo, 145
Albemarle, USS (AV-5), 19
Amatsukaze, 39, 48, 50, 52
  crew of, 77
  damage to, 68
  as out of action, 61
  torpedoes launched by, 59
American Magazine, 171–172
Andrews, R. C., 113
Artesani, John H., 142
Asahi Shimbun, 24
Atlanta, 36, 41, 45, 50, 52, 57
Aulick, 187–188
Baldwin, Hanson
  on Ghormley, 30
  on Guadalcanal, 23–24, 27
  on lulls, 83
  on Philippine landings, 190
  on Solomons, 42
Bartlett, Josiah, 7
Barton, 45, 58, 59, 60
Bates, Douglas P., 56–57
Bates, John H., 108
Bath, Maine, shipbuilding, 14–15
battles
  Ainsworth's tactics for, 145, 154
  Calhoun on, 95
  Fletcher-class destroyers in, 90
  MacDonald on, 45, 52, 154
  O'Bannon in, 52–57
  Vandegrift on, 54
  See also Guadalcanal; Guadalcanal, initiation at; Guadalcanal, naval slugfest at; Kula Gulf confrontations; Philippine landings; Slot, struggle for; Tokyo Express; *specific battles*
Beemus, Dale W., 111
Bell, Frederick J., 13, 122
Bell, Jack, 202
Biegel, Charles N., 110
Bigelow, Elmer C., 197

Black Gang, 43–44, 52
Blitz, 10, 126
Bloody Tarawa, 160
bombardments
  air and naval, 4
  Chesnutt on, 174
  Fahey on, 128–129
  by *Fletcher* and *O'Bannon*, 87–88
  Guadalcanal, 27–28, 35, 92
  Hailey on, 100, 128
  MacDonald on, 99
  McInerney staging, 118
  nighttime, 87–89, 98, 155
  Radford in, 130
  Ransom on, 194
  in Slot, 84
  Starr on, 203
Bramble, Russell, 208, 210–211, 215, 218–220, 236
Breining, Albert L., 109–110
Briscoe, R. P., 87, 94, 100, 114
Brodie, Bernard, 13–14
Brooks, Alvin, 239–240
Brown, Julian P., 31, 35–36, 94
Brown, W. D., 16, 25–26
Burke, Arleigh A., 137, 155–156, 238
Burns, Edward S., 207–209, 211, 217
Bush, USS (DD-529), 216
bushido, 214

Cactus code name, 28, 69, 74
Cactus Striking Force
  end of *De Haven* in, 107–115
  Hailey on, 95–98
  Halsey on, 101
  holding the line, 96
  against Japanese, 98–107
  job for, 93–98
  open fire of, 100
  overview, 92–93
  ships in, 94, 97
Calhoun, Raymond C., 51, 95
California, USS (BB-44), 8
Callaghan, Daniel J., 30, 40–42
  death of, 62–64
  destroyers split by, 67
  force of, 45–47
  giving firing orders, 51
  Vandegrift on, 69
Cant, Gilbert, 32
Catalina Amphibious planes ("Black Cats"), 86, 128
Celmer, Lilian, 171
Chesnutt, Jacob Thomas, Jr.
  on air raids, 130
  on beauty of nature, 121–122
  on being Navy man, 240
  on bombardment, 174
  on carnage, 197–198
  depending upon, 93
  on doing job, 58–59
  on explosions, 196
  on Foster, 179–180
  on getting killed by Tokyo Express, 82–85
  hearing loss of, 235–236
  on hell breaking loose, 79
  on kamikaze attacks, 187
  on living through war, 67
  on Lord's protection, 63
  on McGinnis, 126
  on mines, 203–204
  on paratroopers, 203
  on radar, 58
  on rescue, 80
  on seeing action, 182
  on supplies, 74
  on Tokyo Rose, 185
Chevalier, USS (DD-451), 90–91, 103, 125, 239
  batteries from, 140
  division of, 117
  in Kula Gulf confrontations, 138
  on leave, 168

rescue by, 144
sinking of, 158, 238
tangling with enemy, 102
torpedoes launched by, 157
Chicago, 103, 104, 106
Christmas celebrations, 192–193
Christofferson, Edward A., Jr., 201
Churchill, Winston, 10–11, 239
Cianca, Louis F., 53
CIC. *See* combat information center
CIC Handbook for Destroyers Pacific Fleet, 89
Cleveland, 103
Cloward, Jr. R., 179
Cole, William M., 17, 80
in chart house, 62
Halsey replacing, 81
issuing orders, 57–58
maneuvers by, 59
navigation skills of, 74–75
as pleased with men, 44
radar and, 238
as skipper, 20
timing of, 27
torpedoes launched by, 60, 79
transfer arrangements by, 63
on Wylie, 66
Colhoun, USS (DD-801), 216
Columbia, 103
column formation
Fletcher in, 41–42, 45–47, 182
Jenkins in, 145
Nicholas in, 145
O'Bannon in, 41–42, 45–47, 51, 145
Radford in, 145
La Vallette in, 182
combat information center (CIC), 57, 89, 238
comradeship, 134
Constantino, Hector, 112
Conte, Albert V., 106
Cooper, USS (DD-695), 190
Copahee, 27
Coral Sea, Battle of, 24, 83
Corregidor assault, 195–198, 202–203
crews
Ainsworth training, 86
of *Amatsukaze*, 77
breaking down, 124–125
of *De Haven*, 108
of Desron 21, 5, 117, 239
of *Fletcher*, 17–18, 126
of *Howorth*, 215
MacDonald and, 16, 47, 65, 73, 99, 127, 170, 239
of *Missouri*, 4
of *O'Bannon*, 15, 16, 73, 91, 96
of *Sterett*, 95
superstitions of, 125
of *La Vallette*, 126
Wilkinson on, 66
Crowley, Dennis, 87–88
Curran, James A., 140
Current Tactical Orders and Doctrine, 137
Cushing, 45, 50–52

Dahlke, D. H., 44
Davis, Ralph O., 104
De Haven, USS (DD-469), 83, 90, 93
in Cactus Striking Force, 94
in Condition One or Two, 97
crew of, 108
end of, 107–115
as escort, 99
Hailey on, 113
on leave, 168
sinking of, 111, 238
DeLaureal, Henry, 123, 221–222, 228, 233
Denver, 201–202
depth charges, 5, 75
on early destroyers, 12
Fletcher-class destroyers and, 13, 95

depth charges *(continued)*
of *Laffey*, 56
O'Bannon dropping, 132–133
Wilkes on, 105
Destroyer Squadron 21 (Desron 21)
accomplishments of, 95
citations, 5
clashes with, 4
in Corregidor assault, 196–198
crews of, 5, 117, 239
as escorts, 133
food supply, 224
formation of, 127
Halsey and, 4–5, 148, 162
heroes of, 33
in Kula Gulf confrontations, 159–162
under MacArthur, 175–176
MacDonald on, 118
Nimitz on, 148, 160
O'Bannon on roster of, 116
at Okinawa, 213
in Philippine landings, 184, 188–189
protective screen of, 194
ships of, 20
in Solomon Islands, 158–159
submarines threatening, 131–132
Time magazine on, 135
at Tokyo plains attack, 225–226
U-boats sought by, 122
war record of, 237–238
way paved for, 19
destroyers
Bell on, 122
Callaghan splitting, 67
at Caribbean Sea trials, 14
depth charges on early, 12
as fightingest thing afloat, 119–127
Halsey using, 34
Halsey's fondness for, 12
Hara, T., loving, 119
MacDonald on role of, 26
multiple-duty vessels, 13–14
Nimitz on, 147–148
offensive action preferred, 26
shortage of, 73
in Slot, 93
See also Fletcher-class destroyers
Disputed Passage (movie), 82
dive bombers, 131, 177, 187
See also kamikaze attacks
Doolittle, James H., 108, 231
dropping potatoes story, 132–133
Duke of York, HMS, 227
Dungaree Navy, 122
Dunham, Malcolm M., 66–67, 124
Dunkirk rescue, 10

Eastern Solomons, Battle of, 39
Elam, Leonard, 110
English Channel gun emplacements, 11
Enterprise, 31, 41
escorts
De Haven as, 99
Desron 21 as, 133
Fletcher as, 34–37, 74, 76, 83, 86, 89–91
Nicholas as, 34–37, 74, 76, 83, 86, 89–91, 99
O'Bannon as, 34–37, 74, 76, 83, 86, 89–91, 99
in Pearl Harbor attack, 39
Radford as, 99
in Slot, 84
Wing on, 25
Essick, Joseph P., 105
Everett, John, 27
Everett, Johnny, Jr., 130
explosions
Chesnutt on, 196
in Kula Gulf confrontations, 154–159
on *Radford*, 199–200
on *La Vallette*, 198–199

Fahey, James J., 104, 128–129, 179, 200
Fanning, Ernest G., 228
Fanshaw Bay, USS (CVE-70), 187
Fields, Archie R., 109–111
The First Line (radio program), 148
Fletcher, USS (DD-445), 29
  bombardments by, 87–88
  in Cactus Striking Force, 94
  in column formation, 41–42, 45–47, 182
  crew of, 17–18, 126
  damages to, 238
  desperate situation for, 24
  division of, 117
  elimination of gun batteries by, 196
  embarking for Pacific, 19–20
  as escort, 34–37, 74, 76, 83, 86, 89–91
  exercises on, 20
  fire of, 185
  at Gilbert Islands landing, 167
  in Guadalcanal naval slugfest, 57–61
  gunners of, 44
  at home, 234
  inexperience of, 40
  as "Lucky 13," 66
  in Marshall Islands assault, 174
  meeting enemy, 38
  minesweeping by, 203–204
  officers of, 15
  operating off Cuba, 18
  overhaul of, 222
  radar of, 79
  rescues by, 79–80, 197, 239–240
  size of, 18
  squadron led by, 114
  as target, 43
  tossed into action, 25
  total miles traveled by, 238
  U-boats hunted by, 23
  as vital to success, 108
Fletcher-class destroyers
  arrival of new, 83, 85, 108
  in battle, 90
  as deadliest killer, 12–14
  depth charges and, 13, 95
  gunners on, 13
  most decorated, 20
  preparing for service, 15
  tasks for, 93
  Tokyo Express tangled with, 95
  torpedoes on, 13
Formalhaut, 25–26
Foster, John L., 179–180, 196–197
Fox, Furman, 112
Frank, N. J., Jr., 193–195
Frank, Nicholas J., Sr., 187
Frese, Bernard W., 110–113
friendly planes, 128–129

Gabelman, Warren H., 126, 238–239
Gallery, Philip D., 177, 194, 222
Gambier Bay, USS (CVE-73), 187
Gebhardt, James F., 59
Ghormley, Robert L., 9–11, 19–20
  Baldwin on, 30
  desperation of, 30–31
  on help arriving, 21
  MacDonald on, 30
  night fighting and, 27
  Nimitz replacing with Halsey, 31
  priority dispatch to, 28
Giffen, Robert C. ("Ike"), 103–104, 106
Gilbert Islands, 167
Glaize, Olen D., 226
Good Night Officially: The Pacific War Letters of a Destroyer Sailor (Raines, O.), 236
Gorsline, Burt, 141, 157
Gowen, George, 239
Grant, USS (DD-649), 186
Grayback, 86
Grayson, USS (DD-435), 13, 122

Gregory, P. A., 105
Gressard, Fred, 20, 60, 79
Grimes, Al, 241
Groshart, Gene, 167
Guadalcanal
  Baldwin on, 23–24, 27
  bombardments at, 27–28, 35, 92
  enemy evacuating, 107
  gathering for, 19
  Halsey on re-taking of, 40
  hazards at, 22
  Hirohito on, 37
  Hurd on, 27
  naval balance at, 21
  Nimitz on, 22, 39–40
  Operation Watchtower, 23
  press on, 23
  Ugaki on struggle at, 28–29
  See also Torpedo Junction
Guadalcanal, initiation at
  crew not knowing hell at, 42–47
  Halsey as fightingest admiral, 30–33
  Hara, T., at, 37–39
  hoping for relief at, 27–29
  overview, 25–27
  showdown at, 39–42
  Whisler as country boy at, 34–37
Guadalcanal, naval slugfest at
  confusion during, 49
  Fletcher in battle, 57–61
  Halsey on pride of ships and crews, 64–69
  Juneau disappearing, 61–64
  New York Times on, 69
  O'Bannon in battle, 52–57
  overview, 48–52
gunners
  of *Fletcher*, 44
  on *Fletcher*-class destroyers, 13
  MacDonald on, 131
  of *O'Bannon*, 44, 52, 97
  of *Radford*, 101
Gwin, 144, 154
Hackett, Orivall M., 141–144
Hagy, Charles H., Jr., 43–44
Hailey, Foster
  on bombardments, 100, 128
  on Cactus Striking Force, 95–98
  on *De Haven*, 113
  on detachment, 112
  on no time for mourning, 114
  on red tracers, 111, 131
  on ships boiling along, 99–100
  on sizzling day, 123
  on Slot struggle, 123–124
  on tin-can navy, 102
Hall, Perry, 21
Hall, Richard J., 171
Halsey, William F.
  aggression of, 4
  on Ainsworth, 129
  armada of, 238
  on bombing, 224
  boosting morale, 84
  on Cactus Striking Force, 101
  call from, 51
  on *Chicago*, 106
  Cole replaced by, 81
  correspondence of, 73
  countermeasures of, 38
  as darling of home front, 31–32
  Desron 21 and, 4–5, 148, 162
  destroyers used by, 34
  as fightingest admiral, 30–33
  as fond of destroyers, 12
  four stars received by, 69
  Ghormley replacement by, 31
  on Guadalcanal naval slugfest, 64–69
  high-risk game played by, 45
  home front and, 224–225
  on informal dress, 118
  joint operations of, 138
  on kamikaze attacks, 214
  on lull, 73–74
  on new organization, 94
  on *O'Bannon*, 5–6

operations combined by, 102
opportunities for, 93
orders from, 114
on re-taking Guadalcanal, 40
on retreat, 108
on sailors, 33
Solomon Islands, focused on, 116
strikes ordered by, 98
on surrender, 232
tasks at Guadalcanal, 32–33
thorns in side of, 127
Time magazine on, 32, 68–69
Tokyo Bay entered by, 3, 230, 238
on war's end, 226–227
Whisler on, 227
on Wright, 80–81
Hancock, John, 7
Hanson, Baldwin, 23
Hara, Moichiro, 38, 81
Hara, Tameichi
on being saved from catastrophe, 50
besting of, 241
command of, 120
on confusion, 49
creating arc, 49
destroyers loved by, 119
with family, 82
feeling no triumph, 67–68
grandfather influencing, 38
memoir of, 237
as son of samurai, 37–39
on Tanaka, 81
on Tokyo Express, 76
torpedoes launched by, 60–61, 156–157
visiting mentor, 48
withdrawal of, 51
Hatsuzakura, 228
Hayashi, Ichizo, 214
Hedrick, William C., Jr., 143
Silver Star awarded to, 148
Helena, 36, 41, 45, 62–63, 86, 99
batteries from, 140
salvos fired by, 100
sinking of, 145–146
survivors of, 146–147, 148–150, 169
Henderson, Harry H., 90, 106
Henderson, Olon, 239–240
Heroic Comics, 170
Hiei, 49–50, 52, 53–54, 57, 60
sinking of, 57
Higai, Joji, 102–104
Hill, Andrew, 94, 102, 109, 145
Navy Cross awarded to, 148
Hiraide, Hideo, 24, 232
Hirohito, 3, 83, 107, 119, 156
on Guadalcanal, 37
on kamikaze attacks, 213
Hiroshima bombing, 225
Hitler, Adolf, 10, 18–19, 33
Hollister, W. W., 159
Holmes, Donald, 41, 46–47, 59, 93
home front, 3, 31–32, 92–93, 96, 124, 224–225
Honolulu, 79, 88, 99, 140
Hoover, Gilbert C., 62, 63
Hope, 201–202
Hopewell, 189, 191, 234
rescue by, 197
Hornet, 23
Howell, J. E., 79
Howorth, USS (DD-592), 189, 191, 205
crew of, 215
damages to, 238
end of war for, 219
heading home, 234
at Iwo Jima, 210–212
kamikaze attacks encountered by, 208–209, 218
as new, 206
at Okinawa, 212, 215–218
Huggard, Douglas J., 59
Hughes, USS (DD-410), 190
Hulbert, USS, 8
Huntley, John P., 108

Hurd, Charles, 23, 27
Hyakutake, Harukichi, 27–28

Identification, Friend or Foe (IFF), 188
Imperial Navy, 37, 119
Ironbottom Sound, 42, 51
Iwo Jima, 210–212
Izaki, Shunji, 154–155

Japanese, 39, 228
  Cactus Striking Force against, 98–107
  in Kula Gulf confrontations, 138–145
  O'Bannon as scourge of, 168–172
  Starr on assault of, 225
Japanese Destroyer Captain (Hara, T.), 60
Japanese Fleet, 5–6, 60
Java See, Battle of, 39
Jenkins, USS (DD-447), 90–91, 183
  aircraft repelled by, 186
  in column formation, 145
  damages to, 222, 238
  division of, 117
  fire from, 194
  at Gilbert Islands landing, 167
  at home, 234
  in Marshall Islands assault, 174
  mines sunk by, 185
Jetton, Benjamin F., 145
  Silver Star awarded to, 148
Jintsu, 154
Johnson, Frank L., 81, 87, 128–129, 236
Johnson, Martin, 166
Johnson, Vernice, 171
Juneau, 37, 41, 58, 61–64

Kalinin Bay, USS (CVE-68), 187
Kamada, Shoichi, 68
kamikaze attacks, 3, 4
  allowing little sleep, 209–212
  Bramble on, 210
  Chesnutt on, 187
  Halsey on, 214
  Hirohito on, 213
  Howorth encountering, 208–209, 218
  at Okinawa, 212–221
  overview, 206–209
  in Philippine landings, 187–188, 191–192, 194
  pilot code and, 214
  Raines, O., encountering, 208–209
  Ransom on, 189
  Thompson, W., on, 192
  on *La Vallette*, 189
  Whisler on, 189
Kato, Masuo, 232
Katz, Benjamin J., 90, 147
Keating, Betty, 171–172
Kenney, George, 95
King, Ernest J., 19
Kinkaid, Thomas C., 78
Kirishima, 49–50, 57, 64
Kitkun Bay, USS (CVE-71), 187, 194
Kitts, Willard A., 80
Knight, Lendall, 53
Knox, Frank, 29
Kondo, Nobutake, 64
Kopara, 35–36
Krom, D. E., 79
Kula Gulf confrontations
  Battle of Vella Lavella as, 156–159
  Chevalier in, 138
  Desron 21 in, 159–162
  flames and explosions in, 154–159
  flares in, 101
  Japanese stirred up in, 138–145
  laying down of lives in, 145–148
  MacDonald in, 127
  Nicholas in, 138
  O'Bannon in, 138–139

one-man army in, 148–153
overview, 136–138
prey in, 98
Strong in, 138–139
Kusaka, Jinichi, 104

Laffey, 45, 56
Langley, Willard G., 141
Lanham, Richard N., 56
Leander, 154
Lee, Walter A., 185, 190
Long Lance torpedoes, 131–132, 137, 145, 155
Louisville, 85–86, 103, 104
loyalty, 126
Luck, Goodwin R., 153
Lyndon, Dennis C., 229, 231

MacArthur, Douglas, 95
Desron 21 under, 175–176
New Guinea operations of, 172–177, 181–183
Philippine landings and, 184, 188
Ransom on, 175
retreat of, 195
at surrender, 232
MacDonald, Donald, 6, 33
as assistant naval attaché, 10
avoiding harm, 145
background and education, 7
on battle, 45, 52, 154
on bombardments, 99
cannonside chats by, 121
as catapult officer, 8
chats given by, 180
with Churchill, 10–11
command of, 94
on confidence, 134–135
crew and, 16, 47, 65, 73, 99, 127, 170, 239
on danger, 24
depending upon, 93
on Desron 21, 118
on dropping potatoes, 133
embarking for Pacific, 19
on enemy contact, 42–43
field reports of, 98
first ship assignment, 8
on Ghormley, 30
good luck charm of, 55
on gunners, 131
on hectic life, 127
on home front, 124
on humor, 125
in Kula Gulf confrontations, 127
on London citizens, 11
on loyalty, 126
on morale, 96
naval career of, 235
navigation skills, 21
Navy Cross awarded to, 148
on new ships, 91
on night fighting, 52
as *O'Bannon* commander, 94, 99–100
as *O'Bannon* executive officer, 12
on *O'Bannon* maneuverability, 14
as officer for coding arrangements, 9
in peril, 142
on planes, 43
preparing for service, 14–15
on reality of war, 18
on relief, 101–102
on rescues, 86, 146–147
on role of destroyers, 26
as Roosevelt aide, 9
on *San Francisco*, 61–62
on seeing action, 99
sensing change, 34
on ship in flames, 56
Silver Star awarded to, 66
skills of, 119–120
on Slot struggle, 120
on social schedule, 8–9

MacDonald, Donald *(continued)*
as stabilizer, 126–127
in Task Force 67, 38
TBS use by, 67, 140
Time magazine on, 172
on Tokyo Express, 35, 82
on training, 17
tributes to, 170–171
on war fighting, 15
as worthy man, 81
Mackert, Theodore F., 199
Mahan, Paul E., 222
Mai, Donald W., 201
Manley, USS (DD-74), 22
Mansfield, Jack E., 198
March of Time, 171
Marine Corps Hymn, 14
Marsh, H. M., 105
Marshall Islands assault, 173–174
Maruyama, Masao, 28
Maryland, 187
Masi, J. A., 105
Matsuo, Isao, 214
McBride, William M., 236
McCalla, USS (DD-488), 34
McCarthy, John C., 226, 228, 232, 238
McGee, William T., 105
McGinnis, Robert D., 126
McGoldbrick, J. A., 105
McGrath, Robert J., 15
McInerney, Francis X.
background of, 116–117
bombardments staged by, 118
as commander, 120
on friendly planes, 129
Navy Cross awarded to, 148
orders of, 116
ships juggled by, 118
McLean, Ephraim R., Jr., 90–91, 104, 141–143
Merrill, Aaron S. ("Tip"), 94
Midway, Battle of, 24, 39, 83
Miller, Harry F., 90
Miller, Hugh B., 136–137, 139, 143–144
on Arundel Island, 149–153
Navy Cross awarded to, 153
on rubber raft, 148–149
mines
Chesnutt on, 203–204
Jenkins sinking, 185
minelaying missions, 130
minesweepers, 197, 198
minesweeping, 203–204
Taylor sinking, 185
Thompson, W., evading, 194
Minneapolis, 78–79
Missouri, USS ("Mighty Mo"), 232
crew, 4
as flagship, 3
at war's end, 228–229
Moir, Robert Lee, 112
Monssen, 45, 56
Montgomery, Robert, 113
Montpelier, USS, 103, 179, 198, 200
Moosbrugger, Frederick, 155–156
Mrs. Miniver (movie), 215
Mullany, USS (DD-528), 216
Murray, Glenn, 207
Myers, M. P., III, 199

Nagara, 48–50
Nagumo, Chuichi, 39, 48
Nashville, 86, 99, 177, 193
O'Bannon crashing into, 191
salvos fired by, 100
Navajo, 106
Navy Cross, 148, 153
Nelson, Horatio, 40, 42
New Guinea operations
of MacArthur, 172–177, 181–183
overview, 165–167

Ransom on, 181
as sedate, 183
ship as world in, 177–181
New Orleans, 79
New York Times, 23, 27, 69, 92, 170, 213
Nicholas, USS (DD-449), 4, 5, 29, 114, 239
building of, 15
in Cactus Striking Force, 94
in column formation, 145
commissioning ceremony, 15–16
desperate situation for, 24
dive bombers charging, 131
drills on, 21–22
embarking for Pacific, 18–19
as escort, 34–37, 74, 76, 83, 86, 89–91, 99
as flagship, 117
food supply, 224
at Gilbert Islands landing, 167
heading home, 234
in Kula Gulf confrontations, 138
on liberty, 204
as lucky ship, 238–239
in Marshall Islands assault, 174
new skipper for, 94
at Okinawa, 212
on patrol, 98
preparing for service, 15
Presidential Unit Citation awarded to, 148, 160, 172
rescue by, 226
retreating, 26
suicide witnessed by, 221
at surrender, 231–233
as target, 203
in Tokyo Bay, 230–231
tossed into action, 25
total miles traveled by, 238
as vital to success, 108
at war's end, 223, 229
night fighting
bombardments, 87–89, 98, 155
Ghormley and, 27
MacDonald on, 52
with radar, 87–89
Nimitz, Chester W., 19
asking for performance review, 30
on bombing, 224
correspondence to, 73
on Desron 21, 148, 160
on destroyers, 147–148
on flag officers, 81
on gallantry, 64
on Giffen, 106
on Guadalcanal, 22, 39–40
Halsey replacing Ghormley and, 31
headquarters, 93
keeping at bay, 28
on need for improvements, 83
out to win war against Tokyo Express, 77–82
priority dispatch to, 28
Normandy beaches, 10
Norris, John G., 85
North African landing, 19–20
Northampton, 79–80, 239
Norton-Taylor, Duncan, 142
on enemy guns, 133
on tin-can navy, 138
on torpedoes, 132, 145

O'Bannon, Presley, 14
O'Bannon, USS (DD-450), 3–4, 29
aircraft shadowing, 101
attacks by, 224
batteries from, 140
bombardments by, 87–88
building in Bath, Maine, 15
in Cactus Striking Force, 94
Christmas celebrated on, 193
in column formation, 41–42, 45–47, 51, 145

O'Bannon, USS (DD-450) *(continued)*
crew of, 15, 16, 73, 91, 96
as cruiser support, 103
damages to, 161
desperate situation for, 24
on Desron 21 roster, 116
dive bombers charging, 131
division of, 117
dropping depth charges, 132–133
embarking for Pacific, 19–20
as escort, 34–37, 74, 76, 83, 86, 89–91, 99
exercises on, 20
at first attack site, 18
in Guadalcanal naval slugfest, 52–57
gunners of, 44, 52, 97
Halsey on, 5–6
heading home, 231
heroes of, 241
hunting submarines, 42–43
illumination of, 50
inexperience of, 40
in Kula Gulf confrontations, 138–139
on leave, 168
as legend, 170
as lucky ship, 190
MacDonald as commander, 94, 99–100
MacDonald as executive officer, 12
MacDonald on maneuverability, 14
meeting enemy, 38
as model, 134
Nashville crashed into, 191
new command, 94
at Okinawa, 212
on patrol, 82
preparing for service, 14–15
Presidential Unit Citation awarded to, 160, 172, 231
rescue attempt by, 88
on rest and recuperation trip, 82
as scourge of Japanese fleet, 168–172
supply runs by, 77
as target, 43
Time magazine on, 135
in Tokyo Bay, 230–231
Tokyo Express tangled with, 95
torpedo launch by, 51, 157
tossed into action, 25
total miles traveled by, 238
training on, 17
transfers off, 125–126
U-boats hunted by, 23
as vital to success, 108
at war's end, 223, 226, 229
Ohmae, Toshikazu, 68
Okinawa
Desron 21 at, 213
Howorth at, 212, 215–218
kamikaze attacks at, 212–221
Raines, O., on, 215
O'Neill, Jack, 236–237
Ontani, Inaho, 228
Operation Watchtower, 23

Pacific Fleet, 19, 91
paratroopers, 203–204
Patch, Alexander M., 97
Patton, George S., 9
Pearl Harbor attack, 11–12, 15
as hit-and-run disaster, 33
Japanese carriers and escorts in, 39
losses, 24
Navy hit hard at, 31–32
Yamamoto planning, 102
Pensacola, 79
Peterson, George, 142
Peterson, Vernon A., 153
Pfeifer, Carl F., 142
on abandoning ship, 56
Black Gang and, 44, 52
on hope and work, 53
on playing for keeps, 43

Silver Star awarded to, 66
on Solomon Islands, 74
on tension, 139–140
Philip, George, Jr., 51, 54, 101, 171
Philippine landings
armada in, 190, 193
Baldwin on, 190
Corregidor assault as, 195–198, 202–203
Desron 21 in, 184, 188–189
as horrible experience, 198–205
kamikaze attacks in, 187–188, 191–192, 194
MacArthur and, 184, 188
miraculous survival in, 188–195
overview, 184–190
Phillips, H. I., 170–172
Phoenix, 222
Pitts, Melvin E., 171
Portland, 37, 41, 45
Powers, Frederick D. ("Pinky"), 8
POWs, 233–234
Presidential Unit Citation, 148, 160, 172, 231
Pridmore, James A., 227, 229, 231
PT boats, 114, 151–152, 184
Pullman, James, Jr., 194
Purdy, Frederick W., 141–143

radar
Chesnutt on, 58
Cole and, 238
of *Fletcher*, 79
night bombardment with, 87–89
SG, 41–42, 88
Wylie and, 87–88, 238
Radford, USS (DD-446), 90, 114, 129
in bombardments, 130
in Cactus Striking Force, 94
in column formation, 145
damages to, 202, 238
division of, 117
as escort, 99
explosion on, 199–200
fire support from, 177
at Gilbert Islands landing, 167
gunners of, 101
at home, 234
in Marshall Islands assault, 174
minesweepers screened by, 198
Presidential Unit Citation awarded to, 148, 160, 172
Radio Tokyo, 68
Raines, Orvill, 205
background, 206
Bramble on, 220
death of, 218–221
duties of, 217
goodnight kiss of, 206–207
kamikaze attacks encountered by, 208–209
memory of, 236
on Okinawa, 215
Raines, Ray Ellen, 206–209, 211–212, 215, 219–220, 236
Ralph Talbot, 144
Ransom, Dow H., Jr. ("Doc")
background of, 165
on bombardments, 194
Bronze Star awarded to, 200
civilian career of, 235
on departure, 173
on dive bombers, 177
duties, 166
on Filipinos, 186
first aid training by, 178–179
homecoming of, 205
on horseplay, 174
humor of, 167, 178
on kamikaze attack, 189
on loss of patient, 173
on MacArthur, 175
on medical materials, 176
on New Guinea operations, 181

Ransom, Dow H., Jr. ("Doc") *(continued)*
on news of leave, 168
on routine days, 183
on sinkings, 186
Thompson, W., on, 182
on transports, 184
wounded treated by, 200–202
Real Life Comics, 170
red tracers, 111, 131, 211
Redman, Robert H., 199
Regan, Donald A., 141–143
rescues
Ainsworth ordering, 147
Chesnutt on, 80
by *Chevalier*, 144
Dunkirk, 10
by *Fletcher*, 79–80, 197, 239–240
by *Hopewell*, 197
MacDonald on, 86, 146–147
by *Nicholas*, 226
O'Bannon attempting, 88
by Romoser, 146
by *Taylor*, 147
Rhyne, Willy, 54, 56
reunions attended by, 240–241
on Slot struggle, 122
Rivers, Rudolph, 120
Robards, Jason, Jr., 80
Rodrigos, Maurice, 143–144
Romoser, William K., 90, 129
minelaying missions of, 130
Navy Cross awarded to, 148
rescue mission by, 146
Roosevelt, Franklin D.
awarding four stars, 69
death of, 219
MacDonald as aide to, 9
optimism of, 84–85
professional killers of, 133–135
Ross, USS (DD-563), 185
Roth, Eli, 105
Roupe, R. H., 91, 103, 104
on comradeship, 134
on overwhelming odds, 157
Rowan, John J., 97, 108, 111–113
Ryan, Thomas P., 156

Salinas, USS (AO-19), 8–9
Samuels, Lewis, 114
samurai, 37–39
San Francisco, 36, 41, 44, 45
as death chamber, 66
MacDonald on, 61–62
repairs needed on, 63
sinkings by, 57
Saufley, 140, 187
Scott, Norman, 40–41, 50
death of, 62
Vandegrift on, 69
Selfridge, 157
Setter, James F., 17–18, 46
Sexton, John T., 15
SG Radar. *See* Sugar George Radar
Shigure, 119–120, 156–157
Silver Star, 66, 148
sinkings
of *Barton*, 60
of *Chevalier*, 158, 238
of *Chicago*, 106
of *De Haven*, 111, 238
of *Helena*, 145–146
of *Hiei*, 57
of *Northampton*, 80, 239
Ransom on, 186
by *San Francisco*, 57
of *Strong*, 142–145, 238, 241
Sleepless Lagoon, 95, 96, 98
Slot
bombardments in, 84
destroyers in, 93
escorts in, 84
as hellhole, 123
patrols, 157

pursuits up, 114
risky waters of, 65
rushing down in, 76, 95
Slot, struggle for
air raids during, 129–133
death and destruction in, 127–129
destroyers as fightingest thing afloat in, 119–127
Hailey on, 123–124
MacDonald on, 120
overview, 116–118
Rhyne on, 122
Roosevelt's professional killers in, 133–135
submarines in, 131
Time magazine on, 120
Smith, R. W., 181, 184
fishing trips arranged by, 192–193
Murray on, 207
Soete, G. W., 199
Solomon, Herbert, 112–113
Solomon Islands
advances up, 4
Baldwin on, 42
Desron 21 in, 158–159
diverting ships to, 33
foothold in, 21
Halsey focused on, 116
landings at, 3
Pfeifer on, 74
recapture plans for, 23
showdown in, 39–42
transports to, 26
victory in, 159
See also Guadalcanal; Guadalcanal, initiation at; Guadalcanal, naval slugfest at; Kula Gulf confrontations
Spruance, Raymond A., 212
St. Lo, USS (CVE-63), 187
St. Louis, 86, 99, 138–139, 140, 217
Stark, Harold R., 9
Starr, Douglas, 175, 179
on bombardment, 203
on food supply, 224
on hunger, 234
on Japan assault, 225
on prisoners, 233
on war record, 239
Sterett, USS (DD-407), 21, 45, 50, 51
blown out of water, 52
burying dead of, 63
crew of, 95
Strickland, D., 79
Strong, USS (DD-467), 90
dive bombers charging, 131
division of, 117
duels of, 136
in Kula Gulf confrontations, 138–139
on leave, 168
sinking of, 142–145, 238, 241
torpedo striking, 140–142
submarines
Desron 21 threatened by, 131–132
hunting for, 178
in Ironbottom Sound, 42
O'Bannon hunting, 42–43
in Slot struggle, 131
Wing on echoes, 132
See also U-boats
Sugar George Radar (SG Radar), 41–42, 88
Sullivan brothers, 63
supply runs, 77
surrender
Halsey on, 232
MacArthur at, 232
Nicholas at, 231–233
Taylor at, 231–233

Tachibana, Masao, 130
Takanami, 78–79

talk between ships (TBS), 19, 42, 50, 198, 216
  Giffen using, 104
  MacDonald using, 67, 140
Tanaka, Razio, 76–79, 81
Task Force 18, 103, 104
Task Force 67, 38, 86
Taylor, Robert L., 174
Taylor, USS (DD-468), 4, 90, 103, 123
  aircraft repelled by, 186
  cruise book of, 134
  division of, 117
  enemy captured by, 221–222
  fire support from, 177
  at Gilbert Islands landing, 167
  in Japanese waters, 228
  in Marshall Islands assault, 174
  mines sunk by, 185
  at Okinawa, 212
  rescues by, 147
  at surrender, 231–233
  tangling with enemy, 102
  in Tokyo Bay, 230–231
  at war's end, 223, 229
TBS. *See* talk between ships
Ten Go operation, 213, 216
Thomas, H. W., 79
Thompson, George, 227, 229
Thompson, Wells, 174, 189
  alert to, 198
  on kamikaze attacks, 192
  mines evaded by, 194
  natives reported by, 191
  on Ransom, 182
Time magazine
  on Desron 21, 135
  on Halsey, 32, 68–69
  on MacDonald, 172
  on *O'Bannon*, 135
  on Slot struggle, 120
tin-can navy, 102, 138, 148
Tojo, 107
Tokyo Bay
  Halsey entering, 3, 230, 238
  Nicholas in, 230–231
  O'Bannon in, 230–231
  retreat to, 108
  Taylor in, 230–231
Tokyo Express, 6, 26
  Ainsworth on, 85–89
  in big leagues, 89–91
  Chesnutt on, 82–85
  Fletcher-class destroyers tangling with, 95
  halting, 154
  Hara, T., on, 76
  interception of, 114
  MacDonald on, 35, 82
  Nimitz out to win war against, 77–82
  O'Bannon tangling with, 95
  overview, 73–77
  searches for, 98
  stopping, 169
Tokyo plains attack, 225–226
Tokyo Rose, 124, 134, 185
Tollberg, M. W., 105
Tolman, Charles E., 83, 102, 108–110
Torpedo Junction
  christening of, 25
  dangers in, 26
  intensified efforts in, 28
  voyages across, 34–35, 75, 77, 82, 133
torpedoes, 45
  Amatsukaze launching, 59
  Chevalier launching, 157
  Chicago hit by, 104
  Cole launching, 60, 79
  depth performance errors of, 67
  fired at *Atlanta*, 57
  on *Fletcher*-class destroyers, 13
  Hara, T., launching, 60–61, 156–157

Long Lance, 131–132, 137, 145, 155
Louisville hit by, 104
Norton-Taylor on, 132, 145
O'Bannon launching, 51, 157
oxygen propelled, 39
Strong struck by, 140–142
Wilkinson launching, 55
Wylie on, 60
Toyama, Yasumi, 76
Truman, Harry, 226, 235
Turner, James R., 152
Turner, Richmond K., 38, 40–41, 212

U-boats, 14, 103
Desron 21 seeking, 122
Fletcher and *O'Bannon* hunting, 23
Ugaki, Matome
on American Marines, 24
cohorts of, 37
on destroying enemy, 38
on scattered dreams, 82–83
on struggle at Guadalcanal, 28–29
United States Fleet, 3–4, 19
United States Naval Academy, 7–8

La Vallette, USS (DD-448), 90, 103
Christmas celebrated on, 192
in column formation, 182
crew of, 126
damages to, 202, 238
division of, 117
explosion on, 198–199
as heading home, 204–205
heroes on, 105–106
kamikaze attack on, 189
on leave, 168, 172
library of, 181
in line of fire, 104–105
in Marshall Islands assault, 173–174
minesweepers screened by, 198
on patrols, 185
submarine hunting by, 178
tangling with enemy, 102
task force of, 186
towed to safety, 106–107
Vandegrift, Alexander A., 23
on battle, 54
depleted lines of, 51
forces of, 27, 64–65
help promised to, 33
on need for relief, 28
optimism of, 30–31
on Scott and Callaghan, 69
units of, 40
Vella Lavella, Battle of, 156–159
Vincennes, USS (CA-44), 108

Wainwright, J. W., 231
Waithman, Robert, 169
Wake Island, 23
Wake Island, USS, 216
Walker, E. G., 44
war's end
Halsey on, 226–227
Missouri at, 228–229
Nicholas at, 223, 229
O'Bannon at, 223, 226, 229
Taylor at, 223, 229
Washing Machine Charlie, 98
Washington, 36
Wellings, Joseph H. ("Gus"), 90, 141–144
Werntz, Bobby, 7
West Virginia, USS (BB-48), 198
"What Comes Next in the South Pacific" (Norris), 85
Whisler, Robert, 43
on drills and watches, 35
on fatigue, 123
good luck charm of, 46, 55, 236
at Guadalcanal initiation, 34–37
at gun mount, 100
on Halsey, 227
on heading home, 231

Whisler, Robert *(continued)*
  on kamikaze attacks, 189
  retirement of, 236
  on Smith, 181
  on tasks, 53
  on youth, 40
White Plains, USS (CVE-66), 187
Wichita, 103
Wilkes, Jack, 105
Wilkinson, Edwin R., 14–15, 18
  in command, 51
  on crew, 66
  departure of, 94
  exercises conducted by, 20
  navigation skills of, 43, 52, 56, 74–75
  Navy Cross awarded to, 66
  as pleased with men, 44
  timing of, 27
  torpedoes launched by, 55
Williams, Clem C., 100, 109–112
Wilson, George R., 157
Wing, Virgil N., 16
  on drills, 21–22
  on escorts, 25
  on fortitude and bluster, 36–37
  on submarine echoes, 132
Witten, Chuck, 103–107
Wolfert, Ira, 54–55
Worden, William L., 232
Wright, Carleton, 78–81
Wylie, Joseph C., 17, 33, 41–42
  on bitterness, 75
  in chart house, 62
  Cole on, 66
  as executive officer, 57–58
  handbook compiled by, 89
  on Hoover, 63
  navigation skills of, 21
  radar and, 87–88, 238
  on shooting, 59
  on torpedoes, 60

Yamamoto, Isoroku, 29, 37, 102
Yokota, Minoru, 62
Yomiuri Hochi, 214
Yorktown, USS (CV-5), 108
Yoshihito, Takasaki, 228
Young, Cassin, 57
Yudachi, 60